THE WAR AGAINST
PROSLAVERY RELIGION

The War against Proslavery Religion

ABOLITIONISM AND THE

NORTHERN CHURCHES,

1830–1865

JOHN R. MCKIVIGAN

Cornell University Press

ITHACA AND LONDON

First published 1984 by Cornell University Press.
Published in the United Kingdom by Cornell University Press Ltd., London.

International Standard Book Number 0-8014-1589-6
Library of Congress Catalog Card Number 83-45933
Printed in the United States of America
Librarians: Library of Congress cataloging information
appears on the last page of the book.

The paper in this book is acid-free and meets the guidelines
for permanence and durability of the Committee on Production
Guidelines for Book Longevity of the Council on Library Resources.

Contents

Preface

The War against Proslavery Religion examines the efforts of American abolitionists to persuade northern religious institutions to condemn slavery and to endorse immediate emancipation. The early abolitionists shared the views expressed in 1846 by the widely respected nineteenth-century Presbyterian minister Albert Barnes concerning the crucial role that the churches could play in ending slavery:

> Let the time come when, in all the mighty denominations of Christians, it can be announced that the evil is ceased with them forever; and let the voice of each denomination be lifted up in kind, but firm and solemn testimony against the system—with no mealy words, with no attempt at apology, with no wish to blink at it, with no effort to throw the sacred shield of religion over so great an evil—and the work is done. There is no public sentiment in this land—there could be none created—that would resist the power of such testimony. There is no power *out* of the church that could sustain slavery an hour, if it were not sustained *in* it.

The abolitionists labored from the early 1830s to the end of the Civil War to enlist the support of the churches for their crusade. They pioneered many of the tactics that later generations of radicals and reformers would employ when attempting to goad conservative institutions into endorsing movements for social change. Yet despite the efforts of thousands of antislavery men and women both inside and outside the churches, all but a few small denominations balked at a commitment to uncompromised abolitionist principles and programs. As a result, civil war and government coercion, not moral suasion and church discipline, became the instrument that finally ended slavery in 1865. The reasons for the churches' failure to take the leading role that Barnes and the abolitionists had envisioned for them also go far to explain why subsequently the nation's major religious bodies remained silent for so long concerning the pervasive racial prejudice that prevented black Americans from exercising their full equal rights.

This volume could not have been completed without the assistance of many individuals and institutions: the American Antiquarian Society (Worcester, Massachusetts); the American Baptist Historical Society (Rochester, New York); the Amistad Research Center (New Orleans); the Brown University Archives; the Chicago Historical Society; the Historical Society of Pennsylvania (Philadelphia); the Houghton Library, Harvard University; the Library of Congress; the Massachusetts Historical Society (Boston); the Oberlin College Archives and Oberlin College Library; the Ohio Historical Center (Columbus); the Ohio State University Library; the Presbyterian Historical Society (Philadelphia); the United Methodist Archives Center, West Ohio Conference, United Methodist Church, Bieghly Library, Ohio Wesleyan University (Delaware, Ohio); the International Headquarters of the Wesleyan Methodist Church (Marion, Indiana); the Western Reserve Historical Society (Cleveland, Ohio); and the Yale University Library. Special thanks are due to William Bigglestone, Archivist at Oberlin College, for the generous gifts of his time and of his knowledge of the antebellum period to a visiting scholar.

The editors of the journals involved have kindly permitted me to reproduce material previously published as "The Christian Anti-Slavery Convention Movement of the Northwest," *The Old Northwest: A Journal of Regional Life and Letters* 5 (October–December 1979); and "The Antislavery Comeouter Sects: An Overlooked Abolitionist Strategy," *Civil War History* 26 (June 1980). Portions of Chapter 8, "Vote As You Pray and Pray As You Vote: Church-Oriented Abolitionism and Antislavery Politics," are reprinted from *Crusaders and Compromisers: Essays on the Relationship of the Antislavery Struggle to the Antebellum Party System,* ed. Alan M. Kraut, © 1983 Alan M. Kraut, by permission of the publisher, Greenwood Press, a division of Congressional Information Service, Inc.

I owe a particularly large debt to Professor Merton L. Dillon, whose counsel and encouragement have been invaluable and whose own writing set a high example of precision in thought and style. I am also grateful to many former and current colleagues who took time off from their own work to give me valuable assistance and advice, especially John V. Cimprich, William N. Black, Jessica M. Dunn, and Jason H. Silverman. The last, in particular, provided numerous suggestions that speeded the final stages of writing. John W. Blassingame deserves credit for making the atmosphere of the Frederick Douglass Papers project congenial to scholars with a wide range of interests and backgrounds. Thanks are due to Douglas Gamble, Douglas C. Stange, Nancy Hewitt, Lawrence J. Friedman, and Richard S. Taylor for conversations or correspondence that increased my insight into particular elements of church-oriented abolitionism. Alan M. Kraut, Jane H. Pease, and Ronald P. Formisano have read drafts of portions of this book and offered suggestions that helped to clarify my thinking. Mary E. Lang, a talented copyeditor, deserves credit for giving my prose a badly needed polishing. Janet Soresino typed the manuscript with remarkable speed and accuracy.

Finally, I thank my wife, Madeleine Leveille McKivigan, for finding time in the midst of her own busy career to offer more assistance than she realizes.

JOHN R. MCKIVIGAN

New Haven, Connecticut

THE WAR AGAINST
PROSLAVERY RELIGION

Introduction

The conversion of the churches to the cause of immediate emancipation was the earliest and most persistently pursued goal of the American abolition movement. Abolitionists condemned slavery largely on moral grounds and sought the sanction of established religious institutions for their views. Heavily influenced by evangelical trends, abolitionists branded slave owning a sin that required repentance in the form of immediate emancipation. Abolitionists demanded that the churches testify to slavery's inherent sinfulness by barring slave owners from their communion and fellowship. They believed that by threats of church discipline the denominations could coerce slaveholders to manumit their slaves. Early abolitionists hoped that the churches would become the leading agencies for the eradication of human bondage.

When the abolition movement was still in its infancy, its advocates approached influential clergymen and church associations to obtain their cooperation. They were quite confident when they first appealed to the pulpit, for, as one early abolitionist recalled, they "had attributed the silence of the clergy respecting slavery to the same source with their own former quiescence, partly thoughtlessness, partly ignorance of the essential character and actual workings of the system, and partly preoccupation with subjects nearer home."[1] In addition, the clergy were thought to be sympathetic to reform, for many of them had shown interest in the slavery problem by involvement in the movement to colonize free blacks in Africa. This early optimism, however, was quickly dispelled. For example, William Lloyd Garrison, while still an obscure editor, asked his own minister, the renowned Lyman Beecher, for an endorsement of immediate emancipation only to be told that his zeal "was commendable, but misguided."[2] In the early 1830s this experience was repeated again and again as clergymen and denominations shied away from involvement in the controversial abolition cause.

As a result of clerical indifference and at times outright hostility to the immediate emancipation program, the abolitionists' attitude toward the churches underwent extensive change. Still convinced of the righteousness of their cause, antislavery militants accused religious institutions of thwarting rather than promoting God's will. As early as 1834, abolitionists warned "that the American Church is stained with the blood of 'the souls of the poor innocents,' and holds the keys of the great prison of oppression; and that she can never go forth to millennial triumph until she shall wash her hands from blood—open the prison door—and let the oppressed go free."[3] Modeling themselves on the biblical prophets, abolitionists began a campaign to save the churches from divine retribution by rousing them from their toleration of the "sum of all villainies."[4]

Many aspects of the abolition movement's relations with the American churches are well known to historians. Clergymen and church members are acknowledged to have played leading roles in the early antislavery societies. The antebellum use of the Bible to justify slavery is treated as a significant, though embarrassing, chapter in American religious history. Similar recognition is accorded to those few sects, such as the Quakers, that did not succumb to the general toleration of slavery. The debate over slavery is granted a major role in provoking sectional schism in several major denominations well before the Civil War.[5] Despite this sizable body of knowledge, however, important misperceptions still impair historical understanding of the interaction between abolitionists and the churches.

One such misperception concerns the precise attitude of the northern religious community toward slavery before the Civil War. Historians generally portray the northern churches as expounding antislavery sentiment far in advance of the region's other institutions, especially its political parties. The sectional schisms in the Methodist, Baptist, and other denominations in the 1840s and 1850s are frequently cited as evidence of the growing antislavery militancy of northern church leaders. Similarly, the vigorous denunciations by many northern clergymen of the Fugitive Slave Law of 1850 and the Kansas-Nebraska Act of 1854 are used to make the claim that the churches were helping to lead the revolt against politicians' amoral handling of slavery-related issues.[6]

Such interpretations ignore serious deficiencies in the northern churches' antislavery testimony. For example, northern Methodists and Baptists permitted thousands of border-state slaveholders to remain in their communions after the schisms of the mid-1840s, thereby dramatically undermining their ability to condemn the morality of slave owning. Most other northern denominations similarly tempered their criticism of the institution of slavery by absolving slaveholders of any individual guilt. A few particularly conservative denominations deemed slavery a purely secular matter and stood steadfastly neutral on the issue of its morality. Although some northern churchmen publicly supported antislavery political positions and parties, before the Civil War no major denomination endorsed immediate emancipation. The abolitionists were well aware of these shortcomings. Applying strict, evangelically defined standards of moral responsibility, the abolitionists believed that the northern as well as the southern churches were guilty of sanctioning slavery and should be branded as exponents of a proslavery religion.

Another significant misperception concerning church-oriented abolitionism involves the scope and effectiveness of abolitionist activities in the 1840s and 1850s. Historians are well acquainted with the course of major antislavery efforts before the schism in the original national abolitionist organization, the American Anti-Slavery Society (AASS), in 1840. With the fragmentation of the movement, however, subsequent antislavery endeavors became less coordinated and are therefore harder to evaluate. In accounts of the abolitionists after 1840, the faction that followed the lead of William Lloyd Garrison is usually regarded as the chief heir to the tradition of using moral suasion to reform secular and religious institutions. Citing this group's heterodox religious views and their intemperate denunciations of the churches, historians have usually minimized the effectiveness of Garrisonian agitation on the major religious bodies.

Not much greater success is attributed to the efforts of the abolitionists who broke with the Garrisonians. Some of these non-Garrisonian abolitionists founded their own national organization, the American and Foreign Anti-Slavery Society (AFASS), which attempted to continue traditional lobbying of the churches. Inadequate funds and lack of local auxiliaries, however, severely restricted the capacity of the AFASS to conduct a vigorous antislavery propaganda campaign. The increasing diversion of many abolitionists' attention to political antislavery projects further weakened the AFASS. As a result of these trends, historical accounts portray abolitionist efforts within the churches after the 1830s as diffuse, decentralized, and ineffectual.[7]

Although the schism in the AASS certainly was a setback for the abolitionists, it is inaccurate to conclude that they played little part in the subsequent development of antislavery sentiment in the churches. Close examination of the records left by the Garrisonians reveals that, despite their frequent denunciations of the slavery-tolerating denominations, they still endeavored to reform those churches. The membership of Garrisonian societies after 1840 continued to be made up largely of clergymen and church members who continued to work for abolitionist goals inside their own denominations. In addition, Garrisonian presses and speaking platforms were made available to antislavery churchmen who hesitated to affiliate themselves formally with this faction. Most of all, Garrisonian propaganda never ceased to prod the northern churches and to carry the message that their practices lent moral sanction to slavery.

Careful study of the activities of non-Garrisonian abolitionist groups after 1840 reveals a similar record of uninterrupted antislavery labors in the northern religious community. The increase in political antislavery activities in the 1840s and 1850s did not produce a simultaneous decline in abolitionist activities in the churches. A large proportion of non-Garrisonian abolitionists remained committed to antislavery church reform and used the AFASS to coordinate their activities. This "Christian" abolitionist faction, as many of its members preferred to designate themselves, overlapped considerably with the political abolitionists. Each of the non-Garrisonian groups nevertheless maintained a distinct identity because of separate goals, tactics, and organizations.[8] The unsatisfactory results of the denominational schisms of the mid-1840s spurred Christian abolitionists to undertake further lobbying of northern religious bodies in the hope of bringing about a clear-cut repudiation of slavery. The waning strength of the church-oriented AFASS was thus more apparent than real, for it stemmed from a proliferation and diversification of these Christian abolitionist efforts. Although Garrisonian, political, and Christian abolitionist factions pursued different tactics after 1840, they all contributed to moving the churches closer to abolitionist principles and practices by the coming of the Civil War.

This book attempts to correct these misperceptions and to shed new light on abolitionism's relationship with the churches. Careful examination of the religious principles that helped produce modern abolitionism will reveal what actions abolitionists believed the churches must take to end their toleration for slavery. Because the major antislavery events of the 1830s are well known, the book concentrates on the interrelationships between the abolitionists' frequent failures, the division of their movement, and the changes in their attitudes and tactics in dealing with the churches. Examination of the pre–Civil War schisms in the Presbyterian, Baptist, and Methodist denominations will show why northern religious bodies continued to reject abolitionism even after the departure of most southern members.

With this information as background, it becomes possible to assess the effectiveness of a variety of new church-oriented tactics developed by

abolitionists in the 1840s and 1850s. In those years the Christian abolitionists organized a number of now nearly forgotten religious bodies.
Individuals and entire congregations joined these new sects as a means of
persuading their old churches to adopt a stronger antislavery position. In a
similar fashion, Christian abolitionists set up their own missionary and
religious publication societies in order to draw funds away from the established "benevolent" organizations and thereby pressure the latter to abandon policies indirectly sanctioning slavery. Abolitionists in the 1840s and
1850s sponsored a long series of Christian Anti-Slavery Conventions.
These meetings endeavored to obtain greater support for abolitionist principles among church members and to provide some coordination and
mutual encouragement for religious antislavery reformers. By the late
1850s this interdenominational antislavery cooperation developed permanent organizational structure in the form of the Church Anti-Slavery Society, which remained influential throughout the Civil War in spreading
abolitionist ideas. Finally, the antislavery political parties, along with the
troubled political events of these decades, had a generally un-
acknowledged influence on abolitionist advances inside the nation's
churches. Examination of these varied activities will demonstrate that
church-oriented antislavery activity did not decline after the rupture of the
old abolitionist societies.

Analysis of the abolitionists' principles, goals, and tactics permits an
assessment of their impact on the northern churches. Judging themselves
by their original goals, the abolitionists generally concluded that they had
failed to convert the northern churches into bona fide antislavery agencies
before the Civil War, for all but a few denominations refused to condemn
slaveholding as sinful or to endorse immediate emancipation. This judgment, however, is unduly harsh toward both the northern churches and the
abolitionists. During the late 1850s several northern religious bodies finally did make major advances toward unequivocal antislavery positions.
More important, the northern religious community in general grew more
outspoken in its disapproval of slavery during the 1850s. As the following
chapters will demonstrate, a significant portion of the credit for these
developments should go to the abolitionists, whose continuing agitation
and carefully enunciated principles gave direction to the late-blossoming
antislavery sentiment in the northern churches. Nevertheless, the abolitionists' own appraisal of their achievements should not be too quickly
dismissed. The promptness with which most northern denominations
abandoned the cause of black rights during Reconstruction reveals that
abolitionists were correct to doubt the strength of the churches' belated
commitment to emancipation.

—1—

No Christian Fellowship
with Slaveholders

In the late 1850s Massachusetts abolitionist Charles K. Whipple observed that "the Anti-Slavery movement . . . was at its commencement, and has ever since been, thoroughly and emphatically a religious enterprise."[1] Historians generally agree that moral repugnance for the southern institution was the strongest unifying element in the antislavery campaign. Nowhere did religiously defined convictions and goals play a more prominent role in abolitionists' activities than in their exertions among northern churches.[2] Therefore, students of abolitionism seek to explain how such a morally oriented reform movement quickly came to regard American religious institutions as among its most relentless opponents.

I

At the root of the conflict between the abolitionists and the major American denominations were fundamental disagreements over the morality of slavery and the churches' responsibilities toward the institution. Before the emergence of the modern abolitionist movement in the 1830s, the religious community had judged slavery in terms of its social, political, and economic consequences as well as in terms of its ethical implications. Although many denominations had made antislavery professions in the immediate post-Revolution era, most also had expressed concern for the potentially disruptive effects of emancipation. As a result, American churches were satisfied to encourage gradualist programs of amelioration and voluntary manumission that held out only faint hope for eventual abolition. As described below, many denominations endorsed the Ameri-

—18—

can Colonization Society, whose activities seemed more calculated to rid the nation of free blacks than of slaves.[3] But before the failure of this gradualist approach was widely recognized, new theological trends arose that radically reset the course of the antislavery campaign.

The origins of this great revolution in the American religious climate can be traced to the early nineteenth-century resurgence of revivalistic preaching known as the Second Great Awakening. Like the first Great Awakening movement in the mid-1700s, this evangelistic wave revitalized many United States denominations, especially those that were most free from inhibiting Calvinistic influences, such as the Methodists. Orthodox Calvinism, already undergoing considerable modification among its Congregational and Presbyterian adherents, stressed predestination, the depravity of human nature, and humankind's inability to effect its own salvation. The new evangelicalism replaced Calvinist determinism with the Arminian assumption that every human possessed the free will and moral capability to work out his or her own conversion and redemption. Revivalism retained the traditional Calvinist emphasis on personal sin but used it as a means to heighten the emotional pressure upon the individual to repent his or her sins and accept God's saving grace. Revivalistic notions of personal guilt for sin and of individual responsibility for salvation led many evangelical churchmembers to conclude that immediate and complete repentance for wrongdoing was the only acceptable proof of genuine Christian character.[4]

An important corollary to these new evangelical assumptions was the concept of benevolence. Each new convert to evangelicalism faced the problem of seeking reassurance about the genuineness of his or her conversion after the emotional uplift from the revival had passed. Many of the new Christians found relief from their doubts in the preachings of Charles G. Finney, a Presbyterian minister and the most effective revivalist of his era. Finney taught that salvation was only the beginning of religious experience and that the proper test of love of God lay in overcoming one's self-interest and acting in a benevolent manner toward all humankind. The converts, preached Finney, began a new life in which "they have no separate interests. . . . They should set out with a determination to aim *at being useful in the highest degree possible.*"[5] In addition to helping create a climate of concern for the well-being of others, benevolence implied that any conduct resulting in human misery was morally reprehensible. In the mid-nineteenth century thousands of benevolence-inspired men and women joined a host of voluntary societies founded to reform the behavior of their fellow citizens. These included organizations dedicated to battling such vices as intemperance and prostitution and pursuing evangelistic goals through missionary, sunday school, and religious publication societies.[6]

Another outgrowth of evangelical trends with ramifications for the antislavery movement was the doctrine of perfectionism. Always implicit in revivalism's high estimation of humanity's free will and moral ability, forms of perfectionism appeared in several denominations and spread into secular thought. Finney's call to disinterested benevolence impelled the converted to work for the moral perfection of society. The doctrine of entire sanctification led many Methodists to believe that true Christians could maintain the strictest personal morality in the face of a corrupt world. Secular reformers such as John Humphrey Noyes created entire communities built upon perfectionistic tenets. Although they disagreed on some points, all perfectionists shared an abhorrence for individuals and institutions that tolerated any form of evil.[7] Historians place less emphasis than they once did on the influence of individual perfectionists such as Noyes and Finney upon antislavery leaders, but elements of perfectionism show up in the principles and goals of even the most orthodox Christian abolitionists. The influence of perfectionism helped abolitionists to maintain uncompromising personal moral standards that set both example and direction for the broader antislavery movement.[8]

Millennialism was another theological trend growing out of evangelicalism that had an important impact on antislavery thought. The success of revivals in the United States led many clergymen to predict that their country would be the site of the kingdom of God on earth, prophesied in Revelation in connection with Christ's Second Coming. American millennialists disagreed, however, as to whether the thousand years of temporal order would occur before or after Christ's advent. The premillennialists, or Adventists, believed the Second Coming would precede the millennial age and were pessimistic regarding efforts to reform the world in advance of the time of Christ's direct intervention. Postmillennialism was much more encouraging toward social reform movements, because the coming of Christ was not expected until the ideal society had been prepared on earth. Inspired by postmillennial zeal, reformers believed that no social problem, including slavery, was intractable, because their work was in fulfillment of a divinely ordained plan.[9]

The key difference between the abolitionist ideology that emerged in the 1830s and earlier antislavery thought lay in the abolitionists' judgment that slave owning was "a sin—always, everywhere, and only a sin."[10] Although a few individuals and small sects before the Second Great Awakening had considered slaveholding sinful, the influence of the new theological trends on the immediatism of the 1830s was paramount. Evangelicalism taught that God had given every individual free will and moral ability but that slavery deprived its victims of the unhindered use of these powers and stood as an obstacle to salvation. Those inspired by benevolent principles regarded it as sinful to condone slavery, a system that produced so much human misery, when it could be abolished. Once slaveholding was recognized as a sin, the only acceptable atonement was immediate emancipation, because evangelicalism taught that the Bible required sinners to repent and cease wrongdoing *at once*. Abolitionists refused to consider pleas of mitigating circumstances in the cases of individual slave owners; they denied there could be any acceptable excuse for continuing to sin. Gradualist programs for abolishing slavery had to be discarded because they compromised with evil by sanctioning its temporary continuance.[11]

In addition to the condemnation of slaveholding as a "sin *per se*," the abolitionists pointed out the disastrous effects of slavery on the moral atmosphere of the South and of the nation. Abolitionists charged that slavery conflicted with "those social relations and duties which not only spring from our social nature, but which God has also enjoined by positive enactment," such as those between husband and wife and between child and parent.[12] In like manner, abolitionist writings insisted that slavery barbarized the morals of the masters, for, as one antislavery tract explained, "the 'peculiar institution' has become their God, and whatever protects it right. . . ."[13] Rather than resist slavery's corrupting influence, the abolitionists complained, many southern clergymen openly defended human bondage as compatible with the Bible. Immediate emancipation seemed the only way to save the nation from godlessness and ruin.

Clearly products of contemporary evangelical trends, these moral perceptions about slavery shaped the objectives of abolitionist activity among the nation's churches. It became a matter of primary importance to persuade the denominations to testify to the sinfulness of slave owning. Abolitionists contended that Christians had a duty to bear the same witness against slaveholding as against any other sin. If only the religious bodies would "call it [slavery] by its *right name*, Robbery," one abolitionist declared, professedly Christian masters would be placed under formidable duress to repent.[14] Alvan Stewart, a New York lawyer and early abolitionist, told the Presbyterian General Assembly that failure to declare slave owning sinful represented "moral cowardice." Stewart warned that continued equivocation would place the influence of the church to the side of proslavery forces, for "silence soon becomes acquiescence, which is soon apology, which is soon defence, which is soon vindication,'' leading to the destruction of the reputation and authority of the church.[15]

The acknowledgment of slaveholding's inherent sinfulness was only the first step the abolitionists demanded of the churches. Abolitionists reminded the denominations that nearly all of them professed to follow an interpretation of early Christian practice that reserved full church membership exclusively to the ''visible saints.'' Accordingly, most sects had established strictly defined disciplinary procedures first to interrogate, then to admonish, and finally to expel unrepentant sinners. Already a few small churches, most notably the Quakers, had testified to slavery's inherent sinfulness by taking the first steps toward expelling slaveholders from their fellowship. Abolitionists insisted that the major denominations also treat slave owning as a sin that required church discipline. Opponents of slavery hoped that the slaveholders' consciences might be awakened if threatened with the moral odium of ejection from the Christian body.[16]

James G. Birney, himself a repentant slave owner, testified that if the churches adopted such a method to agitate the slave master's conscience, ''it would be the largest lever that could be used,'' for ''nothing short of the fear of Hell will make him resign his hold.''[17] Kentucky abolitionist minister John G. Fee warned that by accepting slave owners into church membership, ''we become partakers in the guilty practice of slaveholding, and sharers in the future consequences.''[18] Fee also appealed to denominations to discipline slaveholders because ''your usefulness demands it''; that is, he was invoking Finney's benevolent doctrine that God requires the converted to aid those who are suffering.[19] In response to claims that the expulsion of slaveholders would divide and weaken the churches, abolitionists contended that religious bodies must be guided by moral principles, not by expediency. A church risked divine retribution, abolitionists warned, if it forgot that its ''well-being . . . surely does not consist in its extent and numbers, but in the purity of its doctrine and the uniformity and consistency with which they are lived up to.''[20]

The abolitionists' demand that the churches expel slave owners should not be interpreted as primarily an effort to avoid contamination from fellowship with sinners. Although abolitionists were genuinely concerned about the purity of their church communion, their foremost concern was the extinction of slavery. As reformers, they recognized that a church's adoption of a disciplinary rule against slaveholding would mark it as a genuine abolitionist body that had thrown its moral influence behind immediate emancipation. The abolitionists believed that without such an unqualified testimony, antislavery professions by the churches would have little impact on either the slaveholders or the northern public.[21]

Early abolitionists expected the churches to do more than denounce slavery as a sin and bar slaveholders from church membership. They called on the clergy to enter into secular as well as religious discussions as advocates of immediate emancipation. Abolitionists branded as fallacious the contention that slavery was a political rather than an ethical question. They criticized the support of many denominations for the American Colonization Society as an evasion of the moral duty to make uncompromising attacks upon wrongdoing.

The abolitionists also wanted the churches to reform their treatment of blacks. In recent decades, historians such as Jane Pease and William Pease have noted that a large proportion of white abolitionists were not free from the prevailing racial prejudices of their time. Nevertheless the abolitionists took a strong stand against official and unofficial forms of discrimination practiced against blacks in northern churches. In particular, abolitionists denounced the segregation of blacks into separate "Negro pews," because it helped perpetuate the spirit of caste used to justify slavery. The *American Anti-Slavery Almanac* stressed the irreligious nature of making distinctions based on race:

> That hue and those features which the churches . . . publicly deride and blasphemously criticize and scout, by compelling all those who have them to act *apart—because* they have them—God *approves*—they are his own handwriting upon their forms—pronounced by himself "very good"—and to convert them into a BADGE OF DEGRADATION, is monstrous impiety.[22]

The sincerity of such statements is attested by the frequency with which white abolitionists protested discrimination in the churches by joining blacks in Negro pews or by quitting congregations that segregated black communicants. By making the northern churches cease their prejudicial treatment of blacks, the abolitionists hoped to eliminate a significant indirect sanction of slavery.

The abolitionists' heavily moralistic approach to the problem of slavery inevitably led them into clashes with religious institutions long under the influence of racial prejudice and the interests of slaveholders. By strict abolitionist standards, American denominations not only tolerated but in some ways even condoned the practice of slavery. Holding themselves responsible to principles and not to institutions, the abolitionists had no patience with delays in converting the churches into antislavery vehicles.

The abolitionists' efforts would encounter obstacles so deeply rooted in questions of theology, morality, and church polity that they would endure even after the departure of southern communicants from many of the religious bodies. To understand the exact nature of these obstructions, it is necessary to examine the traditional stance of the churches toward slavery, the objections raised to abolitionist moral assumptions, and the unique problems originating in the sectarian pecularities of each major denomination.

II

The modern abolitionist movement began at a time when American churches had just completed a significant recovery in strength and prestige. For a few years after the Revolution, the moral authority of the clergy and churches seemed seriously weakened by the social disruptions caused by that conflict and by the popularity of the deistic beliefs of many founding fathers. Around the turn of the century, however, the revivalistic enthusiasm of the Second Great Awakening had restored waning church attendance and support for religion. During the period 1800–1830, Methodist membership increased sevenfold, and Presbyterian membership quadrupled, Baptist tripled, and Congregationalist doubled. In 1850 approximately one of every seven or eight Americans was an official member of a denomination and two or three times that number attended church with some regularity. According to the testimony of both contemporary observers and historians, the revitalized churches exerted significant influence over the individual, social, and even political and economic behavior of millions of Americans.[23]

Another important feature of mid-nineteenth-century American religion was its diversity. During these years the impact of immigration and conflicting theological trends, such as evangelicalism and "liberal" rationalism, had made the United States into what one contemporary observer described as "a motley sampler of all church history."[24] Among other things, American denominations differed on doctrinal questions concerning free will and individual conscience, on the amount of lay versus ecclesiastical control in church government, and in their ethnic and regional distributions of membership.[25] These considerable differences in theology, polity, and demographic makeup would significantly influence the effectiveness of abolitionism's appeal to the various denominations.

A final important factor in shaping a denomination's receptiveness to contemporary abolitionism was its previous history in dealing with slavery. As the research of David B. Davis reveals, no denomination within the Judeo-Christian tradition could claim a heritage of outright opposition to slavery. With the exception of only a few pietistic sects, churches in the colonial era had displayed a high degree of toleration toward the institution in both the North and the South.[26] In the aftermath of the Revolution, however, the wide acceptance of Enlightenment concepts regarding natural rights and human liberty led several denominations to incorporate condemnations of slaveholding in their disciplines. But this early burst of antislavery vigor in the churches barely lasted out the century, and few denominations actually enforced disciplinary actions against slave-owning members. What remained of church antislavery sentiment concentrated instead on ameliorative programs such as missionary work among the slaves and advocacy of colonization. A brief survey of the standing of slavery in the major religious denominations will document this general pattern of increasing toleration for slavery in post-Revolution church practices.[27]

The Methodist Episcopal church began its life as a separate denomination in the flush of post-Revolution antislavery sentiment. In keeping with the strong expectations of the times, the original Methodist discipline condemned the "buying and selling of men, women, and children." Little effort was made to enforce this rule, however, perhaps because of the widely held conviction that slavery was progressing rapidly toward extinction. Methodism expanded considerably in its first half-century, becoming the second largest denomination in the nation. To maintain this rate of growth, the Methodists gradually ceased efforts to prohibit slave owning in the church except among ministers, and even then only in states permitting manumission. Methodist leaders feared that stronger action against slaveholding would not only cause southerners to bar the denomination's itinerants from access to their slaves but also damage the church's influence as an advocate for projects of amelioration and colonization.[28]

Presbyterian practices toward slavery developed along a roughly similar course. The predominantly Scotch-Irish Presbyterians in the United States first created a national religious organization soon after the Revolution's end. The new denomination adopted both a highly structured church government of sessions, presbyteries, synods, and general assemblies and a discipline that outlined procedures to expel unrepentant sinners from its communion. Although many staunchly Calvinistic Presbyterians were cool toward the more enthusiastic forms of revivalism, the denomination grew to 225,000 members by 1837. The promulgation of a few vaguely worded proemancipation statements in the 1790s did not noticeably affect the Presbyterians' growth. In 1818 the denomination's General Assembly declared that it considered "the voluntary enslaving of one part of the human race by another, as a gross violation of the most precious and sacred rights of human nature, as utterly inconsistent with the law of God.''[29] An accompanying statement critical of immediate emancipation and the lack of any disciplinary actions against slaveholders, however, effectively nullified these antislavery professions. Already the Presbyterians were displaying a tendency to treat slavery as an evil social system for which individual slave owners could not be held morally accountable.[30]

The Baptists were the nation's largest denomination when the nineteenth-century abolitionist movement began. Because the Baptists refused to create a national governing structure, no machinery existed to enact or enforce a denominationwide disciplinary position toward slaveholding. During the Revolutionary era many local Baptist associations had condemned slavery, but there had been much subsequent backsliding. Prominent exceptions to that trend were the various Friends to Humanity associations of midwestern and Kentucky Baptists who had actively opposed the introduction of slavery into their locales early in the century. By the 1830s, however, the powerful influence of slaveholding members and the traditional Baptist reluctance to mix religion with civil affairs had quieted nearly all antislavery voices. In addition, the Baptists had suffered so heavily from divisions over questions of mission policy and theology that there was strong sentiment in all portions of the church against raising another disruptive issue.[31]

The proper position of the church on the question of slavery was a problem facing the predominantly northern Congregationalists and Unitarians as well as the more national faiths. Congregationalism and Unitarianism emerged as separate sects out of the old New England Puritan establishment as a result of theological disputes over the unity of the deity, the divinity of Christ, and the rights of private conscience. Both churches were slow to penetrate the West and gained almost no southern followers. Before its breakup in the 1820s, the old Congregational establishment had given only modest support to emancipation programs in its home region.[32] In the following years, both the Congregationalists and the Unitarians discriminated against northern free blacks and had endorsed colonization schemes. The Congregationalists attracted few if any slaveholding members, but they established a fraternal correspondence and participated in benevolent ventures with other churches that had many slave-owning communicants. The Unitarians' missionary efforts in the South had had little success, but many of their leaders opposed any pronouncement on slavery that might offend potential converts. The Congregationalists and Unitarians demonstrated that considerable distance from slavery was no guarantee of strong sentiment against the "peculiar institution."[33]

Theological liberalism greatly shaped antislavery developments in two other denominations, the Universalists and the Disciples of Christ, or the Christian Church. Universalism denied the Calvinist principle of eternal damnation and professed the salvation of all humankind. This denomination's social ethics combined tolerance and a millennial reliance on God to conquer earthly evils. At their first national convention in 1790, the Universalists called for the abolition of slavery but rejected mechanisms to enforce such ordinances on the church's membership. Instead, Universalists expressed hope that temperate appeals to the slave owners' consciences would produce practical remedies beneficial to both the slaves and the masters.[34]

The Disciples of Christ similarly rejected antislavery action. Founded by seceders from a number of denominations, the Disciples came together in 1832 on a doctrine of scriptural literalism that rejected all humanmade division of Christians. The Disciples' theological tenets incorporated elements of both liberal rationalism and evangelical postmillennialism and achieved popularity through a modified revivalistic preaching style. Though often considered a predominantly border state denomination, more than half of the Disciples' pre–Civil War congregations were in the North. This church took a favorable view, especially as expressed by its leading spokesman Alexander Campbell, of compensated emancipation and colonization. Although Disciple leaders criticized cruel practices accompanying slavery, they declared that the Scriptures did not condemn slaveholding as sinful and so rejected church discipline against masters.[35]

Several major religious bodies did not follow the pattern just described. Liturgical or sacerdotal faiths in the United States, which included Roman Catholics, Episcopalians, and Lutherans, shared a disinclination to admit that slavery was a valid subject for religious discussion or church legislation. The emphasis of these denominations on assent to formal doctrine, traditional confessions, and ritual observances proved far less conducive to involvement in social reform than the requirement of continuous proof of genuine conversion demanded by evangelical faiths. Members of the ritualistic bodies preferred work through their own church organizations to involvement in the interdenominational benevolent societies. Despite the Catholics' unique prohibition of racially discriminatory practices, neither they nor any of the other liturgical denominations hesitated to accept slaveholders into membership. The evangelicals' concept of the denial of religious fellowship to sinners was foreign to these churches, which generally expelled only heretics. Whereas the evangelical bodies at least had shared in the antislavery sentiment common in the late eighteenth century, their liturgical counterparts had a heritage of careful neutrality in the slavery controversy and of implicit toleration of Negro bondage.[36]

Certain other American religious bodies diverged from the general pattern of church practices toward slavery by taking an early stand against it. The Quakers, or Society of Friends, are the best known of this group. Eschewing a formal creed for the guidance of personal revelation or "inner light," the Quakers lived by a moral code that blended elements of quietism with humanitarianism. Although English Quaker founder George Fox had expressed concern over slavery as early as 1657, antislavery sentiments grew slowly among American Friends. In 1758, John Woolman and Anthony Benezet persuaded the Philadelphia Yearly Meeting of Friends to reprove their members for owning slaves. By the 1780s, Quaker slaveholders had either emancipated their bondsmen or quit the sect. Friends dominated the early abolition societies that successfully persuaded the northern states to end slavery, usually by gradual means. The Quakers' pacifistic beliefs, however, made the sect less active in later antislavery movements than their early history would suggest.[37]

Second only to the Friends in terms of early religious antislavery prominence were the Freewill Baptists. This sect was organized in New England in the 1780s as a result of the evangelistic preaching of the Reverend Benjamin Randall. Freewill Baptists broke away from their Calvinist brethren because they could no longer adhere to doctrine of predestination, which denied the freedom of human moral will. In the 1840s, the Freewill Baptists claimed sixty thousand communicants, a large majority of whom were in New England, but with congregations scattered across the North and Canada. Almost from its inception the new denomination barred slaveholders from church membership. In 1827 the Freewill Baptists' General Conference authorized the ordination of blacks as ministers. Although they shunned the major benevolent agencies, which were dominated by Calvinists, the Freewill Baptists were active in their own reform societies and in morally oriented political causes.[38]

A third group of opponents of slavery consisted of the small Scottish Presbyterian sects. The Reformed (Covenanter), Associate (Seceder), and Associate Reformed bodies of immigrant Scottish Presbyterians perpetuated Old World theological and liturgical disputes. To varying degrees, the bodies disapproved of the evangelical practices of most American denominations and disliked cooperating with them in benevolent enterprises. The Covenanters in 1800 and the Seceders in 1811 ordered their members to free their slaves. By the 1820s, however, the latter sect had begun to seek accommodation with mainstream Protestant opinion and made no effort to enforce its discipline on slaveholding members. The western synod of the Associate Reformed Presbyterian church in 1830, the most assimilated of the three Scottish sects, resolved that "involuntary slavery should be removed from the church, as soon as opportunity in the providence of God is afforded to slave owners. . . . "[39] The remainder of the sect, however, continued to tolerate slaveholders in its communions, and the result was a schism in the 1850s. The significance of the Quaker, Freewill Baptist, and most Scottish immigrant sects lay in their demonstration to northern Christians that a denomination could refuse fellowship to slaveholders and still prosper.

This brief survey reveals that with a few exceptions the American churches had come to terms with slavery by the 1830s. Despite antislavery professions in the immediate post-Revolution era, churches soon ceased in practice to be governed by them. Most denominations placated residual antislavery sentiment by labeling slavery an undesirable social institution that should be ended through ameliorative and gradualistic methods. Except for the Quakers and a few other small sects, no American religious denomination in existence during the first quarter of the nineteenth century challenged slaveholding as inconsistent with Christian teachings.

III

The movement for immediate emancipation came into direct conflict with the general toleration of slavery by the early nineteenth-century churches. At the root of this confrontation were fundamental disagreements about the morality of slavery and the churches' proper role in the face of this institution. The abolitionists, who aimed to achieve their goals through religious reform, wished primarily to persuade the churches to take an unqualified stand against slavery. Their opponents held contrary views in varying degrees that formed a kind of continuum.

An unabashedly proslavery faction, mainly but not exclusively southerners, defended slavery on scriptural grounds, claiming that both revealed and natural religion sanctioned slavery. In denominations in which evangelicalism's impact was weak, there was usually a conservative element that declared slavery a secular matter toward which religious bodies should remain neutral. Almost as conservative were northern churchmen who had personal objections to slavery but felt that the denominations should defer to southern consciences on this issue. Perhaps the largest group of northern churchmen could be classified as antislavery moderates.

This faction acknowledged slavery as an evil institution and believed that the churches should support gradualistic programs such as colonization, and later, antiextensionism in order to end it. These moderates, however, objected to the abolitionists' blanket attacks on the character of slaveholders and to their efforts to expel southerners from the churches.[40] Both defenders of slavery and abolitionists believed it essential to prove that their cause was fully compatible with the basic sources of Christian faith. But no matter how common their original ground, there was no reconciling their different ends. Controversy in the churches over the issue of Biblical sanction for slavery continued until the end of the Civil War and the final emancipation enactments.[41]

Whereas both sides in the religious disputes over slavery insisted upon their biblical orthodoxy, the institution's defenders relied particularly heavily on a literal interpretation of the Scriptures. A striking number of prominent northern divines, including Nathan Lord, president of Dartmouth College, Moses Stuart, a professor at Andover Seminary, and John Henry Hopkins, Episcopal bishop of Vermont, joined southerners in finding slavery sanctioned by biblical teaching. These men cited similar pieces of evidence in their preaching and writing. The proslavery biblical scholars identified blacks as the descendants of Ham or of Cain, heirs to curses of perpetual subjugation. They argued that Old Testament patriarchs practiced a system of servitude much akin to American slavery. Slavery also existed at the time of Christ and his apostles, and the defenders of the South pointed out that the New Testament contained no condemnation of the institution. Almost invariably, these writers noted that Saint Paul in several of his epistles had admonished slaves to be obedient to their earthly masters and in one instance even ordered the escaped slave Onesimus to return to his master, Philemon. After arguing that the Bible demonstrated divine approval for slavery, Nathan Lord warned that any human reproach to the institution of slaveholding was "dishonorable to God, and subversive to his government."[42]

Abolitionists and moderate antislavery churchmen countered the attempt to appropriate the Bible to the proslavery cause. Abolitionists rejected the contention that blacks were the heirs of Cain's or Ham's curse or that southern slaveholders had been appointed executors to carry out any such curse. Moderate antislavery ministers, including Henry Ward Beecher and Albert Barnes, strove to show that American slavery was much harsher than that tolerated by the Old Testament Jews, and abolitionists such as George B. Cheever argued that the ancient Hebrew practice was not a type of slavery at all.[43] Abolitionists denied that the New Testament showed that early Christians had countenanced slavery. Instead they insisted that the Bible, especially the New Testament, should be examined for its overriding principles of justice and righteousness, principles that were in complete contradiction to the idea of human bondage. John Rankin, probably the leading Presbyterian abolitionist, summed up this argument: "The whole Bible is opposed to slavery. The sacred volume is one grand scheme of benevolence. Beams of love and mercy emanate from every page, while the voice of justice denounces the oppressor, and speaks to his awful doom."[44]

Parallel to the debate over the Bible's position on slavery was a dispute over whether natural religion, the other accepted source of revelation, sanctioned human bondage. Abolitionist arguments relied heavily on Enlightenment concepts of natural law, inalienable human rights, and the innate goodness of all humans. Such concepts, however, were promising targets for religious defenders of slavery. Not only did the abolitionists' humanitarian philosophy conflict with Calvinist views on the fallen state of man, charged orthodox slavery proponents, but it also ignored evidence of moral corruption visible in almost every aspect of society. Proslavery churchmen defended the system as a divinely established institution by which the most depraved and dangerous individuals and groups could be brought under the influence of civilization and religion. Slavery, claimed one of its northern clerical apologists, was "a wholesome ordinance, on the whole, and for the punishing and restraining of vice, and the encouragement of virtue, to the more certain attainment of the ends of God's natural and moral providence."[45] Until Christ's Second Coming removed the sources of humanity's inherent imperfection, to abolish slavery would be to tamper with divine intentions.

In the debate over the revealed nature of slavery, proslavery and antislavery spokesmen frequently exchanged the accusation that their opponents' ideas encouraged the spread of infidelity. Some antislavery reformers did hold unconventional religious views. The charge that abolitionism was a heterodox movement, however, also stemmed from the clash over biblical interpretation. Because the antislavery argument denied the literal meaning of several scriptural passages, critics reproached abolitionism for teaching men that "the Bible is an unintelligible book" and that "the writing upon the wall, may be from God, but the impression is, according to their confidence in the interpreter."[46] Abolitionists, in turn, accused slaveholders of being secret skeptics, hypocritically seeking to enlist the church and the Bible as their defenders. It was this religious sanction for human bondage, abolitionists charged, that turned some opponents of slavery against orthodox Christianity.[47]

Many churchmen who sided with the abolitionists against claims of

divine sanction for slavery rejected the latter's contention that slaveholding was intrinsically sinful. One commonly expressed objection held that
slavery was a morally neutral institution that had to be judged according to
the circumstances surrounding each individual case. This viewpoint conceded that the Bible contained no express condemnation of slavery, but at
the same time it affirmed that slaveholding was bound by the same scriptural regulations that governed all relationships between people. Conservative churchmen acknowledged that slaveholding was often a source of
sinful abuses, but they laid the blame to erring individuals, not to the
system. These conservatives feared that if the church expelled slaveholders as sinners it would release them from all moral restraints and
ameliorative influences.[48] Not surprisingly, after a few years of trying to
reverse these opinions, the abolitionists began charging that expediency
governed the moral determinations of such church leaders.

Even moderate antislavery churchmen dissented from the abolitionist
description of slaveholding as an unqualified sin. These antislavery moderates contended that some slave owners could not be held morally
accountable for their actions. One expression of this viewpoint acknowledged grounds on which slaveholders could escape the guilt attached to
their position. For example, if an individual became an owner of slaves
involuntarily, perhaps through inheritance, and found himself legally prohibited from manumitting them, he was not to be adjudged a sinner.
Antislavery moderates sometimes claimed that a master who recognized
the evil of slavery would be morally correct to delay freeing his slaves if
circumstances made such an action detrimental to their welfare. But even
in cases in which the temporary deferment of emancipation brought no
stigma of sin, true Christian masters were to deal with their servants in
accordance with the notion that "their slaves, though legally property, are
morally and actually men" and never to mistreat or exploit them for "gain
or convenience."[49]

Edward Beecher, a member of the distinguished Presbyterian clan,
advanced a similar assertion that slaveholding was an "organic sin."
Beecher recognized the sinfulness of owning human property but denied
that slaveholders were sinners. The moral responsibility for the organic
sin of slavery, according to Beecher's doctrine, lay with the society that
passed laws to sustain the system, not with the individual masters.[50]
Abolitionists, however, rejected Beecher's and all other moral arguments
that qualified the belief that slave owning was a sin per se. Abolitionists
contended that any compromise about the sinfulness of slave owning
encouraged southerners to manufacture excuses for delaying emancipation

and hindered the churches from taking disciplinary actions against slave-holders.

Another subject of debate was the reformers' demand that the religious institutions cease all practices that lent moral forbearance to slavery. In particular, most denominational leaders rejected abolitionist proposals to bar slaveholders from church membership regardless of the Christian piety they evinced. Liturgical denominations refused to deny fellowship to slaveholders because the idea that individuals could be held responsible for the sins of other church members was contrary to their established doctrines. In many denominations, sweeping guidelines on acceptable moral behavior were opposed as infringements upon the local autonomy of lower judicatories. Even moderate antislavery churchmen argued that slaveholders' consciences could be enlightened better inside the religious bodies than outside them. The question of religious fellowship with slave owners would be the most important point of contention between abolitionists and moderate antislavery churchmen.[51]

Other objections to the abolitionists' religious principles and goals related to more worldly considerations. Many church leaders hesitated to endorse any position on slavery that might drive away southern members. Such caution is attributable both to feelings of denominational pride and to fears that divisive public quarrels would jeopardize confidence in the church's moral leadership. Northern church opponents of abolitionism also expressed concern about offending members of their own congregations on the slavery question. They frequently disparaged the abolitionists' violent denunciations of slave owners on the grounds that such language fostered "the worst passions, in the Reformer himself, in the slaveholder, in the slave, and in the whole community."[52] Both popular revivalists and local ministers complained that preaching against slavery would interfere with their work of a purely religious nature. In the later years of the antislavery campaign, some denominational spokesmen rationalized their churches' inaction on the slavery question by citing their fear of identifying the church with the growing heterodoxy of a portion of the abolitionists.[53] If the churches ever were to be enlisted in the abolition movement, some way would have to be found to demonstrate that continued toleration of slavery, and not antislavery agitation, was the greater threat to their institutional strength.

A final major obstacle faced by abolitionists in the churches was the strong support given by their moderate rivals to more gradualistic antislavery programs. When abolitionism and proslaveryism began making their disruptive appeals, antislavery moderates deprecated both views as "ultraisms'' and professed to maintain the scripturally grounded, traditional position of the churches toward slavery.[54] Antislavery moderates placed greater confidence than did the abolitionists in the reasonableness and Christian character of the slaveholder. Many moderates insisted that the most effective way to reform slave owners was to "speak to them as friends,—as those influenced by the high principles of the gospel of Christ; and with a regard to *their* highest good, as well as to the good of the suffering slaves."[55]

Church leaders opposed to abolitionism rejected calls for immediate emancipation and favored a variety of more gradual programs, including apprenticeship periods to prepare slaves for the responsibilities of freedom, compensation for masters, and colonization. The last of these programs was a serious competitor with abolitionism for the support of the churches. Organized in 1816, the American Colonization Society (ACS) attracted a varied constituency of politicians, merchants, southern planters, and evangelical reformers for its program of transplanting freed blacks to Africa. The ACS copied many of the techniques of other benevolent reform societies, targeting church groups for the appeals of its agents, choosing clergymen such as the Reverend Ralph R. Gurley and Robert Finley to oversee day-to-day operations, and holding annual business meetings in New York City during the same week as those of the religious organizations. The ACS appealed to the religious community by emphasizing the opportunity that colonization provided for the Christianization of heathen Africa. Especially in the 1820s and 1830s, the colonizationists were successful in attracting endorsements and financial contributions from religious bodies. In 1832, for example, the New York Baptist Association requested that its congregations take up a collection for the ACS, "believing that . . . the Colonization of the free people of colour on the coast of Africa, will prove the means of great good to them and the injured natives of that benighted continent."[56]

Many of the abolitionists had originally supported the ACS but drastically revised their opinion of colonization during the 1830s. Enlightened in part by free blacks' rejection of the ACS, the abolitionists reexamined colonization and found it to be not only an impractical but also an immoral scheme. On the latter account, they accused the ACS of inflaming racial prejudice by disparaging the accomplishments of free blacks. William Lloyd Garrison, for instance, noted the inconsistency of the ACS's promise to evangelize Africa by sending it the same free blacks that the society castigated as "an illiterate, degraded and irreligious population."[57] The abolitionists concluded that the ACS was at heart a proslavery organization because it scrupulously avoided any official endorsement of emancipation or criticism of the slaveholders. Although some abolitionists regarded the churches' backing for colonization as further evidence of slavery's corruption of those institutions, others expressed confidence that religious bodies would anathematize the ACS once awakened to its moral failings.

Although a few northern churchmen such as Lyman Beecher attempted to reconcile abolitionists and colonizationists, each group so thoroughly defamed the other's moral character that any form of cooperation became inconceivable. The abolitionists deeply wounded northern colonizationists by questioning the sincerity of their desire to see slavery extinguished. ACS advocates, in turn, branded abolitionists as fanatics whose view of slavery as a personal rather than a national sin undermined the chances of bringing about the sectional cooperation deemed essential to any benevolent program, but especially to one that aimed at eventual emancipation. Colonizationists also regarded white Americans' racial prejudice as unchangeable and considered blacks doomed to inferior status unless they emigrated. The strength of this last opinion in the northern mind was ultimately the abolitionists' biggest obstacle to ending support for the ACS from the religious community.[58] Although antislavery moderates such as the colonizationists devoted far less of their time to the slavery question than did the abolitionists, their influence, especially in church leadership circles, made their programs powerful rivals for the support of the religious public. Despite the variety of obstacles confronting them, during the 1830s the abolitionists launched what they hoped would be a quick drive to enlist the churches in their campaign.

—2—

Donning the Prophet's Mantle

No decade of the antislavery campaign has been more thoroughly studied than the 1830s. These years witnessed the final consolidation of the principles of immediate emancipation in the United States and the formation of an organized movement to act upon them. During the 1830s the abolitionists developed most of the methods of reaching and converting a mass audience that they would employ for the rest of their campaign. By means of their lecturing agents, petition drives, and the circulation of countless pages of printed materials, the abolitionists attracted thousands of followers. Throughout the same period, however, the targets of abolitionist efforts, the individual slaveholders and the great national institutions, rejected antislavery appeals. In addition, the early abolitionists had to endure attempts to silence antislavery agitation by mob violence and by legal and ecclesiastical enactment. By the end of the decade, the abolitionists would be forced by the strength of their opposition to reconsider the movement's original moral suasion strategy.

I

In the early 1830s the new, evangelically inspired perceptions of the immorality of slavery produced an organized movement to abolish the institution. Some individuals, however, had already attempted to generate popular antislavery attitudes. Eighteenth-century Quakers such as John Woolman and Anthony Benezet had endeavored to expose the moral, social, and economic disadvantages of slavery. Many Revolutionary era evangelicals had joined in these attacks on slaveholding as a corrupt worldly practice incompatible with genuine Christian spirit. These early agitators had had varying degrees of success in persuading their churches to adopt and to enforce disciplinary rules against slaveholding, but their efforts had been in large part responsible for the gradual eradication of slavery in the northern states after independence. Societies formed by Quakers and the other early enemies of slavery, such as the American Convention for Promoting the Abolition of Slavery and Improving the Condition of the African Race, endeavored to sustain the post-Revolution sentiment for emancipation past the end of the century.[1]

The growing cotton-based prosperity of slavery and the continuing strength of racial prejudice, however, quickly subverted such antislavery feeling as survived. Aside from a few small sects such as the Quakers, churches ignored their earlier antislavery testimony and welcomed slave owners into their communions. Church leaders argued that the conversion of the master and the slave would guarantee an end to the undesirable aspects of slavery. Similarly, much antislavery sentiment was diverted into proposals to aid blacks by Christianizing Africans, an idea that encouraged support for the American Colonization Society. By the 1820s, only northern free blacks and a few whites such as the itinerant Quaker publisher Benjamin Lundy kept alive an uncompromised opposition to slavery.[2]

The new evangelical religious trends began a revival and a transformation of the antislavery movement in the early 1830s. One of those influenced by the evangelical view of slavery was William Lloyd Garrison, a onetime associate of Benjamin Lundy. In 1831 Garrison founded his own newspaper, the *Liberator,* in Boston and went beyond Lundy in repudiating colonization and demanding immediate emancipation. At approximately the same time in New York City, a group of wealthy and benevolent-minded businessmen, including the silk merchants Arthur and Lewis Tappan, also came to believe that owning slaves was sinful and that nonslaveholders had a duty to awaken the South to its errant ways. These New Yorkers launched an antislavery newspaper, the *Emancipator,* and hired Elizur Wright, Jr., as a full-time secretary to correspond with others who might be enlisted in their cause. The news in late 1833 that the British Parliament had emancipated the slaves in the West Indies served as the final impetus for bringing together the American opponents of slavery. New England Garrisonians, New York reformers, free blacks, and Quakers met in Philadelphia in December 1833 and founded the American Anti-Slavery Society. This convention marked the beginning of a new phase in the campaign to end slavery in the United States.[3]

In the next six and a half years, the AASS expanded rapidly. Auxiliaries were founded in fifteen states and territories and in hundreds of counties, cities, and villages. In 1838 the AASS claimed a membership of about a quarter million. The regional growth of the abolitionist movement, however, was far from uniform. Though launched by small groups of immediatists in Boston, Philadelphia, and New York, during the 1830s the AASS drew the bulk of its membership from rural areas and small towns. In particular, western Massachusetts, southern Vermont and New Hampshire, upstate New York, and northeastern Ohio, all areas noted for religious revivals in the 1820s and 1830s, proved fertile ground for abolitionist recruitment.[4]

During the 1830s some significant regional variations emerged in the religious affiliations of early abolitionist leaders. In New England, especially outside the Boston area, Methodists and Baptists rather than the descendants of the colonial establishment, the Congregationalists and Unitarians, predominated in antislavery activities. In contrast, abolitionist sentiment remained relatively dormant among New York Methodists and Baptists until late in the decade, allowing Presbyterians and Congregationalists to dominate the movement in both New York City and upstate. Presbyterians also took the leading role in early Pennsylvania abolitionist circles except in Philadelphia, where they were joined by numerous Quakers. In the northern or "upper" region of the Midwest, settled heavily by New England migrants, the Congregationalists proved the most active antislavery denomination. In the more southern counties of the Old Northwest, Hicksite Quakers and a small number of Presbyterians and Baptists who had left birthplaces in the slave states became the mainstays of organized abolitionism. With only a few exceptions, the abolitionist movement appears to have grown most rapidly among the leading evangelical denominations in each region of the North.[5]

Roughly the same pattern of religious affiliations present in the abolition movement at large shows up in the leadership of the AASS. The long lists of largely honorary officers annually elected by the society included members of nearly every religious faith in the country, but important patterns of relative denominational support are readily apparent. (See Table 1.) The evangelical religious groups supplied by far the largest numbers of abolitionist leaders, with the Congregationalists and Presbyterians alone contributing nearly half of the more than three hundred officers of the AASS from 1833 to 1840. In contrast, not a single Roman Catholic or Lutheran has been identified in that group. Similarly, very few Unitarians and Freewill Baptists are found among the AASS leadership, despite New England's heavy representation. The influence of the Quakers, who played a major role in the founding of the AASS in 1833, apparently declined, for their share of officers dropped from approx-

Table 1. Religious affiliations of the officers of the American Anti-Slavery Society, 1833–1840

Denomination	1833 (%)	1834 (%)	1835 (%)	1836 (%)	1837 (%)	1838 (%)	1839 (%)	Total 1833–40 (%)
Orthodox Quaker	2 (2.1)	2 (1.4)	1 (0.7)	1 (0.7)	1 (0.9)	1 (0.8)	3 (1.9)	4 (1.3)
Hicksite Quaker	6 (6.4)	11 (7.5)	8 (5.9)	8 (5.7)	3 (2.7)	5 (3.9)	9 (5.6)	17 (5.3)
Quaker (faction undetermined)	10 (10.6)	10 (6.8)	7 (5.2)	6 (4.3)	11 (9.7)	8 (6.2)	8 (5.0)	23 (7.2)
Freewill Baptist	2 (2.1)	2 (1.4)	2 (1.5)	2 (1.4)	—	—	1 (0.6)	3 (0.9)
Scottish Presbyterian	1 (1.1)	1 (0.7)	1 (0.7)	1 (0.7)	—	—	—	2 (0.6)
African Methodist Episcopal Zion	—	1 (0.7)	1 (0.7)	1 (0.7)	—	—	—	1 (0.7)
Congregational	24 (25.5)	35 (23.8)	33 (24.4)	33 (23.6)	29 (25.7)	31 (24.0)	34 (21.1)	73 (23.0)
New School Presbyterian	8 (8.5)	19 (12.9)	17 (12.6)	19 (13.6)	20 (11.7)	25 (19.4)	28 (17.4)	44 (13.8)
Old School Presbyterian	1 (1.1)	2 (1.4)	2 (1.5)	1 (0.7)	—	1 (0.8)	1 (0.6)	3 (0.9)
Methodist Episcopal	1 (1.1)	2 (1.4)	3 (2.2)	4 (2.9)	2 (1.8)	3 (2.3)	8 (5.0)	10 (3.1)
Baptist	6 (6.4)	14 (9.5)	15 (11.1)	12 (8.6)	7 (6.2)	10 (7.8)	14 (8.7)	24 (7.5)
Unitarian	4 (4.3)	6 (4.1)	5 (3.7)	6 (4.3)	5 (4.4)	5 (3.9)	5 (3.1)	8 (2.5)
Universalist	1 (1.1)	1 (0.7)	1 (0.7)	1 (0.7)	—	—	—	1 (0.3)
Adventist	—	—	1 (0.7)	1 (0.7)	1 (0.9)	1 (0.8)	—	1 (0.3)
Swedenborgian	1 (1.1)	1 (0.7)	1 (0.7)	1 (0.7)	—	—	—	1 (0.3)
Deist	—	1 (0.7)	—	—	—	—	—	1 (0.3)
Antislavery Come-outer	—	—	1 (0.7)	1 (0.7)	1 (0.9)	1 (0.8)	1 (0.6)	1 (0.3)
Protestant Episcopal	3 (3.2)	4 (2.7)	5 (3.7)	4 (2.9)	3 (2.7)	2 (1.6)	2 (1.2)	7 (2.2)
German Reformed	—	—	1 (0.7)	1 (0.7)	—	—	—	1 (0.3)
Undetermined	24 (25.5)	34 (23.1)	30 (22.2)	37 (26.4)	30 (26.5)	36 (27.9)	45 (28.0)	93 (29.2)
Total	94 (100)	147 (100)	135 (100)	140 (100)	113 (100)	129 (100)	161 (100)	318 (100)
Total ministers	34 (36.2)	61 (41.5)	54 (40.0)	52 (37.1)	38 (33.6)	46 (35.7)	50 (31.1)	117 (36.8)

imately one-fifth of the first year's slate to one-eighth at the decade's end. Although these incomplete statistics should not be taken as proof that any particular denomination was inclined or disclined toward abolitionism, they do reveal an evangelical bias within the AASS leadership that came to play an important role in shaping the direction of the antislavery campaign.

The early leaders of the AASS envisaged that the nation's churches would play a key role in the destruction of slavery. The abolitionists naturally turned to the Protestant denominations for support because of the strong religious orientation of most antislavery leaders and because of the churches' cooperation with other benevolent movements. Because they viewed slavery from a moral perspective not widely shared, the immediate abolitionists desired the endorsements of established religious institutions for their program. In the early years of their campaign, most abolitionists deemphasized secular arguments for emancipation to avoid compromising the character of their movement as a "spiritual conflict, with spiritual weapons and for spiritual ends. . . . "[6]

Under the direction of its New York–based executive committee, which included both ministers and benevolently inclined businessmen, the AASS undertook a great propaganda effort to enlist the churches in its crusade. In addition to the *Emancipator,* which became the organ of the national society, and the *Liberator,* which remained in Garrison's hands, new antislavery newspapers and journals were founded and widely circulated. These journals and a host of abolitionist tracts presented the antislavery argument in a moralistic language calculated to appeal to an audience accustomed to evangelistic rhetoric. The friends of the abolitionist cause went to great lengths to get their literature into the hands of potentially sympathetic church members.[7]

It was by the spoken and not by the printed word, however, that the abolitionist message most effectively reached the unconverted. The AASS and its state and local auxiliaries combined publication activities with the employment of itinerant lecturers. These lecturing squads, including the almost legendary "Seventy" recruited by the charismatic abolitionist orator Theodore Weld and sent out by the AASS in 1836 and 1837, had a high proportion of ordained ministers and seminary students. The training and written instructions of these early agents encouraged them to stress the moral arguments against slavery. Their reports and letters reveal that they particularly sought to address congregations and religious conventions. Despite opposition from unsympathetic religious and civic leaders, these early agents spread the antislavery gospel into many previously unreached areas.[8]

In addition to propaganda activities, abolitionists tried to appeal to the religious denominations through inside channels. Individual abolitionists asked their ministers to read announcements of antislavery meetings or to offer prayers for the oppressed. Special attempts were made to win endorsements from prominent clergymen and leading revivalists. When the ministers were hesitant, abolitionists asserted that the antislavery question was as appropriate a topic for discussion in the churches as was temperance, chastity, or any other moral reform cause. In congregations where they achieved an initial hearing, abolitionists attempted to set up regular prayer meetings for the slave and then to form local antislavery societies. To further these efforts in the local churches, the *Emancipator* advised its readers: "Abolitionists, to be successful, must be men of deep piety; if all our actions be not in accordance with the principles we profess, we give reason to our opponents for standing aloof from us, and suspect[ing] us of insincerity."[9] The same article also warned abolitionists not to be overly "censorious" toward dissenting brethren. This last suggestion, however, would prove impossible for abolitionists to follow, as most churches continued to shun the slightest antislavery commitment.

The abolitionists lobbied higher-level ecclesiastical judicatories as well as individual congregations. In 1835 and 1836 the AASS called on its members to memorialize the governing bodies of their denominations "to pass resolutions condemning slavery as a sin, and to take such other measures as are proper to effect its speedy removal. . . . "[10] Antislavery agents attended the conferences, assemblies, and conventions of the various denominations in the mid-1830s to plead the case for abolition among delegates who would give them a hearing. Within only a few years some northern areas began sending representatives with outspoken antislavery views to these church conferences. Agents and members of the antislavery societies sponsored special conventions in various denominations to coordinate abolitionist endeavors within the sects.[11] In retrospect, these activities can be viewed as the first steps toward the sectional division of several church bodies.

In addition to the efforts made inside their denominations and local congregations, abolitionists adopted several special tactics in the 1830s to win over the religious community at large to antislavery principles. For example, they sought the endorsement and active cooperation of the interdenominational network of voluntary societies that solicited and distributed funds for missionary, religious publication, and moral reform causes. Abolitionists asked that these benevolent societies, in their publications and missionary efforts, condemn the slaveholder as sinner and succor his victims. In addition, abolitionists called on these bodies to cease all practices that lent moral countenance to slavery, particularly the acceptance of financial contributions from slave owners. Despite friendly appeals and less friendly threats to end contributions to the organizations, abolitionists failed to enlist the benevolent societies in the antislavery campaign in the 1830s.[12] Chapter 6 will examine abolitionist activities among these bodies in greater detail.

Another special tactic adopted by abolitionists in the 1830s was the organization of interdenominational conventions and societies of antislavery church members. Mixed conventions of laymen and clergymen and exclusively clerical conventions "for discussion and prayer on the subject of immediate emancipation" were held in New England throughout the decade.[13] In Philadelphia in 1838, a group of abolitionist members of evangelical denominations joined together in a Church Union Anti-Slavery Society to overcome the predominantly conservative influence of the clergy. This new society was organized because the older, Quaker-dominated antislavery organizations in the city refrained from religious exercises out of deference to the principles of the Society of Friends. The Church Union Anti-Slavery Society remained on friendly terms with Quaker abolitionists but adopted practices calculated to appeal to the broader evangelically minded community.[14] The following year, some New York City abolitionists, led by Lewis Tappan and James G. Birney, founded an Evangelical Union Anti-Slavery Society on the Philadelphia model. With members representing at least five denominations, the new society declared slaveholding to be sinful and charged that except for a few "empty resolutions" the northern churches tolerated slavery as much as "the professed Christians of the slave states."[15] Although these organizations proved short-lived, the idea of interdenominational antislavery conventions and societies would be periodically revived down to the Civil War in the effort to interest the churches in active opposition to slavery.

A final tactic utilized by early abolitionists in their dealings with the churches was to seek the sanction of foreign, particularly British, religious bodies for antislavery principles and objectives. The American antislavery societies sent circulars to British churchmen to solicit their prayers and sympathies. After the success of their own emancipation campaign, British denominations needed little prompting from American abolitionists to petition American churches to take antislavery action. Antislavery periodicals in this country gave publicity to the numerous remonstrances sent by British denominations to their American counterparts. The Massachusetts Anti-Slavery Society applauded these foreign rebukes for startling "the dull ear of the American church. . . ."[16]

Probably the greatest service by non-Americans to the abolitionist cause in the United States churches came from the World Anti-Slavery Convention held in London in June 1840. More than five hundred delegates attended from Great Britain, continental Europe, the United States, and the Caribbean. Historians principally remember this gathering for Garrison's refusal to take part in the proceedings after female delegates were denied seats. The London convention, however, should be noted for its stern condemnation of the toleration shown slavery by American churches. In a resolution presented by the British clergyman John Angell James, the convention recognized slaveholding to be sinful regardless of mitigating circumstances and declared it to be the "incumbent duties" of Christian bodies "to separate from their communion all those persons who, after they have been faithfully warned in the spirit of the Gospel, continue in the sin of enslaving their fellow creatures. . . . "[17] In their subsequent struggles in the various denominations, American abolitionists had the great advantage of being able to cite endorsement from some of the most respected figures in world Protestantism for abolitionist principles.

II

The abolitionists achieved varying degrees of success in their labors in the American religious community during the 1830s. The antislavery movement attracted adherents from the clergy and laity of nearly every denomination in the country. With a few exceptions, however, the governing bodies of those churches withheld official support for immediate emancipation. An examination of abolitionist exertions in the major denominations during the 1830s will reveal the principal obstacles that antislavery forces would labor to overcome until the commencement of the Civil War.

Evidence of the difficulties that abolitionists faced in dealing with the churches can be seen in their failure to obtain the unqualified support of even the small sects with long-standing antislavery traditions. The AASS had few complaints regarding the Freewill Baptists' enthusiasm for abolitionism. A predominantly New England faith, the Freewill Baptists did not have a significant southern constituency to placate in the slavery debate. Although their congregational polity made it impossible to establish a uniform rule barring slave-owning members, they found other ways to signal their opposition to slavery. The denomination's periodical, the *Morning Star,* began advocating immediate emancipation as early as

1834. The Freewill Baptists' General Conference declared slavery sinful in 1835 and endorsed the principles and methods of the AASS in 1837, recommending that the denomination's ministers and lay members "use all proper means to promote [abolitionism's] interest."[18] The *Emancipator* hailed the Freewill Baptists' "prosperity in every department of Christianity" as an example to other denominations that abolitionism would not conflict with a church's well-being.[19]

The abolitionists' success among the immigrant Scottish Presbyterian sects was mixed. The Reformed Presbyterian church had barred slaveholding members ever since its establishment in the United States in 1800. During the 1830s the Reformed Presbyterians endorsed immediate emancipation and repudiated their earlier endorsement of colonization. The Associate Synod Presbyterians adopted a disciplinary rule against slave owning in 1831 but did not enforce it until the 1840s, whereupon southern members seceded. The Associate Reformed Presbyterians attracted enough southern communicants to establish a separate synod in 1803 and subsequently declined to take disciplinary action against slaveholding. The northern Associate Reformed Presbyterians declared slave owning a civil issue and rejected the moral grounds of the abolitionists.[20]

Quaker support for modern abolitionism similarly fell below expectations produced by that sect's long antislavery tradition and by its leading role in the British antislavery movement. As noted above, Friends made up a noteworthy proportion of the officers of the AASS and of the active abolitionists in New Jersey, Delaware, eastern Pennsylvania, and several areas of the Midwest. In addition to successfully compelling all church members to emancipate their slaves, the Society of Friends provided leadership in efforts to induce all opponents of slavery to abstain from "purchasing and selling, using and consuming the products of slave labor."[21] Despite this enduring antislavery tradition, a majority of both the orthodox and the theologically more liberal Hicksite wings of Quakerism refused to affiliate with the abolitionists. The conservative Friends expressed fear that to sanction abolitionism would conflict with traditional Quaker pacifistic principles and would jeopardize the sect's precarious social respectability. As early as 1834, Garrison complained that the Friends had "degenerated from their parent stock."[22]

Of the major Protestant denominations, the early abolitionists had the highest hopes for rapid antislavery advances among the Presbyterians, because that church had as recently as 1818 condemned slavery as "utterly inconsistent with the law of God."[23] Even before the formation of the

AASS, proabolition Presbyterians, particularly northwesterners such as John Rankin and Samuel Crothers, had petitioned their denomination's General Assembly for enforcement of the long-ignored antislavery discipline. The large proevangelical or New School wing of the Presbyterian church proved as sympathetic to abolitionism as to other benevolent reforms. This was especially true in western New York and the northern, or "upper," regions of the Midwest, where many antislavery Congregationalist ministers and laymen had united with Presbyterians under terms of the Plan of Union of 1801. Presbyterian abolitionists, who made up a large share of the early leaders of the AASS, persuaded many of the New School–dominated presbyteries and synods to declare slavery sinful and to call for immediate emancipation. AASS agent Theodore Weld lobbied at the Presbyterian General Assembly in 1835 and believed that a quarter of the delegates, including several from the border states, were already sympathetic to his cause.[24]

The antislavery campaign among the Presbyterians, however, suffered a serious setback when the General Assembly of 1836 rejected a report that called for the censure of slaveholders. The majority at that assembly, including more than half the northern delegates, declared that such forceful antislavery action "would tend to distract and divide" the denomination.[25] Antiabolition sentiment among northern Presbyterians sprang from a number of sources. Nearly all theological conservatives rejected the abolitionists' tenet that slaveholding was sinful, on the grounds that it was an evangelically inspired position that lacked a scriptural basis. Even in the New School wing, a sizable faction preferred gradualistic antislavery plans such as colonization, hoping to unite the broadest possible range of benevolent reformers. One of the strongest proponents of the latter position was Lyman Beecher, who as president of Lane Seminary in Cincinnati had had his moderate views repudiated by a majority of his student body led by Theodore Weld in the widely reported Lane debate of 1834. Beecher and other antiabolitionist northern Presbyterians nevertheless remained confident that they upheld their denomination's tradition of testimony against the evil nature of slavery and of support for its eventual extinction.[26]

Presbyterian abolitionists were not moved by the antislavery professions of their opponents and claimed that the proceedings of the General Assembly of 1836 demonstrated the "inroads the spirit of Slavery has made on the Church of Christ."[27] Though discouraged, abolitionists vowed to continue their struggle until the triumph of emancipation. A final showdown over abolitionism, however, was forestalled by a schism in the Presbyterian church in 1837. This division resulted from disputes over the new evangelical doctrines in which the slavery question played only a secondary role.[28]

The Methodist antislavery heritage had never been completely extinguished, and the encouragement of British Wesleyans helped revive the abolitionist movement in this denomination in the early 1830s. Talented young Methodist ministers from New England such as LaRoy Sunderland, George Storrs, and Orange Scott organized local Wesleyan Anti-Slavery Societies and served the AASS as officers and lecturing agents. By the mid-1830s the abolitionists had captured control of several Methodist annual conferences in New England and sent Storrs, Scott, and other antislavery militants to the 1836 General Conference to agitate for the enforcement of the denomination's traditional rules against slaveholding. The New England Methodist abolitionists also dispatched agents to New York and the Midwest to convert their fellow churchmen in those regions to antislavery principles.[29]

Despite some initial successes, the Methodist abolitionists soon encountered opposition. The 1836 General Conference not only rejected the petitions to review church discipline regarding slaveholding but also censured Scott and Storrs for delivering abolitionist lectures during the conference. With the assistance of the bishops, conservative northern Methodists launched a counterattack against abolitionists in the denomination. Outside the New England conferences, prominent abolitionist ministers were either banished to the least desirable circuits or suspended entirely from their preaching duties. In a similar manner, editors of denominational periodicals sympathetic to abolitionism were replaced, and those journals were closed to further antislavery articles. A number of annual conferences even adopted rules to forbid ordination to anyone confessing to proabolition sentiments.[30]

Several factors explain the strength of conservatism among northern Methodists. Southerners made up an important segment of this truly national denomination's membership. Many annual conferences overlapped free and slave territories, and itinerant ministers, dependent on the church for salaries and pensions, had learned to suppress controversial antislavery opinions that could offend slaveholders. In addition, a substantial portion of Methodist laymen in the Midwest had been born in the South and had no patience with abolitionist preaching. Conservative northerners also recognized the dangers that abolitionism posed to church unity and felt no compunction in using the denomination's great institutional power to crush internal enemies. Theologically, Methodism's perfectionist strains, or holiness, emphasized personal sanctification rather than participation in

social reform. Methodist conservatives charged that the abolition movement was a product of a Presbyterian and Congregational benevolent
"ultraism" that threatened the unity of the church and the nation.[31]

In the face of official opposition, Methodist abolitionists increased their
efforts. In addition to forming more local Wesleyan Anti-Slavery Societies, abolitionists held regional conventions to coordinate antislavery
activities within the denomination. Scott, Storrs, Luther Lee, Edward
Smith, and other abolitionist agents braved official sanctions to carry the
antislavery message to Methodists in New York and the Midwest. When
their work was barred from denominational periodicals, they founded
their own newspapers and published additional articles in the AASS
organs. Some Methodist abolitionists became so angered at the conservatives' obduracy that they seceded and formed independent congregations
or joined denominations more sympathetic to antislavery principles. The
AASS *Emancipator* warned the Methodist hierarchy in 1838 that the
latter's attempts to preserve denominational unity by suppressing antislavery discussion were a failure because they "had pacified nobody at the
North, and satisfied nobody at the South."[32]

The loose structure of the Baptist denomination presented major obstacles to abolitionism. Antislavery societies had difficulty convincing northern Baptists that they shared in the guilt of southern slaveholding church
members. Abolitionists denied that the lack of a strong central organization relieved northern Baptists from the moral obligations of denouncing
slave owning as sinful and barring slaveholders from their pulpits and
communion tables. Abolitionist propaganda warned that nonslaveholding
Baptists, unlike northern Methodists and Presbyterians, must bear full
culpability for church practices that condoned slavery, because no
"Bishops, Conferences, or General Assemblies, have imposed the burden
upon them."[33]

Theological disagreements among Baptists also complicated the abolitionists' efforts within this denomination, especially in the Northwest. In
rural frontier areas, a sizable proportion of Baptist congregations clung to
a strict predestinarian faith that opposed both evangelicalism and organized prosletyzing. In general, these anti-mission Baptist congregations
rejected antislavery agents as meddlesome outsiders and abolitionism as
an impious challenge to a divinely ordained social order. Another group of
western Baptists who refused support to the abolitionists were the Friends
of Humanity, although they themselves had a long antislavery tradition.
By the 1830s, however, the Friends of Humanity had adopted a premillennialist doctrine that led them to turn their attentions from solving worldly
problems to maintaining the purity of the small sect.[34]

Despite these obstacles, the abolitionists succeeded in stirring up a great controversy among Baptists. The Baptist preachers Elon Galusha, Cyrus P. Grosvenor, and Nathaniel Colver became prominent early abolitionists and made antislavery lecturing tours among their coreligionists for the AASS. As early as 1836, antislavery Baptists in New England began meeting in conventions that aimed at purifying the denomination "from the reproach of cherishing in its bosom the sin of slavery."[35] Although their church lacked the strong central organization of the Methodists and Presbyterians, conservative Baptists took steps to quell antislavery discussion. For example, the Baptist Board of Foreign Missions, which solicited funds to support overseas evangelical efforts, suppressed proabolition remonstrances from British Baptists for more than a year. The Baptist General Tract Society, another widely supported denominational benevolent body, required its agents to pledge not to enter the slavery debate. The officers of several Baptist societies issued public circulars that affirmed their organizations' neutrality toward slavery. In the face of such opposition, Baptist antislavery conventions in the late 1830s began to discuss the necessity of secession if the churches remained obdurate.[36]

Although several thousand Congregationalists from the rural regions of New England joined the antislavery society in the 1830s, the figures of authority in this denomination resisted abolitionist appeals. Some Congregationalists objected strongly to the abolitionists' blanket condemnation of the slaveholder's moral character. For example, the Connecticut State Congregational Association was willing to condemn "the buying and selling of slaves for selfish ends" but implicitly acknowledged that there was moral justification for engaging in slaveholding temporarily.[37] Similarly, although some local congregations seconded abolitionist demands that the denomination cease all forms of fellowship with churches with large slaveholding memberships, the New England state Congregational associations refused all such requests. The preaching of itinerant antislavery lecturers offended the theocratic ideals of the Congregational clergy, and several state ministerial associations barred abolitionist agents from their pulpits in actions that the AASS dubbed ecclesiastical "gag laws" after the comparable treatment given to abolitionist petitions by the United States Congress. Despite evidence of growing support for abolitionism among New England Congregationalists in the 1830s, the most influential clergy and laymen continued to express hope that programs of colonization and amelioration could end slavery without the disruptions of church and state that immediate abolition might cause.[38]

The abolitionists had greater success among Congregationalists outside the denomination's traditional New England home ground. Although most

Congregationalists in the West had joined Presbyterian churches in accordance with the terms of the Plan of Union, several colonies of transplanted New Englanders persisted in retaining their traditional church polity. Seeking means to demonstrate their superior purity over Presbyterian rivals, these western Congregationalists frequently adopted unqualified rules against fellowship with slaveholders in their churches and ministerial associations. Probably the best-known stronghold of Congregational abolition in the West was Oberlin College, in Ohio. Founded in 1833, this school acquired its antislavery reputation in 1835, when a majority of the Lane rebels transferred there to complete their ministerial training. None other than the great revivalist Charles G. Finney was professor of theology and later president at Oberlin. Although Finney encouraged his students to concentrate on evangelical rather than antislavery activities, a generation of Oberlin-trained ministers would play a leading role in abolitionist activities among western Congregationalists. Thanks to their clear-cut antislavery stand, western Congregationalists attracted a steady trickle of defectors from Presbyterianism. Freed of the establishment heritage of their New England coreligionists, western Congregationalists could take an uncompromising stand on a most divisive social issue.[39]

Although none of the churches most affected by evangelicalism accepted the entire AASS program during the 1830s, the abolitionist movement made considerable progress in each of them. The abolitionist record among the theologically more liberal denominations was less successful. As already noted, many individual Unitarians had enlisted in New England antislavery societies, but these men and women failed to win an endorsement for abolitionism from the church establishment. One important reason for most Unitarians' disinclination toward abolitionism was their antinomian theology, which, in contrast to evangelicalism, did not attribute social problems such as slavery to personal sin. This same individualistic strain caused the Unitarian spokesman William Ellery Channing to advise his coreligionists to stay aloof from all types of benevolent reform movements because they diminished the moral influence of the individual. Unitarian conservatives also denied that it was within the powers of their denomination officially to condemn slave owning, because its loose church polity delegated all authority to the local congregations. Rejecting immediate abolition as likely to harm both the slave and the master, Unitarians instead endorsed gradualism, compensation, and colonization as more acceptable antislavery programs.[40] The abolitionists' failure to win acceptance even from the professedly antislavery Unitarian clergy of New England would have a decisive impact on the direction of the movement.

Abolitionist efforts in the 1830s made little progress in other theologically liberal denominations. Northern Universalist leaders rejected
the abolitionist contention that slavery was a product of personal sin and
instead described it as an undesirable social institution. The abolitionist
demand that churches expel slaveholding members was dismissed as totally foreign to the denomination's tolerant practice of opening communions
to all. Although a few individual Universalists joined the AASS, their
church displayed little sympathy toward the evangelically inspired principles of the abolitionists.[41] In like manner, Alexander Campbell, the spiritual leader of the Disciples of Christ, rebuked the abolitionists' proscriptive moralism as a danger to the ideal of Christian unity. Reflecting the
denomination's large southern membership, antislavery sentiment among
Disciples during the 1830s rarely went beyond endorsements of colonization.[42]

Abolitionist activity in the ritualist religions during the 1830s proved
equally unrewarding. Although abolitionists circulated the endorsement of
immediate emancipation by Irish Catholic patriot Daniel O'Connell, it
brought few American Catholics into the antislavery movement. Some
Catholic priests agreed with antislavery goals, but preferred not to associate with a movement dominated by evangelical Protestants, who often
possessed anti-Catholic prejudices. Episcopalian bishops wielded their
considerable powers to keep all discussion of the potentially disruptive
slavery question out of church sessions. When the black Episcopalian
minister Peter Williams, Jr., of New York City became active in the
AASS, warnings from his church hierarchy forced him to withdraw. Even
Episcopalian laymen such as William Jay, who served in several abolitionist offices in the 1830s, were rarities in antislavery ranks. The
Lutheran General Synod rejected all discussion of abolition in its councils
as an exclusively secular question but repeatedly issued public endorsements of the colonization program during these years. With a few exceptions, abolitionists failed to awaken members of the liturgical denominations to antislavery activism.[43]

III

This survey reveals that the principles of abolitionism had attracted a
small but vocal minority in the northern religious community. Evidence of
the limited impact of abolitionist efforts in the churches in the 1830s can
be seen in the failure of all major denominations and even some of the
traditionally antislavery sects to adopt the strict standards advocated by

the abolitionists. A number of factors account for this limited success. As noted in the preceding chapter, many of the objections to abolitionist principles and practices were stated primarily in theological terms. A closer analysis, however, reveals that a number of sociocultural and institutional factors interacted with theological issues to erect complex barriers against the progress of abolitionist efforts.[44]

To a large extent, the acceptance or rejection of abolitionism by a particular religious body seems to be correlated with its stand on some broader theological issues. The degree to which evangelical doctrines had affected a denomination generally determined its receptivity to abolitionist arguments. For example, ritualist, liberal, and strict Calvinist churches all objected to one or more aspects of the abolitionists' evangelically inspired claim that slaveholders were inherently sinners and that the churches had a moral obligation to purify their communions by expelling them. But even a strong evangelical orientation, was no guarantee of denominational adoption of abolitionist principles. Whereas postmillennialist fervor seemed to encourage reformist activities, premillennialist groups such as the Baptist Friends of Humanity turned their attention away from worldly social problems. The evangelical doctrine of human perfectionism in some denominations encouraged involvement in benevolent and reform movements, but in others, including the Methodists, it caused a more inward-directed striving for holiness.

Theological attitudes governing the composition of church membership also seemed to correlate with a predisposition to move toward or away from abolitionism. Denominations with considerable tolerance for human imperfection generally rejected the abolitionist condemnation of the slaveholder as sinner. This group included ritualist churches such as the Roman Catholics and Episcopalians; Universalists, who believed in the potential salvation of all; and Disciples, who strove for the unification of all professing Christians. At the other extreme, religious bodies with a desire for a scrupulously purified communion of believers generally rejected abolitionist principles that would add new, nontheological tests of fitness for membership. Among the latter bodies were predestinarians such as the Anti-Mission Baptists, strict Calvinist groups such as the Old School Presbyterians, and premillennialist groups. Abolitionists fared best in the 1830s among denominations that struck a balance between a near-universal and a highly exclusive membership standard.

A denomination's tradition with regard to social activism had a discernible impact on its response to abolitionism. Episcopalians, New England Congregationalists, and Unitarians, with their status as established churches, were slow to shed their defensive attitude toward the existing social order. These denominations were cautious about taking any position on controversial issues that might jeopardize their links to the social and economic elites. Another category of churches disinclined toward social activism were small sects with pietistic traditions such as the Quakers. These sects not only preferred to withdraw from worldly corruption but also discouraged their members from associating with nonmembers in any projects with religious overtones.

Traditions of social ethics also affected the degree of success that abolitionists achieved among denominations with strong Old World heritages. Although immigration to the United States had stabilized during the early nineteenth century and would not begin again in significant numbers until the mid-1840s, several denominations had become well established by the time of the first decade of abolitionist agitation. The largest of these, the Roman Catholic, the Lutheran, and the Dutch Reformed faiths, had all been established churches in Europe and were disinclined to set any membership test that would exclude large numbers of otherwise pious individuals. On the other hand, the Scottish Presbyterian sects shared a dissenting Calvinist tradition that inclined them toward strict disciplinary rules. Even among the latter bodies, however, some leaders rejected a ban against slaveholding members as a secular and not a religious issue. The heritage of most immigrant faiths therefore inclined them against abolitionism.

Ecclesiastical structure of polity also played an important role in the progress abolitionists made in different denominations. The decentralized structure of denominations such as the Baptists, Congregationalists, and Unitarians delegated to local jurisdictions the authority to determine standards for membership. As a result, abolitionists were able to attract many converts in those churches but remained powerless to establish uniform antislavery practices in them. At the other extreme, denominations such as the Episcopalian and Roman Catholic churches, where the clergy possessed all or nearly all authority, provided abolitionists no direct means to influence church practices. It was in denominations with a federated structure that the abolitionists were able to make greatest headway, because once in control of a few local judicatories they could dispatch delegates and address petitions to higher authorities to demand the establishment of strict antislavery rules.

Another aspect of church government that affected the abolitionists' campaign in the 1830s was the power of a denominational hierarchy to suppress antislavery debate within church councils. Roman Catholic and Episcopalian bishops forbade their clergy to participate in organized abolitionist activities. Methodist bishops lacked the same sweeping authority but used their considerable influence to persuade many local conferences to discipline or expel persistent antislavery agitators from the ranks of their preachers and lay moderators. Through its control over all editorial appointments, the Methodist General Conference was also able to keep abolitionist articles out of its large network of newspapers and periodicals. Even in denominations with substantial local independence, conservatives found means to discourage abolitionist agitation. In New England, Congregational ministerial associations tried but failed to bar itinerant abolitionist speakers from their pulpits. Among Baptists and Disciples, abolitionist influence was curtailed by a systematic purging of antislavery agitators from all positions of influence in the denominational missionary and publication societies.

In addition to active suppression by church authorities, important facets of inherent institutional conservativism stood as obstacles to abolitionism. Conservatives in all faiths feared debate over slavery as a threat to denominational strength and status. Identification with an unpopular social movement such as abolitionism would almost certainly penalize a church in terms of both membership and financial contributions. In evangelical denominations, there was opposition to divisive issues that would end cooperation among the churches. In former dissenting denominations such as the Methodists, Baptists, and even the Quakers, abolition was viewed warily as a threat to hard-won social respectability.

Certain demographic factors also came into play. As already noted, religious bodies with recent Old World connections, with the exception of a few small sects, demonstrated almost no concern for the slavery issue. Another significant demographic factor was the size and influence of southern membership in a denomination. Southern antislavery sentiment had declined to inconsequential levels since the Revolutionary era. Most members of religious bodies that preserved their antislavery traditions, such as the Quakers and the Baptist Friends of Humanity, had migrated from the South in striking numbers in the early nineteenth century. As a result of these trends, southern members of the major national denominations formed significant minority blocs that steadfastly opposed even a modest strengthening of antislavery church doctrines. Even the presence of only a few southern congregations in a denomination such as the Unitarians caused conservatives to decry the disruptive impact of abolitionism. Southern influence likewise was strongly felt in denominational and interdenominational benevolent organizations because southerners had been major financial patrons of those organizations.

Southern attitudes toward slavery also affected church debates in more indirect ways. In the Midwest, especially in regions adjacent to the slave states, the membership of the Methodists, Baptists, Disciples, and several other denominations was composed primarily of migrants from the South who retained strong antiblack and proslavery sentiments. Although some exceptional antislavery groups and individuals existed among these "Butternut" Midwesterners, the dominant tendency of this population was to resist any abolitionist-sponsored actions to impugn the morality of slaveholding. In addition to these native southerners, many northern clergymen had been educated with slave owners in colleges and seminaries and had taught or preached in the slave states at some point in their careers and, as a result, were disinclined to agree with blanket condemnations of their intimate acquaintances. Finally, southern influence was felt through the great economic power that slavery exerted over the entire nation. Many northern merchants, bankers, and cotton-mill investors had large financial interests in slavery. As major contributors to religious and benevolent institutions, these men used their influence to promote the status quo where slavery was concerned and thus to operate against antislavery programs that would reflect negatively on the character of their enterprises. The power of these prosouthern forces proved to be a major obstacle to antislavery advances in churches in the lower Midwest and in urban commercial centers across the entire North.

A final factor that affected the success of abolitionist efforts in the 1830s was the traditional relationship of denominations toward slavery. Abolitionism had very little impact in this period either among religions with a history of neutrality toward slavery, such as the "immigrant" denominations, or among churches founded since the decline of Revolutionary era antislavery sentiment, such as the Universalists or the Disciples. Denominations that had already removed slaveholders from their membership by their own disciplinary action, such as the Quakers, or as a result of northern emancipation, such as the Congregationalists and Unitarians, felt little need to endorse to abolitionist principles. Abolitionist agitation stimulated the most intense debate among such churches as the Methodists and Presbyterians, whose traditional antislavery disciplinary rules had come to be ignored by the 1830s. Even in those bodies, however, most northern leaders argued that support for colonization and for ameliorative programs for the slaves was more in keeping with their churches' historic antislavery professions than was abolitionism. The bitterness of the debate in the churches during the 1830s between the abolitionists and other northerners who regarded themselves as genuine opponents of slavery produced such a polarization of attitudes that subsequent concessions by either side seemed almost impossible.

The abolitionists themselves made a rather mixed assessment of their success in dealing with the religious community in the 1830s. The annual reports of the AASS recognized that abolitionist efforts had provoked an ongoing public discussion in the North concerning the churches' relation to slavery. Although nearly every church continued to extend fellowship to slaveholders, abolitionists applauded the growing minorities in most denominations who repudiated the practice.[45] But despite these advances, the churches fell far short of the leading role in the antislavery movement that the abolitionists had originally envisioned for them. Toward the end of the decade, the leaders of the abolitionist movement reevaluated their goals and tactics. This reassessment significantly contributed to the internal debate that split the AASS in 1840 and turned many abolitionists against further dealings with the churches.

—3—

Garrisonianism, the Churches,
and the Division of
the Abolitionist Movement

As a result of the disappointment about their modest achievements in reforming the churches in the 1830s, a great debate over strategy took place within the abolition movement. The significant role that bishops and ministers had played in the churches' rejection of abolitionist entreaties produced a growing anticlerical sentiment among a large number of abolitionists. Even many orthodox abolitionists began to consider whether cutting their ties with unrepentant church organizations would be preferable to risking spiritual contamination. Some abolitionists blamed the heterodox social and religious beliefs of their co-workers for the churches' distance from the movement. Furthermore, as doubts increased about the likelihood of the churches' quick conversion to abolitionism, a growing number of antislavery advocates began to suggest secular approaches, such as an independent political party, as better means to change public opinion. The advent of these new and conflicting ideas presaged the end of the old American Anti-Slavery Society in a bitter schism that would have great impact on the subsequent course of abolitionism in the churches.

I

The 1830s are remembered as a decade of intellectual ferment when many long-established institutions and beliefs came under question. A host of new movements flourished in the crosscurrents of imported European romantic thought and the revivalistic quest for personal holiness. Advocates quickly appeared for drastic revisions in family and economic patterns, religious practices and creeds, and the powers of governments and church bodies. Garrison, attracted to many of these reforms and always a champion of free discussion, opened his *Liberator* columns to articles from proponents and opponents of the latest radical positions. Regarding society's other faults to be as much products of sin as slavery was, Garrison adopted a perfectionistic creed epitomized in his inquiry "whether 'total abstinence' from *all* sin is not as obligatory as it is from one sin."[1]

A large proportion of active abolitionists, particularly in New England, also became mainstays of the movements stemming from this radical perfectionism. This group acquired the title "Garrisonians" because of their deference to Garrison's senior standing as a reformer and because of the central role of his *Liberator* in advertising their views. The Garrisonians included many first-rate minds and dedicated reformers such as Henry C. Wright, Nathaniel P. Rogers, Wendell Phillips, Edmund Quincy, Parker Pillsbury, and Maria Weston Chapman, all of whom cooperated with Garrison on the basis of shared principles.

A recent study of the leadership of the Garrisonian abolitionists found them to be a predominantly Boston-based group from diverse socioeconomic backgrounds but with most sharing an antinomian or liberal religious upbringing, education or training in a profession, and a longstanding disinclination toward politics. During the 1830s and afterward, these frequently ostracized reformers developed close personal bonds to one another and especially to Garrison, who functioned much like a father figure to his colleagues. As a consequence of the Unitarian or Quaker heritage of most Garrisonian leaders, the group felt no strong commitment to the established benevolent institutions sponsored by the evangelical community. Instead the Garrisonians emphasized the responsibility of every individual to strive for a universal reform of social ills. As a result, no cause—from sexual equality to dietary reform—lacked Garrisonian champions. Such activities caused considerable consternation among the more religiously orthodox and socially conservative abolitionists, who feared that the antislavery movement would be irreparably damaged by association with even less popular movements.[2]

Particularly worrisome to other abolitionists were the positions that the Garrisonians adopted toward political responsibilities and women's rights. Many Garrisonians endorsed pacifistic or "nonresistant" practices, on the grounds that the use of coercive force conflicted with Christian principles and was responsible for most of the world's ills, including slavery. Strict adherents to this view refused to vote, denying that governmental means could bring about true reforms. During the late 1830s Garrison devoted an increasing proportion of the *Liberator*'s columns to the peace cause, particularly to reports on the operations of the newly founded New England Non-Resistance Society.[3] In the same years, Garrisonian men generally took advanced stands on the role of women in public affairs. The social mores of the early 1830s had excluded antislavery women from AASS membership and had forced them to found their own auxiliary organizations. In 1837 two female abolitionists, Angelina and Sarah Grimké, challenged this separation, braving considerable abuse to lecture to audiences of both sexes. The controversy surrounding the Grimkés led Garrisonians to question old assumptions about feminine roles and eventually to endorse full participation for women in all abolitionist activities.[4]

Another source of controversy in abolitionist circles was the hostility of many leading Garrisonians toward the nation's churches. In part this attitude reflected the impact of perfectionism on the theological views of Garrison, Henry Wright, James Boyle, and a number of other abolitionists. In the late 1830s, these individuals filled the *Liberator* with articles rejecting the observance of the Sabbath, the authority of the clergy, and the divine inspiration of the Bible.[5] More important, though, were the disappointment, frustration, and anger caused by the cool reception abolitionism encountered in most denominations. The unrelenting opposition of the majority of the ministry to the abolitionist program led the Garrisonians to denounce the clergy in violent language that deeply disturbed the religious public. A series of clashes with the New England clergy in the mid-1830s that helped foster these sentiments warrants a brief examination.

In January 1835 a group of Congregational ministers and merchants attempted to create a new antislavery organization as a rival to the AASS. The American Union for the Relief and Improvement of the Colored Race was founded on a platform that attempted to use supporters of abolition, colonization, and other programs aimed at aiding the free blacks and the slaves. The American Union claimed that the antislavery message would gain a more receptive hearing, especially in the South, if it abandoned its harsh accusations against the moral character of slaveholders and the churches that granted them membership. The new society especially singled out Garrison's *Liberator* for unnecessary virulence toward ecclesiastical opponents. A few committed antislavery men, including Arthur Tappan, were attracted temporarily to the American Union. Most abolitionists, however, heeded the *Emancipator*'s warning not to "leave [the] firm ground" of recognizing slavery as sinful to plunge into "quagmires of expediency and policy," and the moderate body soon ceased to exist.[6]

The following year, William Ellery Channing, the most influential Unitarian of his day, issued another challenge to abolitionist principles and measures. In a widely discussed pamphlet, Channing conceded that slavery was a system of great evil. Because he did not share the evangelically inspired moral assumptions of the abolitionists, however, Channing refused to place the blame for social ills on the behavior of individuals. To drive the slaveholders away from the good influences of the churches and to assail them with vituperative language Channing deemed counterproductive. Garrison denounced Channing's works as "Ishmaelitish," and other abolitionists complained of the Unitarian's "fanciful separation" of the responsibility of the slaveholder from the wrongs he committed. The warm reception for Channing's arguments by a broad segment of the New England clergy, despite the abolitionist attempts at rebuttal, was another indication to Garrisonians that the churches' moral sense had become corrupted by slavery.[7]

The full extent of disapproval for Garrisonian practices within the religious community became apparent in 1837, when many proabolition ministers joined protests against the *Liberator*'s attitude toward the churches. A complaint by the Congregational General Association of Massachusetts that it was improper for female abolitionists to address mixed audiences sparked a succession of "Clerical Appeals" aimed at curbing this and other Garrisonian "excesses." The first appeal, signed by five ministers, including two members of the Massachusetts Anti-Slavery Society, berated the Garrisonians' use of a language of "hasty, unsparing, almost ferocious denunciation" offensive to the Christian spirit.[8] Later appeals criticized Garrisonian participation in unorthodox religious and social causes. All the appeals implied that Garrisonian antislavery practices displayed disrespect for the church and clergy and therefore only increased antiabolitionist feeling among the religious public.[9]

The accusations of the clerical appeals alarmed and angered the Garrisonians, who claimed to see little validity in the grievances cited in them and responded primarily by assailing their opponents' motives. The Massachusetts Anti-Slavery Society charged that the signers of the appeals had forfeited all claims to the trust of truehearted antislavery men, because they had demonstrated "a man-pleasing and not a God-pleasing spirit" in promoting conciliation with the slavery-defending churches.[10] Garrisonian anticlerical rhetoric reached new heights in exhortations to abolitionists to resist the dictation of antislavery tactics by "spiritual popes" chiefly concerned with the protection of the moral authority of their offices.[11]

When the Garrisonians applied to the executive committee of the AASS for support to rally abolitionist sentiment against the clerical appeals, they discovered that the New York–based group was sympathetic to the charges against them and not disposed to intervene. The officers of the national society had joined in earlier replies to the American Union and to Channing, because fundamental abolitionist principles had been challenged. In the case of the clerical appeals, however, the New Yorkers found considerable validity in the accusations against the Garrisonians. The religious affiliations of the AASS's active officers (president, treasurer, secretaries, and members of the executive committee) were predominantly orthodox, and a large proportion of them were ordained clergymen. (See Table 2.) The moving spirits of the AASS executive committee included the Tappan brothers, William Jay, James G. Birney, and Joshua Leavitt, who had worked together for years in numerous benevolent and evangelical projects. These men feared that the Garrisonians' behavior jeopardized the AASS's chance to obtain sanction for abolition from the religious institutions that they regarded as the cornerstone to successful reform efforts. Most of these men probably shared the suspicions of William Jay, the organization's corresponding secretary, toward the Garrisonians:

> The Anti-Slavery Soc[iet]y is avowedly a *Christian* Society. On this fact rests our hope of divine assistance & on this alone rests our confidence in each other. I do not trust any coadjutor who [does] not act with us from Christian principles. . . . I do not depend on any man as an abolitionist who does not act from a sense of religious obligation.[12]

Table 2. Religious affiliations of the active officers (president, treasurer, secretaries, and executive committee members) of the American Anti-Slavery Society, 1833–1840

Denomination	Total (%)
Hicksite Quaker	1 (5.9)
Congregational	5 (29.4)
New School Presbyterian	6 (35.3)
Baptist	1 (5.9)
Protestant Episcopal	2 (11.8)
Undetermined	1 (5.9)
Total	17 (100)
Total Ministers	7 (41.2)

Several New York abolitionists accused the *Liberator* of maliciously judging the entire ministry of New England by the proslavery opinions of a few clergymen. Publicly the *Emancipator* and the executive committee remained neutral in the controversy over the clerical appeals because they regarded the affair as primarily local and personal and believed it to be a distraction from more serious work. Privately, important abolitionists such as Elizur Wright and Birney hoped that the Garrisonians might secede and thus remove an incubus from the national society.[13]

The refusal of the AASS executive committee to condemn publicly the clerical appeals added to tensions among abolitionists and served to increase Garrisonian anticlericalism. Garrison wrote Lewis Tappan to demand an explanation for the "strange, inexplicable, pernicious silence" of the New Yorkers, which he warned was universally interpreted as approval for the appealants' charges.[14] To his brother-in-law, George W. Benson, Garrison complained that there was "too much sectarianism at [the] headquarters. There appears to be 'something rotten in the State of Denmark.'"[15] The Garrisonian-dominated Massachusetts Anti-Slavery Society protested that many of the so-called orthodox among the abolitionists desired to erect religious tests for membership in their organization. The Garrisonian body condemned such proposals as certain "to distract antislavery societies, and to turn their efforts against each other instead of slavery."[16]

II

The furor over the clerical appeals proved to be only the first of a series of divisive quarrels in abolitionist ranks during the late 1830s. A number of questions divided the abolitionists into hostile and contentious factions during these years. Heated opposition had arisen to Garrisonian attempts to win recognition of an equal status for women in the abolition societies. The antifeminists feared that abolitionism would be handicapped in conservative social and religious circles by a connection with an even less popular cause. In the same period, abolitionists who advocated the formation of an antislavery political party desired to purge the Garrisonians from the AASS. These political-minded abolitionists believed that the nonresistant views and extremist reputations of the Garrisonians posed major obstacles for the new program. As will be seen, these issues reinforced the growing division among antislavery forces over the question of whether or not to continue efforts to abolitionize the churches. The forces that opposed feminism and that favored political antislavery action could unite with those that sought new church-oriented abolitionist tactics. The Garrisonians were able to oppose all three as advocates of proscriptive measures that would force dissenting abolitionists out of the AASS.[17]

After a short period of relative calm following the clerical appeals, controversy again erupted in New England antislavery circles between Garrisonian and more church-oriented abolitionists. When the 1838 New England Anti-Slavery Convention voted to accept women as members, many Congregational ministers protested. At the January 1839 annual meeting of the Massachusetts Anti-Slavery Society, clerical abolitionists led by the Reverends Charles T. Torrey, Orange Scott, Nathaniel Colver, and Amos A. Phelps failed in efforts to prohibit the participation of women and to censure the Garrisonians for not voting. Unable to turn the old state organization against Garrison and the *Liberator*, the Garrisonians' opponents founded their own body, the Massachusetts Abolition Society, and issued their own newspaper, the *Massachusetts Abolitionist*. Advocates of the Massachusetts Abolition Society traveled throughout the state to charge that the Garrisonians had abandoned abolitionism for crusades "against human government, the ministry, all the theological institutions, etc."[18] The new society's agents charged that Unitarians and nonresistants dominated the old society while the opinions of abolitionists from more orthodox sects went ignored. The Massachusetts Abolition Society, however, soon proved to be a disappointment to anti-Garrisonian abolitionists in the state and nationwide. The new society expended its energies in assailing various Garrisonian heterodoxies and made little progress in launching new church or political antislavery programs.[19]

The *Liberator* examined the Massachusetts Abolition Society and declared that "the new organization is the third edition of the 'American Union'—the 'Clerical Appeal' being the second."[20] The Garrisonians regarded the new society as another attempt by the northern ministry to create a vehicle for soothing their uneasy consciences without having to take any decisive action against slavery. Garrisonians especially deplored what they perceived as the Massachusetts Abolition Society's manipulation of the "spirit of sectarianism" to seduce a few truehearted friends into their "schismatic" and "disorganizing" venture.[21] The greatest danger posed by the new society, according to Garrisonians, was its complete domination by the ministry. The Massachusetts Anti-Slavery Society warned abolitionists that "neither the management of the anti-slavery cause, nor that cause itself, belongs to any professional class."[22] Rallying their forces around opposition to clerical dictation, Garrisonians maintained the loyalty of a large portion of the New England abolitionists.[23]

The failure of the anti-Garrisonian campaign in New England caused the church-oriented abolitionists to consider ways of reorganizing the antislavery movement in order to separate themselves from the Garrisonians. Before the formation of the Massachusetts Abolition Society, Lewis Tappan had recommended that Garrison's Boston opponents organize an Evangelical Union Anti-Slavery Society on the Philadelphia and New York City models, in which abolitionists with heterodox religious views would not be welcomed. On the national level, Tappan discussed plans with other abolitionists for members of evangelical denominations to unite in a new voluntary society, modeled after the highly centralized American Board of Commissioners for Foreign Missions. Still other abolitionists suggested replacing the old national society with a loose federation of denominational antislavery societies. Exponents of the various formats promised that the new organizations would be more effective in church circles because they would not have the stigma of unorthodox and anticlerical elements, which the non-Garrisonian abolitionists blamed for much of the resistance to the AASS.[24]

The Garrisonians reacted with predictable hostility to all these suggestions. The officers of the Massachusetts Anti-Slavery Society protested that a reorganization of the antislavery societies along denominational lines would put the movement under the control of the very churches it was trying to reform. Garrison denounced these schemes as "high treason against our glorious cause," because they compromised abolitionist principles to win "*respectability* and *popularity*."[25] If such plans had been introduced at the Philadelphia Convention of 1833 that formed the American Anti-Slavery Society, Garrison declared, no national society ever would have been formed. The Garrisonians took an adamant position against all membership tests, religious or political.[26]

The final schism in the AASS came over the women's rights issue, not religious tests. By the end of the 1830s, non-Garrisonian abolitionists had despaired of inducing their opponents to leave the national society voluntarily and attempted to purge the radicals. After a standoff at the 1839 annual meeting of the AASS, both factions marshaled their supporters for the next year's gathering. Large delegations were recruited from the New York and Philadelphia Church Union Anti-Slavery Societies to attend the climactic 1840 annual meeting. Garrisonians reported that their New England abolitionist rivals made furious efforts to rally to their side "*every* minister, influential deacon, or active sectarian. . . . "[27] For their part, the Garrisonians chartered a steamship to carry sympathetic delegates from Massachusetts to the New York City meeting. The showdown in the convention came when the Garrisonians won a close vote on a resolution to permit women to serve as officers of the society. In reaction, the minority bolted and formed their own abolition organization, the American and Foreign Anti-Slavery Society.[28]

The cause of the fissure in abolitionist ranks deserves close scrutiny. The consensus of historians examining this problem is that all abolitionist factions regarded the women's question as a symbol of more substantial differences. Historians also have concluded that the chief source of divisiveness in the movement was the dispute over the propriety of launching an antislavery political party.[29] Such an interpretation, however, overlooks the contribution of disagreements over religious antislavery tactics in the destruction of abolitionist unity.

By 1840 many prominent Garrisonians had renounced the moral authority of the churches and clergy. The Christian abolitionists retained the movement's original hope to convert the nation's religious institutions into antislavery vehicles and viewed the Garrisonians' theological heterodoxy and anticlerical outbursts as handicaps to antislavery efforts in the churches. A majority of Christian abolitionists similarly regarded the Garrisonian introduction of the women's rights question into antislavery activities as an unnecessary affront to the conservative sensibilities of the clergy. This church-oriented faction cooperated closely with abolitionists committed to political activism in the unsuccessful attempt to force the Garrisonians out of the AASS. The proportion of effort given by each non-Garrisonian faction is impossible to discern because their memberhsip overlapped considerably. The best evidence of the strength of the religiously motivated opposition to Garrisonianism in 1840 was the persistence of church-oriented abolitionist activities until the Civil War, as later chapters will demonstrate.

III

The schism in the American Anti-Slavery Society had a great impact on the attitudes and tactics of Garrisonian abolitionists in the religious sphere. Under Garrisonian control, the AASS became outspokenly critical of even the slightest display of toleration toward slavery by the churches. A growing proportion of the active leaders of the post-1840 AASS severed all connections with established religious institutions. At the same time the Garrisonians branded the seceders from the AASS as a clergy-dominated faction more concerned with denying the extent of the churches' culpability for slavery than with ending it. This uncompromising stand helped reinforce the public's perception of the Garrisonians as bitter enemies of all forms of organized religion.

The Garrisonians defined religious fellowship strictly and maintained that antislavery churches must bar not only slaveholders but also anyone who defended or abetted slavery. Because so few denominations even approached this standard, the AASS under its new Garrisonian leadership could unflinchingly resolve in 1840 that the American "Church ought not to be regarded and treated as the Church of Christ, but as the foe of freedom, humanity and pure religion, so long as it occupies its present position."[30] In 1850 the Garrisonian Massachusetts Anti-Slavery Society reiterated this theme by declaring that the American denominations were not authentic Christian bodies and that abolition required "nothing less than a Reformation of the Religion . . . of the Country."[31]

The most vociferous spokesperson for the Garrisonians' uncompromising attack on the churches was Stephen S. Foster, a New Hampshire resident who quit his studies for the Congregational ministry to become a full-time abolitionist lecturer. In his widely quoted work, *The Brotherhood of Thieves; or, A True Picture of the American Church and Clergy* (1843), Foster described slavery as a "social crime" that the small number of slaveholders could not sustain without the countenance of "northern watchdogs," particularly the churches and clergy.[32] Like the early abolitionists, Foster regarded the clergy as "the manufacturers of our public sentiment" who held "in their hand the key to the great prison-house of Southern despotism, and can 'open and no man shut, and shut and no man open.'"[33] Because he doubted that the ministry and the churches were prepared to take any actions that might weaken "their glorious ecclesiastical Union," Foster counseled abolitionists to make war upon the time-serving religious authorities.[34]

Another Garrisonian who gained a national reputation for his vehement rhetoric in assailing the church was Parker Pillsbury, Foster's longtime lecturing partner in New Hampshire. In *The Church As It Is; or, The Forlorn Hope of Slavery* (1847), Pillsbury declared: "Our religion has been found at war with the interests of humanity and the laws of God. And it is more than time [that] the world was awakened to its unhallowed influence on the hopes and happiness of man, while it makes itself the palladium of the foulest iniquity ever perpetrated in the sight of heaven."[35] These and similar vituperative denunciations of the nation's churches by such other Garrisonians as Abigail Kelley Foster, Wendell Phillips, Nathaniel P. Rogers, and Charles King Whipple were frequently reprinted by antiabolitionist editors as evidence of abolitionist infidelity.[36]

Not only their language, but also the theological views of many Garrisonians evidenced a widening rupture with orthodox religion. In the 1840s and 1850s, AASS members played highly visible roles at a series of Church, Ministry, and Sabbath Conventions, where they challenged the infallibility of the Bible, the spiritual authority of the clergy, and the sanctity of the Sabbath. Many Garrisonians espoused the doctrine of nonresistance, which orthodox Christians regarded as a perversion of Christ's gospel of peace. Because the AASS had no religious tests, the society attracted conspicuously large numbers of Unitarians, spiritualists, feminists, communitarians, and other theological and social radicals.[37] The Garrisonians' connection with these assorted heterodox movements and the virulence of Garrisonian criticism of the churches encouraged many contemporaries and several twentieth-century historians to assume that the AASS was an infidel organization. Typical accounts in the religious press of a Garrisonian convention noted little besides "the vulgarisms, and infidel slang, the coarse ribaldry, the kicks and curses aimed at the ministry, Church, Bible, etc."[38]

The Garrisonians had little success in rebutting these charges. AASS spokespersons denied that their society, in its collective capacity, was responsible for the religious views of individual members. Wendell Phillips contended that the AASS had never attacked the Bible or the churches per se, only the use of their authority to shield slavery. Although a few Garrisonians endeavored to defend their theological views, most heeded William Lloyd Garrison's warning that the accusation of infidelity was "an old device to divert attention from the true issue" of slavery and abolition.[39]

The most controversial approach adopted by the Garrisonians toward the churches was their variant of the practice of "comeouterism." At the beginning of the antislavery movement, abolitionists had worked from inside religious bodies. By the late 1830s and early 1840s, however, many abolitionists began to despair that the churches could be made into antislavery vehicles. As an alternative, these abolitionists revived the ancient Christian practice of "coming out" of religious associations deemed evil rather than risking spiritual contamination by attempting to purify them.[40] Both Garrisonian and Christian abolitionists adopted a variety of comeouter tactics. These included local congregations' renunciation of all ties to higher bodies that admitted slaveholders to fellowship, the creation of new denominations with constitutions that prohibited slave-owning members, and individual abolitionists' separation from all religious connections as a protest against the latters' complicity in slavery.

Although some Garrisonians participated in the formation of antislavery congregations and sects, the third and most radical form of comeouterism won the adherence of such prominent Garrisonians as Stephen S. Foster, Parker Pillsbury, Nathaniel P. Rogers, Maria Weston Chapman, Henry C. Wright, and Garrison himself. Such a course appealed to the anticlerical and perfectionistic religious views of this faction. In addition, as skilled propagandists, these Garrisonians recognized that excommunicating one's church for the sin of abetting slavery was a dramatic gesture sure to agitate the religious community.[41]

One of the best examples of the Garrisonians' comeouter propaganda was the public letter of Wright to his Newbury, Massachusetts, congregation, which declared:

> I am deeply and sorrowfully impressed with the belief that by your opposition to the Anti-Slavery enterprise, and by your silence in regard to the wrongs of the slave and the guilt of the slaveholder, you, as a church, are doing more to make our holy religion the scorn and execration of mankind than all that Jew, or Heathen, or Infidel, ever did or can do. While you thus continue by your silence or otherwise to sustain this system of wrong and outrage—I cannot regard you as a christian church: and I DO HEREBY RENOUNCE YOU AS A CHRISTIAN CHURCH. This resolution is formed in view of the day when I am to meet the imbruted slave and his guilty oppressors and their abettors before Heaven's tribunal. It is deliberately formed and never will be retracted till, as a *church,* you have humbled yourselves before God and the slave, repented and made restitution by bearing an open and constant testimony against slavery.[42]

Not all cases of Garrisonian comeouterism were voluntary. Because of his abolitionist activities, Pillsbury's ministerial association revoked his license to preach; only then did he retaliate by excommunicating the entire association. Foster's congregational church in Hanover, New Hampshire, expelled him for having become "a disorganizer and a leveller" as well as an abolitionist.[43] Numerous Hicksite Quaker members of the AASS were similarly discharged from their yearly meetings for refusing to desist from their antislavery agitation.[44]

Some Garrisonians experimented with an even more aggressive form of comeouterism. In the early 1840s, Foster, Pillsbury, Abigail Kelley, and a few other Garrisonians invaded churches and disrupted Sunday services with unannounced and usually undesired antislavery lectures. The usual reward for such efforts was a rapid and sometimes violent ejection, even from Friends' meetinghouses. Although they were universally condemned in religious circles, these radical comeouters believed that their tactics forced even the most reluctant churchmen to reflect on the question of slavery. In his memoirs, Pillsbury claimed that "nothing like or unlike it, before or afterward, so stunned the whole people, until John Brown, with his twenty heroes, marched on Harpers Ferry and challenged the supporters of slavery to mortal combat."[45] Most Garrisonian comeouters, however, regarded secession from the churches as sufficiently vivid testimony and eventually discarded the more dramatic practices.

In secular as well as religious affairs, Garrisonians adopted increasingly radical stances after 1840. Garrison's *Liberator* championed perfectionism not as a question of theology but as "sound morality" essential to the success of all reform movements.[46] Garrisonian males not only endorsed the theory of sexual equality but selected such women as Abigail Kelley, Lydia Maria Child, and Maria Weston Chapman for responsible positions as lecturers, editors, secretaries, and treasurers. By the late 1830s nonresistant principles had led many Garrisonians to refuse to vote. In the next decade, the AASS advocated the dissolution of the federal union to separate the North from the guilt of sustaining a proslavery Constitution. Although a few exceptionally anarchistic abolitionists such as Nathaniel P. Rogers broke with the AASS as too conservative, the Garrisonians did little to appease the more cautious elements of the antislavery movement.[47]

Despite a modest degree of rapprochement in later years, the Garrisonians retained many bitter feelings toward the abolitionists who quit the AASS in 1840. The *Liberator* blasted the seceders' new American and Foreign Anti-Slavery Society as a body created by the "clergy and their retainers."[48] Garrisonians accused the "new organization" of compromising traditional antislavery principles—particularly the duty not to tolerate fellowship with slaveholders or their apologists or abettors—in order to placate the clergy's fears of disrupting church unity. Garrisonians also complained that many seceders had quickly lost all interest in abolitionism except for antislavery politics.[49] Regarding their opponents as compromising, priest-ridden, and thirsting after political office, Garrisonian leaders opposed any reconciliation with their former abolitionist colleagues unless the latter repented of their erring ways.

In the mid-1840s the most radical Garrisonians pushed to have the AASS and its auxiliaries formally endorse their perfectionist doctrines. Typical of the comeouter resolutions adopted by Garrisonian conventions was the following, passed by the 1843 annual meeting of the Massachusetts Anti-Slavery Society:

Resolved, That the Church or minister that refuses to treat the sin of slaveholding, which is the sum of all other sins, its perpetrators and abettors, near and remote, direct and indirect, as they do all other sins and sinners, is not a Church of Christ, or a minister of the gospel; and that it is the duty of all true abolitionists to withdraw all support or countenance from such ministers and Churches.[50]

In 1844 the AASS anniversary gathering declared nonresistance "a duty" and endorsed disunionism on the grounds that "political union in any form between a slaveholding and a free community must necessarily involve the latter in the guilt of slavery."[51] These last two resolutions passed over protests by David Lee Child, Ellis Gray Loring, and others that such judgment of the conduct of fellow abolitionists was "eminently sectarian, intolerant, and presumptuous."[52]

IV

The American Anti-Slavery Society's increasingly hostile public stance toward religious and governmental institutions has led many historians to minimize the Garrisonians' contribution to the overall antislavery movement. According to this interpretation, the Garrisonians, by placing ideological purity ahead of practical achievement, converted the AASS from an effective instrument for abolition into an isolated and ridiculed "holy fraternity." Since the late 1960s, a number of influential studies have attempted to rehabilitate the Garrisonians' historical reputation, but they have concentrated almost exclusively on the group's political activities.[53] A close inspection of AASS operations after 1840, however, reveals that the Garrisonians also made significant contributions to the antislavery campaign in the nation's churches.

One reason for historians' underestimation of the Garrisonians' role in church-oriented abolitionist affairs is their failure to investigate systematically the religious practices of individual AASS members. The result has been the persistence of the popular but mistaken image of the AASS as a society whose leaders had renounced and abandoned all religious institutions. An examination of the religious affiliations of the 238 men and women who served as officers of the AASS from 1840 to 1864 reveals several surprising statistics. (See Table 3.) Although there is little or no biographical information available for many of these individuals, at least 134, or 56.3 percent, were church members; only 21, or 8.8 percent, were comeouters. Even if all of the 83 Garrisonians whose religious affiliations cannot be ascertained were comeouters, they still would account for only a minority of the society's leadership. Of the 45 Garrisonians holding pol-

Table 3. Religious affiliations of the officers of the American Anti-Slavery Society, 1840–1864

Denomination	1840 (%)	1845 (%)	1850 (%)	1855 (%)	1860 (%)	1863 (%)	Total 1840–65 (%)
Orthodox Quaker	1 (1.2)	—	—	—	—	—	2 (0.8)
Hicksite Quaker	8 (9.5)	10 (14.5)	11 (17.7)	5 (12.8)	5 (11.6)	5 (11.1)	22 (9.2)
Quaker (faction un-determined)	12 (14.3)	9 (13.0)	6 (9.7)	1 (2.6)	1 (2.3)	2 (4.4)	19 (8.0)
Freewill Baptist	1 (1.2)	—	—	3 (7.7)	2 (4.7)	2 (4.4)	5 (2.1)
Wesleyan Methodist		2 (2.9)	1 (1.6)	—	—	—	3 (1.3)
Progressive Friend		2 (2.9)	2 (3.2)	3 (7.7)	2 (4.7)	—	6 (2.5)
Union Church	2 (2.4)	—	—	—	—	—	4 (1.7)
African Methodist Episcopal			1 (1.6)				2 (0.8)
Congregational	12 (14.3)	5 (7.2)	3 (4.8)	2 (5.1)	3 (7.0)	3 (6.7)	17 (7.1)
New School Presbyterian	2 (2.4)	1 (1.4)	1 (1.6)	—	—	—	5 (2.1)
Methodist Episcopal	2 (2.4)	—	—	—	—	—	3 (1.3)
Baptist	6 (7.1)	1 (1.4)	1 (1.6)	1 (2.6)	—	—	11 (4.6)
Disciple of Christ		—	—	—	—	—	2 (0.8)
Adventist	1 (1.2)						1 (0.4)
Unitarian	6 (7.1)	5 (7.2)	5 (8.1)	7 (17.9)	6 (14.0)	7 (15.6)	19 (8.0)
Universalist		1 (1.4)	—	—	—	—	1 (0.4)
Swedenborgian	1 (1.2)	1 (1.4)	2 (3.2)	1 (2.6)	—	—	2 (0.8)
Spiritualist		1 (1.4)	1 (1.6)	1 (2.6)	1 (2.3)	1 (2.2)	3 (1.3)
Free Thinker	1 (1.2)	—	—	—	—	—	2 (0.8)
Antislavery Come-outer	2 (2.4)	4 (5.8)	5 (8.1)	3 (7.7)	7 (16.3)	7 (15.6)	21 (8.8)
Undetermined	27 (32.1)	26 (37.7)	23 (37.1)	13 (33.3)	16 (37.2)	14 (31.1)	83 (34.9)
Total	84 (100)	69 (100)	62 (100)	39 (100)	43 (100)	45 (100)	238 (100)
Total ministers	8 (9.5)	6 (8.7)	4 (6.5)	5 (12.8)	4 (9.3)	4 (8.9)	31 (13.0)

icy-shaping offices (president, treasurer, secretaries, and members of the executive committee) in contrast to honorary offices (vice-presidents and managers), 27, or a full 60 percent, are known to have been church members. (See Table 4.) Despite the strongly anticlerical statements made by some Garrisonians, at least 31, or 13 percent, of the AASS officers can be identified as active ministers during their terms as AASS officers.

Several factors account for the discrepancy between the accepted perceptions of Garrisonians' religious behavior and the reality. Some evidence of Garrisonian anticlericalism exists in the fact that only 3, or 6.7 percent, of the 45 highest-level AASS officers (Samuel May, Jr., William H. Channing, and John T. Sargent) were clergymen, and all three were Unitarians. A possible trend toward Garrisonian comeouterism may be discernible from the slow but steady decline in the proportion of identified church members among AASS officers, from 64.3 percent in 1840 to 56.5 percent in 1845 to a low of 46.5 percent in 1860. Most significant was the type of denomination with which churchgoing Garrisonians were affiliated. Sixty-three, or approximately half, of the 125 Garrisonians who remained in the churches were members of either the traditionally antislavery denominations such as the Quakers or the new comeouter congregations and sects founded in the 1840s. The other half were divided between 36 members of evangelical denominations such as the Congregationalists, Presbyterians, Methodists, and Baptists and 25 members of theologically liberal denominations, principally Unitarians. The proportion of members of the major evangelical churches declined from 40.7 percent in 1840 to only 15.8 percent in 1860, while the proportion of Unitarians and other liberal Christians increased from 13.0 percent to 36.8

Table 4. Religious affiliations of the active officers (president, treasurer, secretaries, and executive committee members) of the American Anti-Slavery Society, 1840–1864

Denomination	Total (%)
Hicksite Quaker	7 (15.6)
Quaker (faction undetermined)	3 (6.7)
Progressive Friend	1 (2.2)
Union Church	1 (2.2)
Unitarian	13 (28.9)
Adventist	1 (2.2)
Antislavery Comeouter	8 (17.8)
Undetermined	10 (22.2)
Total	45 (100)
Total ministers	3 (6.7)

percent. These statistics suggest that many of the evangelical abolitionists' charges of Garrisonian infidelity can be attributed to sectarian bias.

The Garrisonians boasted of the AASS's lack of membership tests, and the statistics on their religious practices confirm that claim. Just as large numbers of Garrisonians continued to vote despite the AASS's endorsement of nonresistance, so a majority of the society's officers ignored its exhortation to come out of the churches that tolerated slavery. Numerous leading Garrisonians stood by their old denominations and worked to end their proslavery practices. For example, Garrisonians such as the Reverends Samuel Joseph May and his nephew Samuel May, Jr., were proponents of antislavery action in the American Unitarian Association. Other Garrisonians retained membership in the traditionally antislavery Quaker and Freewill Baptist denominations and worked to bring their practices more into line with the strict standards of the AASS. Most significantly, Garrisonians not only remained in the Reformed Presbyterian church and some comeouter sects but also won exemptions for those bodies from blanket condemnations of the churches at AASS conventions.[54] Later chapters will describe at greater length the contributions of the Garrisonians to the antislavery campaigns inside these and other denominations.

In addition to the lobbying by individual Garrisonians in their denominations, the AASS continued to employ many other time-honored methods of moral suasion to awaken the churchgoing public to the evil nature of slavery. In their literature and lectures, Garrisonians still preached the original AASS doctrine that slave owning was a sin and that there was no Christian alternative to immediate emancipation. AASS newspapers, annual reports, and traveling lecturers continued to elaborate on how northern religious bodies condoned slavery through their fellowship of slave owners and discrimination against blacks. Garrisonians applauded clergymen and politicians who interjected moral considerations into the public debates over government policies toward slavery. During the 1850s the Garrisonians invited prominent ministers such as Henry Ward Beecher and George B. Cheever to address their conventions in order to encourage them to adopt more stringent abolitionist positions. The society also devoted considerable efforts to persuading foreign denominations to terminate fellowship with proslavery American churches.[55] Several Garrisonians touring Britain in 1846 and 1847 generated favorable publicity for the antislavery movement by their campaign to convince the Free Church of Scotland to return financial contributions from American slaveholders.[56]

Although they remained suspicious of the character of the AASS schismatics, Garrisonians often took part in new church-oriented antislavery tactics devised by their abolitionists rivals after 1840. As already noted, some Garrisonians joined with antislavery Christians in forming comeouter sects to protest the toleration of slavery in the established denominations. AASS members also played a limited role at several of the interdenominational Christian Anti-Slavery Conventions sponsored by their abolitionist opponents. Garrisonian as well as Christian abolitionist presses published literature calculated to encourage churchmen to reform the practices of the religious benevolent societies that attempted to remain neutral toward slavery. Later chapters will assess in more detail the Garrisonian contribution to each of these church-oriented antislavery efforts.

A strong case can be made that the 1840 schism in the AASS did not damage antislavery efforts in the churches. Garrisonians neither compromised original religiously inspired principles nor lessened the society's commitment to moral suasion. Garrisonian writers and lecturers endeavored to demonstrate that the practices of most denominations aided and abetted slavery. A large proportion of Garrisonians remained in their old denominations, particularly in the theologically liberal bodies, in order to labor for adoption of abolitionist religious practices. Other Garrisonians utilized comeouterism as a valuable propaganda gesture to expose church inaction against slavery. Because the Garrisonian-controlled AASS concentrated upon changing public opinion, its agitation had important indirect impact on the churches. Given the fact that Garrisonian labors helped to strengthen northern antislavery sentiments, the AASS must be credited with helping to make the churches more receptive to abolitionist advances. Just as the Garrisonians can be regarded as helping to prepare the way for the Republicans in politics, so the AASS's activities contributed to moderate antislavery gains in the northern churches.

—4—

Church-Oriented Abolitionism and the Sectional Schism in the American Churches

Few other incidents in the history of the antislavery movement are so well known as the sectional schisms in the Methodist Episcopal church in 1844 and in the Baptist denomination in 1845. Historians regularly cite the divisions in these and in other denominations in the 1840s and 1850s as evidence of growing antislavery sentiment in the North. Historical accounts rely on contemporary observers as diverse as Henry Clay, John C. Calhoun, and John Quincy Adams, all of whom attributed these denominational dissolutions to an increasing divergence between North and South on the moral question of slavery. These accounts maintain that the denominational divisions transformed the northern churches into powerful antislavery exponents well before the Civil War.[1]

Such an interpretation ignores the opinion of the abolitionists, who closely monitored every facet of the religious community's relations toward slavery. Despite their quarrels over other questions, nearly all abolitionists agreed that the sectional schisms in the Baptist, Methodist, and other denominations did not represent significant antislavery advances. For example, Garrisonian abolitionists such as Parker Pillsbury responded to the claim that northern antislavery had caused the church schisms with the remark, "Grosser fraud and falsehood was never told."[2] Christian abolitionists arrived at the similar conclusion that the motive of the denominational separations was one "not of principle, but of policy."[3] This was a discouraging assessment for the latter group, most of whom had continued to work inside their churches for antislavery reforms since quitting the American Anti-Slavery Society in 1840.

I

Historians have customarily ignored or dismissed the activities of the Christian abolitionists. Although lively historiographical skirmishes have occurred over the Garrisonians' contribution to the success of the antislavery campaign, few students of abolitionism credit their church-oriented opponents with any important accomplishments. The American and Foreign Anti-Slavery Society (AFASS), formed by seceding members of the AASS, is typically portrayed as "a museum of old abolitionists" that could neither keep most of its founders active nor attract a younger generation to the time-honored methods of battling slavery.[4] Even historians critical of the Garrisonians dismiss the AFASS as a "transitional" or "auxiliary" vehicle to the new political abolition movement.[5] In contrast to the Garrisonians' public feud with the nation's religious institutions, AFASS relations with the churches have been described as "fairly peaceful if not always cordial" and as improving rapidly once the northern churches began to progress toward antislavery positions.[6] According to many recent historians, the new organization's approach to abolitionism was insufficiently radical or innovative to arouse the northern conscience from its long-established patterns of indifference and sufferance toward slavery.[7] A close scrutiny of antislavery activities within the northern religious community, however, shows that these charges against the AFASS must be qualified or dismissed altogether.

The accomplishments of the AFASS are even more impressive when weighed against the handicaps under which that body labored in its first years. The failure of the opponents of Garrisonianism to capture control of the AASS in 1840 put them at the disadvantage of not only having to create a second national abolition society, but also having to justify the need for one. The AFASS was launched in the midst of a severe economic depression that cut heavily into potential contributions. Moreover, by 1840 revivalistic enthusiasm had passed its peak, and the spirit of interdenominational cooperation had declined. The society's male-only membership policy cost it the support of the growing number of female abolitionists and of those men sympathetic to the feminist cause. Many experienced non-Garrisonian abolitionist leaders, including Henry B. Stanton, Joshua Leavitt, and James G. Birney, joined the AFASS but devoted the bulk of their energies to political antislavery labors. Other nationally prominent abolitionists such as Theodore Weld and William Goodell, together with the officers of many local and state antislavery societies, refused to align themselves with either of the rival national abolition societies.[8]

The first major hurdle for the AFASS was to establish itself as a vehicle independent from the new antislavery Liberty party. Among the early leaders of the AFASS, political abolitionists such as Birney, Stanton, and Leavitt concluded that the churches were "so entirely identified with the rest of the community, that we are not likely to see them taking a stand, on any subject, greatly in advance of the body of the people." The trio believed that the only likely ways to carry the churches forward were "those means which affect the mass of the people," meaning political action.[9] Many Christian abolitionists, however, shared the antebellum religious community's mistrust of politics as sordid and compromising. For example, Lewis Tappan, the editor of the society's periodical, the *American and Foreign Anti-Slavery Reporter*, feared that involvement in "independent nominations" would "lead abolitionists away from the moral and religious aspects of the cause" and taint the abolition movement in the eyes of high-minded churchmen who frowned upon political scheming.[10] After a struggle for control of the *Reporter* in the summer of 1841, the politicians conceded active management of the society to the Christian abolitionists, who remained convinced that changing church opinion was the key to progress toward emancipation.[11]

Under the influence of William Jay, Amos Phelps, and other abolitionists who conscientiously supported both religious and political antislavery activities, the position of Tappan and of the AFASS toward the Liberty party slowly changed. In 1842 the society's *Reporter* began giving favorable coverage to Liberty party activities. Immediately before the 1844 election, the *Reporter* praised the high antislavery principles of the Liberty party and of its presidential candidate, Birney, but stopped short of an outright endorsement. At its annual meeting in May 1845, the AFASS overcame its final qualms and called upon all abolitionists to "secede from the political parties, Whig and Democratic, to which they belong, and unite their efforts with the Liberty party for the overthrow of slavery and the restoration of the principles of liberty."[12] Although the AFASS continued to concentrate most of its energies on antislavery church reform, support for the Liberty party became a regular part of the society's program. The antislavery political forces, in return, gave valuable assistance to abolitionist activities in the churches, as will be described in Chapter 8.

Despite its support for political abolitionism, the AFASS retained a primarily religious orientation. The main reason for this orientation was the heavy involvement of the society's leadership in the nation's churches and benevolent organizations. Although the religious affiliations of twenty-two of the eighty-nine men (24.7 percent) who served as AFASS officers (president, vice-presidents, secretaries, treasurer, and members of the executive committee) cannot be ascertained, every one of the remaining sixty-seven individuals was an active church member. (See Table 5.) Unlike their Garrisonian rivals, no officer of the AFASS appears to have "come out" of a proslavery denomination without having immediately joined another church more sympathetic to abolition. The large majority of AFASS leaders were drawn from the evangelical denominations. Only two Quakers, John G. Whittier and Arnold Buffum; one Unitarian, William Kirkland; and two Episcopalians, William Jay and James Mc-Cune Smith, can be identified among the society's officers. In contrast, the Congregationalists alone supplied at least twenty-seven officers (30.3 percent), including Phelps, Simeon S. Jocelyn, George Whipple, and Arthur and Lewis Tappan. The other major evangelical denominations were represented at a minimum by eleven New School Presbyterians (12.4 percent), nine Baptists (10.1 percent), and eight Methodists (9.0 percent). In addition to their church memberships, Tappan, Jay, Leavitt, and many other AFASS officers were stalwarts of the interdenominational benevolent societies, such as the American Bible Society and the American

Table 5. Religious affiliations of the officers of the American and Foreign Anti-Slavery Society, 1840–1854

Denomination	1840 (%)	1845 (%)	1850 (%)	1853 (%)	Total 1840–1854 (%)
Orthodox Quaker	1 (2.5)	—	1 (4.3)	1 (3.6)	2 (2.2)
Freewill Baptist	—	—	—	1 (3.6)	1 (1.1)
Wesleyan Methodist	—	1 (4.8)	1 (4.3)	1 (3.6)	2 (2.2)
American Baptist Free Mission Society	—	—	—	1 (3.6)	2 (2.2)
Union Church	1 (2.5)	1 (4.8)	2 (8.7)	1 (3.6)	3 (3.4)
African Methodist Episcopal Zion	—	1 (4.8)	1 (4.3)	—	1 (1.1)
Congregational	10 (25.0)	7 (33.3)	11 (47.8)	12 (42.9)	27 (30.3)
New School Presbyterian	9 (22.5)	3 (14.3)	—	1 (3.6)	11 (12.4)
Old School Presbyterian	1 (2.5)	1 (4.8)	1 (4.3)	1 (3.6)	1 (1.1)
Methodist Episcopal	5 (12.5)	—	—	1 (3.6)	6 (6.7)
Baptist	7 (17.5)	—	—	1 (3.6)	6 (6.7)
Unitarian	—	1 (4.8)	—	—	1 (1.1)
Protestant Episcopal	1 (2.5)	1 (4.8)	1 (4.3)	2 (7.1)	2 (2.2)
Undetermined	5 (12.5)	5 (23.8)	5 (21.7)	6 (21.4)	22 (24.7)
Total	40 (100)	21 (100)	23 (100)	28 (100)	89 (100)
Total ministers	18 (45.0)	6 (28.6)	10 (43.5)	12 (42.9)	37 (41.6)

Tract Society, which supplemented regular church activities. Perhaps the strongest indication of the key role of religion in the lives of the AFASS officers is the fact that thirty-seven (41.6 percent) were ordained clergymen and many more were deacons and lay preachers. At least eight of these clergymen were black; blacks were statistically far more visible in leadership roles in the AFASS than they were in the Garrisonian AASS.[13]

Many AFASS officers were selected because of their active part in the antislavery movements within the churches during the 1830s and 1840s. Drawn from both the clergy and laity, these men were the editors of antislavery religious periodicals, the founders of denominational abolition societies, and the perennial advocates of motions for action against slavery and against racial discrimination at church conventions. These Christian abolitionists made the denominational antislavery societies into affiliates of the AFASS, thus largely compensating for the organization's dearth of state and county auxiliaries. By sharing membership in the AFASS, antislavery activists in the various faiths pledged themselves to one common program to end the toleration of slavery by the northern churches.[14]

The key figure in the leadership both of the AFASS and of many church-oriented abolitionist ventures was Lewis Tappan. Son of a Northampton, Massachusetts, storekeeper, Tappan had followed his older brother Arthur to New York City, where together they operated a prosperous silk-importing firm. When the brothers' partnership was dissolved in 1841, Tappan established a credit-rating agency that later evolved into the Dun & Bradstreet Company. After a youthful flirtation with Unitarianism, Tappan returned to the orthodox faith of his forebears. Deeply impressed by evangelical ideals of disinterested benevolence as preached by Charles G. Finney, Tappan gave generously of his time and money to nearly all the religiously inspired reform movements of the 1820s and 1830s. It was Tappan's strong religious faith that drew him into abolitionism and permitted him to remain confident that the movement would eventually convert other benevolent-minded individuals. Despite his religious orientation, Tappan was flexible enough to cooperate with political abolitionists and to seek support from such nonevangelical groups as New York City's early labor radicals. A dedicated administrator and a liberal financial patron of a variety of antislavery organizations, Tappan held first place in the ranks of Christian abolitionists down to the Civil War.[15]

The strong commitment of the AFASS leaders to a church-oriented abolitionist strategy played an important role in blocking a reconciliation with the Garrisonians. Despite agreement with the Garrisonians on basic principles concerning the sinfulness of slaveholding and the churches' moral responsibilities toward slavery, Christian abolitionists shared the suspicions of other northern churchmen about the theological orthodoxy of the AASS leaders. The AFASS declared itself the only abolition society open to men of orthodox religious views because the AASS required its members to "vilify the ministry of the church, [and] abandon the religious persuasion with which they are connected."[16] Lewis Tappan proclaimed that "good men" could not join the Garrisonians in "a crusade of the impenitent against the church."[17] Tappan and several other evangelical abolitionists, however, betrayed a prejudice against all forms of liberal theology in their private disparagements of the Garrisonians as "Unitarians, Universalists, [and] Nothingarians" who acted "under the guise of a profession of Christianity."[18] The failure of several attempts to reunite the abolitionist factions in a common "Anti-Slavery League" was due as much to religious antagonism as it was to quarrels over political programs.[19]

While they assailed Garrisonian infidelity, the Christian abolitionists also scrupulously guarded their own faction's religious reputation. Many criticized Gerrit Smith, a major contributor to the AFASS, for making political antislavery speeches on the Sabbath. Elizur Wright was replaced as editor of the newspaper of the Massachusetts Abolition Society, an AFASS auxiliary, because of his theological liberalism.[20] The AFASS members believed that only by demonstrating their own orthodoxy could they expect to disprove the popular presumption that heterodoxy was an inherent corollary of abolitionism. A survey of the northern religious press discloses that the moderate antislavery editors usually acknowledged the Christian abolitionists' religious soundness, whereas more conservative editors generally branded all abolitionists as infidels.[21]

Although AFASS supporters demonstrated an intense concern for their religious reputations, it did not follow that their criticism of the churches was less severe than that of the Garrisonians. The society's *Reporter* testified that the churches' lenient attitude toward the crimes of slavery was "highly derogatory to the honour of religion" and damaging to the moral character of the clergy.[22] The society regularly declared that the major northern churches shared in the sin of slavery by their refusal to condemn it and praised the few denominations and individual ministers who opposed such a "time-serving ecclesiastical policy."[23] At its annual meetings the AFASS firmly endorsed the expulsion of slave owners from religious fellowship, as in this resolution adopted in 1841:

> *Resolved,* That we earnestly recommend to the churches and Christian so-
> cieties of every name, the duty of bearing decided testimony against the

abomination of slavery, by refusing the privileges of membership and communion to all who are guilty of that sin, or who justify the practice, until they give evidence of repentance. . . .[24]

The AFASS also denounced the racial prejudice and procolonization sentiment that remained prevalent in northern religious circles.[25] Contrary to Garrisonian accusations, there is no evidence that the AFASS demanded any less of the churches than did the AASS when dealing with purely slavery-related matters.

Despite limited financial resources, the AFASS attempted to sustain the moral suasion campaign of the old AASS. The society's *Reporter* appeared only sporadically, and its publication was suspended completely in 1846. The AFASS, however, had greater success with the circulation of its other major publications: the *Liberty Almanac*, edited by Joshua Leavitt, and the society's annual reports, written by Lewis Tappan. The latter work, in particular, attracted wide praise as a thorough chronicle of the activities of antislavery reformers in both the religious and the political spheres. As a supplement to the society's own publications, AFASS secretaries wrote hundreds of articles for sympathetic political newspapers, advocating antislavery church reform. The AFASS regularly recruited prominent church figures to draft antislavery pamphlets and petitions, which attracted widespread notice because of their authority. The society likewise learned to attract large audiences to its public meetings by advertising such well-known figures as Charles G. Finney, Henry Ward Beecher, Frederick Douglass, and John P. Hale as featured speakers. Although the AFASS could afford to hire only a few lecturing agents, those selected were generally assigned to labor among members of their own denominations, where they could be most effective.[26] By such creative methods, the AFASS was able to stretch its resources to support an aggressive propaganda campaign among northern churchmen.

The AFASS also successfully maintained another traditional tactic of the old AASS, the rallying of foreign support for the American abolition campaign. AFASS leaders, particularly Lewis Tappan, established fraternal relations with the officers of the British and Foreign Anti-Slavery Society and the Canadian Anti-Slavery Society. Through these connections, the Christian abolitionists lobbied foreign Protestant churches to bar visiting Americans from their religious fellowship unless those individuals were genuinely antislavery. The AFASS also encouraged Britons to protest the failure of the Free Church of Scotland and of the international Evangelical Alliance to bar slaveholding members or contributors. By the late 1840s the AFASS faction had far outdistanced its Garrisonian rivals in enlisting the cooperation of the heavily church-oriented foreign abolition societies.[27]

AFASS members also developed new methods to challenge the established churches' toleration of slavery. Many Christian abolitionists joined the Garrisonians in seceding from their old slavery-tainted religious connections. Unlike the anti-institutional radicals in the AASS, the Christian abolitionist comeouters quickly formed new congregations and sects that combined antislavery practices with orthodox creeds. Pro-AFASS abolitionists similarly founded their own missionary and religious publication societies to protest the established bodies' neutral attitude toward slavery in those endeavors. Christian abolitionists also sponsored interdenominational Christian Anti-Slavery Conventions to encourage and coordinate the increasingly diverse efforts against slavery in the churches. In all these activities, AFASS adherents demonstrated greater ingenuity than their Garrisonian rivals in finding new means to further the abolitionist cause in the churches. The influence of these new tactics will be explored in later chapters.

After the 1840 schism in the AASS, the church-oriented activities of the Christian abolitionists simultaneously expanded and decentralized. The AFASS attempted to provide coordination to the various new religious antislavery projects as well as to conduct its own propaganda campaign against the churches' toleration of slavery and racial discrimination. The proliferation of sectarian and benevolent abolitionist organizations and the competition from antislavery politics, however, diverted energy and finances away from the AFASS. By the late 1840s, active membership had dwindled to a hard core in New York City and the immediate surrounding region. In 1855 this debilitating trend finally forced the Christian abolitionists to dissolve the AFASS. By that time, though, the many new church-oriented abolitionist institutions, founded and nurtured by AFASS members during the 1840s and 1850s, had matured sufficiently to conduct their antislavery labors without the benefit of a national overseeing body.

II

Although AFASS members experimented with new church-oriented tactics, they concentrated most of their efforts in the early 1840s on traditional methods of lobbying within church channels. Unforeseen developments in the churches in the mid-1840s, however, led Christian abolitionists to doubt the effectiveness of their long-standing strategies for reforming religious bodies. When the slavery agitation of these years produced sectional divisions of several large denominations, Christian abolitionists expected that the northern wings of these churches would then adopt abolitionist standards. The failure of northern religious leaders to advance beyond a lukewarm antislaveryism—even after mass defections of southern church members—disappointed abolitionists and forced a reconsideration of future church-oriented antislavery tactics.

No consensus ever existed among abolitionists as to whether their movement should work to bring about schisms in the churches, but such an outcome had always been implicit in their demand that slaveholders be barred from Christian fellowship. From the mid-1830s on, abolitionists' hopes to use the churches as agencies to carry antislavery arguments into slaveholding territory declined as northern conservatives united with southerners to restrict free discussion in the nation's religious, as well as political, institutions. When influential northern churchmen stated fears that antislavery actions would threaten denominational unity and obstruct the progress of religion, even Christian abolitionists began to express a preference for a divided church "unless the cause be betrayed for the sake of unscriptural peace and inglorious and unchristian ease."[28]

The denominational schisms most often identified with antislavery agitation were those of the Methodists in 1844 and the Baptists in 1845. The division of the Presbyterian denomination in 1837, however, also had an important impact on church-oriented abolitionist tactics. The causes and consequences of this division offered important lessons to the abolitionists about the complex obstacles that confronted antislavery church reform. The relative importance of the factors causing the Presbyterian separation is a subject of debate among historians. The Presbyterian General Assembly of 1837 explained its expulsion of four northern synods on the grounds that those judicatories had deviated from the church's traditional Calvinism. In particular, the conservative majority charged that those synods had become corrupted through their adoption of revivalistic preaching styles and their cooperation with liberal-minded Congregationalists in missionary and other benevolent projects. The widely accepted thesis of historian C. Bruce Staiger, however, contends that these synods had also been the ones most outspoken against slavery. Staiger suggests that the expulsions were actually the product of a covert deal between southerners and orthodox northerners to purge the church of a common enemy.[29]

A later interpretation by John W. Christie and Dwight L. Dumond contradicts Staiger and minimizes the role of abolitionism in the 1837 schism. Christie and Dumond contend that as early as the General Assembly of 1818, the Presbyterians had established an unspoken policy of opposing slavery in theory while tolerating it in practice. These authors find no satisfactory evidence that antislavery Presbyterians dissented strongly enough from the denomination's consensus on slavery to have caused a schism.[30] The subsequent inaction of both Presbyterian factions on the slavery issue soon caused abolitionists to interpret the events of 1837 from a viewpoint similar to Christie's and Dumond's.

The fate of antislavery efforts within the larger and theologically more orthodox Old School Presbyterian denomination revealed both the power of northern conservative antiabolitionism in the churches and the need for reformers to adopt new tactics to deal with that sentiment. Although southerners accounted for only one-third of the Old School Presbyterian membership, many northerners joined them in suppressing all discussion of slavery in their national church councils. The northern conservatives, including Joshua Wilson and Charles Hodge, decried both abolitionist and proslavery doctrines as "fanatical" and favored gradual emancipation and colonization as the least disruptive solution to the slavery program.[31] Despite the dominant position of these conservatives in the denomination, a few veteran abolitionists such as Samuel Crothers, James Dickey, Thomas E. Thomas, and Erasmus D. McMasters sided with the Old School after the Presbyterian schism. This small Christian abolitionist minority, centered in the Chillicothe Presbytery of southern Ohio, regularly sent remonstrances to the Old School General Assemblies calling for enforcement of the churches' 1818 antislavery discipline.[32]

The persistent petitioning by the abolitionist faction finally forced the Old School General Assembly of 1845 to define the church's position on slavery. With only thirteen negative votes, the Old School governing body resolved that although the church disapproved of the many evils accompanying slavery and hoped for its eventual extinction, the Bible gave no sanction for barring slaveholders from Christian communion. The General Assembly went on to warn that "modern abolitionism" threatened the peace of all churches and "so far from removing the evils complained of tend[ed] only to perpetuate and aggravate them."[33] The strength of northern conservative opposition to abolitionism would eventually force some antislavery Old School Presbyterians to abandon their church.

Although only a few southern presbyteries allied themselves with the New School, or theologically more evangelistic, Presbyterians, that body proved itself nearly as solicitous as the Old School toward slaveholding members. In the church's early years, the New School General Assemblies sidestepped the troublesome question by delegating authority over the slavery question to lower judicatories. As a result, several western presbyteries excluded slaveholders from their pulpits and communions. Pressure for a definitive statement finally forced the General Assembly of

1846 to acknowledge slavery's oppressive character, but at the same time the body proclaimed it unfair "by general and promiscuous condemnation" to declare all slaveholders sinners and unfit for church membership.[34]

Northern conservatives in the denomination such as Sydney E. Morse, editor of the *New York Observer,* praised the New School General Assembly's action for its "latitude of construction," but the move caused deep divisions in the antislavery forces.[35] Strict abolitionists in both the AASS and the AFASS denounced the ruling as a compromise that fell far short of long-established antislavery principles. Many abolitionists suggested comeouterism to antislavery New School Presbyterians, either along Garrisonian lines or into other denominations or even into a new antislavery Presbyterian sect. Most New School Presbyterians who claimed to disapprove of southern oppression, however, argued that further agitation from inside the denomination, not secession, would better encourage antislavery reform.[36] A serious problem was emerging for abolitionists over church-oriented antislavery tactics. Given the failure of even predominantly northern and professedly antislavery churches to sever their ties to slavery, abolitionists had to decide whether to continue their efforts from within or from outside those bodies.

III

The abolitionists in the Methodist Episcopal church soon faced such a dilemma. In the 1830s, Methodist abolitionists failed to persuade their denominational authorities to expel slaveholders for violating the long-ignored discipline against the "buying and selling of men, women and children."[37] Despite their rejection of abolitionism, the Methodist church councils continued to pay lip service to their antislavery heritage by endorsements of colonization and by missionary work among the slaves. Eventually, however, the efforts of northern conservatives to uphold this modest antislavery tradition in the face of growing pressure from abolitionists and from proslavery southerners backfired and caused a series of secessions.[38]

The year 1840 marked a turning point in the antislavery campaign in the Methodist Episcopal church. Despite intensive abolitionist lobbying, the Methodist quadrennial General Conference of that year not only rejected all antislavery petitions but also increased official discrimination against black church members. In protest, Methodist abolitionists held denominational antislavery conventions and founded a permanent national organization, the American Wesleyan Anti-Slavery Society, in October 1840. Within another year, Methodist abolitionists also established a weekly periodical, edited by the Reverend Orange Scott, and an antislavery missionary society.[39] Perhaps because Scott, LaRoy Sunderland, George Storrs, and other organizers of this new movement had been prominent in launching the AFASS, the Garrisonians either ignored these activities or ridiculed them as ineffective. In contrast, the AFASS and the Liberty party press praised and publicized the growth of the abolitionist spirit among these Methodists. The AFASS even hired members of the American Wesleyan Anti-Slavery Society as lecturing agents among their own denomination.[40]

Despite assistance from the AFASS, Methodist abolitionists made little progress. The denominational antislavery society could rarely get its proceedings reported in the Methodist press. Several antislavery Methodist ministers were suspended from preaching as punishment for their abolitionist preaching and writing. With the official machinery of the denomination turned against them, many Methodist abolitionists despaired of ever converting their church. Influenced by the perfectionistic strain in Methodist theology, Scott and other antislavery reformers concluded that, because their labors had no foreseeable success, it would be "a sin for us to remain longer in the church."[41]

A steady trickle of antislavery-motivated secessions from the Methodist Episcopal church occurred during the late 1830s, but the November 1842 call for organization of a new abolitionized Methodist church, signed by Scott, Sunderland, and Jotham Horton, precipitated a large-scale exit. Within two years the new Wesleyan Methodist Connection grew to nearly fifteen thousand members. The *True Wesleyan,* the organ of the new sect, boasted that "the influence of [antislavery] seceders is, to say the least, tenfold to what it would be by remaining in churches where, by necessity, they must sanction by example, the system of slavery."[42] Wesleyans also claimed that membership in their venture afforded Methodists an opportunity to escape moral culpability for toleration of slavery without the need to participate in the more infidel comeouterism of the Garrisonians.[43]

Ironically, the mass departure of the abolitionist Wesleyans only shortly preceded the secession of most southerners from the Methodist Episcopal church. Although conservative northern Methodists claimed to be glad to be rid of the "restless spirit" and the "distraction" that the antislavery agitation had produced, they took steps to discourage antislavery moderates from joining the Wesleyans.[44] The bishops permitted a number of Methodist antislavery conventions to meet in New England without official harassment. The editors of several northern Methodist newspapers opened their columns to antislavery articles. At the same time, however, the conservatives warned antislavery zealots that the adoption of undiluted abolitionist doctrines would destroy the church's powerful influence in behalf of ameloriation and gradual emancipation.[45]

The test of the conservatives' conciliatory policy came at the Methodist General Conference of 1844. For a week, delegates at the conference debated what action the church should take toward Bishop James O. Andrew of Georgia, who had become a slaveholder in violation of one of the few antislavery rules that the church still observed. Attempts by northern conservatives to arrange a compromise with southern delegates failed because the latter wanted to use the issue to discover the extent of abolitionist infiltration of the denomination. With 18 northern delegates siding with the South, the conference voted 110 to 63 to suspend Andrew from his episcopal duties as long as he remained a slaveholder. Although this was an extremely mild reproof, most southerners considered it an official acknowledgment that the denomination attached a moral stigma to slave owning. Offended southern delegates announced their intention to secede, and the General Conference adopted a Plan of Separation to divide church resources equitably. The following year the Methodist Episcopal Church, South, was organized in Louisville, Kentucky.[46]

The northern majority at the 1844 General Conference clearly refused to give a positive moral sanction to slaveholding, which militants in both sections interpreted as the real issue at stake in the Andrew affair. The growing strength of abolitionist sentiment in many annual conferences and the possibility of still more secessions to the Wesleyans prodded northern church leaders to resist any further compromise of the denomination's antislavery traditions. The actions of the General Conference and the subsequent southern secession, however, did not induce the denomination to adopt abolitionist religious principles and practices. In fact the northern wing of Methodists soon repudiated the Plan of Separation and began competing with the Methodist Episcopal Church, South, for members in the border states. At least four thousand slaveholders from local conferences in those regions believed conservative reassurances that the northern Methodist church was not an abolitionist body and retained their affiliations.[47]

Abolitionists scrupulously monitored the Methodist schism. Wesleyans were surprised by the actions of the General Conference of 1844 against Bishop Andrew but declared them products of "expediency," not of genuine antislavery sentiment. The *True Wesleyan* complained that nothing had been done to exclude the thousands of slaveholding ministers and members from the border states who chose not to secede.[48] The Garrisonians' Massachusetts Anti-Slavery Society observed that "the Northern Methodists received their just reward for their wicked attempts to preserve the unity of the Church at the expense of justice and right, in seeing the Church rent in twain by even the feeblest breath of agitation."[49] One Liberty party newspaper aptly summed up the doubts of all non-Garrisonian abolitionist factions by wondering of the Andrew affair "what has been gained, for if sound *principle* has not advanced, little has really been gained."[50] The moderate antislavery position developed by the northern Methodists, as in the case of the New School Presbyterians, fell far short of the standards set by the abolitionists for the churches.

IV

The connection of the abolitionists to the Baptist schism of 1845 roughly paralleled their dealings with Methodist antislavery developments. The Baptist commitment to a maximum of autonomy for individual congregations greatly complicated abolitionist endeavors. Baptist antislavery forces could press their demands at the local level, but there was no body with the authority to establish or to enforce a policy on slavery for the entire denomination. Large numbers of Baptists, however, cooperated in voluntary societies for the support of missions and religious publication ventures. Abolitionist efforts among the Baptists therefore concentrated on demands that those organizations repudiate all ties with slave owners by refusing their contributions and forbidding their appointment as missionaries.

After several years of agitation at local levels, Baptist abolitionists gathered at the American Baptist Anti-Slavery Convention in New York City in April 1840. Longtime abolitionists Nathaniel Colver, Duncan Dunbar, Charles W. Denison, Elon Galusha, and Cyrus P. Grosvenor gave focus to the meeting's antislavery sentiment. The American Baptist Anti-Slavery Convention and its state auxiliaries met annually to discuss how their denomination's "benevolent societies should be instantly purged from all their guilty connection with slavery. . . ."[51] To add weight to their protests, Baptist abolitionists founded a provisional committee in 1842 to collect and distribute funds for missionary activities from church members no longer willing to cooperate with slaveholders in the regular societies. The AFASS aided this movement by appointing Denison as a special agent to travel among his fellow Baptists organizing local denominational antislavery societies. Only the Garrisonians crit-

icized the Baptist abolitionists for retaining membership in denominational mission societies while endeavoring to reform those bodies. The
prominence of such longtime opponents of Garrisonianism as Nathaniel
Colver in the American Baptist Anti-Slavery Convention heightened
AASS suspicions about the commitment of Baptist abolitionists to the
principle of denying Christian fellowship to slaveholders.[52]

The Baptist crisis over slavery came to a head in the early 1840s. In
both the Baptist Triennial Convention, which oversaw foreign missions,
and the American Baptist Home Missionary Society, conservative northerners experienced growing pressure from both abolitionists and southerners. To demonstrate their organization's opposition to abolitionism, the
Triennial Convention of 1841 rejected demands to expel slaveholders
from benevolent activities and dropped abolitionist agitator Elon Galusha
from the organization's managing board. At the next Triennial Convention in 1844, a conservative majority tried to placate both northern and
southern militants by resolving that "in cooperating together as members
of this Convention in the work of Foreign Missions, we disclaim all
sanction, either express or implied, whether of slavery or antislavery."[53]

In 1845 Alabama Baptists tested the antislavery sentiment of the Board
of Foreign Missions of the Triennial Convention with an inquiry whether
it would appoint slaveholding missionaries. The board had never been
faced with this problem. After several disputatious meetings, the board
decided that it could never make such appointments because it "would
imply approbation of slavery."[54] In an effort to retain southern support,
the board assured slave owners that it nevertheless still welcomed their
membership and contributions. This reply so infuriated southern Baptists
that they promptly seceded and launched their own foreign missionary
projects.[55]

In 1845, under the guidance of Francis Wayland, president of Brown
University, northern conservatives reorganized the Triennial Convention
into the American Baptist Missionary Union. To stifle further antislavery
agitation, the new organization made its managers responsible only to a
select group of life members and not to small contributors or representatives of individual congregations. The founding convention also rejected
all amendments to the organization's constitution that would erect barriers
to reunification with southern Baptists or prohibit slaveholders from becoming members, officers, or missionaries of the body. Wayland pronounced himself satisfied that the constitution was "purely for missions"
and "equally free from slavery and antislavery."[56]

The American Baptist Home Mission Society similarly debated the
question of supporting slaveholding missionaries. In 1845 the society

agreed to a sectional division of its resources "upon amicable, honourable, and liberal principles."[57] In the following year, the organization adopted a new constitution that gave its board complete control over the selection and location of missionaries. Baptist abolitionists failed in attempts to amend the constitution to instruct the society's missionaries not to serve congregations with slaveholding members.[58]

The reaction of conservative northern Baptists creates doubts about the antislavery character of the missionary societies' reorganizations. Conservatives such as Wayland, Spencer H. Cone, and John Mason Pack denied that the societies had deviated from their long-standing neutrality toward slavery and instead blamed the breakups on southern insistence upon proslavery policies. In opposing antislavery membership tests for the new societies, several nonabolitionist northerners expressed their willingness to accept southerners as members and contributors provided that the latter made no demand for slaveholding missionaries. Wayland spoke for most conservative northern Baptists when he denounced as "false in principle and unchristian in practice" any church action that automatically treated slaveholders as sinners.[59]

The reorganization of Baptist missionary societies after the southern secession caused a division over tactics among the denomination's abolitionists. As early as 1843, a militant faction in the American Baptist Anti-Slavery Convention had founded a permanent organization, the American and Foreign Baptist Missionary Society, whose constitution incorporated abolitionist principles regarding religious fellowship with slaveholders. Unable to agree on a course of action, the American Baptist Anti-Slavery Convention dissolved itself after the sectional schism of the regular missionary societies. Many veteran leaders of the Baptist antislavery movement, including Colver and Galusha, remained in the established missionary organizations. Although they preferred more explicit bars against fellowship with slave owners, these abolitionists asserted that the established societies' practices were effectively separated from all connections with slavery. In contrast, supporters of the American and Foreign Baptist Missionary Society resolved to keep their organization functioning until the constitutions of the Missionary Union and the Home Missionary Society "have been so defined that their antislavery character shall be distinctly marked."[60] In 1846 the American and Foreign Baptist Mission Society changed its name to the American Baptist Free Mission Society and claimed to be the only unquestionably antislavery benevolent channel in the denomination.

Non-Baptist abolitionists had difficulty assessing the Baptists' complicated series of schisms and reorganizations during the 1840s. Christian abolitionists initially expressed pleasure over the events of 1844 and 1845 but later complained when the reorganized Baptist societies rejected explicit exclusion of slave owners from fellowship. In 1853 the AFASS concluded that although "many sincere Anti-Slavery men" remained in those mission bodies, "that connection . . . prevents to a great extent the effective development of their antislavery tendencies."[61] Although Nathaniel Colver remained active in the AFASS, that organization established close working ties with the American Baptist Free Mission Society. The Garrisonian AASS predicted that abolitionists who remained in the regular missionary bodies would fail to bring those societies to an uncompromising antislavery position. The Garrisonians, however, also questioned the consistency of the Free Mission group in continuing to permit fellowship in local congregations with the supporters of the old societies. Although northern Baptists had taken a stronger stand against slavery, abolitionists inside and outside the denomination could not agree whether or not further antislavery efforts were necessary.[62]

V

Most historians regard the sectional schisms in the Methodist and Baptist churches as evidence of the increasingly antislavery attitude of the North in the 1840s. The abolitionists' appraisal of those events, however, raises serious questions about the strength of antislavery sentiment involved. There is considerable validity in the abolitionist charge that southern proslavery intransigence, not northern antislavery militancy, forced the final church divisions. It was southerners who raised the immediate issues that led to the schisms of the mid-1840s, the acceptance of a slaveholding bishop in the Methodist church and the appointment of slaveholding missionaries in the Baptist societies. The abolitionists were not even in a position to lead resistance to those demands, for the most active of them had already seceded by the mid-1840s. Even conservative northern Methodists and Baptists blamed southern firebrands for forcing the denominations to depart from their neutrality on the question of fellowship with slaveholders.[63]

There is also substantial evidence to support the abolitionists' charge that after the schisms of 1844 and 1845 neither the northern Methodists nor Baptists adopted an uncompromising antislavery position. Even after the departure of most southern members, the northern wing of each denomination declined to declare slave owning inherently sinful or to subject the practice to church discipline. By not disciplining slaveholders as they did habitual drunkards, thieves, and adulterers, these religious bodies sacrificed their most powerful means to attempt to persuade slave owners to manumit their bondsmen. Proof of the weakness of the northern Baptists' and Methodists' antislavery professions was the ability of thousands of slaveholders to remain in the religious fellowship of each church until the Civil War. Given the churches' failure to adopt an unqualified moral position, their cautious antislavery statements likewise had a greatly reduced impact on the northern public's toleration of slavery.

Despite the overall accuracy of the abolitionists' specific charges, it is possible to interpret the church schisms as advances in northern antislavery sentiment. While rejecting the abolitionist position that slaveholding was inherently sinful, northern Methodist and Baptist church leaders upheld their denominations' traditional position of regarding slavery as an evil social system that should be gradually extinguished. These northern churchmen could not in good conscience accede to southern demands that the denominations certify the moral rectitude of slaveholding by appointing slave owners as missionaries and bishops. In short, under pressure from the abolitionists and proslavery southerners, northern Methodists and Baptists abandoned their studied neutrality toward slavery and reaffirmed the long-ignored modest antislavery traditions of their denominations. Although some southerners remained in fellowship with both bodies, the schisms helped to sharpen sectional polarization and freed northern Methodists and Baptists to speak and act more aggressively against slavery in later years.

The significance of the Methodist and Baptist divisions as antislavery measures becomes clearer from comparison with other denominations' positions toward slavery in the mid-1840s. Neither of the supposedly antislavery denominations could approach the standards set by the Quakers, the Freewill Baptists, and most Scottish Presbyterian sects in refusing to sanction slavery by accepting slaveholders as members. Compared with the official neutrality toward slavery maintained by the liturgical sects and by the archconservative Old School Presbyterians, however, the actions of the northern Methodists and Baptists were undeniably antislavery gestures and statements. Northern Baptists and Methodists were most similar to the predominantly northern New School Presbyterian, Congregational, and Unitarian denominations in their treatment of the slavery question. Although many individual New School Presbyterians, Unitarians, and Congregationalists adopted strong antislavery views, all these denominations refused to accept the fine points of abolitionist principles on the sinfulness of slave owning and on the church's duty to discipline slaveholding members.[64] In the mid-1840s, these five groups composed a moderate antislavery majority within the northern religious community. (See Table 6.)

These modest antislavery gains failed to satisfy the religiously defined standards of the abolitionists. The failure of the Methodist and Baptist schisms to end the toleration of slavery in either body led abolitionists to disagree further over tactics for church reform. Although the Garrisonians hoped that the religious separations might hasten a similar political break-up, they nevertheless protested the northern churches' continued complicity with slavery. That the northern church members could refuse to take decisive antislavery actions even after the southerners seceded was additional proof to the Garrisonians that traditional religious institutions were totally corrupt and that abolitionists had no alternative but to leave them.[65]

For Christian abolitionists, after more than a decade of agitation within the churches, the unsatisfactory outcome of the denominational schisms produced disagreements over future church-oriented antislavery strategy. Some Christian abolitionists remained in their old church connections and cooperated with more moderate antislavery church members in efforts to move the denominations closer to abolitionist standards. Many other Christian abolitionists renounced further agitation inside the churches and founded new religious organizations free from all connection with slavery. The next three chapters will examine the new tactics employed by the abolitionists to persuade the northern religious community to take stronger actions against slavery.

Table 6. Membership in the principal religious denominations in the United States, 1849

Denomination	Total numbers
Methodist Episcopal	629,660
Methodist Episcopal, South	465,553
Baptist	664,566
Old School Presbyterian	179,453
New School Presbyterian	155,000
Congregational	193,093
Dutch Reformed	32,840
German Reformed	69,750
Protestant Episcopal	72,099
Lutheran	149,625
United Brethren	15,000
Evangelical Association	15,000
Unitarian	30,000
Roman Catholic	1,190,700

Source: Methodist Episcopal Church, *The Methodist Almanac for the Year of Our Lord, 1849* (New York, 1849), 21.

—5—

Abolitionists and
the Comeouter Sects

Beginning in the 1840s, a new phenomenon emerged in the Christian abolitionist campaign in the nation's churches: the antislavery comeouter sect. As noted in Chapter 4, a segment of Methodist and Baptist abolitionists seceded and formed their own religious organizations to protest the slow advance of antislavery sentiment in their old denominations. The dramatic sectional schisms in those churches in 1844 and 1845 did not halt this trend. By the mid-1850s there were at least six major comeouter sects: the Wesleyan Methodist Connection, the American Baptist Free Mission Society, the Free Presbyterian Church, the Franckean Evangelical Lutheran Synod, the Indiana Yearly Meeting of Anti-Slavery Friends, and the Progressive Friends, as well as many independent antislavery congregations. In a distinct but analogous movement, black Christians founded their own separate churches, such as the African Methodist Episcopal church and the African Methodist Episcopal Zion church, to protest the proslavery prejudice of the major denominations. The creation of these comeouter sects by tens of thousands of antislavery Christians was a dramatic protest against the churches' failure to correct their proslavery and racist practices.

I

The antislavery comeouter sect movement derived its main inspiration from the abolitionists' theological arguments against fellowship with slaveholders. Like the early abolitionists, the comeouters believed that slave owning was sinful and that the churches were guilty of tolerating sinners in their membership. After years of unsuccessful effort to reform the religious denominations, many zealous abolitionists resolved to heed the biblical injunction, "Come out from her, my people, that ye receive not of her plagues."[1] Comeouters considered separation from a contaminated religious body to be not only a means of protecting one's own soul, but also a forceful testimony to alert the churches to their unsafe and unchristian course. The comeouter sects cited the precedents of earlier Christians, from the fourth-century Donatists to the leaders of the Protestant Reformation, who had felt impelled to secede from a sinning church and to form new communions restricted to the uncorrupted. Following the example of these previous reformers, the comeouter sects attempted to establish uncompromised institutional bases from which to carry on the work of freeing the churches from their sins.

The comeouter sect movement has received scant attention from historians because it is seldom distinguished from a practice of Garrisonian abolitionists also dubbed "comeouterism." As observed earlier, some members of the post-1840 American Anti-Slavery Society repudiated all ties with organized Christian bodies. These abolitionists were motivated by anticlerical and perfectionistic religious beliefs as well as by the desire to protest the churches' complicity with slavery. Although only a minority of Garrisonians formally abandoned their old denominations, those coming out included many of the most prominent spokesmen for the AASS. Few of the Garrisonians who seceded from the major denominations were content to affiliate with the comeouter sects. The AASS pronounced that of all the comeouter bodies only the Progressive Friends measured up to the AASS's rigid standards for religious and political behavior.[2] Most members of the comeouter sects, in turn, shied away from association with Garrisonians because of the latters' reputation for theological heterodoxy. Thus, in practice the two forms of antislavery comeouterism remained distinct.[3]

The relationship between Christian abolitionists and the comeouter sects also needs careful examination. The AFASS interpreted abolitionist religious obligations broadly enough to give sanction both to the members of the comeouter churches and to the antislavery reformers who remained in their old denominations. The AFASS constitution urged its adherents to observe "the duty of embracing every suitable opportunity for exhibiting . . . slavery's utter incompatibility with the spirit of Christian religion," but the society never defined this exhortation as requiring abolitionists to secede from religious connections.[4] In fact, leading Christian abolitionists disagreed among themselves about the propriety and effectiveness of comeouterism.

Several factors mitigated against comeouter activity among abolitionist churchmen. Often the denominational affiliation of the AFASS member helped guide his personal views toward comeouterism. Because the Congregational and Baptist denominations lacked a central authority to expel sinning members, many Christian abolitionists chose to remain in these churches despite the absence of a discipline against slaveholding. Similarly, the small number of abolitionists in the Protestant Episcopal church rejected secession for any reason as incompatible with their belief in a universal "Catholic and Apostolic" church.[5] Geographic factors also played a role: abolitionists showed less interest in secession from a denomination in whose local judicatories their influence was strong, as was the case for Methodists in New England or Baptists and Presbyterians in the upper Midwest. In rural areas, the handfuls of potential antislavery comeouters had to be willing to accept the considerable burdens of supporting their own congregations. Among clergymen, the probable loss of financial security and social prestige as a result of secession from the established denominations dissuaded the timorous or less committed.[6]

Not all Christian abolitionists harbored such scruples or fears regarding religious comeouterism.[7] Some even attempted to create a single unified abolitionist sect through the Union Church movement in upstate New York and western New England in the 1830s and 1840s. In this hotbed of revivalism, considerable numbers of ministers and church members were read out of their denominations for perfectionistic theological excesses. Disregarding previous religious affiliations, these theological radicals gathered into Union Churches dedicated to the eradication of all sin. When antislavery veterans William Goodell and Gerrit Smith joined this movement in the late 1830s, they helped make abolitionism the most prominent test of godliness in the Union Churches. Emphasis on complete separation from sinners, and particularly from slave owners, replaced correctness in ritual and belief as the binding force in the Union Churches. Church Unionists argued that by seceding from the old denominations and joining the new nonsectarian congregations, Christians could advance the causes of church reform and of emancipation simultaneously. For Goodell and Smith and a small circle of abolitionists who followed them, the Union Churches constituted purified assemblies whose example would ultimately reform their communities.[8]

Although more than forty Union Churches were established, the phenomenon faded after the 1840s because of the decline in revivalistic enthusiasm and lack of interest among most abolitionists. The *Liberator* applauded the antisectarianism of the Union Churches but charged that Goodell and Smith seemed intent on making the new congregations into religious auxiliaries for the third-party movement. Only a few Garriso-

Table 7. Estimated membership in comeouter sects and traditionally antislavery religious bodies, 1850

Group	Total members
Wesleyan Methodist Connection	20,000
American Baptist Free Mission Society	10,000
Free Presbyterian Church	3,000
Franckean Evangelical Lutheran	3,500
Indiana Yearly Meeting of Antislavery Friends	2,500
Progressive Friends	1,000
Union churches	1,000
Society of Friends (noncomeouter)	90,000
Freewill Baptists	55,000
Scottish Presbyterian sects	65,000

nians, such as the Reverend Luther Myrick of Cazenovia, New York, joined Union Churches. The similarly small proportion of Christian abolitionists who joined these bodies suggests that little inclination to compromise doctrinal beliefs existed even among militant opponents of slavery. (See Table 7.) Lewis Tappan explained his skepticism about the Union Church to Goodell: "There is not, I fear, religion enough in the great body of Xian abolitionists, to continue to act as a Church harmoniously and rigorously."[9] The unwillingness of abolitionists to join in a unified church venture to promote their movement opened the way for the creation of the antislavery comeouter sects.

II

As noted in Chapter 4, the comeouter sect movement first began on a significant scale with the formation of the Wesleyan Methodist Connection in May 1843. This new antislavery church had six thousand charter members and claimed fifteen thousand by 1845. After the southern secession from the Methodist Episcopal church, however, Wesleyan growth slowed dramatically. Particularly in the more sparsely settled Midwest, Methodist comeouters lacked sufficient numbers to sustain Wesleyan congregations in many rural communities and were forced to join other antislavery denominations. Although the Wesleyan sect extended from New England to Iowa during the mid-1850s, the total membership of its ten annual conferences numbered only a little over twenty thousand. In their first decade, the Wesleyans also suffered the loss of all three of their founders, with Orange Scott dying, Jotham Horton returning to the Methodists, and LaRoy Sunderland abandoning orthodox religion for spiritualism.[10]

As a means of survival, the Wesleyans developed several new sources of strength. Because they were often the only religious body in the vicinity free from fellowship with slaveholders, Wesleyan congregations attracted members from non-Methodist as well as Methodist backgrounds. The Wesleyans were able to resupply themselves with talented officers because many of their ministers had gained leadership experience in the religious antislavery campaigns of the 1830s within the Methodist Episcopal church. Finally, the comeouter Methodists established close ties with the abolitionist American Missionary Association, which acted as a ready-made channel for the denomination's mission energies and aided struggling Wesleyan congregations.[11]

The Wesleyan Methodist Connection was firmly grounded on abolitionist and comeouter principles. Wesleyan conferences denounced slaveholding as inherently sinful and charged "that the practice of endorsing the Christian character of slaveholders by fellowshipping them as Christians and treating them in any way as the children of God, is giving the most direct encouragement and support to slavery."[12] As long as the major denominations continued to condone slavery in this way, Wesleyans argued, secession from the corrupted churches was a Christian duty. Wesleyan leaders such as Lucius Matlack defended comeouterism not only as a moral obligation but also as the most effective means to "exert an influence upon the religious community of the land . . . in favor of the oppressed."[13]

In their official publications, the Wesleyans declared that antislavery sentiment was the *"principal, leading, and controling"* motive for the secession from the Methodist Episcopal church.[14] Nevertheless, the new sect developed other features of denominational polity and theology that distinguished Wesleyans from their old colleagues. Because of their former troubles with hierarchies, the Methodist comeouters created a highly democratic form of church government. An even more important innovation was the Wesleyans' increasingly perfectionistic rules of conduct for church members. By 1848, the Wesleyans had formally acknowledged their adherence to the doctrine of "entire sanctification," or Christian perfectionism, by enacting disciplinary condemnations of alcohol, tobacco, and secret societies.[15]

An important phase of the Wesleyans' abolitionist activity was the comeouters' protests against proslavery practices in the Methodist Episcopal church. Wesleyan propaganda exposed the fact that approximately four thousand slaveholders remained in the border conferences of the northern Methodist body. Although discipline had been enforced against a slaveholding bishop in 1844, Wesleyans pointed out that Methodist laymen and ministers guilty of the same offense remained unchastised. Orange Scott declared that the Methodists were as wrongfully connected with slavery as ever: "The only difference is there are not so many slaveholders in the northern M. E. Church, but the fellowship of slaveholders is as actual and as sinful."[16]

The Wesleyans made other contributions to the abolitionist movement. They attempted a well-publicized campaign to plant antislavery congregations in the South. North Carolina Quakers' distribution of Wesleyan antislavery tracts among local Methodists created interest in the comeouter denomination. From 1847 to 1851, and again from 1857 to 1859, Wesleyan missionaries labored in western North Carolina and Virginia to establish congregations that denied fellowship to slaveholders. The Wesleyans reported considerable success in these efforts, while never compromising abolitionist principles. On both occasions, these missions ended when southerners expelled Wesleyan preachers for circulating antislavery tracts and aiding runaway slaves.[17]

Despite these varied antislavery endeavors, the Wesleyan Methodist Connection experienced poor relations with the Garrisonian wing of the abolition movement. At its organizing convention, the Wesleyan sect rejected a rule to prohibit fellowship not only with slaveholders but also with all members of denominations that condoned slavery. Regarding this question "as one of those nice points of Christian practice on which it would be difficult to legislate," the Wesleyans allowed local congregations to decide the matter on the merits of individual cases.[18] The Garrisonians never forgave the Wesleyans for that equivocation. The *National Anti-Slavery Standard,* official organ of the AASS, acknowledged the new sect's antislavery professions but told the Wesleyans that in implicitly condoning fellowship with the religious abettors of slavery "you are not true to your standard."[19]

Garrisonians also charged that the Wesleyans' political behavior conflicted with nonresistant and disunionist principles. The *Liberator* contended that in their frequent endorsement of antislavery political candidates the Wesleyans acknowledged allegiance to a constitution sheltering slavery. Several leading Wesleyans, including James M. Walker and Richard Illenden, became converts to Garrisonianism and eventually withdrew from the comeouter sect. In addition, a small minority of Wesleyans adopted the Garrisonian position on nonresistance and remained in the denomination to agitate for a change in its political practices.[20]

The Wesleyans defended their practices against the Garrisonian on-slaught. Instead of replying to the criticism of their fellowship policies, Wesleyans launched a counterattack on the AASS's qualifications to judge religious practices. The Wesleyans equated Garrisonianism with infidelity and warned that slavery would never be ended except through the instrumentality of a purified Christian church. Scott, Matlack, and a majority of Wesleyans rejected disunionism and denied that voting implied condonement of proslavery government activities. The Wesleyans dismissed Garrisonian "no-human government, no-organization, anti-church, anti-Sabbath, and anti-ministry notions, as the quintessence of transcendental nonsense."[21]

In contrast, the Wesleyans maintained close ties with the organizations of other Christian abolitionists. Scott and Luther Lee, another Wesleyan minister, were influential members of the AFASS executive committee. The financial assistance of the American Missionary Association provided valuable support to the Wesleyans' southern missionary endeavors. Wesleyan conventions and newspapers counseled voting for antislavery candidates as a moral obligation. As these varied activities attest, the comeouter Wesleyan sect became the Christian abolitionists' primary vehicle for antislavery agitation among the Methodists in the 1840s and 1850s.[22]

III

A second group of abolitionists that may be considered an antislavery comeouter sect was the American Baptist Free Mission Society (ABFMS). As previously noted, antislavery Baptists began seceding from their denomination's home and foreign missionary societies even before the sectional division of those bodies in 1845. Thereafter the ABFMS became the rallying point for Baptist abolitionists who remained dissatisfied with the antislavery position of their church's established or regular societies. The exact number of Free Mission Baptists is impossible to estimate. The society's own claim to represent one-sixteenth of all northern Baptists may be accurate, for it approximates the ratio of contributions received by the ABFMS and by regular Baptist mission treasuries.[23]

The ABFMS combined in one organization all the religious functions that customarily united Baptists on the national level. Through its central board and treasury, the ABFMS dispatched foreign missionaries to Haiti, Jamaica, Burma, Canada, and Japan and home missionaries to congregations from New Hampshire to Kansas. The same board also managed the printing and distribution of newspapers, Bibles, religious books, and tracts. The Free Mission Society established local auxiliaries across the North that both collected funds and appointed missionaries. Though not directly affiliated with the ABFMS, New York Central College, in McGrawville, New York, and Eleutherian College, in Lancaster, Indiana, were founded by Free Mission Baptists and were open to students of all races. By competing with the regular societies for the contributions of antislavery Baptists, the ABFMS hoped to compel the established benevolent institutions to adopt strict regulations against all forms of religious fellowship with slaveholders.[24]

The comeouter Baptists conducted an intensive propaganda campaign against the toleration of slavery in the denomination's established mission and publication societies. Free Mission Baptists called for cessation of support for the denomination's Bible societies, which still solicited southern contributions, elected slaveholders as officers, and refrained from distributing Scripture to slaves. ABFMS spokesmen similarly charged that, to avoid offending southerners, the American Baptist Publication Society never printed a word against slavery. Comeouter Baptists condemned the regular missionary societies for continuing to accept donations from slave holders and for permitting slave masters to join mission congregations. The ABFMS claimed that the only way for the Baptist rank and file to reform their societies was to shift their benevolent contributions to unquestionable antislavery channels.[25]

The ABFMS spared no effort to affirm that it was an uncompromising enemy of slavery. Its constitution declared: "This Society shall be composed of Baptists, of acknowledged Christian character, who are not slaveholders, but who believe that involuntary slavery, under all circumstances, is sin, and treat it accordingly. . . ."[26] Circulars of the new society announced that the organization would refuse to fraternize with slaveholders or knowingly accept contributions from them. The Free Mission group claimed to be the only faithful descendants of the Baptist abolitionist movement of the 1830s and early 1840s and criticized those early antislavery leaders who retained their connection with the regular mission societies. ABFMS spokesmen upheld traditional abolitionist principles in their newspapers, tracts, and sermons. Writings by Free Mission Baptists against secret societies and war also revealed perfectionist tendencies that the group never formally acknowledged.[27]

In addition to their propaganda, the Free Mission Baptists utilized more active means to agitate the antislavery question in their denomination. The ABFMS successfully appealed to several missionaries of the regular societies to transfer their loyalties to the comeouter organization. The Reverend Edward Mathews carried the ABFMS antislavery gospel into slave-holding Kentucky and Virginia before being violently expelled for preaching to slaves without their masters' permission.[28] In the 1850s many New York Free Mission Baptists ceased to take part in their state association because it continued to endorse the regular benevolent societies. In southern Ohio and Indiana, Baptist abolitionists seceded from their local associations because a majority of the ministers and churches in those bodies continued to extend fellowship to visiting slaveholders. More than a dozen Midwestern congregations joined together to form the Free Regular Baptist Association on a platform that condemned "the prevailing sins of covetousness, slavery, war, intemperance, licentiousness, secret societies . . . and in favor of Free Missions and Free Churches."[29]

Like the Wesleyans, the American Baptist Free Mission Society's relations with other abolitionist groups were complicated by questions of correct antislavery behavior. Garrisonian abolitionists questioned the consistency of some Free Mission Baptist practices. Applying their strict interpretation of antislavery religious obligations, Garrisonians charged the Free Mission Baptists with indirectly sanctioning slavery by continuing to share their pulpits and communion tables with northern Baptists who had refused to sever fraternal church relations with slaveholders.[30] Even Christian abolitionists such as William Goodell worried that most members of the ABFMS endangered their cause by continuing their fellowship with nonabolitionist Baptists.[31]

Most Christian abolitionists, however, cordially cooperated with the Free Mission Baptists. The annual reports of the AFASS listed the ABFMS as a bona fide proabolition religious body, and the periodical of the American Missionary Association declared that the Free Mission Baptist organization "differs from our society only in being denominational."[32] Several comeouter Baptists served the AFASS as officers and agents. By the 1850s, the American Baptist Free Mission Society had achieved roughly the same standing in the abolitionist movement as the other comeouter church ventures.

IV

The third comeouter sect generated by abolitionist agitation of the religious community was the Free Presbyterian Church. After the split in the Presbyterian denomination, both Old School and New School church authorities avoided any antislavery gesture that might anger their southern membership. Abolitionist withdrawals from the Old School Presbyterians began when the 1845 General Assembly declared "that Slavery under the circumstances which it is found in the Southern portion of this country is no bar to Christian communion."[33] Antislavery comeouterism among New School Presbyterians began in 1846, when their General Assembly overruled its Cincinnati synod's suspension of a proslavery minister. In reaction, eleven midwestern ministers renounced New School Presbyterian jurisdiction. Led by longtime abolitionist John Rankin, these ministers founded the independent Free Presbytery of Ripley. Soon numerous antislavery Old School and New School Presbyterians were enrolling in the comeouter venture. In November 1847 the Presbyterian comeouters formally united into the Free Synod of Cincinnati, later renamed the Free Presbyterian church.[34]

Although no record has survived of the exact number of Free Presbyterian church members, the sect counted more than seventy ministers and licentiates in seven presbyteries stretching from eastern Pennsylvania to Iowa in the mid-1850s. Southern Ohio remained the stronghold of the sect throughout its history, and many congregations farther west were founded by migrants from that region. Between meetings of the Free Synod, denominational periodicals such as the *Free Presbyterian, Christian Leader*, and *Free Church Portfolio* linked the widely scattered congregations. The Free Presbyterians also united in support of Iberia College, in Ohio, which admitted students of all races. Rather than create their own mission board, the Free Presbyterians made their sect an auxiliary to the American Missionary Association and thereby received much-needed funds to maintain ministers in struggling congregations.[35]

The career of one Free Presbyterian minister, the Reverend George Gordon, is illustrative of the difficulties facing all the comeouter sect members. Born near Washington, Pennsylvania, in 1806, Gordon trained for the ministry at Western Theological Seminary, in the same state. He sided with the theologically conservative Old School in the Presbyterian schism and served as a pastor for several of its congregations in Ohio and Pennsylvania. In 1850 Gordon quit the Old School to join the Free Presbyterian church and defended his action in a pamphlet, *Secession from a Pro-Slavery Church a Christian Duty*, which expressed his complete conversion to abolitionist principles. Though named president of the Free Presbyterians' Iberia College, Gordon found it necessary also to preach at two congregations thirty miles apart to make enough money to support his family. Besides his work for the comeouter sect, Gordon participated in regional interdenominational antislavery conventions and in abolitionist political campaigns. In 1860 Gordon joined a mob that prevented the rendition of a fugitive slave and was subsequently jailed. This incarceration broke Gordon's health and hastened his death, but he regarded his conduct as guided by *"the express will of God as revealed in the Scriptures,* a standard clearly opposed to the fugitive slave enactments."[36]

Three principles summarize the antislavery creed of George Gordon and other members of the Free Presbyterian church: abolitionism, comeouterism, and perfectionism. The Free Presbyterians claimed to be merely enforcing the traditional Presbyterian recognition of the sinfulness of slavery when they ruled that "no person holding slaves, or advocating the rightfulness of slaveholding, can be a member of this body."[37] The Presbyterian comeouters interpreted this prohibition to exclude from their communion not only slave owners but also members of churches with slaveholding members and even those who voted for slavery-tolerating political candidates. The Free Presbyterians defended their coming-out as the last resort open to Christians who, after years of effort, had concluded that their churches were hopelessly corrupt. The *Free Presbyterian* charged that antislavery churchmen who failed to secede inadvertently misled the public about their denomination's true proslavery character. The Free Synod's original confession of faith listed aggressive war, membership in secret societies, and intemperance as well as slaveholding as sinful behavior. In keeping with such perfectionistic beliefs, the Free Presbyterians warned other abolitionists that only a general moral reformation of the entire country would solve the problem of slavery.[38]

The most valuable contribution of the Free Presbyterian church to abolitionism was its relentless exposure of the proslavery practices of the major Presbyterian denominations. The Free Presbyterians charged that since 1845, when the Old School Presbyterian General Assembly declared slaveholding insufficient grounds for expulsion, proslavery ministers had rushed to join that denomination. The *Free Church Portfolio* reported that northern "cotton-hearted Hunkers" in the Old School Presbyterian church endeavored to silence the few remaining abolitionists in the denomination lest potential southern converts be frightened away.[39] The *Free Presbyterian* accused the New School of being even more hypocritical than the Old School, because the New School denounced slavery as evil but still hesitated to discipline slaveholders. The same periodical predicted that New School leaders would not condemn slave owning as sinful until they calculated that their denomination would "lose more members by retaining slaveholders than by casting them out."[40]

Abolitionist principles also governed Free Presbyterian dealings with other denominations. The antislavery question entered into the competition between Free Presbyterians and Congregationalists for the allegiance of defectors from western New School Presbyterian judicatories. Free

Presbyterians claimed a more consistent antislavery record because they supported the abolitionist American Missionary Association whereas most Congregationalists still cooperated with the slavery-tainted New School Presbyterians in missionary projects. In contrast to their unfriendly attitude toward the major Calvinist denominations, the Free Presbyterians established fraternal ties with the Scottish Presbyterian sects and with the other small proabolition churches and benevolent societies.[41] Only by scrupulously maintaining antislavery standards in church relations did the Free Presbyterians expect to influence other denominations to adopt abolitionist principles.

The Garrisonians appreciated the Free Presbyterians' concern for correct antislavery church relations. The AASS had criticized Wesleyan Methodists and Free Mission Baptists for giving indirect countenance to slavery by their church practices. But the Garrisonians applauded the Free Presbyterian discipline that denied communion not only to slaveholders but also to all members of churches that shared fellowship with slave owners. Although the Free Presbyterians disapproved of the AASS disunionist political views, the Garrisonians acknowledged that most Presbyterian comeouters at least voted consistently with their sect's antislavery principles.[42]

Where Free Presbyterians and Garrisonians differed was in their estimations of the relative importance of religious orthodoxy to the abolitionist movement. The Free Presbyterians complained that the extreme position of many Garrisonians on the Sabbath, the Bible, and the clergy caused church members to regard abolitionism as a movement of infidels. Spokesmen for the Free Presbyterians frequently warned that unless the nation's religious bodies ceased giving shelter to slaveholders, the "Garrisonian type of antislavery sentiment will sweep the masses of the people away" from the churches.[43] The Garrisonians, in reply, disavowed hostility to Christianity but admitted to being enemies of the "sectarian bigotry" displayed by Christian abolitionists such as the Free Presbyterians.[44]

In contrast, the Free Presbyterians worked closely with the Christian abolitionist faction, which shared their conception of antislavery reform as a religiously orthodox and church-oriented movement. Although no Free Presbyterian served as an officer in the AFASS, both groups traded endorsements and cooperated in such projects as the distribution of antislavery tracts. The Free Presbyterian church functioned as an auxiliary to the American Missionary Association. Presbyterian comeouters played leading roles in interdenominational Christian Anti-Slavery Conventions held across the Midwest in the 1850s to promote religious antislavery principles. Free Presbyterians became staunch supporters of antislavery political

parties in the 1840s and 1850s. Although the number of Free Presbyterians remained small, their unceasing agitation made the sect an
important antislavery agency among Calvinist-inclined churchmen.[45]

V

Another small comeouter sect produced by the conflict over slavery was
the Franckean Evangelical Lutheran Synod. Before the Civil War, American Luthern governing bodies cautiously avoided all discussion of slavery,
deeming it a purely secular question. In protest to this inaction and to the
strong procolonization sentiment in their denomination, a group of
Lutheran abolitionists in western New York seceded from the church in
1837. The comeouter Lutherans created their own independent Franckean
Synod with a constitution incorporating both abolitionist terms for fellowship and perfectionistic protemperance provisions. By 1850, the Lutheran
abolitionist sect had grown to number twenty-five ministers, fifty congregations, and more than thirty-two hundred communicants. In their
public resolutions, the Franckeans protested the growing strength of the
"Slave Power" in religious and political affairs and pledged themselves
to work "in all proper channels, to oppose, arrest, and overthrow this
system of despotism. . . ."[46] As early as 1840, the Franckean Synod
endorsed the AFASS. While maintaining their own home mission board,
Franckean Lutherans generously contributed to the overseas projects of
the abolitionist American Missionary Association. The comeouter activities of the Franckean Lutherans demonstrate that Christian abolitionism could penetrate even ritualist and immigrant religious groups.

VI

As described earlier, the traditionally antislavery Quakers displayed
little enthusiasm for abolitionism in the 1830s and 1840s. In 1842, for
example, a conservative majority in the Indiana Yearly Meeting of
orthodox Quakers disqualified eight members from all offices in the meeting as punishment for abolitionist activities. Instead of quietly accepting
this punishment, the censured Quakers seceded. Led by longtime abolitionists Levi Coffin and Charles Osborn, the comeouter Quakers formed
the independent Indiana Yearly Meeting of Anti-Slavery Friends, which
eventually grew to over two thousand members in forty local meetings in
several states.[47] The Quaker comeouters defended their secessions by

charging that the leaders of the Indiana Yearly Meeting had been seduced into abandoning their antislavery heritage by commercial dealings with the South and by racial prejudice against blacks. The parent yearly meeting had erred in censuring abolitionists, the comeouters explained, because genuine antislavery principles "lead to Anti-Slavery action, and you cannot cease from the latter without sacrificing the former."[48]

The Anti-Slavery Friends heeded their own admonition. Levi Coffin and other comeouter Quakers in Indiana participated in the Free Produce movement and the Underground Railroad. The Indiana Anti-Slavery Friends petitioned the state and federal governments and other denominations opposing slavery and discrimination against blacks. Both the AASS and AFASS favorably compared the labors of the Anti-Slavery Friends to the inactivity of most of the sect. The comeouters' prodding finally created a more receptive attitude toward abolitionism among orthodox Friends, and the Indiana schism healed itself just before the Civil War.[49]

Just as among orthodox Friends, yearly meetings of the theologically more liberal Hicksite Quakers also harassed proabolition members. For example, three leading pro-Garrisonian Hicksite Quakers, Isaac T. Hopper, James S. Gibbons, and Charles Marriott, were expelled from the New York Yearly Meeting in 1842 for their antislavery activities. Beginning in Indiana in the mid-1840s and spreading across the Midwest and Pennsylvania, Hicksite abolitionists seceded and founded their own loose organization, the Congregational or Progressive Friends. This new comeouter group rejected doctrinal tests, an ordained ministry, and any form of racial or sexual discrimination. In particular, the Progressive Friends repudiated the "*quiet testimony*" of other Quakers against slavery in favor of more active methods of helping slaves. The Congregational Friends' meetings became forums not only for antislavery action but also for a wide range of reform causes such as temperance, women's rights, and the abolition of capital punishment.[50]

Unlike the other antislavery comeouter sects, the Congregational Friends established close ties with Garrisonian abolitionists. Numerous Garrisonian abolitionists, including Joseph A. Dugdale, Oliver Johnson, and Thomas McClintock, joined the Progressive Friends. Congregational Friends' gatherings passed resolutions praising the Garrisonian AASS and endorsing disunionism. The *Liberator* reported favorably on this comeouter group. Garrison himself addressed a meeting of Congregational Friends and later remarked, "There is something about progressive Quakerism for which I feel a special attachment."[51] In contrast, Christian abolitionists seldom associated with the Progressive Friends because of the comeouter Quakers' toleration of unorthodox religious, social, and political views.

VII

Another group of independent congregations and sects that testified against the conservatism of the major denominations on the race and slavery questions were those bodies founded by antebellum black Christians. Historians have documented in great detail the practices of racial discrimination that drove some blacks to create their own separate religious institutions. There is some disagreement, however, as to whether these black churches participated aggressively in the abolitionist movement.[52] A comparison of the practices of the black churches with those of the predominantly white antislavery sects sheds some light on this issue.

The nation's two oldest black denominations, the African Methodist Episcopal church (AME) and the African Methodist Episcopal Zion church (AMEZ), were founded in the early nineteenth century to protest the racism rather than the proslavery attitudes of white Methodists. Though predominantly northern, both bodies maintained a number of struggling congregations in the slave states. Leaders of these churches, such as AME bishop Richard Allen, played prominent roles in the earliest protests against the program of the American Colonization Society. In later years, however, both denominations held back from official endorsements of abolitionist religious principles. For example, as late as 1856, the AME General Convention rejected a proposed regulation to bar slaveowning members, because church leaders feared that such a radical step would endanger their southern missionary efforts. Partially compensating for this official caution, however, was the active participation of such prominent African Methodist clergymen as Christopher Rush and Jermain W. Loguen of the AMEZ and Daniel A. Payne of the AME in both local and national antislavery projects. Perhaps even more important was the activity of the less well-known AME and AMEZ churchmen and women who operated the Underground Railroad and the vigilance committees, campaigned for the repeal of discriminatory laws and ordinances, and founded institutions that provided free blacks with the opportunity to acquire and exercise new skills.[53] Though falling short of strict abolitionist practices, the African Methodists nevertheless contributed significantly to the campaign against slavery.

Like the African Methodists, some black Baptists in the North and in the border states grew dissatisfied with unequal treatment in mixed churches and established their own religious institutions. The largest of these was the quasi-national American Baptist Missionary Convention (ABMC), which was founded in 1840 and grew to number forty-six ordained ministers and twenty-one licentiates by 1860. The ABMC not only supported a domestic missionary program but also dispatched ministers to preach in Sierra Leone. The black Baptist convention's best-known leaders were the Reverends Leonard Grimes of Boston and Chauncey Leonard of Washington, D.C. Because it sought to protect members of its border-state congregations from retribution, the ABMC muted its public statements regarding slavery. In 1853, however, the ABMC resolved to "put forth our united efforts for the abolition of Slavery, the annihilation of the A[merican] C[olonization] Society, the removal of intemperance and all other kindred evils. . . ."[54] By the end of the decade, the ABMC had also publicly acknowledged slaveholding to be sinful and refused to accept slave-owning ministers in its pulpits. The ABMC and other northern black Baptist organizations stopped short of severing fellowship with northern white Baptist local and state associations. Nevertheless, because of the Baptists' loose denominational structure, black organizations such as the ABMC can be regarded as having adopted most of the functions of antislavery comeouter sects.

No separate black sects arose in the other major denominations before the Civil War. Black Episcopalians, like their white fellow church members, rejected comeouterism as theologically indefensible. Racial prejudices generally forced northern black Presbyterians and Congregationalists to form their own local churches. Although black Presbyterian and Congregational clergymen met irregularly in an informal ministerial association, they retained their affiliations with the white-controlled denominations. Nevertheless, black Presbyterians and Congregationalists founded the Union Missionary Society to protest the proslavery policies of their denominations' mission programs. With the assistance of white patronage, black Presbyterians and Congregationalists and, to a lesser extent, black Episcopalians were more able to take an active role in the abolitionist movement than were the African Methodists and black Baptists, who remained encumbered with the need to build and protect their own denominational institutions.[55]

A large majority of these black church members preferred cooperation with the antislavery projects of the theologically more orthodox leaders of the Christian abolitionist faction to cooperation with Garrisonian projects. Black clergymen, including Christoper Rush, Theodore Wright, James W. C. Pennington, and Samuel Cornish, served as officers of the AFASS. The black American Baptist Missionary Convention associated closely with the comeouter American Baptist Free Mission Society. The Union Missionary Society eventually merged with the abolitionist American Missionary Association. Most white and some black abolitionists regretted the creation of separate black sects but recognized that their success might counteract the anti-Negro and proslavery sentiments of the major denominations.[56] Though neither organized to promote nor always governed by abolitionist religious principles, the AME, the AMEZ, and possibly black Baptist groups such as the ABMC nevertheless aided the antislavery movement in the churches in many of the same ways as the predominantly white comeouter sects.

VIII

The role of the antislavery comeouter sects in American church history needs to be assessed. Sociologists studying the creation of new religious sects have found that those bodies arose to supply spiritual guidance for individuals who had lost faith in the ability of existing religious institutions to provide valid answers to the question "what shall we do to be saved?" This interpretation accounts for much of the comeouter abolitionists' behavior. Abolitionists denounced the nation's churches for having become corrupted by association with slavery. Believing that slaveholding was a sin, comeouter abolitionists felt obliged by evangelical moral standards either to cease all practices sanctioning that inequity or to jeopardize their salvation. Even though many of the comeouter sects adopted perfectionist disciplines on other moral questions, correct antislavery practices remained their key test of true Christian character. Through secession and the formation of separate antislavery sects, the comeouters attempted to awaken the established churches to the duty of abolishing human bondage. The comeouters believed that, with the moral power of the nation's religious institutions arrayed against slavery, emancipation would be inevitable. The antislavery comeouter bodies were rare examples in church history of sects formed to promote social rather than theological reform.[57]

The establishment of the comeouter sects became an important new tactic in antislavery church reform. Abolitionist-motivated secession provided a dramatic means to protest the northern denominations' perceived toleration of slavery. The comeouter sects allowed Christian abolitionists to separate themselves from reproachful relations with slaveholding sins and yet to retain familiar religious practices. Abolitionists could point to the new denominations as evidence that churches could survive and prosper without the fellowship of slave owners. Even the Garrisonians could single out the Progressive Friends as a religious body meeting the strictest standards of nonfellowship with slaveholders.

Not many historians have examined the activities of the antislavery comeouter sects, and those that have generally minimize the seceders' impact on the policies of the major denominations.[58] Chapter 9 will consider the influence of the comeouter sects and of the other new religious abolitionist tactics devised during the 1840s and 1850s. The next three chapters will demonstrate that comeouter churchmen actively participated in the entire sphere of religious abolitionist projects and were among the most dependable antislavery voters. In addition, the comeouter sects provided the Christian religious campaign with a far stronger institutional base than the financially strapped AFASS had ever been able to supply. Though never large in membership relative to the major denominations, the comeouter sects magnified their influence by the central role they played in the overall Christian abolitionist movement.

—6—

Abolitionism and
the Benevolent Empire

The voluntary benevolent society was an important new phenomenon in early nineteenth-century American religious life. These interdenominational organizations supplemented the efforts of the regular churches to disseminate the teachings of evangelical Protestantism and the ideals of virtuous Christian living. Benevolent-minded churchmen joined together in such bodies as the American Home Missionary Society and the American Board of Commissioners for Foreign Missions to aid struggling congregations in the United States and abroad. Many of the same people also cooperated in the American Bible Society, the American Tract Society, and the American Sunday School Union to put the Scriptures and other religious and moral works into the hands of the unconverted.

This broad range of charitable and evangelical projects received the endorsement and assistance of many of the economic and political, as well as religious, leaders of the country. The costs of these institutions were borne by wealthy patrons and by periodic collections in local congregations. Because Baptists, Methodists, and Episcopalians maintained their own sectarian missionary and religious publication societies, Presbyterians and Congregationalists provided the greatest share of support for the interdenominational ventures. Although some historical interpretations stress social control and status anxiety as major motivating forces for these activities, the societies viewed themselves as products of the evangelically inspired principles of disinterested benevolence.[1]

It was in the area of Christian principle that the benevolent societies ran afoul of the abolition campaign. Whereas the benevolent effort envisioned itself as a national movement that embraced all Protestant Christians, the abolitionists objected to any definition of a bona fide Christian that included slaveholders. By abolitionist standards, the benevolent organizations erred in many respects. Antislavery reformers complained that these societies accepted the "wages of sin" in the form of contributions from slaveholders and appointed slave owners as officers and agents. Abolitionists also charged that the societies neither preached nor published a word against slavery. Antislavery reformers denied that any Christian benevolent organization could be neutral upon as serious an ethical question as slavery. Lewis Tappan concluded that the moral respectability lent to slavery by the benevolent societies' fellowship with slaveholders "propped up and kept in countenance" that "iniquitous system."[2]

I

The abolitionists believed that no benevolent organizations gave greater moral aid and comfort to slavery than the two interdenominational missionary associations, the American Board of Commissioners for Foreign Missions (ABCFM) and the American Home Missionary Society (AHMS). The origins of both societies predated the rise of modern abolitionist sentiment, the ABCFM having been founded in 1811 and its domestic counterpart in 1825. After the division of the Presbyterian church in 1837, these missionary societies were primarily cooperative ventures between evangelically oriented Congregationalists and New School Presbyterians. In theory both associations were responsible to their contributing members. In practice, however, the executive committees of each society managed selection procedures so as to ensure their annual reelection virtually intact. Wary of the sectional antagonisms engendered by abolitionism, these self-perpetuating bodies of clergymen and wealthy philanthropists never expressed sympathy for any antislavery measure stronger than colonization. At the same time, the missionary associations avoided taking any stand on moral questions touching slavery that might either discourage southern donations or impinge on the ecclesiastical authority of the cooperating denominations. Thus both missionary societies adopted policies that abolitionists regarded as sanctioning slavery.[3]

Individual abolitionists, not the antislavery societies, initiated the earliest efforts to reform the American Home Missionary Society in the 1830s. Ministers, congregations, and lower-level church judicatories sent the AHMS directors remonstrances requesting changes of policies toward slavery. The AHMS, however, resisted being prodded into a position offensive to southerners and to northern conservatives. In particular, the domestic missionary body attempted to remain officially neutral on the question of the sinfulness of slaveholding. To act otherwise, the society's officers claimed, would violate the prerogative of ministers and denominations to "dictate terms of church membership."[4] Under mounting pressure from antislavery churchmen, the AHMS obliquely acknowledged the evils attached to slavery by ceasing to appoint slave-owning missionaries in the mid-1840s. Despite this concession, the society continued to accept contributions from slaveholders and to welcome them into mission churches.[5]

Early abolitionist agitation of the ABCFM generally paralleled that of the domestic missions. Groups of abolitionist churchmen addressed remonstrances to the board, requesting it to sever all ties with slavery, no matter how indirect. In 1841 and 1842 the ABCFM tried to appease antislavery sentiment by declaring that it would "sustain no relation to slavery which implies approbation of the system. . . ."[6] In 1844, however, the board conceded the accuracy of abolitionist charges that its missionaries to the western Indian tribes accepted slaveholders into their congregations. In reaction to this admission, the Reverend Amos A. Phelps, corresponding secretary of the AFASS, led a petition drive to pressure the board to order an end to that practice.[7]

At its 1845 annual meeting in Brooklyn, New York, the ABCFM rejected these remonstrances. Though acknowledging the system of slavery to be a social evil, or an "organic sin," the board denied the fairness of automatically treating every slaveholder as a sinner. Instead, in its "Brooklyn Report," the board defended the missionaries' independence to judge each applicant for church membership on the basis of personal piety.[8] Abolitionists denounced the logic of the board's organic sin concept as arguing "that provided a sin be only sufficiently prevalent to have become a recognized institution, it ceases to be a sin. . . ."[9] After an unsuccessful effort in 1846 to get the ABCFM to reconsider the "Brooklyn Report," a large portion of Christian abolitionists adopted a "double policy" of continuing to lobby the board while simultaneously launching their own full-scale missionary projects.[10]

II

Even before the "Brooklyn Report," many abolitionists had abandoned the American Board of Commissioners for Foreign Missions to found their own antislavery missionary bodies. In 1839, the sympathy of much of the northern public was attracted to the plight of the *Amistad* captives. These men were recently enslaved members of the Mendi tribe of Nigeria who had successfully revolted while being shipped to Cuba on the Spanish ship *Amistad*. The self-emancipated Mendians, however, were unable to navigate the vessel and drifted into United States waters, where they were arrested for piracy. After a highly publicized legal battle, the Supreme Court freed the Mendians in March 1841. Christian abolitionists attempted to induce the ABCFM to appoint missionaries to accompany the Mendians back to Africa. The board, however, balked at the abolitionists' demand that donations for the proposed Mendi mission be kept in a special fund closed to slaveholders' money.[11]

Thus rebuffed, church-oriented abolitionists initiated their own effort to Christianize Africa and attracted support from far beyond militant antislavery circles. This project soon evolved into the Union Missionary Society, with black minister James W. C. Pennington as president, Lewis Tappan as corresponding secretary, and opposition to religious fellowship with slaveholders as its guiding principle.[12] Antislavery churchmen founded two more organizations in the early 1840s, the Western Evangelical Mission Society and the West Indian Missionary Committee, to finance missions respectively to the Northwestern American Indians and to the Jamaican freedmen. In the mid-1840s, supporters of these three societies decided to merge their efforts into a single interdenominational antislavery missionary society.[13]

In 1846, Christian abolitionists who had despaired of reforming the established missionary institutions sponsored two conventions to promote the cause of "Bible Missions" and founded the American Missionary Association (AMA). The AMA embodied long-standing abolitionist principles in its public condemnation of "the spirit of caste" and in its policy never "to receive the known fruits of unrequited labor or to welcome to its employment those who held their fellow beings as slaves."[14] Pre–Civil War AMA officers included many veteran Christian abolitionists such as Lewis Tappan as treasurer, the Reverend Simeon Jocelyn as secretary for domestic missions, and the Reverend George Whipple as secretary for foreign missions and editor of the society's periodical, the *American Missionary*. Under the direction of these men, the AMA established several denominational auxiliaries, primarily among the comeouter sects, and a number of regional auxiliaries. Funds for the new society's projects came chiefly in small donations, with Congregationalists being the most generous contributors.[15]

Historian Clifton H. Johnson, who has best chronicled the pre–Civil War activities of the AMA, contends that the association was neither conceived of nor used primarily as a vehicle for the propagation of abolitionist principles. Instead, Johnson stresses that the AMA functioned as a genuine missionary outlet for those whose views of slavery prevented them from cooperating in good conscience with established missionary agencies.[16] Although Johnson's conclusion accurately describes the routine operations of the AMA, the association's important contributions to the antislavery movement in the churches can not be dismissed. The AFASS and important individual abolitionists, including William Goodell, George Cheever, and Lewis Tappan, testified that the AMA's refusal to fellowship with slaveholders set a valuable example for other religious institutions. By the mid-1850s, Tappan even came to believe that abolitionist finances and energies could be better spent on the AMA than on the AFASS.[17] The AMA also aided the religious antislavery campaign in several other ways.

The AMA performed a key role in the abolitionist agitation for reform of both the American Board of Commissioners for Foreign Missions and the American Home Missionary Society. The abolitionists appealed to the consciences of the older societies' missionaries about their financial ties to slaveholders' contributions. At the same time, the AMA reminded AHMS missionaries that their congregations' requirement to take up collections for the parent society resulted in their indirect subsidization of mission stations in the slaveholding South. Abolitionists publicized the fact that several of these missionaries and their congregations switched affiliation to the AMA. Advocates of the AMA similarly labored to overcome the loyalty of Congregational and New School Presbyterian contributors to their traditional missionary organizations. To do so, AMA supporters exposed the toleration of slavery in the operations of the AHMS and ABCFM. The AMA's competition for benevolent contributions functioned as a major incentive for other missionary societies to adopt stronger antislavery positions.[18]

The AMA also became an important instrument for Christian abolitionists to lobby the nation's churches for antislavery action. The abolitionist missionary society established close ties with the comeouter sects and served as the foreign missionary vehicle for the Wesleyan Methodists, Free Presbyterians, and Franckean Lutherans. In addition, the AMA gave crucial financial assistance to Wesleyan, Free Presbyterian, and non-denominational Union churches of antislavery churchmen. Only the comeouter Baptists preferred their own organization, the American Baptist Free Mission Society, to working through the AMA. The availability of AMA funds to such comeouter movements spurred the antislavery campaigns inside the major denominations by posing the threat of subsidies to future secessionists.[19]

Of the major denominations, the New School Presbyterians and the

Congregationalists were the most greatly affected by the AMA's antislavery agitation. By offering financial aid to struggling congregations dependent upon the AHMS, the AMA enabled several antislavery western churches to secede from the New School Presbyterians in protest against fellowship with slaveholders. These defectors usually affiliated with the Free Presbyterians or the Congregationalists. Though eastern Congregationalists tended to remain loyal to the older societies, many western Congregationalists, particularly ministers trained by Charles G. Finney at Oberlin, favored the AMA. Rivalry between the AMA and the established missionary societies offered abolitionists an important opportunity to pressure the Congregational and New School Presbyterian establishments to take stricter antislavery positions.[20]

In addition to its regular home missionary operations, the AMA established and publicized a number of special missions chosen to serve as "exemplifications" of the "practicability" of Christian abolitionist principles.[21] The AMA conducted several missions to the free blacks in the North and in Canada, in the hope that the spiritual guidance and education provided would help dispel prejudice against blacks. When competition began between pro- and antislavery settlers in Kansas and other western territories, the AMA dispatched missionaries to preach an abolitionist Gospel to bolster the morale of free state emigrants.[22]

The special domestic missions of the AMA that attracted the greatest popular interest were those in the slave states. AMA funding helped make possible the work of Wesleyan Methodist missionaries in North Carolina. The longest-running AMA mission in the South was that conducted by the Reverend John G. Fee. The son of a slave-owning Kentucky planter, Fee had been converted to abolitionism while studying at Lane Seminary in the early 1840s. He quit the New School Presbyterian ministry in 1845 after being censured for his antislavery sermons and began his career as an AMA missionary. After preaching in various parts of Kentucky, he settled at Berea, in Madison County, and founded a congregation and a college on uncompromised antislavery and anticaste standards. Though frequently shot at and beaten, Fee remained active in a wide range of Christian and political abolitionist projects. When southerners violently expelled all AMA missionaries and agents during the panic following John Brown's raid on Harpers Ferry, the association sent Fee and other "exiles" on lecturing tours across the North as living testimony to the brutal nature of slavery.[23]

The AMA was an important agency in the Christian abolitionist campaign. Through its varied activities, the AMA supplied coordination to antislavery work both in the benevolent societies and in the religious denominations. Even normally hostile Garrisonians conceded that the

AMA provided abolitionists with a channel for mission contributions that was unquestionably free from complicity with slavery.[24] Not all antislavery churchmen, however, abandoned the old interdenominational mission societies for the AMA, and agitation for reform continued inside the ABCFM and the AHMS until the Civil War.

III

The transferal of the loyalties of many abolitionists to the American Missionary Association marked the beginning of a new phase of the antislavery campaign in the American Board of Commissioners for Foreign Missions. In a sense, the AMA supporters had joined the Garrisonians as outside critics of the board's countenance of slavery. Whether they envisioned the AMA as a permanent replacement for the board or as a means by which to reform the older body, many abolitionists diverted their financial contributions to the comeouter society. Despite these secessions, a number of other Christian abolitionists, including Jonathan Blanchard, William Jay, and George Cheever, remained inside the board for several more years and continued to press for antislavery action.[25]

Opposition to abolitionist demands came from two distinct groups within the ABCFM. The more conservative faction argued that the board should stick to missionary work and ignore slavery, on the grounds that it was a political rather than a religious question.[26] A moderate group professed antislavery feelings but resisted the abolitionists' demand that the board treat all slaveholders as sinners. The moderate faction claimed that the ABCFM could be more instrumental in ending slavery if allowed to preach Christian principles to both masters and slaves. This last contention appalled abolitionists, who protested that such fraternal treatment by the board would serve only to ease the consciences of slave owners.[27]

The ABCFM could not shake off abolitionist complaints against fellowship with slaveholders in its Cherokee and Choctaw missions. The Reverend Selah B. Treat, one of the board's secretaries, created considerable controversy when he recommended that missionaries give special scrutiny to the Christian character of slaveholding Indians who desired to join their congregations. Conservative board supporters immediately protested that Treat's actions violated the independence of missionaries. The volume of complaints against Treat's statement led the board's managers to issue a public explanation that the secretary had expressed "opinions" and not "instructions" to the missionaries. The ABCFM declared that it still stood by the position of the "Brooklyn Report" that slaveholding per se was no bar to good Christian standing.[28] Both the AASS and Christian abolitionists condemned this ruling as capitulation to the interests of slavery and noted that so-called antislavery churchmen quietly acquiesced in that action.[29]

Throughout the 1850s, abolitionists kept alive the issue of the board's mission to Indian slave owners. In 1858 the ABCFM decided to rid itself of "increasing embarrassments and perplexities" by dropping its missions among the Choctaw and Cherokee.[30] Attempting to sidestep the entire debate over fellowship with slave owners, the board justified its closing of the Indian mission on the sole ground that the tribes had been successfully Christianized. The organization's missionaries to the Indians, however, denied any such success and claimed instead that they were victims of a surreptitious attempt to appease antislavery critics. Abolitionists concurred with the missionaries' judgment and branded the board's action a "remarkable evasion" of "the responsibilities connected with their long indulged complicity with slavery."[31] As if to confirm abolitionist accusations, the ABCFM in its annual meetings of 1859 and 1860 refused requests that it publicly condemn the contemporary agitation for reopening the slave trade.[32] Although the American Board of Commissioners for Foreign Missions had dropped its most flagrant ties to slavery by the time the Civil War began, the society continued to reject the religious principles and practices of the abolitionist movement.

In many respects, the later phase of the slavery dispute in the American Home Missionary Society paralleled that in the ABCFM. Abolitionists had many complaints against the AHMS but concentrated their attack upon its acceptance of slaveholders into southern missionary congregations. In the ensuing debates, some of the society's defenders voiced strong opposition to abolitionism while others claimed that the home missionary effort in the South would help end slavery.[33] Growing sectarian rivalry between New School Presbyterians and Congregationalists added to the society's problems. Offended by Congregational badgering over slavery, Presbyterians shifted some of their missionary contributions to their own Church Extension Society. A rising denominational consciousness, as well as antislavery sentiment, accounts for the large shift of Congregational missionary donations to the AMA. The 1852 Albany convention of Congregationalists endorsed the AHMS but resolved that only missionaries of known antislavery opinions should be sent into the South.[34]

In response to these trends, the AHMS chose to placate Congregational antislavery sentiment by gradually reducing the number of its missionaries in the slave states until in 1856 there were only fifteen. In December of that year, the society's executive committee went even further by resolving not to "grant aid to churches containing slaveholding members unless evidence be furnished that the relation is such as, in the judgment of the Constitution, is justifiable, for the time being, in the peculiar circumstances in which it exists."[35] Although Garrisonians and AMA leaders protested that this action still fell short of an outright prohibition of all religious fellowship with slaveholders, antislavery moderates called it a vindication of their noncomeouter policies. Particularly in the Midwest, many AMA supporters were sufficiently pleased with the AHMS's stiffer rules regarding slaveholding to shift the bulk of their mission contributions back to the older society.[36]

Whereas many abolitionists believed that the AHMS had not become sufficiently antislavery, a number of conservative northern churchmen held the opposite conviction. These antiabolitionist northerners founded a new benevolent association, the Southern Aid Society, to collect money for struggling slave state congregations abandoned by other missionary organizations. At its peak the new society was aiding churches in fourteen southern states. Abolitionists and antislavery moderates condemned the mercenary motivation of the northern businessmen who liberally contributed to the Southern Aid Society. The controversy over the society's toleration of slavery prevented it from obtaining financial support from northern religious circles to rival that of either the AHMS or the AMA.[37]

By the time of the Civil War, abolitionist agitation had drastically changed the policies of the American Board of Commissioners for Foreign Missions and the American Home Missionary Society. Both societies had ceased employing slaveholding missionaries. By a variety of means, both the board and the AHMS had also eliminated slaveholders from their mission congregations. Although neither body erected a formal bar against donations from slave owners, the societies' new practices made such contributions extremely rare. Nevertheless, abolitionists remained dissatisfied because both organizations continued to refuse to treat slaveholding as inherently sinful. Until the established societies made the necessary reforms, Christian abolitionists proclaimed their own American Missionary Association the only mission organization that did not sanction slavery.

IV

The abolitionists' agitation within the nation's religious publication societies proved less successful than their labors to reform the missionary bodies. Greater numbers of conservatives on the slavery question, especially Episcopalian, Old School Presbyterian, and Dutch Reformed church members, supported the publication societies than supported the missionary bodies. The complicated system of management of the Bible, tract, and Sunday school organizations created additional difficulties for abolitionists, because their administrations were even more immune than those of the mission associations to pressure from the average contributor. The abolitionist principle of no fellowship with slave owners, though easily applied to the operations of missionary societies that supported congregations of Christians, seemed less applicable to the printing and distribution of Bibles and other religious material.[38] These obstacles persuaded Christian abolitionists to work for less rigorous antislavery goals in the hope of enlisting the cooperation of more moderate opponents of slavery. Although this "Popular Front" strategy accomplished less than originally hoped, it produced several important antislavery advances in the religious publication field.

The American Tract Society (ATS) was the abolitionists' primary target among the religious publication bodies. Founded by a merger of regional societies in Boston and New York City in 1825, the ATS annually printed and distributed millions of pages of moral exhortatory pamphlets and books during the 1850s. The real control of the ATS lay in its publishing committee composed of five or six ministers, each representing a different denomination and each possessing a veto against the printing of any given work.[39]

Instead of complaining about the thousands of slaveholding contributors to the American Tract Society, the abolitionists concentrated their protests against even more flagrant proslavery practices. Specifically, they charged the ATS with publishing tracts against every evil or sinful practice except those associated with slave owning. Abolitionists similarly complained that the ATS censored even the mildest antislavery reference or allusion from its reprints of established religious works. One abolitionist editor labeled these policies evidence of the "readiness" with which "the conductors of the large printing establishments of the land 'bend the pliant hinges of the knee' in meek submission to [the] Moloch of oppression."[40] Despite a mounting number of churchmen who repeated these charges, the officers of the ATS refused even to acknowledge the calls for reform until 1852.

Confronted with the indifference of the ATS officers to antislavery protests, a small group of western Christian abolitionists met in Cincinnati in 1851 and founded their own antislavery religious tract organization, the American Reform Tract and Book Society (ARTBS). The new body argued in a public address that the established religious publication societies were "so trammelled by pecuniary interests" that antislavery churchmen needed their own vehicle to spread the unpopular truths of abolitionism.[41] Midwestern Congregationalists and Free Presbyterians supplied the greatest number of active officers and agents to the Cincinnati-based ARTBS, but contributions came from antislavery churchmen in nearly all denominations. Eastern Christian abolitionist organizations also recognized the value of the ARTBS, and both the AFASS and AMA endorsed the new tract society.[42]

Though hard hit by the depression of 1857, the ARTBS catalog grew to over a hundred titles by the end of the decade. The society distributed over four million pages of religious literature in 1859. In its first years, the ARTBS mainly published works that dealt with the moral questions surrounding slavery, as these representative titles reveal: *Hebrew Servitude and American Slavery, Fellowship with Slavery, Colonization,* and *Slavery and the Bible.* After 1857 the ARTBS sought broader support by adding the entire standard range of religious and moral tracts, books, and Sunday school materials to its catalog of publications. In addition, the ARTBS published its own periodical, the *Christian Press,* which became an influential advocate for religious and political abolitionism. The ARTBS had no distribution system of its own but depended on the efforts of sympathetic Christian abolitionists, particularly AMA missionaries and colporteurs, to spread its tracts and books throughout the North and even into the border states.[43]

In its various publications, the American Reform Tract and Book Society advocated the fundamental moral principles of abolitionism in an uncompromised form. Such views served the purpose of clearly setting the ARTBS apart from the American Tract Society but gave the new organization an extremist image. Some ARTBS backers worried that undiluted radicalism handicapped the society in soliciting financial support from moderate antislavery churchmen. Severely hurt by the economic contraction of the late 1850s, the ARTBS was floundering in 1858 when the antislavery agitation in the ATS came to a head.[44]

Although many western antislavery radicals abandoned the American Tract Society in the early 1850s, eastern Christian abolitionists continued to work to reform the established publishing body for several more years. Lewis Tappan, William Jay, and other abolitionists repeatedly called public attention to the society's refusal to print any statement critical of slavery or of any practice attached to it. In 1852 the managers of the ATS finally responded to this criticism with a declaration that their constitution allowed them to print only material "calculated to receive the approbation of all evangelical Christians."[45] In the opinion of the ATS officers, that clause ruled out all publications touching on the controversial topic of slavery. To conciliate northern feelings, the American Tract Society's annual meeting in 1856 resolved that nothing in the organization's constitution prohibited the publication of works that exhorted masters to treat their bondsmen according to Christian precepts. Inundated by southern objections in response, however, the ATS publishing committee unanimously decided to authorize no such work.[46]

This history of unrelenting resistance to northern antislavery sentiment set the stage for a dramatic showdown at the American Tract Society's convention in May 1858. In a rare show of cooperation, Christian abolitionists met beforehand with antislavery moderates in an attempt to map out a common strategy for the convention. The abolitionists, led by Lewis Tappan and George Cheever, argued that the entire antislavery group must demand that the ATS condemn slave owning as a sin. The moderates, including Baptist Francis Wayland and Congregationalist Leonard Bacon, balked at this undiluted dose of abolitionist principles; they wanted instead to censure the publishing committee for its disregard of the previous year's decision to circulate works on the duties of masters.[47]

All factions on the slavery question rallied as many supporters as possible for the annual meeting at the Reformed Dutch Church of New York City in May 1858. The American Tract Society's constitution, however, restricted voting rights to substantial contributors. The all-out abolitionist position lost heavily because even the antislavery moderates spoke and voted against it. Soon after that ballot, the combined antislavery forces failed by more than a five-to-one margin to defeat a resolution endorsing the performance of the publishing committee. The victorious conservatives then reelected every member of that body, including the Reverend Nehemiah Adams of Boston, a notorious apologist for slaveholders. The Garrisonian *Liberator* scornfully concluded that the entire reform movement in the ATS had been foredoomed because it had been "compromising in character" and therefore "utterly unreliable" to bring about any genuine antislavery advances.[48] After the debacle in 1858, prospects for changing the ATS through internal agitation appeared slim.

The unwillingness of the conservatives who dominated the American Tract Society to make even slight concessions forced moderate antislavery churchmen into taking uncharacteristically strong counteraction. Soon after the ATS's annual meeting in 1858, its Boston auxiliary announced that it would no longer contribute to the parent society and that it would begin to print its own tracts. In May 1859 the Bostonians formally seceded and established themselves as an independent organization, the American Tract Society, Boston. The new organization announced that its primary objective would be to carry out the plan originally adopted by the American Tract Society's annual meeting of 1857, to publish tracts that advocated "those moral duties which grow out of the existence of slavery, as well as those moral evils which it is known to promote. . . ."[49] The

Boston tract society printed a number of works that fitted that description but that also avoided any discussion of the character of slaveholders or ways to abolish slavery.

Noting those shortcomings, the abolitionists warned that the new society did not merit its reputation as an antislavery organization. One Garrisonian writer branded the American Tract Society, Boston, a dangerous "palliative" that deluded its patrons into discounting the necessity of the "radical cure" of expelling slaveholders to deal with the "disease" of slavery that infected the northern church.[50] Christian abolitionists worried that the Boston society would attract contributions away from their own organization, the American Reform Tract and Book Society. The ARTBS issued public circulars to complain that whereas the Boston group published works only upon the "Duties of Masters," the abolitionists' society "takes up Slavery itself, especially as it exists among us, and exposes its inherent sinfulness and enormous evils."[51] The rivalry between the Boston and Cincinnati societies reached its climax at the Northwestern Reform Tract Convention, held in Chicago in October 1859. This meeting arranged a compromise that created an agency for a united solicitation effort in the Northwest and left both societies free to decide on the content of their tracts.[52]

Despite competition for benevolent contributions from two rival antislavery tract societies, the managers of the American Tract Society remained opposed to the adoption of any policy that would alienate the confidence of the South. Eastern merchants and politicians joined Episcopalians, Old School Presbyterians, and conservative members of other denominations in endorsing the ATS's neutral position on slavery. At the society's annual meetings in 1859 and 1860, backers of the publishing committee easily defeated the antislavery faction's new rallying cause—the issuance of a tract against the slave trade. Despite persistent internal and external antislavery pressure, before the Civil War the American Tract Society refused to print a single word against any aspect of human bondage.[53]

Another religious publication organization that abolitionists attempted to reform was the interdenominational American Bible Society (ABS). Even though this society had both slaveholding officers and patrons, the abolitionists first concentrated on correcting an even more glaring example of the organization's toleration of slavery. The ABS, founded in 1816, had as its professed goal to supply every family in the United States with a copy of the Scriptures. By the 1830s, hundreds of thousands of dollars contributed by benevolent-minded Protestants had gone into that ambitious project. In the middle of that decade, the American Anti-Slavery

Society began to complain that few of these Bibles reached southern slaves. In 1834 the AASS offered to aid the American Bible Society in raising $20,000 to correct this situation. The managers of the ABS, however, declined to undertake such a campaign, contending that their organization's constitution denied the national body jurisdiction over the distribution policies of local southern auxiliaries.[54]

Such self-serving reasoning outraged abolitionists. In the 1840s Christian abolitionists, led by Joshua Leavitt and Henry Bibb, promoted a campaign of donations to the American Bible Society specifically designated for financing distributions to southern blacks. As a propaganda vehicle, the "Bibles for Slaves" drive gave Christian abolitionists the opportunity to convince northerners of the depraved nature of an institution that denied its victims even the comfort of reading the Scriptures. The Garrisonians, however, scoffed at the project. An AASS gathering derided the distribution of Bibles to slaves in the southern states, where laws forbade them to learn to read, as being as much "a burlesque of a philanthropic enterprise" as supplying the blind with spectacles.[55]

The Bibles for Slaves campaign failed to move the American Bible Society. The society accepted and recorded the contributions in a fund labeled "for the slaves," but because of continued southern resistance little money was spent for that purpose. In another example of the come-outer trend, abolitionist churchmen abandoned the ABS in growing numbers during the late 1840s and the 1850s. In 1848 the American Missionary Association started its own Slaves' Bible Fund, and its missionaries and colporteurs distributed copies of Scriptures to bondsmen in Kentucky. To counter this competition, the managers of the ABS occasionally counseled its southern auxiliaries to supply the spiritual needs of literate blacks. Though accomplishing little, these gestures proved sufficient to retain the loyalty of the large majority of benevolent-minded northerners. On the whole, the abolitionist agitation of the American Bible Society failed to produce any significant concession to northern antislavery sentiment.[56]

Antislavery activities in one additional religious publication society, the American Sunday School Union, deserve brief mention. Founded in 1824, the interdenominational union printed and circulated hundreds of religious and moral works for juveniles. Like the American Tract Society, the union refrained from involvement in the slavery debate but attracted little abolitionist attention until 1848, when it dropped Thomas Gallaudet's *Jacob and His Sons* from its catalog in response to southern complaints against the work's harsh description of Joseph's sale into slavery. Both abolitionists and moderate antislavery churchmen protested this submission to slaveholders' demands. In the 1850s the ARTBS began printing its own line of antislavery Sunday school materials, and antislavery Congregationalists founded their own society for the same purpose. Although this competition caused the American Sunday School Union to suffer financial losses, that organization joined the Bible and tract societies in refusing before the Civil War to publish works against slavery.[57]

V

Questions surrounding the issue of slavery, especially those concerning fellowship with slaveholders, disturbed other agencies of interdenominational religious cooperation in addition to the mission and publication societies. Probably the most spectacular example of this problem occurred in the deliberations of the Evangelical Alliance during the late 1840s. The alliance grew out of an attempt to form an international and interdenominational association to promote the spread of evangelical Protestantism. This movement began when a British group issued a call for a world Protestant convention in August 1846. Over nine hundred clergy and church members, including seventy-seven from the United States, attended the London gathering. Among the Americans were prominent northern ministers such as Lyman Beecher, Stephen Olin, Samuel H. Cox, and Edward N. Kirk. In addition, several slaveholders, including the Reverend Thomas Smyth of South Carolina, participated. The appearance of the slaveholders offended the moral sensibilities of a number of the meeting's sponsors. A motion to bar slave owners from membership in the Evangelical Alliance soon disrupted the proceedings of the London convention.[58]

After American delegates caucused to discuss this problem, slaveholder Smyth reported with gratified surprise that "patriotic feelings" had led most northerners to oppose the proposed prohibition.[59] Most northern delegates defended this position as opposition to sweeping judgments about any class of professing Christians without regard to individual circumstances. Several northerners, however, also hinted that a United States auxiliary of the Evangelical Alliance could take more effective antislavery action on its own if not subject to foreign dictation. With the United States delegation adamant against rules involving slaveholders, the convention gambled on the antislavery sentiment of most American churchmen and voted to allow each national affiliate to form its own membership policy.[60]

All factions of American abolitionists reacted with hostility to news of the London convention's decision to include slaveholders. Both Garrisonian and Christian abolitionists charged that the British had been duped by those American delegates who claimed to be active opponents of slavery. Several Garrisonians were touring England at the time of the London meeting and organized well-attended rallies to protest the countenance afforded slaveholders by the Evangelical Alliance. The AFASS sent a *Remonstrance* to Britain complaining that the alliance's action on the fellowship question had been hailed in this country "as a complete triumph of the American policy of building up religious institutions, which shall be precluded, by their very constitution, from bearing an effective testimony against slavery."[61]

The abolitionists also launched a barrage of criticism against the churchmen who tried to establish an American auxiliary to the Evangelical Alliance. True to abolitionist predictions, this group considered a motion to bar slaveholders but settled for a mild declaration that slavery was a "stupendous evil" that Christians should endeavor to end.[62] This action pleased almost no one. Abolitionists charged that the Evangelical Alliance's position fell far short of the Christian's duty to rebuke and exclude sinners. Southerners and other conservatives branded the statement on slavery's evils as unwarranted interference in secular matters and as submission to British meddling in American affairs. Having offended partisans on both sides of the slavery question, the American branch of the Evangelical Alliance failed completely in its projects for united Protestant activism.[63]

The moral questions raised by the abolitionists affected at least one other interdenominational benevolent organization. Despite its sponsorship of social activities, the Young Men's Christian Association possessed a strongly evangelistic orientation, especially in the years before the Civil War. Abolitionists saw no reason to exempt this new society from the moral obligation not to accord fellowship to slaveholders. Despite abolitionist protests, the convention founding the YMCA adopted a constitution that forbade discussion of divisive topics such as slavery. Although antislavery pressure induced a few local affiliates in the North to secede from the national association, a minor resurgence of revivalism in the late 1850s helped the YMCA to expand despite abolitionist opposition.[64]

By their own strict standards, the Christian abolitionists' campaign failed to reform any of the interdenominational benevolent societies into antislavery institutions. Nevertheless, the labors of the abolitionists and some moderate antislavery allies, both inside and outside the benevolent organizations, achieved several minor successes. Although none of these societies came into total alignment with abolitionist principles by the time of the Civil War, antislavery advances at least drove most southerners from the major interdenominational missionary societies. In the instances in which the benevolent institutions continued practices that in abolitionists' view lent moral countenance to slavery, a number of rival societies were established that attracted the contributions of the many antislavery northern church members.

The abolitionist campaign in the benevolent societies also made an important contribution to the overall antislavery movement in the churches. The benevolent organizations were major national institutions, and antislavery activities in them attracted coverage and comment in the secular as well as in the religious press. The interdenominational character of the missionary and publication societies allowed the abolitionist agitation of those bodies to have broad impact. Members of a wide range of Protestant faiths had to consider seriously whether cooperation with slaveholders helped or hurt their favorite benevolent projects. Changes in missionary society policies toward slaveholders affected the internal affairs of every denomination whose ministers received financial support from the societies. Most significantly, the abolitionists' success in encouraging moderate antislavery churchmen to question *actively* the positions of the benevolent institutions toward slavery encouraged similar activism inside many denominations. The grudging acknowledgment of slavery's moral defects by several benevolent organizations created a more hospitable climate in the northern churches within which the abolitionists could call for the cessation of all practices that they claimed sanctioned human bondage.

—7—

Interdenominational
Antislavery Endeavors

A third new tactic that emerged in the later years of the Christian abolitionist movement was the sponsorship of interdenominational religious antislavery conventions and societies. After the breakup of the American Anti-Slavery Society in 1840, the American and Foreign Anti-Slavery Society could not provide the centralized direction to church-oriented abolitionist efforts that its predecessor had. In the 1850s Christian abolitionists, particularly in the Northwest, resorted to holding interdenominational Christian Anti-Slavery Conventions in an attempt to restore some coordination to their religious and political enterprises. These gatherings were aimed at the conversion of northern church members with vaguely antislavery sentiments to thoroughgoing religious abolitionist principles. Many of these conventions similarly called on northern antislavery politicians to apply stricter ethical standards to their opposition to slavery. In the late 1850s these attempts to supply moral guidance to religious and political antislavery endeavors finally crystallized into a permanent organization, the Church Anti-Slavery Society. Reports of these various interdenominational antislavery activities provide additional evidence that the Christian abolitionist campaign in the churches continued in force until the Civil War.

Garrisonian abolitionists played an important though distinctly secondary role in these interdenominational antislavery conventions and societies. A few such gatherings permitted AASS advocates to introduce resolutions that vindicated the Garrisonian positions respecting churches and politics. More often, the interdenominational antislavery gatherings barred the infidel Garrisonians from membership, creating doubts among AASS spokesmen as to the new movement's commitment to abolitionism.

The editor of the *National Anti-Slavery Standard* expressed typical Garrisonian misgivings about the Christian Anti-Slavery Conventions: "Experience has taught us to distrust, as altogether unreliable, the antislavery professions of men who are always careful to repel the cooperation of men whose religious opinions differ from their own. Such men we have usually found subordinating the cause of the slave to the interests of their sect."[1]

Because the Christian abolitionists made large claims for these conventions, the AASS subjected the gatherings and later the Church Anti-Slavery Society to careful scrutiny. Though far from satisfied, the Garrisonian press more than once expressed pleased surprise at the advanced stands that Christian abolitionists were willing to endorse. The opinions of the Garrisonians provide important contemporary criteria by which to evaluate the interdenominational antislavery conventions and the Church Anti-Slavery Society.

I

Abolitionists in the 1850s had several precedents for forming interdenominational conventions and societies to promote antislavery church reform. Ministers and church members had played prominent roles in the early AASS, and most antislavery gatherings of that period had had a distinctively religious cast. In the late 1830s both Philadelphia and New York City had short-lived antislavery societies, limited exclusively to church members. Although these societies later participated in maneuvers to form antislavery organizations inhospitable to the anticlerical Garrisonians, the original purpose of the new bodies was to convert area ministers to abolitionist principles. The Union Church movement in upstate New York, discussed in Chapter 4, had evolved from a series of interdenominational Christian Anti-Slavery Conventions in the early 1840s.[2]

At least a dozen Religious or Christian Anti-Slavery Conventions were held in New England from 1842 to 1849 and infrequently thereafter. To appeal to the broadest possible range of the religious antislavery public, these New England gatherings generally avoided taking stands on controversial questions such as the sinfulness of slaveholding and fellowship with slaveowners. In several states these meetings functioned as adjuncts to the Liberty party movement, with the religious and political conventions scheduled to reinforce each other's attendance. Garrisonian abolitionists subjected these conventions to considerable criticism, especially after one of them expelled Stephen Foster for not meeting the description of its call for "ministers and church members."[3] Although an occasional interdenominational antislavery convention was held in the East in the 1850s, the movement there faded as many non-Garrisonian abolitionists became preoccupied with the growing political antislavery movement, particularly the Free Soil campaign of 1848.

The outcome of that campaign, with its diluted platform, unprincipled politicians, and disappointing results, revitalized northern abolitionists' interest in church-oriented endeavors. Among those looking for new ways to battle slavery was a committee of Ohio and Indiana antislavery veterans who issued a call for a "Convention of Christians" to meet in Cincinnati in April 1850, "to consider upon the connection of the American Church with the sin of Slaveholding."[4] The group of fifteen who signed the call included twelve clergymen from eight different denominations. The committee's leaders were prominent abolitionist churchmen such as Quaker Levi Coffin, Free Mission Baptist William Brisbane, Free Presbyterian Jonathan Cable, and Congregationalist Charles Boynton. In their correspondence and circulars, the callers denied that they were a "disorganizing element" but acknowledged that they were prepared to discard slavery-corrupted ecclesiastical forms in order to "save the *Church*."[5]

The Cincinnati committee sent personal invitations to many leading Christian abolitionists and antislavery politicians but significantly omitted Garrisonians. The two thousand responses to the invitation committee's request for endorsements was an indication of the widespread interest in the gathering. The convention received letters from Lewis Tappan, Gerrit Smith, James G. Birney, Cyrus P. Grosvenor, John Rankin, William Jay, and other important antislavery figures. With only a few exceptions, these correspondents advised that the meeting adopt strong resolutions favoring religious comeouterism as the last resort of antislavery Christians.[6]

To gather for the four-day convention, more than 150 ministers and church members braved threats of a riot from unsympathetic Cincinnatians. Two Free Soil politicians, Samuel Lewis of Ohio and Stephen C. Stevens of Indiana, chaired the sessions. The moving spirits of the gatherings, however, were clergymen, particularly midwesterners Boynton, Brisbane, Rankin, John G. Fee, and Edward Smith, and two visiting easterners, William Goodell and George Whipple. Wesleyans, Free Mission Baptists, Free Presbyterians, and comeouter Quaker as well as most established denominations were represented. The convention's atmosphere was kept solemn through opening and closing prayers. To satisfy the scruples of Reformed Presbyterian delegates, presiding officers allowed neither applause nor psalm singing.

The convention's discussions addressed a broad range of topics. Referring to the debate in Congress on the proposed Compromise of 1850, several speakers argued that government policy toward slavery needed an acknowledged moral foundation. Whipple, the corresponding secretary of the American Missionary Association, exposed the slavery-tolerating practices of other missionary societies. The most important discussions in the convention, however, related to questions of church relations with slavery. Goodell, Rankin, and Fee, all comeouters, argued in favor of a resolution that sanctioned secession "from all the churches, ecclesiastical bodies, and missionary organizations, that are not fully divorced from the sin of slaveholding" and that pledged those present to "come out from among them unless such bodies shall speedily separate themselves from all support of, or fellowship with, slaveholding."[7] After a lengthy debate, this radical resolution passed unanimously when the small number speaking against it abstained.

The Cincinnati gathering had significant repercussions. The Garrisonian press had closely followed this new antislavery development and complimented the convention for its unequivocal condemnation of religious fellowship with slaveholders. The AFASS and other Christian abolitionist propagandists such as Goodell expressed optimism that the meeting would give a "fresh impulse" to antislavery agitation in the churches.[8] More important were the reactions of the various religious groups. The comeouter sects were happiest with the convention. The Reverend Edward Smith wrote, in a letter to the *True Wesleyan*, organ of the Methodist comeouters, that the "Convention came to Wesleyan ground."[9] The Free Mission Baptist *Christian Contributor* declared that the Cincinnati convention would have "the most powerful influence" for secession from proslavery churches.[10]

In other denominations, attitudes toward the Cincinnati convention varied according to the source's degree of commitment to abolitionism. Several Congregational and New School Presbyterian newspapers praised the antislavery sentiment of the Cincinnati delegates but not the meeting's enthusiasm for comeouterism. Most of the press of these and other northern denominations, however, was much more critical. The Cincinnati *Presbyterian of the West* denounced the deliberations of the convention as a "species of wholesale declamation and denunciation which has characterized the Abolitionists for years past."[11] The colorful Illinois Methodist preacher Peter Cartwright visited a session of the Christian Anti-Slavery Convention and dismissed its membership as "composed of a heterogeneous mass of disaffected, censured, or expelled preachers" and its comeouter principles as "clearly disorganizing and revolutionary in their nature, and in all their tendencies."[12]

Despite its mixed reception, the Cincinnati gathering stimulated anti-

slavery churchmen to increased activity. In the summer of 1850, interdenominational antislavery conventions in Ottawa, Illinois, and Medina,
Ohio, took an advanced position on the duty of churches to separate
themselves from slavery. In May 1851, Indiana abolitionists held a Christian Anti-Slavery Convention in Indianapolis on the day preceding a political gathering called to oppose the adoption of antiblack amendments to
the state constitution. The Indianapolis religious meeting not only endorsed abolitionist church practices but also reinforced the political con-
clave by declaring opposition to racial discrimination and to the newly
passed Fugitive Slave Law.[13] These events encouraged western abolitionists to make plans for even larger interdenominational antislavery religious projects.

II

The most important Christian Anti-Slavery Convention of 1851, and of
the entire movement, took place in Chicago that July, called by a committee from the previous year's Cincinnati gathering. The Chicago convention attracted the presence of major eastern abolitionists such as Lewis
Tappan, George Whipple, and William Goodell by a promise to empha-
size the slavery question as it related to both the missionary societies and
the churches. This prospect greatly worried supporters of the established
interdenominational evangelical associations, the American Board of
Commissioners for Foreign Missions and the American Home Missionary
Society. The predominantly Presbyterian and Congregational backers of
those two bodies held their own convention in Chicago shortly before the
Christian Anti-Slavery Convention in order to deny that their societies
gave any sanction to slavery.[14]

Despite such opposition, more than 250 delegates from eleven states
met in Chicago, including the renowned revivalist Charles G. Finney of
Oberlin, who infrequently attended abolitionist meetings. Nearly every
denomination had one or more representatives at the gathering, but Congregationalists and members of comeouter sects predominated. The Reverends Jonathan Blanchard of Knox College in Illinois, John G. Fee of the
American Missionary Association station at Berea, Kentucky, and
William Brisbane of the Free Mission Baptists led the arguments on the
convention floor that individual church members shared responsibility for
the sins sanctioned by their church. Over and over again, various comeouters charged that antislavery sentiment had abated among abolitionists
who had failed to secede from established churches. The large number of

delegates from the regular denominations who endorsed these views, especially New School Presbyterians, seemed a portent of further secessions.[15]

The convention's public address accused all the major denominational missionary societies of practices that gave "respectability to slaveholding."[16] Free Mission Baptists successfully persuaded the convention to reject the plea of noncomeouter Baptist abolitionist Nathaniel Colver to exempt his denomination's missionary operations from that sweeping condemnation. The Chicago convention similarly attacked the toleration of slavery by the interdenominational American Board of Commissioners for Foreign Missions and the American Home Missionary Society. Most of the convention's Presbyterian and Congregational delegates proclaimed their preference for the American Missionary Association. The convention also passed resolutions against the Fugitive Slave Law and the moral deficiencies of the major political parties.[17]

The pronouncements of the Chicago convention attracted nationwide comment. The meeting's attack on the relationship of the missionary societies to slavery provoked well-publicized exchanges between abolitionist churchmen and northern defenders of the established mission organizations. Among Baptists, for whom the question of missions held particular importance, the Free Mission Society's press expressed pleasure that a predominantly non-Baptist convention had endorsed the comeouters' charges against the denomination's regular mission boards. Most regular Baptist newspapers, however, applauded Nathaniel Colver's reply in the same convention to the comeouters' arguments. The Chicago *Watchman of the Prairie,* for example, claimed that northern Baptists "are ten years ahead of other denominations in their freedom from the charge of supporting or sympathizing with slavery through their mission organizations."[18] Among Congregationalists and New School Presbyterians, similar exchanges took place over the correct slavery policies for the ABCFM and the AHMS. A sign of the growing influence of abolitionist principles was the fact that the defenders of the established missionary bodies usually did not attack the practice of denying fellowship to slaveholders but instead claimed that their societies already adhered to it.[19]

Christian abolitionists believed that, in addition to promoting the antislavery cause in the missionary enterprises, the Chicago Christian Anti-Slavery Convention had aided their purposes in other ways. Abolitionists cited the criticism of the Chicago gathering by many professedly antislavery clergymen as evidence that the latter were "more attached to a sect, than they are opposed to slavery."[20] The enthusiasm for interdenominational antislavery cooperation stimulated by this meeting soon led midwestern Christian abolitionists to found the Cincinnati-based American Reform Tract and Book Society and a regional auxiliary to the American Missionary Association.[21] The callers of the Chicago convention claimed that their effort had helped to increase the pressure on the major denominations and on the missionary societies for antislavery actions, not just antislavery professions.

Among abolitionists, only Garrisonians believed that the Chicago meeting fell short of its promise. The western Garrisonian *Anti-Slavery Bugle* berated the Chicago gathering for claiming to be *"Christian and religious"* when it advocated comeouterism but then described the followers of Garrison as *"Infidel"* for having done the same thing.[22] The *Bugle* also charged that the abolitionist churchmen would not have taken such high ground had it not been for the prodding of Garrisonians, who held antislavery truth "paramount to the interests of church or government."[23] But despite these criticisms, the Garrisonians generally agreed with other abolitionists that the Chicago convention had added to the pressure for antislavery reform on northern religious bodies.

Although the Chicago meeting was the high point of the Christian Anti-Slavery Convention movement, at least a dozen similar gatherings were held throughout the 1850s. Congregationalists from Oberlin College and the Free Presbyterians sponsored several small interdenominational antislavery conventions in Ohio and western Pennsylvania from 1851 to 1855. These gatherings took a strong stand against fellowship with slaveholders in church or missionary connections. An Illinois Christian Anti-Slavery Convention was held annually during the early 1850s and endorsed an uncompromising political as well as religious abolitionist program.[24] In 1852 Lewis Tappan attended a Religious Anti-Slavery Convention in Augusta, Maine, where a resolution was passed counseling disobedience to the Fugitive Slave Law. This gathering also adopted the strongest endorsement yet obtained from the eastern antislavery clergy of refusing church fellowship to slave owners. Garrisonians who observed this convention, however, claimed that the fellowship resolution had passed only "in the confusion, at the final adjournment" through a maneuver by Tappan and a few others.[25] Garrison's *Liberator* criticized a Boston Christian Anti-Slavery Meeting in 1857 as a meeting of churchmen whose antislavery principles were so weak that most remained in denominations that still welcomed slaveholders into their fellowship.[26] The eastern interdenominational antislavery projects continued to be less popular and less abolitionist in principle than those in the western states.

An interesting by-product of the western interdenominational abolitionist gatherings was a well-publicized series of annual antislavery conventions in Cincinnati from 1851 to 1855. Though frequently labeled "Christian" antislavery conventions in the contemporary press, these meetings were called under the auspices of the Ladies' Anti-Slavery Circle of Cincinnati and managed to bring together moderate and radical antislavery political figures, proabolition church leaders, and Garrisonians. The Cincinnati meetings did not shun discussion of religious antislavery questions. These conventions usually endorsed the expulsion of slaveholders from all religious institutions. Representatives of comeouter sects demanded—and got—exemptions for their denominations from Garrisonian-sponsored resolutions branding the whole American church as proslavery. The political viewpoints expressed at these conventions varied from Garrisonian disunionism to arguments that slavery was unconstitutional. Free Soilism, however, as advocated by politicians in attendance such as George Julian, won the warmest reception from the delegates. The proceedings of the Cincinnati antislavery conventions revealed that militants in all abolitionist factions agreed that religious principles, if not religious institutions, still had a role to play in emancipation cause.[27]

III

A lull in interdenominational antislavery activities occurred in the mid-1850s. The growing acceptance of antislavery principles in several northern churches encouraged abolitionists to concentrate instead upon intradenominational agitation. More important, the political antislavery activities of the new Republican party, which opposed the extension of slavery, attracted unprecedented participation by Christian abolitionists. Interdenominational antislavery efforts, however, revived in 1859, when an Ohio State Christian Anti-Slavery Convention was held in Columbus in August and a Northwestern Christian Anti-Slavery Convention met in Chicago that autumn.

The Ohio State Christian Anti-Slavery Convention hoped to guide the antislavery movement back to its original religiously inspired principles. The attendance by a strong delegation from Oberlin and the participation of Joshua R. Giddings, leading Republican antislavery radical, highlighted the convention. The gathering demanded in its resolutions that the antislavery political movement return to moral arguments and adopt a stronger platform in favor of emancipation and racial equality. The convention criticized northern conservatives, including Republicans, who counseled obedience to proslavery legislation such as the Fugitive Slave Law. The convention's public address asserted the right of "Christian men" to bring the slavery question, "supposed by some to be exclusively political, to the test of morality and religion."[28]

An indication of the Columbus meeting's overriding concern with the political situation was its comparatively restrained pronouncements on religious antislavery questions. The convention proclaimed the importance of prayer in the antislavery campaign and defined the moral evils inherent in slavery but took no stand on the question of fellowship with slaveholders, despite the large number of comeouters and other church radicals present. Although Garrisonians chided this concentration upon the political rather than ecclesiastical obligations of antislavery Christians, the meeting won heavy praise from other abolitionist circles.[29] The Columbus convention was evidence of the growing conviction among antislavery churchmen in the late 1850s that their greatest aid to the emancipation cause lay in lobbying northern politicians to take more principled stands on the issue.

In October 1859 a Northwestern Christian Anti-Slavery Convention was held in Chicago as part of a week of religious antislavery activities, including an anniversary of the American Missionary Association and a convention of abolitionist churchmen who desired to reform the American Tract Society. As in 1851, the Chicago convention brought together leading western Christian abolitionists and several like-minded easterners, such as Lewis Tappan and George B. Cheever. This convention went further than the Columbus gathering; it passed resolutions endorsing the expulsion of slaveholders from all religious institutions and warning that the "integrity and perpetuity" of the church would be in danger unless it opposed slavery.[30] Convention speakers exhorted ministers to preach against slavery and to form permanent church-oriented antislavery organizations.

Like the Columbus gathering, the Chicago convention took strong stands on political matters. In particular, it passed resolutions that denounced the Fugitive Slave Law and recent suggestions for reopening the slave trade. After a heated debate, a majority of convention delegates voted to "deplore" the violence of the recent Harpers Ferry incident and to recommend instead "the use of moral and peaceful means for the abolition of slavery."[31] With the 1860 presidential election approaching, Republican aspirant Salmon P. Chase privately wrote to caution delegates to the convention "who are in earnest for practical success next year . . . not to go too far" by insisting that a Republican administration actively intervene against slavery "in order to satisfy the demands of moral principle."[32] Although the gathering passed resolutions that protested "compromising platforms" and the selection of candidates chiefly on the basis of their "availability," most speakers declared their intention of working

—136—

within the Republican party, as Chase had hoped.[33] The highly political orientation of both of these later interdenominational antislavery ventures demonstrated the increased willingness of Christian abolitionists to work through both secular and religious channels.

IV

A final example of interdenominational abolitionists effort was the Church Anti-Slavery Society, founded in the spring of 1859. Although the new society quickly grew to include several hundred ministers and church members, the major sources of its inspiration and activities were two Congregational ministers, George B. Cheever and his brother Henry. The Cheever brothers had been members of the old AASS but had dropped out of the active antislavery movement before 1840 because of their disdain for the Garrisonians' religious views. After ministerial work in his native New England, George Cheever relocated in New York City, where he first edited the *New York Evangelist,* a leading religious newspaper, and then became pastor of the wealthy Church of the Puritans. During the 1840s Cheever established a reputation both as a dynamic preacher and as a leading pamphleteer in the protemperance and anti-Catholic causes. In the 1850s he became a regular contributor to the New York *Independent,* an influential Congregational periodical. The younger Cheever brother, Henry, had less success as a clergyman but finally established himself in a congregation in Jewett City, Connecticut.[34]

Events in the 1850s drew the Cheever brothers back into the antislavery movement. They joined many other ministers in denouncing proslavery governmental actions such as the Fugitive Slave Law and the Kansas-Nebraska Bill. The Cheevers, however, also criticized the new Republican party for its low moral tone on the slavery issue. In the mid-1850s, both George and Henry Cheever became leading figures in efforts to induce the various benevolent societies and the Congregational state associations to sever all religious fellowship with slaveholders. In addition to these activities, George Cheever began to write widely circulated books and tracts that advanced essentially the same moral arguments against slavery as had the early abolitionists of the 1830s. His *Guilt of Slavery and the Crime of Slaveholding* was perhaps the most scholarly expression of the abolitionist assertion that the Bible did not sanction slavery. Moderate antislavery Congregationalists such as the editors of the *Independent* frequently censured and censored George Cheever's uncompromising abolitionist pronouncements.[35]

After the dissolution of the AFASS in the mid-1850s, the Cheever brothers saw a need for a new national organization to coordinate Christian abolitionism. In the fall of 1858 they conferred with New England friends about the possibility of establishing a new abolitionist society exclusively for ministers and church members. A convention to launch such an organization was planned for Worcester, Massachusetts, in March 1859. To prevent attendance by potentially disruptive Garrisonian abolitionists, the organizers issued invitations by means of a private circular instead of a public call. In the meantime, to give direction to the meeting's deliberations, George Cheever prepared a declaration of sentiments and Henry Cheever a constitution for the proposed new body.[36]

Approximately fifty delegates attended the Worcester gathering, with Massachusetts alone supplying more than half. After two days of sessions the convention founded the Church Anti-Slavery Society (CASS) and selected Henry Cheever for the key office of secretary of the organization. In its first public address the organization adopted orthodox abolitionist principles. For example, it endorsed by resolution the "total extinction [of slavery] to be demanded at once."[37] The convention also declared it the duty of Christian churches to refuse fellowship to slaveholders and their defenders. Although several delegates objected to the proposed condemnation of slaveholding as "inherently" sinful, a large majority nonetheless voted to retain that crucial qualifier. The new abolition society announced that its distinctive goal was not merely to end the churches' complicity with slavery but actively to enlist them in the antislavery crusade.[38]

The commitment of the Church Anti-Slavery Society to uncompromised Christian abolitionist principles was ensured by its selection of officers. Congregational minister John C. Webster, a longtime supporter of the American Missionary Association and of political abolitionism, was the CASS president from its founding through the end of the Civil War. The redoubtable Lewis Tappan sat on the executive committee and participated vigorously in its discussions. The Christian abolitionist sentiment of the Cheever family was well represented in the CASS leadership, with Henry serving as the society's secretary and his brother-in-law, Ichabod Washburn of Worcester, Massachusetts, serving as the society's treasurer. Although George Cheever held no formal office in the CASS, he frequently traveled and lectured in its behalf and was a regularly featured speaker at its anniversaries. These veteran abolitionists helped provide leadership to the many members of the CASS who were relatively new to the antislavery movement.[39]

The Church Anti-Slavery Society experienced a healthy growth in the two years from its founding to the start of the Civil War, thanks especially to the lecturing and writing of Henry Cheever, who became its general agent as well as secretary in July 1859. The CASS established local auxiliaries in several New England towns, New York City, Philadelphia, Pittsburgh, and points as far west as Illinois. From scattered newspaper reports and from its few surviving official records, the society appears to have drawn supporters from across the denominational spectrum, with Congregationalists and members of the small abolitionist sects enrolling in the greatest numbers. (See Table 8). The new society attracted a large attendance at its public anniversaries and annual meetings by scheduling speeches from antislavery luminaries such as Wesleyan minister Daniel Worth, just expelled from North Carolina; Henry Wilson, the Republican governor of Massachusetts; and John Brown, then only of Kansas fame. Several important clergymen never previously associated with an abolitionist organization, including New School Presbyterian Albert Barnes and Methodist Episcopalian Gilbert Haven, gave endorsements to the Church Anti-Slavery Society.[40]

Besides attempting to draw church members into its ranks, the Church Anti-Slavery Society found other ways to work for antislavery reform in the religious community. Henry Cheever attended dozens of Congregational and New School Presbyterian assemblies throughout the Northeast in order to stimulate discussions of the churches' responsiblity for slavery. To foster antislavery sentiment in local congregations, the CASS encouraged abolitionists to form quarterly or monthly prayer meetings for the enslaved. Henry Cheever wrote to the Ohio State Christian Anti-Slavery Convention and George Cheever traveled to the companion Chicago gathering to recommend that western religious abolitionists join forces

Table 8. Religious affiliations of the officers of the Church Anti-Slavery Society, 1859–1864

Denomination	Total (%)
Freewill Baptist	1 (2.9)
Scottish Presbyterian	1 (2.9)
Free Presbyterian	1 (2.9)
Independent Methodist	1 (2.9)
Congregational	17 (48.6)
New School Presbyterian	2 (5.8)
Methodist Episcopal	3 (8.6)
Baptist	2 (5.8)
Undetermined	7 (20.0)
Total	35 (100)
Total ministers	16 (45.7)

with the CASS. When the editors of many denominational newspapers and periodicals ignored the new society, the CASS successfully turned to the political antislavery press for coverage. The *National Principia,* edited by the radical political abolitionist William Goodell in New York City, became the unofficial organ of the society.[41]

The Church Anti-Slavery Society quickly allied itself with the various antislavery reform movements in the religious community. The CASS regularly praised the comeouter sects' efforts to convert their parent denominations to an antislavery position. The press of the comeouter sects, in turn, favorably reported the new abolitionist group's activities. Speakers at the society's meetings warned the benevolent institutions that proslavery attachments would prove fatal to their labors. Many who joined the new antislavery organization also contributed to the abolitionist American Missionary Association. The Church Anti-Slavery Society exerted pressure on the interdenominational publication institutions by subsidizing the printing of religious antislavery tracts that the established bodies had rejected.[42] The CASS made great strides before the Civil War in establishing itself as the AFASS's heir as the coordinator of Christian abolitionist activities.

The Church Anti-Slavery Society also attempted to mobilize the churches' moral power as an influence on government policy toward slavery. It frequently passed resolutions against the Fugitive Slave Law, the *Dred Scott* decision, and numerous additional legislative or judicial actions that denied equal rights to black Americans. Leaders of the CASS chastised Garrisonian disunionism as an evasion of northern responsibility for slavery. On the question of supporting one political party, however, sentiments among members of the society were so divided that no official position was taken in elections. Many of the society's members were fervent Republicans, but others, including the Cheevers, refused to vote for the new party until it recognized the justice of immediate emancipation. Not until the Civil War began did the CASS overcome its internal political divisions and become an effective lobbying force.[43]

Although Henry Cheever frequently remarked that the CASS was not founded as an enemy to any existing abolitionist organization, troubled relations soon developed between the new society and the Garrisonians. Both Cheevers praised the AASS's fidelity to the cause of the slave, but they and other Church Anti-Slavery Society spokesmen concluded that the heterodox theological views of most Garrisonian leaders rendered that class of abolitionists incapable of fostering antislavery sentiment in the American churches. The Garrisonians, in turn, regarded the CASS's claim to be the only "distinctively and exclusively Christian" abolitionist association as an implicit attack on their own organization.[44] Garrisonian spokesmen objected to the Church Anti-Slavery Society's assumption of the right to define what principles were Christian and branded that attitude as one more in line with the teachings of the Pharisees than with those of Jesus Christ. The AASS press defended the necessity of keeping the emancipation movement free from religious tests and questioned how the CASS hoped to aid the slaves by slandering other abolitionists. The Garrisonians especially complained that while the new society's members refused to cooperate with the supposedly infidel AASS, they nevertheless continued to support churches and benevolent societies that offered fellowship to the assuredly anti-Christian slaveholders. The Garrisonians also described the Church Anti-Slavery Society's political behavior as inconsistent on the grounds that the religious abolitionists were occasionally cordial to the Republicans.[45]

Despite this exchange of criticism, Garrisonians surprisingly conceded that the antislavery position of the Church Anti-Slavery Society was "far in advance of any stand yet taken by the popular churches," and "second in thoroughness only to the platform of the American Anti-Slavery Society."[46] As in the case of the AASS's relations with the comeouter denominations, the Garrisonians could acknowledge that other groups had honest antislavery intensions, yet they continued to point out that excessive concerns for sectarian matters could interfere with abolitionist effectiveness.

The AASS's qualified endorsement of the Church Anti-Slavery Society was just one sign of a growing reconciliation between Garrisonian and Christian abolitionists in the late 1850s. A few abolitionists such as Samuel J. May, John G. Whittier, and Ellis Gray Loring had occasionally found ways to bridge the gaps between the various abolitionist camps. In the late 1840s and early 1850s, proposals advanced by Whittier, James Freeman Clarke, and others for reuniting Garrisonian, religious, and political abolitionists had come to naught.[47] Several trends during the late 1850s, however, made possible a partial reconciliation of abolitionist factions. The demise of the AFASS in 1855 removed a focus for the bitterness between partisans of the 1840 abolitionist schism. The adoption of more liberal religious views by such prominent non-Garrisonian abolitionists as James G. Birney, Theodore Weld, Gerrit Smith, and Elizur Wright blurred old theological divisions inside the movement. The political events of the 1850s also drew abolitionists together in the role of friendly critics of the new moderate antislavery political parties.[48]

Most of the initiative for reconciliation came from the Garrisonians.

Former schismatics such as William Goodell, Beriah Green, Gerrit Smith, and Samuel Aaron were welcomed back to the AASS's meetings and platforms. Younger leaders of the antislavery movements in the churches during the 1850s, including Henry Ward Beecher, Hiram Mattison, and Gilbert Haven, also were invited speakers at Garrisonian conventions. Although the managers of the new interdenominational abolitionist gatherings and organizations remained somewhat wary of the infidel reputation of the Garrisonians, the war of words between the two groups never approached the level of the years around 1840. Instead both groups found common ground in working to convert the moderate antislavery sentiment in northern churches into support for abolitionist principles and programs.[49]

Just as Christian abolitionists discovered ways to cooperate with their former Garrisonian rivals, they also learned techniques to influence the political dimensions of the antislavery movement during the 1850s. The controversial issues of that decade increased the desire of Christian abolitionist organizations to apply strict ethical standards to political affairs touching slavery. Most of the Christian Anti-Slavery Conventions, for example, sought means to encourage northern politicians to consider the moral dimensions of government policy toward slavery. The experience accumulated in these and other efforts would enable the religious community to exert well-organized pressure upon government officials to eradicate the oppressive system when the Civil War presented the opportunity to do so. As the following chapters will show, the various interdenominational abolitionist endeavors had an important impact in furthering both ecclesiastical and political antislavery sentiments before and during the Civil War.

—8—

Vote as You Pray and Pray as You Vote: Church-Oriented Abolitionism and Antislavery Politics

From the 1840s onward, the antislavery movement in the United States became progressively more involved in questions of political action. In the 1830s, abolitionists employed moral suasion tactics to try to awaken other Americans to the sin of slaveholding. After years of failure in these efforts, many abolitionists turned to more conventional political practices to advance the cause of immediate emancipation. At the same time, sectional disagreements over government economic policy and over the disposition of western lands added to the attention accorded to slavery in public debate. Several pieces of controversial legislation and episodes of premeditated violence fired political hostility between northerners and southerners. Ultimately these sectionally divisive events led to civil war, but not before they had also influenced the progress of the abolitionist campaign in the nation's religious institutions.

I

Although the founders of the American Anti-Slavery Society concentrated their earliest efforts on working for the conversion of the churches to antislavery principles, they also soon discovered political processes to advance their cause. Abolitionists petitioned legislatures and offered antislavery testimony to any lawmaking body willing to take up the subject. Antislavery groups interrogated political candidates to determine whether any had acceptable views on slavery-related issues. When no candidate expressed antislavery sentiments, abolitionists often protested by "scattering'' their ballots among write-in candidates. The early abolitionists nevertheless refrained from making their own nominations for fear of compromising the moral character of the antislavery movement.[1]

In the late 1830s, however, many abolitionists reassessed their opposition to an independent antislavery political party. After half a decade of effort, their moral suasion campaign had converted few slaveholders or religious institutions to abolitionism. In contrast, the abolitionists' petition campaigns had enrolled the support of thousands for limited antislavery measures, such as abolition in the District of Columbia and prohibition of the interstate slave trade. Attempts to suppress abolitionist agitation by legal or violent actions had backfired, strengthening moderate antislavery feelings in the North. This combination of trends convinced a significant number of abolitionists that an antislavery political party could tap these new northern sentiments. A series of conventions in 1839 and 1840, called to explore the potential for coordinated antislavery political action, led to the founding of the Liberty party and to the nomination of veteran abolitionist James G. Birney for president.[2]

As discussed in Chapter 3, the opposition of leading Garrisonian abolitionists to an antislavery third party, as well as other disagreements, had led to the schism in the AASS in 1840. To a degree infrequently recognized by historians, there also was considerable hesitancy among Christian abolitionists to give public support to the fledgling Liberty party. Many of these abolitionist churchmen shared the antebellum religious community's mistrust of politics as sordid and compromising. A majority of the early leaders of the American and Foreign Anti-Slavery Society feared that the new party would distract attention from the moral aspects of the antislavery campaign. Christian abolitionists also were sensitive to the Garrisonians' charge that the Liberty party was founded as an attempt to protect the churches from potential disruptions by diverting antislavery reform into politics.[3]

Another reason for the reluctance to support the Liberty party was the strong allegiance of many abolitionists and other reform-minded northern Christians to the Whig party. The same evangelical trends that had awakened churchmen to movements such as temperance and abolitionism in the 1820s and 1830s had also drawn them into politics on the Whig side. Through its requirement of continuous proof of conversion, evangelical theology inclined its adherents toward both religious and political efforts to eliminate sin. Compared to the laissez-faire ideology of the antebellum Democrats, the Whigs' moralistic rhetoric and occasional support of sabbatarian and prohibition measures was highly attractive to evangelical voters. Even on the issues of slavery and racial discrimination, northern Whig politicians often took positions that won the sympathy of proabolition evangelicals. The Liberty party challenged the Whig claim on evangelical voters and sparked heated disputes. Rather than risk offending churchmen with strong partisan loyalties, the AFASS and other Christian abolitionist groups initially preferred a policy of strict political neutrality.[4]

The Liberty party attempted to win the active support of antislavery churchmen by advancing a program that retained much of the abolitionist movement's traditional emphasis on the moral and ethical aspects of the slavery question. Although some political abolitionists tried to introduce economic considerations into their party's arguments against slavery, the Liberty platform in the presidential elections of 1840 and 1844 differed little from those of the old antislavery societies. The abolitionist political party condemned not only slaveholding but also the nation's pervasive racial prejudice as an affront to God's laws. It called for the immediate abolition of slavery wherever constitutionally possible and for the repeal of all racially discriminatory legislation as both a religious and a political duty. By characterizing slavery as "a great question of public morality," Liberty party spokesmen hoped to win the votes of churchmen who believed politics should be conducted in accordance with Christian principles.[5]

After pointing out the moral implications of slavery-related political issues, the Liberty men denounced those who still refused to vote for the new antislavery party. In their battles with the Garrisonians, the political abolitionists charged that nonresistant principles conflicted with what the 1844 Liberty platform described as "the moral and religious duty" to vote for antislavery candidates. The third-party spokesmen also censured the Garrisonian policy of advising those abolitionists who persisted in voting to support the candidate of the major parties who had the strongest antislavery stance.[6] Liberty men complained that this practice was based on the unacceptable "axiom, that politics, of necessity, must be impure—that they must be conducted on principles of mere expediency, and that moral principle, for the time being, must be laid aside."[7]

The Liberty party also attacked Christian abolitionists who continued to vote for the Whigs and Democrats. Political abolitionists asserted that both of the major parties were subservient to slave interests and hence unfit for support from antislavery Christians. Liberty men denounced the practice of voting for the less objectionable Whig or Democratic candidate as an immoral "least-of-two-devils doctrine."[8] Congregational minister Jonathan Blanchard reported being one of many veteran abolitionists forced to "run a regular gauntlet" of moral condemnations from Liberty party champions for "the sin of voting for [Whig William H.] Harrison" in 1840.[9] To capture and hold the loyalties of proabolition churchmen, third-party advocates developed the argument that ethically consistent Christians must "vote as they pray"; in other words, those opposed to holding fellowship with slaveholders in their churches should likewise refuse to vote for candidates and parties that took no stand against slavery. An Indiana Liberty party newspaper summarized this argument with the admonition: "Vote as you pray. You must do it, or be recreant to your country, recreant to your religion, recreant to your God."[10]

In addition to defining the moral responsibilities of voters in relation to slavery, the Liberty party encouraged the churches to undertake antislavery reform. Liberty party conventions regularly endorsed the view that slavery was inherently sinful. Occasionally these meetings also recommended that the churches cease all religious fellowship with slaveholders. In 1842 the nominating convention of the New York Liberty party called on church members to renounce the "sin of patronizing pro-slavery preachers."[11] Liberty party newspapers also served as forums for public discussion of purely church-related abolitionist questions. In particular, the third-party press provided invaluable publicity to the antislavery movements in the Methodist and Baptist churches, where denominational editors habitually censored news of abolitionist activities. Although most Liberty party editors refrained from endorsing the controversial practice of comeouterism, they applauded the ability of the new abolitionist sects to "goad" the old denominations toward stronger antislavery positions.[12]

Liberty party leaders did not merely express support for the principles of abolitionism in church affairs. James G. Birney, the party's presidential nominee in 1840 and 1844, wrote *The American Churches: The Bulwark of Slavery,* an uncompromising exposé of proslavery church practices. Liberty party politicians such as Presbyterian Birney, Methodist Samuel Lewis of Ohio, Unitarian John Pierpont of Massachusetts, Congregationalist Owen Lovejoy of Illinois, Presbyterian Alvan Stewart of New York, and Congregationalist Samuel Fessenden of Maine were also prominent campaigners for antislavery reform in their denominations. The Liberty party's efforts to remake the churches into proabolition vehicles set an important precedent for later antislavery political organizations.[13]

The Liberty party's moralistic propaganda and program and its endorsement of antislavery reform in the churches gradually overcame the hesitation of most Christian abolitionists to support the new party. Although the AFASS constitution condemned Garrisonian nonresistance and proclaimed the moral obligation of antislavery voting, the society initially refused to ally itself with the Liberty party. As described in Chapter 4, the attitude of AFASS leaders toward the Liberty party steadily warmed until the society gave the political abolitionists' vehicle an unqualified endorsement in 1845. Although the AFASS continued to concentrate the majority of its limited propaganda resources on antislavery church reform, support for the Liberty party and its candidates became a regular part of the society's program.

Another source of support by Christian abolitionists for the Liberty party came from the Christian or Religious Anti-Slavery Conventions held in New York and New England in the 1840s. Although discussion of religious antislavery questions generally received priority, these gatherings also possessed an important political dimension. Most of the New York Christian Anti-Slavery Conventions limited themselves to a general statement that voting should be governed by moral antislavery principles; however, some openly endorsed the Liberty party. For example, a convention in Hamilton, New York, resolved that "those who admit the sinfulness of slavery . . . and yet vote for oppression, or for those who are connected with pro-slavery parties, are guilty of most gross inconsistency; and are undeserving the name Christian patriots, and unworthy to be recognized as the true friends of down-trodden humanity."[14] In Maine, Connecticut, and Vermont, the Christian Anti-Slavery Conventions functioned as adjuncts to the Liberty party movement, with religious and political gatherings scheduled to reinforce each other's attendance.[15]

Antislavery politics also played an important role in the operations of the religious comeouter bodies. Many of the new Union Churches made antislavery voting a requirement for membership. Gerrit Smith, William Goodell, and Beriah Green, the most prominent figures in the Union Church movement, were all leaders in the New York Liberty party. Goodell, the major propagandist for this movement, stressed the need for abolitionists to behave consistently in their religious and political lives by abandoning old slavery-tainted affiliations to join the Union Churches and the Liberty party. Garrisonian newspapers, in contrast, complained that Goodell and Smith were attempting to transform these new congregations into religious auxiliaries for the third-party movement.[16]

The comeouter sects also committed themselves to political action against slavery. Although a Garrisonian minority existed in several of these bodies, comeouter sect officers and editors generally opposed the policies of nonresistance and disunion. In fact the leaders of the comeouter sects were among the foremost proponents of the Christian abolitionist argument that antislavery churchmen had a religious duty to use all means—moral and political—to abolish slavery. The Free Presbyterian church made it a disciplinable offence for sect members to vote for any candidate "guilty of the crimes of slaveholding, dueling, or other scandalous offences against the law of God."[17] The conventions and newspapers of the Free Presbyterians, Wesleyans, and Free Mission Baptists all counseled voting for antislavery candidates as a moral obligation. As a result of this prompting, comeouter sect members took an active interest in Liberty party affairs.[18]

The Liberty party had a small but discernible impact on the voting habits of northern church members. In recent years, American political historians have developed sophisticated quantitative techniques to measure the voting behavior of various religious, social, and economic groups. For the early period of antislavery politics, however, data sufficiently accurate for such research methods are difficult to locate. The small size and geographic dispersion of the membership of Christian abolitionist institutions renders discernment of their voting patterns through statistical analyses impossible. Enough evidence exists, however, to permit historians to gain some insight into antebellum voting preferences of the larger denominations. Although their evidence is fragmentary, these studies have shown that antislavery voters tended to belong to the evangelical denominations, especially the Methodist, Baptist, Congregational, and New School Presbyterian churches. By thrusting a new ethically defined issue into politics, the Liberty party challenged the Whig hold on the evangelical vote. Once convinced of the evil nature of slavery, these morally inclined voters would be tempted to support the Liberty Party. But the small support for Liberty party presidential candidate Birney—seven thousand votes (0.29 percent) of the total popular vote in 1840 and sixty-two thousand votes (2.31 percent) in 1844—showed that the single issue of slavery was not yet strong enough to cause significant evangelical defections from the Whigs.[19]

Abundant contemporary sources, however, document that the Liberty party did attract enthusiastic support from one group of evangelical antebellum churchmen, the Christian abolitionists. The gradual but steady movement of the AFASS into the Liberty party camp has already been documented. Except for reports of a small nonvoting Garrisonian faction among the Wesleyans and in some Union Churches, the antebellum press contains few notices of members of the highly evangelical religious comeouter groups supporting any other party. In contrast, the abolitionist press frequently denounced the continuing allegiance of the older antislavery churches, the Quakers and Freewill Baptists, to the Whig and Democratic parties, respectively. Public support for the Liberty party was also quite strong among western Congregationalists, especially those who had severed fraternal relations with the Presbyterians during the 1840s in protest against Presbyterian conservatism on antislavery as well as on theological issues. Among the northern religious and benevolent bodies, the Christian abolitionist groups were alone in their public endorsements of the Liberty party. By the mid-1840s, an informal alliance had developed between the forces of political and religious abolitionism.[20]

II

Fundamental disagreements over how to build upon the Liberty party's limited success in the mid-1840s eventually destroyed the unity of the political abolition movement. A faction led by Salmon P. Chase, Gamaliel Bailey, and Henry B. Stanton advocated electoral cooperation with moderate antislavery groups in the major parties. The Mexican War and the subsequent opposition of many northerners to permitting slavery in the western territories provided a ready issue for the construction of an antiextensionist coalition in the election of 1848. In a complicated series of intraparty battles, the procoalition forces outmaneuvered all opponents and merged the Liberty party with antiextensionist Whigs and Democrats, creating the new Free Soil party. Unlike the Liberty party, the Free Soilers gave no endorsement to immediate abolition or to equal rights for blacks. In fact many Free Soilers held strong negrophobic sentiments and supported antiextensionism as a means of keeping black labor—free or slave—from the territories.[21] What the Free Soil party offered in lieu of the Liberty party's high standards was a potentially vast expansion of antislavery influence, albeit of a limited nature, in the political system.

Not all Liberty men could accept the compromised antislavery position of the new party. As early as 1845, Birney, Goodell, Elizur Wright, and Gerrit Smith had proposed to broaden the Liberty party platform into a program of universal reform. Calling themselves the Liberty League, this faction also took the position that the Constitution did not sanction slavery and that therefore Congress had the power to abolish slavery everywhere in the Union. Although the Liberty League failed to capture control of the Liberty party or to block the Free Soil merger, members vowed to continue to work for their undiluted abolitionist program. In 1848 the Liberty League ran Gerrit Smith for president in opposition to the Free Soil and major party candidates. Despite its lack of electoral success, the Liberty League continued to function under a variety of names until the Civil War.[22]

The Free Soilers and Liberty League members represented contrasting approaches to antislavery politics. The Liberty Leaguers presented a host of philosophical, legal, and historical arguments to support their cardinal tenet that slavery was unconstitutional, but the capstone of their case was the contention "that slavery is so evidently contrary to the paramount law of nature, to justice, to fundamental morality, and the law of God, that it never was, and never can be legalized; and that no legislature nor monarch possesses the power to make it legal."[23] Because they defined slaveholding as both sinful and illegal, the Liberty Leaguers could tolerate no compromise on any political question touching slavery. Thus the Liberty League charged the Free Soil movement with sanctioning the sin of slaveholding on the grounds that the antiextension platform recognized slavery's right to remain undisturbed in the South.

The Free Soilers, however, found several ways to defend antiextensionism as a morally responsible policy. They pointed out that the Liberty League's view of slavery as unconstitutional conflicted with the generally accepted belief that the federal government could not abolish slavery where it already existed. Free Soilers also observed that Americans commonly believed their country had a divine mission to Christianize the world. The spread of slavery to the West jeopardized this mission by threatening to pervert the Christian character of the nation. Free Soilers therefore maintained that their program to arrest the expansion of slavery served an important moral purpose, not merely the selfish interests of the North. Although the Free Soilers took no official position on the rights of blacks, many party members and newspapers exhorted their fellow citizens to abjure racially discriminatory practices. In comparison to the Whigs and the Democrats, the Free Soilers allowed moral considerations to take an unquestionably larger role in declarations of their party position toward slavery. George Julian, the antiextensionists' candidate for vice-president in 1852, defended his party's platform on the grounds that it "embodies the unfashionable political virtue of recognizing the distinction between right and wrong, and the government of the world by a Providence."[24]

Although both the Liberty League and the Free Soil party claimed to take a highly ethical approach to political issues, the Free Soilers trailed their rivals in the old Liberty party's role of encouraging antislavery reform in the northern churches. The high point of Free Soil action in this regard was a resolution passed by the party's 1852 national convention declaring "that slavery is a sin against God and a crime against man, which no human enactment nor usage can make right."[25] Unlike the original political abolitionists, the Free Soilers refrained from stating that Christians should deny fellowship to slaveholders. In their personal church relations, most leading Free Soilers remained in denominations that tolerated slavery. Although Free Soil newspapers frequently reported on church affairs, their editors hesitated to endorse as a moral duty either the expulsion of slaveholders from religious fellowship or the secession of antislavery Christians from proslavery denominations.[26]

The Liberty Leaguers campaigned far more actively than the Free Soilers against church complicity with slavery. In their newspaper editorials, political platforms, and convention resolutions, the Liberty Leaguers gave clear, unqualified endorsements to the doctrines of slavery's inherent sinfulness and of the Christian's obligation not to remain in communion with slaveholders. Liberty Leaguers placed the major blame for the proslavery tone of the nation's politics on the churches and warned "that so long as the Church and ministry stumble at the problem, whether or not 'the sum of all villanies' is *malum in se*—it is not strange that graceless politicians should stumble at the problem whether the temple of the Holy Ghost can be legislated into a commodity of lawful merchandise."[27] Like the old Liberty party, the Liberty League viewed the antislavery agitation of both religious and political institutions as one inseparable movement.

The only dissension in Liberty League ranks over questions of proper antislavery church relations concerned the practice of comeouterism. The Liberty Leaguers condemned the Garrisonian variant of comeouterism as an evasion of moral responsibility. Although the Liberty League's newspapers publicized the activities of the comeouter sects, they did not endorse the establishment of new antislavery denominations. In their private lives, many leading Liberty Leaguers were exponents of the nondenominational Union form of comeouter congregation. Goodell, in particular, publicly feuded with the leaders of the comeouter sects over their "sectarianism."[28]

It is revealing to compare the political support garnered by the Free Soilers and by the Liberty Leaguers from antislavery northern churchmen. The results of the presidential elections of 1848 and 1852, in which the two parties competed, tell much of the story. The 1848 Free Soil ticket of Martin Van Buren and Charles Francis Adams received 290,000 votes, compared with only 2,500 for the Liberty Leaguers. Four years later, the antiextension party's totals dropped to 156,000, but Goodell, the Liberty League's presidential nominee, received so few ballots that no state reported them.[29] Two important facts can be deduced from these election results: first, the small size of the Liberty League vote indicates that most antislavery churchmen chose the more moderate antislavery political position; and second, the Free Soilers attracted considerable support from northerners who had never backed the abolitionist position in religion or politics.

Documentary evidence tends to confirm these conclusions. In May 1848 the AFASS endorsed John P. Hale, the first presidential candidate of the procoalition faction, but remained neutral in the contest between the Free Soilers and Liberty Leaguers. Although the American Missionary Association regularly passed resolutions encouraging its supporters to vote against slavery, it never officially endorsed a specific candidate. As individuals, the officers of both societies divided their support between the moderate and radical antislavery parties. This ambivalence so angered Gerrit Smith and many other Liberty Leaguers that they halted their financial contributions.[30]

Midwestern Christian abolitionists demonstrated less hesitation in supporting the Free Soilers rather than the Liberty Leaguers. Prominent Free Soil politicians George Julian and Stephen C. Stevens of Indiana and Samuel Lewis of Ohio played leading roles at the Christian Anti-Slavery Conventions in the early 1850s. These meetings condemned the major-party politicians for their role in the passage of the Fugitive Slave Act of 1850 and helped popularize the "higher law" argument against its enforcement. Although delegates to the conventions criticized the low moral tone of the Free Soil program, they still voiced no support for the Liberty League. The Cincinnati-based American Reform Tract and Book Society's *Christian Press*, under the editorship of the Reverend Charles B. Boynton, applauded the Liberty League's contention that slavery was unconstitutional but nevertheless endorsed the Free Soilers.[31]

Although Goodell believed that most of the Liberty League's support came from voters who had quit proslavery churches, even in those come-outer groups many preferred the Free Soilers. Smith's and Goodell's strong advocacy of the interdenominational Union Church movement had alienated many of the churchmen struggling to create the various come-outer sects. Although the comeouter denominations' press generally acknowledged the Liberty League's superior principles, the majority of comeouter sect editors endorsed the Free Soilers as the only realistic hope for political abolition. A Free Mission Baptist periodical praised the "moral effect" of the Free Soilers' antiextension platform and predicted that if slavery were to "be inhibited from entering upon ground where it is not . . . its existence in the slave states will soon cease, as though taken away 'without hands.' "[32] The traditionally antislavery denominations, the Quakers and Freewill Baptists, generally abandoned their allegiance to the old major parties only to shift support to the Free Soilers. This lack of backing for the Liberty League among even the most militantly abolitionist churches underscored the general lack of enthusiasm for radical antislavery politics in the northern religious community.

Whereas the Liberty League had difficulty establishing a base of support among abolitionist church groups, the Free Soilers made important gains among members of the major Protestant denominations. Though unwilling to accept the abolitionist position that slaveholders were sinners who must be expelled from Christian communion, a growing number of northern antislavery moderates acknowledged that slavery was an undesirable moral evil that should be peacefully extinguished. Many of these churchmen found in the Free Soil party an acceptable outlet for their cautious antislavery sentiment. A large portion of the northern religious press endorsed the moral character of the antiextension program. The Free Soilers attracted many nationally prominent moderate antislavery ministers such as Henry Ward Beecher, Leonard Bacon, and Theodore Parker, who had never voted for the Liberty party.[33] These moderate antislavery Christians became a valuable bloc in the Free Soil ranks, and their influence helps to explain why the new party so readily dropped the Liberty party's endorsement of abolitionist religious practices.

III

Historians have long noted the repercussions on northern public opinion of events such as passage of the Fugitive Slave Law and the Kansas-Nebraska Act, the "Bloody Kansas" feuding, and the Harpers Ferry raid. As more and more northerners became alarmed at what they perceived as aggressive acts by the "slave power," the fortunes of antislavery political parties rose. These events and the northern reaction to them also produced a perceptible increase in antislavery activism among the clergy and other church leaders. Because of differences in theology, polity, political traditions, and demographic makeup, however, the degree of this change varied from denomination to denomination. These developments would lead to increasing interaction between the political and religious antislavery movements in the late 1850s.

The first important event of the 1850s that helped stimulate antislavery sentiment in the northern churches was the passage of the Fugitive Slave Law of 1850. Debate over this legislation was extensive. The northern clergy cited legal, constitutional, and political objections to the law, but their most telling complaints were against the requirement that individual citizens assist in capturing runaways. Clerical opponents of the Fugitive Slave Law recalled the Old Testament law of the Jews: "Thou shalt not deliver to his master the servant [who] is escaped from his master to thee. . . ."[34] To help reenslave fugitives was to give direct personal aid

—153—

to the abominable system of slavery, and many northern ministers denied
that any secular authority could command such collusion. In their sermons
and writings, scores of clergymen proclaimed that their first duty was to
the higher law of God and that therefore they could not obey the Fugitive
Slave Law.[35]

Despite such promising signs, large numbers of northern ministers defended the Fugitive Slave Law of 1850. Conservative clergymen warned
that the preservation of the Union depended on the North's compliance
with the Constitution's provision for the rendition of escaped slaves. More
than one minister described Paul's epistle to Philemon as an inspired
commandment to obey the Fugitive Slave Law. Supporters of the legislation of 1850 described government as God's instrument to order man's
relations and counseled obedience to all properly established laws. These
conservatives acknowledged the existence of a higher law, but argued that
the constituted authorities, not personal whim, were sounder and safer
judges of God's precepts.[36] One historical study comparing northern ministers who defended the Fugitive Slave Law with those who opposed it
finds that the former were older, from the socially dominant denominations of their region, and from churches with theologies that placed less
emphasis on individual conscience.[37]

Several features in the controversy over the Fugitive Slave Law of 1850
worked to the advantage of the antislavery movement in the churches. The
strength of opinion against the legislation forced articles on the subject
into religious periodicals that hitherto had maintained strict silence toward
slavery. The well-publicized series of renditions of captured runaways
created unprecedented sympathy for the plight of the slave. Although
many ministers who spoke out against the Fugitive Slave Law continued
to oppose abolitionism, their actions nonetheless made antislavery expressions more respectable in religious circles.[38]

The northern clergy reacted even more strongly against the Kansas-
Nebraska Act of 1854, which repealed the Missouri Compromise ban on
slavery in western territories north of 36°30'. Citing economic, political,
and moral arguments, antislavery congressmen appealed to northerners to
protest the measure publicly. Free-state ministers responded to this call in
unprecedented numbers. Even some defenders of the Fugitive Slave Law
spoke out against the Kansas-Nebraska Act. Clergymen complained that
the new law violated established sectional compromises and threatened to
disrupt the peace of the Union. Ministers also repeated the argument that
the extension of slavery would perpetuate the system with all its attendant
evils and thereby further corrupt the moral character of the nation. In
addition to writing and preaching against the act, thousands of northern

clergymen signed memorials to Congress that denounced the legislation. To help ensure the antislavery complexion of Kansas, ministers and congregations also contributed to the societies aiding free-state settlers in the territory. Abolitionist and antislavery politicians hailed these activities as an indication that the northern churches were "waking up at last to a sense of their duty."[39]

Proponents of the Kansas-Nebraska Act, and particularly its chief sponsor, Democratic Senator Stephen A. Douglas of Illinois, reacted with hostility to this clerical onslaught. Douglas charged that abolitionists and Free Soilers had induced northern ministers "to desecrate the pulpit, and prostitute the sacred desk to the miserable and corrupting influence of party politics."[40] A number of clergymen joined the Democratic press in echoing Douglas's attack on political preaching. Even more ministers, however, defended their right to speak out on political issues that touched on moral questions. The editor of one normally conservative Baptist newspaper claimed that clergymen had not only the "*right*" but also the "*duty,* as ministers, charged to 'declare the whole counsel of God,' in certain circumstances to weigh schemes of public policy in the balance of the sanctuary."[41] Abolitionist churchmen had endured the same kind of criticism for years, and they defended the clergy opposing the Kansas-Nebraska Act. Antislavery politicians also affirmed ministers' responsibility to preach against evil wherever it occurred, and claimed that only the friends or dupes of slaveholders contested that legitimate clerical role. Although the Kansas-Nebraska Act passed despite this protest, the re-opened issue of slavery in the territories greatly increased antislavery activism among northern church leaders.[42]

Another secular trend that affected antislavery opinion in the northern churches was the increasing use of violent tactics by participants on both sides of the slavery debate. The plight of fugitive slaves led many northern churchmen to break the law to assist them. A few antislavery activists went even further, aiding slaves to escape and battling authorities to release captured runaways. The sectional rivalry for the Kansas territory often resulted in hostile clashes between pro- and antislavery settlers. The Kansas free-state faction looked to the North for arms to contend with southern encroachments. The most important incident of antislavery violence was John Brown's raid on the federal arsenal at Harpers Ferry. After a short but bloody fight, Brown's attempt to start a slave rebellion ended in his capture and execution.

The sentiments of northern churchmen were deeply divided by these events. Even many antislavery ministers and religious periodicals recoiled from the violence committed in the name of their cause. The participation of clergymen in several well-publicized slave rescues attracted both praise and censure in northern religious circles.[43] Because most northerners blamed the violence in Kansas upon proslavery aggression, there was much support for the free-state settlers from the religious press and ministry.[44] Conservatives predictably damned the Harpers Ferry incident, and many antislavery moderates denied that Brown represented responsible northern opinion. Nevertheless, a surprisingly large number of clergymen defended not only Brown's motives but also his methods. Methodist Gilbert Haven, for example, placed the ultimate blame for the Harpers Ferry bloodshed on "the violent enslavement of forty hundreds of thousands of our kindred. . . ."[45] Most veteran abolitionists remained committed during the 1850s to peaceful antislavery tactics, but younger men in the antislavery ranks began to espouse more revolutionary actions. The attention paid by recent historians to this last phenomenon, however, should not obliterate the substantial evidence that most abolitionists maintained an intense campaign of moral suasion throughout the violent decade.[46] In fact, the strong antislavery emotions stirred by the troubled times would greatly assist the abolitionists' efforts to end church sanction for the southern system.

IV

The popularization of antislavery sentiment in the 1850s helped produce a major transformation of northern politics. At the same time, the rise of nativism as a salient question among many voters weakened traditional party allegiances. The greatest casualty of the divisive political issues of the 1850s was the Whig party. No longer able to satisfy either northern or southern militants, the Whig party performed poorly in the 1852 election and disintegrated amidst the turmoil accompanying the Kansas-Nebraska act. At the same time, passage of this controversial bill strengthened the popularity of antiextensionism among northerners. In 1854 the Free Soilers merged with recent converts to antiextensionism from the Whigs and Democrats to form the Republican party. The new party attracted a broad range of voters, including many who were more concerned with economic development and freedom from competition with black labor than with ending slavery. The presence of these conservative and racist elements worried antislavery churchmen that the new party might abandon all consideration for the moral aspects of the slavery question.[47]

The Republicans' positions on the ethical duties of antislavery northerners alleviated many of the fears of the Christian abolitionists. The new party's leadership included a large radical faction, including Joshua Giddings, George Julian, Henry Wilson, Thaddeus Stevens, Charles Sumner, and Salmon Chase. Although these men emphasized the economic oppression inherent in slavery, they also acknowledged the immorality and inhumanity of the institution. Republican spokesmen advocated antiextensionism not just as a means to confine slavery but also as an unquestionably constitutional program to hasten the extinction of the institution. Republicans extolled the ethical merits of an absolute ban on slavery's growth that would affix an unequivocal stigma to the system. Though seldom challenging the pervasive racial prejudice, Republican rhetoric nevertheless was superior to the demagoguery practiced by northern Democrats.[48]

In addition to agitating political issues in a moral context, a number of prominent Republicans worked actively for antislavery reform in the northern churches. Rather than risk offending moderate antislavery churchmen, in its platforms the Republican party avoided official comment upon ecclesiastical affairs. Most Republican leaders belonged to denominations that still condoned fellowship with slaveholders and took no part in abolitionist efforts to end that practice. There were significant exceptions, however, particularly among Republicans who had been active in earlier third-party ventures. Giddings, Julian, and Wilson all attended interdenominational antislavery gatherings and endorsed those gatherings' work in both the religious and political spheres. In public lectures, Chase declared that political toleration for slavery would end as soon as "every Christian Church [resolved] to stand up in the sacred majesty of a solemn testimony against slavery; to free themselves from all connection with the evil and [to] utter a calm, deliberative voice to the world."[49] The Republicans' most valuable assistance to abolitionist churchmen came from party newspapers such as Gamaliel Bailey's *National Era,* which publicized the activities of religious antislavery movements that often went unmentioned in the denominational press.

A hard core of political abolitionists opposed the Republicans' diluted antislavery program. In 1855 the Liberty League reorganized itself as the American Abolition Society and absorbed the American and Foreign Anti-Slavery Society. This event marked a formal reconciliation between the Smith-Goodell faction and the coterie of New York City Christian abolitionists, including Lewis Tappan and William Jay, who had managed the AFASS and still directed the American Missionary Association. The American Abolition Society denounced slavery as "sinful, illegal, and unconstitutional" and acknowledged "the duty of Christians to hold no

—157—

church relations that involve religious fellowship or ecclesiastical connection with slaveholders."[50]

In addition to conducting a limited propaganda effort, the American Abolition Society ran its own political nominees under the banner of the Radical Abolitionist party. The Radical Abolitionists used Gerrit Smith's presidential candidacies in 1856 and 1860 primarily to assail the moral deficiencies of the Republicans' antiextension program. Whereas the Republicans conceded that the Constitution tolerated slavery where it already existed, Goodell declared that the Bible did not allow northerners "to recognize any such States' rights as the sovereign right to make merchandize of men's souls."[51] Republicans responded to such criticism by accusing the Smith-Goodell group of "moral dilettantism" in refusing to "come down from their perch on platforms which embraced all the moralities, to work on one which only said to slavery 'not another foot of territory.'"[52] The *National Era* protested that "a political party is not a philanthropic association" and therefore could neither define slaveholding as a sin nor justify unconstitutional measures merely to satisfy the dictates of individual consciences.[53]

Although Christian abolitionists frequently echoed Radical Abolitionist criticism of the Republicans' weak stands on the moral questions of emancipation and racial equality, more and more of them in the late 1850s decided to support the moderate antislavery party. Even leaders of the comeouter sects, who preached that religious principle must govern a Christian's voting, endorsed the Republicans' limited antislavery position. Frequently these groups conceded that they were "discouraged with the diluted notions of the anti-slavery-for-white-men-party."[54] Nevertheless, most comeouter churchmen believed that they could elevate the Republican program by cooperating with the advanced antislavery element of the party. For example, veteran Free Mission Baptist William H. Brisbane pledged to "get into harness" for Salmon Chase's campaign for the Republican presidential nomination in 1860 because his election would be "no half way victory" for antislavery principles but "the result of a direct and well understood issue."[55] Events in the 1850s convinced many in the antislavery sects that the Democrats must be driven from control of the federal government at all costs. These considerations led the majority of Christian abolitionists to believe that they faithfully served the antislavery cause by helping to elect Republicans. The editor of a Free Presbyterian journal aptly expressed that sentiment: "All great enterprises, especially those which are moral in their character and aim, reach success through a slow and painful process. . . . The election of Lincoln we well know is not the equivalent to the abolition of slavery but it will be a long step toward that result."[56]

The other Christian abolitionist institutions either endorsed the Republicans or adopted a neutral position. Despite the reconciliation between Gerrit Smith and the leaders of the American Missionary Association, the antislavery benevolent organization continued to refuse to endorse candidates. ARTBS publications praised the Radical Abolitionists' interpretation of slavery as unconstitutional but nevertheless supported Republican candidates. The political loyalties of members of the Church Anti-Slavery Society, founded in the late 1850s, were too divided for the organization to endorse either the Republicans or the Radical Abolitionists. Privately George Cheever railed against the cautious tone most antislavery ministers adopted "out of fear of damaging the miserable cause of a most purely selfish and unprincipled republican party."[57] The drift of Union Church members toward the Republican party led to Gerrit Smith's adoption of increasingly heterodox views on the Bible and church organization and to Goodell's complaint that those bodies had been "seduced into political compromises fatal to their purity."[58]

Often the Christian abolitionists' criticism of the Republicans was aimed at encouraging the new party to take a less diluted antislavery position. The midwestern Christian Anti-Slavery Conventions in Columbus, Ohio, and in Chicago in 1859 stated profound disappointment that Republican platforms and candidates emphasized economic and sectional rather than moral arguments against slavery.[59] Giddings, a leading Republican radical, attended the Columbus convention and implored the churchmen to bring pressure upon the temporizers in his party. The more cautious Chase also applauded these meetings but privately advised antislavery clergymen not to hold the Republicans to a morally defined code for antislavery actions.[60] Despite the Christian Anti-Slavery Conventions' criticism of the Republicans, few delegates at the meetings announced their readiness to defect to another political party.

Christian abolitionists also acted individually to urge Republicans not to compromise the ultimate goals of emancipation and racial equality. They corresponded with Republican leaders, counseling them on the moral obligations of the slavery question. Sermons and religious newspaper articles discussed the duty of voting for antislavery candidates. Abolitionist churchmen who were aligned with the Republicans rallied behind those party leaders perceived to be most vehemently antislavery. Giddings and Julian were the usual favorites of abolitionists pursuing this tactic. After tireless courting, Chase also attracted the backing of several prominent abolitionist ministers in his unsuccessful attempt to capture the 1860 Republican presidential nomination.[61]

The results of the 1856 and 1860 elections reveal that nearly all Christian abolitionists joined the Republican fold. Though defeated in 1856,

Republican presidential candidate John C. Frémont carried all but five northern states. Four years later, Republican Abraham Lincoln was elected president by a minority of the popular vote but with an outright majority in every free state except California, Oregon, and New Jersey. The success of the Republicans was concurrent with the final collapse of the Radical Abolitionist party. In 1856 the Radical Abolitionist ticket received at most a few thousand votes. When Gerrit Smith began advocating a "Religion of Reason" in 1860, the Radical Abolitionist party fell apart. Rather than support a man of suspected orthodoxy, many Radical Abolitionists, including Goodell, sat out the election. Only a few diehards like Lewis Tappan, Frederick Douglass, and George Cheever voted for Smith.[62]

An important element in the Republican victory was the unprecedented degree of public support received from moderate antislavery Christians. Among northern churchmen, former Free Soilers enrolled en masse in the new party. Many northern clergymen and editors of religious periodicals actively campaigned for the Republicans, just as they had earlier spoken out against the Fugitive Slave Law and the spread of slavery into the territories. In addition, the Republicans recruited many first-time antislavery voters from among influential churchmen such as Henry W. Bellows, Francis Wayland, Gardiner Spring, Leonidas L. Hamline, and Dudley A. Tyng. Often, but not exclusively, former Whigs, these men expressed alarm at the growing power of slavery in national affairs. The growing willingness of northern churchmen to act against slavery contributed significantly to Lincoln's election.[63]

The close ties that developed between the political and ecclesiastical antislavery movements would have two important consequences. As events of the 1840s and 1850s made many free-state churchmen into antislavery voters, these northerners also took stronger stands against the toleration of slavery in their religious institutions. At the same time, whether on the side of the Radical Abolitionists or of the Republicans, antislavery churchmen actively demanded that the government treat slavery as a moral problem. As the next chapter will show, these same churchmen would redouble their pressure during the Civil War until the religious bodies finally acknowledged the sinfulness of slaveholding and the Republican administration agreed to make emancipation the goal of the North's military effort. It was therefore appropriate that the political and religious antislavery campaigns would not end until the Thirteenth Amendment had once and for all abolished human bondage.

—9—

Abolitionism and the Advance of Religious Antislavery Practices, 1845–1860

As discussed in Chapter 4, the highly publicized sectional divisions of several large religious denominations caused many contemporaries and most historians to overestimate the strength of antislavery sentiment in the northern churches during the 1840s and 1850s. In the decade and a half before the beginning of the Civil War, however, there was a significant growth of antislavery sentiment in many northern denominations. This antislavery progress in the churches is attributable to a combination of factors. Both the Garrisonian and Christian abolitionist societies maintained the propaganda campaign begun in the 1830s. Some abolitionists also continued to lobby in person at local and national denominational councils. In addition, Christian abolitionists employed three important new tactics to influence religious institutions in the 1840s and 1850s: the creation of comeouter sects, the agitation of benevolent institutions, and the sponsorship of interdenominational antislavery conventions and societies. These religious activities were aided by the sectionally divisive events of these years, which created more antislavery feeling in the North and encouraged political leaders to cooperate with church-oriented abolitionist efforts.

In addition to the abolitionists' efforts and the political climate, several ecclesiastical developments in the 1840s and 1850s aided the antislavery campaign in the churches. With a few exceptions, British denominations actively encouraged their American counterparts to adopt stringent policies against religious fellowship with slaveholders. During this time also, many northern churchmen became deeply involved in other religiously inspired reform movements such as temperance, sabbatarianism, and anti-

Catholicism. Like abolitionism, these campaigns utilized both moral suasion and political means to exact correct behavior. The abolitionist drive benefited from this increased willingness of church members to apply moral standards to secular affairs.[1]

Of surprisingly little help to Christian abolitionism was the temporary upsurge of revivalism in the late 1850s. Compared with participants in the great evangelical wave at the beginning of the century, revivalists in this later religious awakening displayed little enthusiasm for controversial issues such as abolitionism. Both Garrisonian and Christian abolitionists complained that revival prayer meetings often banned discussion of the potentially disruptive slavery question. A few abolitionists even challenged the sincerity of this revival movement because of the prominence of slaveholders and proslavery northerners among the new converts. Nevertheless, many abolitionists reported that they participated effectively in the revival without having to compromise their abolitionist doctrines.[2]

Under the pressure of abolitionist agitation and of the shifting political and religious trends, important developments took place in the northern churches' position toward slavery during the 1840s and 1850s. As a result of the differences in theology, polity, and demographic makeup described in Chapter 2, the impact of these forces varied considerably from denomination to denomination. Overall, the moral climate of the northern religious community became less hospitable to slavery in these decades. When weighed by either church-oriented or Garrisonian standards, however, most northern denominations stopped considerably short of adopting abolitionist principles and practices before the Civil War.

I

Although the Quakers, Freewill Baptists, and most Scottish Presbyterian sects adopted disciplines that barred slaveholding members, abolitionists had criticized those denominations for not taking an active part in the antislavery campaign of the 1830s. This situation had improved significantly by 1860. The Freewill Baptists launched a denominational antislavery society in 1842 to convert all church members to support of immediate emancipation. Freewill Baptist clergymen signed public petitions against slavery and against government policies supporting it. Most Freewill Baptists abandoned their traditional Democratic political allegiances to back first the Free Soilers and then the Republicans. The Freewill Baptists also undertook a mission to aid fugitive slaves in Canada and actively disseminated propaganda against religious fellowship with slaveholders. These vigorous antislavery efforts led even Garrisonian abolitionists, who had earlier criticized the denomination, to announce that the Freewill Baptists were adopting policies that "go far toward exonerating the Connexion from the guilt of sustaining Slavery."[3]

Despite their strict sectarianism, the Scottish Presbyterians also played a more active role in the abolition campaign in the 1840s and 1850s. Of the three sects, the Associate Synod, the Reformed Synod, and the Associate Reformed Synod, only the last had failed to enforce church discipline against fellowship with slaveholders by 1840. Eastern and southern resistance to church pronouncements on secular affairs, including slavery, finally provoked midwestern Associate Reformed Presbyterians to secede and combine with the Associate Synod to form the United Presbyterian church upon uncompromising abolitionist religious principles. The Christian abolitionists maintained good relations with the groups merging into the United Presbyterian church because those churchmen had been long-time supporters of antislavery political candidates and participants in the interdenominational Christian Anti-Slavery Conventions and the Church Anti-Slavery Society.[4] The Garrisonians, in contrast, were most pleased with the antislavery behavior of the Reformed Presbyterians, or Covenanters. Most members of this sect refused to swear oaths or vote because they regarded the United States government to lack God's sanction, as evidenced by the federal protection afforded slavery. The Covenanters had no faith in antislavery politics; they expected that proabolition parties "must become, in time, just what the other parties are."[5] The Garrisonians recognized and acknowledged that here was a denomination "practically carrying out the motto of the American Anti-Slavery Society—'No Union with Slaveholders, either religious or politically.' "[6]

The Quakers advanced more hesitantly toward an active abolitionist stance during the 1840s and 1850s. Efforts to abstain from all products of slave labor died out among the Friends. Few Quakers spoke out against proslavery government policies such as the Fugitive Slave Law. Because many Friends still feared that immediate abolition would result in violence, they supported plans for compensated emancipation and colonization. Persistent abolitionist criticism and two antislavery comeouter movements, however, finally emboldened many Friends to act in accordance with their antislavery tradition. By the late 1850s, most Yearly Meetings of Friends ceased disciplining members who became active abolitionists. Although they lamented the sectional turmoil, Friends voted more and more with the antislavery parties, especially the Republicans. Such actions helped to heal the schism among Indiana Orthodox Friends over the antislavery question and quieted abolitionist charges against Quaker acquiescence in the great national sin.[7]

The Quakers, Freewill Baptists, and Scottish Presbyterians were thus among the few sects that most nearly met the abolitionists' requirements for unadulterated antislavery churches. Not only did those denominations deny membership to slaveholders, but they also actively aided the abolition movement. To this small number of churches could be added the various comeouter sects and several small German immigrant denominations such as the Evangelical Association and the United Brethren in Christ. The Garrisonians still occasionally criticized the political practices and the negligent enforcement of the disciplines against slaveholding in some of these denominations. Nevertheless, in the late 1850s the Garrisonians acknowledged the existence of "exceptional cases" among the predominantly proslavery American denominations. With less hesitation than the Garrisonians, Christian abolitionists accredited these small bodies as genuine antislavery denominations and cited them as examples to other northern churches. Although several major denominations made significant advances in opposing slavery before 1860, this handful of thoroughly abolitionized sects composed the vanguard of the antislavery movement in the churches before the Civil War.[8]

II

The abolitionists were least successful in their dealings with the ritualist and the old-line Calvinist denominations. Among the ritualist sects, the Roman Catholic church had become the nation's largest denomination by the 1850s, as a consequence of the massive Irish and German immigration to America. Despite these numbers, almost no Catholic priests or laymen joined the abolition movement. The recent immigrants resented the nativist and anti-Catholic sentiments that many abolitionists shared with other Protestants of the period. Catholic voters developed close ties to the Democrats, who generally opposed nativism as well as antislavery. Historically, the Catholic church had tolerated slavery, and the American hierarchy's studied silence on the question implied no change in that policy. Catholics expelled only heretics from membership and therefore erected no barriers against slaveholders. Abolitionists protested that the Catholics' official neutrality toward slavery lent moral sanction to the institution. A visiting Irish priest, Father Theobald Mathew, came under particularly strong attack from American abolitionists when he refused to add antislavery remarks to his well-received temperance lectures. The Catholic press defended Mathew by repeating the charges about abolitionist infidelism, in particular labeling Garrison "not only a traitor to God, but also to his country."[9] Such vilification was representative of Catholic opinion regarding the abolitionists in the antebellum era.

The Protestant Episcopal church was another ritualist denomination that attempted to remain neutral on the slavery question. In many sections of the country, the Episcopalians were an elite denomination whose upper-class membership felt little attraction toward controversial social reform movements such as abolitionism. Alarmed at the schisms plaguing other denominations, one Episcopalian editor warned his fellow churchmen "that to intermeddle with it [slavery] would not only seriously endanger the safety of our Union, but produce a division in our own Church."[10] Some northern Episcopalians, including Bishop John Henry Hopkins of Vermont, made no pretense at conservatism but publicly defended slavery as sanctioned by the Bible. A few northern Episcopalians, led by William Jay and his son John, battled racial discrimination in church councils and supported the antislavery cause in the benevolent societies and in politics. Abolitionists praised these exceptional Episcopalians but ranked that church among the most faithful friends of slaveholders. The Episcopal church remained sectionally united until the start of the Civil War, and even then the northern branch refrained from criticism of slavery or slave owners.[11]

Several denominations of non-English-speaking Protestant immigrants also displayed extreme conservatism on the slavery question. Like other liturgical churches, the Lutheran General Synod deemed the question of slavery inappropriate for consideration by an ecclesiastical body. Most Lutheran leaders were strong supporters of the American Colonization Society and the Democratic party. Though Calvinist rather than ritualist, the German and Dutch Reformed churches also avoided taking any stand on slavery beyond endorsing colonization. Abolitionists condemned these denominations for their indifference to slavery's evils and sent special lecturers and literature to disseminate an antislavery gospel among the German-speaking churchmen. Several Lutheran synods in New York, Ohio, and Pennsylvania followed the example of the Franckeans and seceded to protest their denomination's slavery policies. Although a growing number of Lutheran, German Reformed, and Dutch Reformed church members adopted abolitionist principles in the 1840s and 1850s, none of these denominations ever officially condemned slavery or advocated abolition.[12]

The largest Protestant denomination that successfully resisted abolitionist demands was the Old School Presbyterian church. After the schism among the Presbyterians in 1837, the Old School branch inherited most southern church members as well as the least evangelical northerners. Although the church continued to profess allegiance to the antislavery Presbyterian discipline of 1818, Old School leaders interpreted this statement as favoring gradualism and colonization rather than abolitionism. In

1845 the Old School Presbyterian General Assembly acknowledged the evil of slavery but declared that the Bible did not sanction the exclusion of slaveholders from the church. Old School spokesmen described their church as a genuine antislavery body opposed to both proslavery and abolitionist fanaticism. By such a conservative policy, the Old School claimed, the church could win the slaveholders' confidence and eventually persuade them to manumit their slaves. In the meantime, the Old School Presbyterian church would act as a bulwark against the disunionists in both sections who threatened the nation's remaining political and spiritual bonds. [13]

The abolitionist agitation of the 1840s and 1850s had little effect on the Old School Presbyterians. After the General Assembly's action on slavery in 1845, several dozen antislavery ministers deserted the Old School for the Free Presbyterian church. Old School leaders, however, successfully minimized this defection by charging the comeouter sect with fanaticism on the fellowship and political antislavery questions. The Old School's defenders denied that the Free Presbyterians could help the slaves by slandering the slaveholder's Christian character with blanket condemnations. The religious antislavery conventions and societies attracted few Old School Presbyterian participants because that denomination's press skillfully dismissed those bodies as comeouter ventures. Both in their own and in interdenominational mission and publication boards, the Old School Presbyterians contended that the adoption of abolitionist principles would impede benevolent work. Northern Old School ministers' denunciations of political preaching did not prevent them from publicly counseling obedience to the Fugitive Slave Law. The political antislavery movement had little impact on most Old School Presbyterians, who continued to vote with the Democrats before and throughout the Civil War. Despite the abolitionists' efforts, the frequency and fervor of antislavery pronouncements by Old School judicatories steadily declined in the two decades before 1860. [14]

The Old School Presbyterians took firm steps to prevent a resurgence of antislavery discussion in their church councils. When American Congregational associations and British Presbyterian churches persisted in sending antislavery remonstrances to the Old School General Assemblies, all fraternal correspondence was halted. [15] Punitive action was taken against the small antislavery minority inside the denomination. The principal proabolition stronghold in the Old School was the Cincinnati synod, with its leaders the Reverends Erasmus D. McMasters and Thomas E. Thomas, both professors at the New Albany Theological School. Conservatives, led by two staunch colonizationists and Democrats, the Reverend

Nathan L. Rice and wealthy layman Cyrus P. McCormick, attacked New Albany as an abolitionist institution. In 1859 Rice got the General Assembly to assume control over New Albany and to accept a $100,000 endowment from McCormick to move the seminary to Chicago. The Old School selected Rice as president of the new Northwestern Theology Seminary and purged proabolition instructors from the faculty. The antislavery minority vowed to fight on, but its influence had been effectively curtailed. With abolitionism completely overpowered in the denomination, thousands of slaveholders remained undisturbed in the Old School Presbyterian church until the Civil War.[16]

III

While conservatism on the slavery question held sway in the ritualist and the old-line Calvinist denominations in the 1840s and 1850s, abolitionists made significant advances among the more evangelical faiths. The pressure of the new antislavery church tactics had its greatest effect in these denominations. Abolitionists helped many moderate antislavery churchmen overcome doubts about the need to discipline unrepentant slaveholders in their denominations. More important, abolitionist agitation and the darkening political climate of the 1850s encouraged increasing numbers of northern religious leaders to give stronger voice to their disapproval of slavery. In the late 1850s, the growth of aggressive antislavery sentiment in the churches produced several more sectional schisms.

As noted in the discussion of the Presbyterian schism of 1837, the New School church did not become a strongly antislavery denomination after its separation from the Old School faction. Several thousand slave-owning southern Presbyterians sided with the more evangelistic New School after the church division. Also in the New School were numerous northern conservatives, including the Reverends Samuel H. Cox, an apostate abolitionist; Sidney E. Morse, editor of the influential *New York Observer;* and Amasa Converse, editor of the Philadelphia *Christian Observer*. These predominantly East Coast conservatives were proponents of colonization and opponents of all new church legislation on the subject of slavery.[17] Also in New School ranks were numerous antislavery moderates who acknowledged the great evil of slavery but objected to the abolitionists' sweeping condemnation of all slaveholders as sinners. Abolitionist strength in the denomination had been weakened by the defection of comeouters to more unequivocally antislavery churches. Many other abolitionists, however, remained inside the denomination and labored to convince antislavery moderates to take more decisive action against slaveholders.[18]

Abolitionists utilized both traditional and new church-oriented antislavery tactics to reform the New School Presbyterian church. Abolitionist propaganda ridiculed the New School for enforcing church discipline against such innocuous practices as "promiscuous dancing" and horse racing but not against slaveholding. New School Presbyterians in New York and the Midwest played important roles in the Christian Anti-Slavery Conventions and worried denominational leaders by their endorsements of comeouterism as a last resort for antislavery reformers. The abolitionist agitation of the benevolent institutions deeply divided the New School Presbyterians. As noted in Chapter 6, conservatives supported the established societies' officers, whereas moderates frequently allied themselves with abolitionists in working for antislavery goals less extreme than severing fellowship with slaveholders. Likewise, on political antislavery issues, northern New School spokesmen expressed quite different opinions. The editors of the *New York Observer* and Philadelphia *Christian Observer* counseled obedience to the Fugitive Slave Law, whereas many New England and western synods and presbyteries endorsed the higher law doctrine. After the Kansas-Nebraska Act, however, northern New School members became notably more active in both the political and the religious antislavery campaigns.[19]

The greatest single factor that motivated the New School Presbyterians to adopt stronger antislavery positions was the mounting number of pro-abolition churchmen quitting the denomination. Perhaps two dozen abolitionist ministers came out from the New School and joined the Free Presbyterian church in the late 1840s. During the same period several entire midwestern presbyteries threatened secession unless the General Assembly took prompt and firm action against slavery. When the denomination continued to temporize, scores of ministers and churches in western New York and northern Ohio, Indiana, and Illinois switched affiliation to Congregational associations with strict rules barring slave owning. The defection of this heavily "Yankee" element as a consequence of the slavery issue jeopardized the Plan of Union between Presbyterians and Congregationalists in the West. In fact many New School conservatives suspected that Congregationalists raised the fellowship question in the American Home Missionary Society and in the correspondence between the two churches "in order to break in on the integrity and order of sister denominations."[20] Abolitionist observers predicted that the

New School would expel slaveholders only when faced with the potential of a greater loss of northern church members.

The combination of all these forces resulted in the gradual movement of northern New School Presbyterians toward the abolitionist position. The denomination's attempt in the mid-1840s to delegate authority over the slavery question to lower-level judicatories had only stimulated northern synods and presbyteries, especially in the Midwest, to petition the General Assembly for a firm stand on the issue. In the late 1840s and early 1850s, the New School's General Assemblies debated these petitions as well as such resolutions as the one introduced by Indiana abolitionist George Bassett in 1849 to have the denomination declare, "Slaveholding is a sin against God and man, and should be treated by the Christian Church as other gross immoralities."[21] Antislavery moderates voted with conservatives and southerners to defeat measures like Bassett's that might ultimately have expelled slaveholders, but they joined with abolitionist delegates to pass milder resolutions critical of slavery.

At the General Assembly of 1853, however, this coalition of abolitionist and moderate antislavery delegates took an action with more decisive consequences than even its backers had anticipated. Over the objections of northern conservatives and southerners, the General Assembly voted to condemn Christians who became slave owners for reasons other than "unavoidable necessity" and to require presbyteries to report the numbers of such individuals in their membership. Although the measure stopped short of the abolitionist position that slaveholding was intrinsically sinful, the requirement that southern Presbyterians investigate the circumstances of their slaveholding was regarded as highly offensive. Southern presbyteries either ignored the General Assembly's request for such reports, repeated in 1855 and 1856, or replied that they believed slave owning to be morally unobjectionable. Antislavery moderates in the denomination, such as Albert Barnes, responded indignantly to the southerners' claim, and the General Assembly of 1857 censured the Presbytery of Lexington, Kentucky, for proslavery pronouncements. In reaction to this ruling, southern New School Presbyterians seceded and formed the United Synod of the Presbyterian Church, with seven presbyteries and fifteen thousand communicants.[22]

Although a de facto separation occurred between New School Presbyterians and slaveholders in the late 1850s, abolitionists nevertheless disallowed that the denomination had assumed a sufficiently antislavery position. Abolitionists observed that New School leaders denied that their church had adopted a stronger antislavery discipline and instead blamed the schism on proslavery extremists. In 1859 the Free Presbyterians offered to merge with the New School if the latter would adopt an explicit rule barring all slaveholders from membership. The New School, however, rejected these terms, and its General Assembly said nothing more on the subject of slavery until 1862. Both Garrisonian and Christian abolitionists agreed that the New School Presbyterians continued to hinder the progress of emancipation by refusing to rebuke slaveholders as sinners.[23]

The suspension of a slave-owning bishop had provoked the schism in the Methodist Episcopal church in 1844. Despite the secession of sixteen southern annual conferences, the Methodists took no stronger steps toward ending fellowship with slave owners. In fact northern Methodists repudiated the Plan of Separation negotiated by the General Conference of 1844 and competed with the newly formed Methodist Episcopal Church, South, for the allegiance of denomination members in the border states. Conservative Methodists endeavored to convince northerners that the denomination was sufficiently antislavery while assuring southerners that slaveholders would not be expelled from the church. These conservatives voiced approval for colonization as a gradual and safe means of emancipation. They also denied that slaveholding was inherently sinful and opposed rules that condemned slave owners without regard to extenuating circumstances. This conservative position succeeded in holding thousands of southerners in the Methodist Episcopal church after 1844. At the same time, conservative leaders such as the Reverend Abel Stevens tried to mollify antislavery critics by contending that the church's continued toleration for slave owning was not intended "for its restricted *perpetuation,* but for its amelioration and final 'extirpation.' "[24]

Such claims persuaded few abolitionists to drop their demands for disciplinary action against slaveholders. Garrisonian and Christian abolitionist propagandists charged that, because the northern Methodist denomination still had slave-owning members, "its difference from the Southern Church will be one of degree only, and not of kind."[25] The Wesleyan Methodist Connection continued to draw away antislavery Methodists, though in much diminished numbers after 1844. A small number of Methodists also participated in the interdenominational abolitionist projects, especially the Church Anti-Slavery Society. Intra-denominational pressure from a much larger group of Methodist abolitionists succeeded in forcing open the columns of the church's official periodicals to discussion of the moral aspects of slavery-related political questions.[26]

This persistent abolitionist agitation slowly revived the dormant slavery debate in the denomination. The bishops and important conservative ministers such as Stevens, George Peck, and Nathan Bangs managed to suppress antislavery dissent at the General Conferences of 1848 and 1852. Methodist abolitionists, however, destroyed this enforced calm by publishing exposés of the prevalence of slaveholding in border conferences and of the official harassment of antislavery ministers in those districts. A new generation of Methodist abolitionists, including Gilbert Haven, William Hosmer, John Twombly, and Hiram Mattison, argued the case against fellowship with slave owners to a growing northern audience. Particularly in New England, western New York, and the upper Midwest, the rejuvenated Methodist abolition movement won new adherents through its propaganda efforts and through the organization of denominational antislavery conventions and societies. By the late 1850s, northern conservatives had lost control of a majority of the regional annual conferences to the advocates of a stronger denominational policy against slavery.[27]

Antislavery Methodists were divided over how to expel slaveholders without violating the church's constitution. A highly perfectionist element desired a change in the denomination's General Rules, whereas more cautious reformers believed that a reinterpretation of the discipline on slavery would be sufficient. As a result of lack of cooperation between these two antislavery groups, motions to rewrite the General Rules were defeated in the conferences of 1856 and 1860. The latter conference, however, amended the discipline to declare the "holding of human beings to be used as chattels" as grounds for expulsion from fellowship. Conservatives, however, destroyed the impact of this action by persuading the General Conference to acknowledge the ruling as merely "advisory."[28]

The action of the General Conference of 1860 had wide-reaching consequences. A number of dissatisfied New York abolitionists seceded and formed the Free Methodist Church, with a perfectionistic discipline that included a rule against fellowship with slaveholders. Despite eastern conservative reassurance that the new discipline on slavery was unenforceable, practically all border-state Methodists defected to the Methodist Episcopal Church, South, during the summer and fall of 1860.[29] Garrisonians and Christian abolitionists closely followed the antislavery movement in the Methodist denomination and agreed with the conservatives that no clearly stated bar to slaveholding members had been erected. William Goodell observed that the Methodists' "purification" from slavery would not be a "finality" until the "man stealers" were formally excommunicated.[30] Although its official position still stopped short of adopting abolitionist standards, the Methodist Episcopal church, like the New School Presbyterians, had effectively ended fellowship with slave owners before the Civil War.

IV

Falling somewhere between the churches making no progress toward severing fellowship with slaveholders and those achieving at least the form of the abolitionist position in the years between 1845 and 1860 was a diverse group of denominations including the Unitarians, Universalists, Disciples of Christ, Congregationalists, and northern Baptists. The theology of the Congregationalists and Baptists was traditional Calvinism modified by revivalism; that of the Unitarians and Universalists reflected the contemporary liberal trends; and that of the Disciples evinced a unique blend of both elements. The Universalists and Disciples of Christ had nationwide memberships, the Congregationalists and Unitarians were predominantly New Englanders, and Baptists were found throughout the North. One similarity among these denominations, however, was the lack of a strong central church government to enforce a common discipline on all members. This characteristic proved the major obstacle to the acceptance of abolitionist demands for the expulsion of slaveholders. Although antislavery sentiment grew in all these denominations during the 1840s and 1850s, none of them satisfied abolitionists that it had satisfactorily ceased all practices that sanctioned slavery.

Evaluation of the Unitarian position toward slavery in the years 1845–1860 is complicated by the denomination's traditional deference to the rights of individual conscience. Slaveholders may have joined the few southern Unitarian congregations, but the denomination had no power to discipline members. Unitarians opposed the condemnation of all slaveholders as sinners, because such a judgment made no allowance for the circumstances of particular cases. In addition, most Unitarians stayed aloof from reform societies because they believed that membership in such bodies diminished the moral influence of the individual reformer. Unitarians argued that the most effective way to eradicate a social evil such as slavery was by "a long process of organic growth" during which rational persuasion could be brought to bear upon the misguided.[31]

As a result of such individualism, Unitarians differed widely in their relations with the abolition movement. Some of the most important Garrisonians, including Samuel J. May, Francis Jackson, Lydia Maria Child, and Samuel May, Jr., were Unitarians. The Reverends Theodore Parker,

James Freeman Clarke, and Moncure Daniel Conway never joined abolitionist societies but actively participated in the antislavery campaign. William Ellery Channing, the most influential Unitarian minister of his day, publicly attacked slavery but deemed the abolitionists' sweeping condemnations of slaveholders counterproductive. Other leading Unitarian clergymen, such as Francis Parkman and Ezra Stiles Gannett of Boston and Orville Dewey of New York City, remained colonizationists despite criticism from the abolitionists.[32]

The new church-oriented abolitionist tactics developed in the 1840s and 1850s had little impact on the Unitarians. Prejudice against the liberal denominations ran high among the evangelical Christian abolitionists. The sponsors of the interdenominational antislavery conventions and societies seldom invited Unitarians to their gatherings. Unitarians were not welcome in the benevolent societies either and so were unaffected by the antislavery reform movements there. The Fugitive Slave Law and the Kansas-Nebraska Act stimulated debates among Unitarians, but the denomination refused to take any official position on such political questions.[33]

Ironically, Garrisonian abolitionists became the leading antislavery agitators inside the Unitarian denomination in the 1840s and 1850s. While on a speaking tour in England, Samuel May, Jr., convinced British Unitarians to remonstrate against the toleration shown slavery by their American counterparts. Samuel May, Jr., his older cousin Samuel J. May, and other Garrisonians labored repeatedly to persuade the American Unitarian Association, the denomination's missionary and publication society, to condemn slavery. Garrisonians championed Theodore Parker, whose extreme theological liberalism and antislavery views had alienated many of his fellow Unitarians. Under this influence, a majority of Unitarian ministers, acting in a purely individual capacity, signed antislavery petitions. In 1857, delegates from Unitarian societies in Kentucky and Missouri seceded when the Conference of Western Unitarian Churches resolved that slavery was "evil and wrong" and "doomed by God to pass away" through the influence of Christian teachings.[34] In a similar manner, most of the other small Unitarian congregations in the South collapsed or defected in reaction to the denomination's growing antislavery reputation. The denomination, however, still refused to endorse the antislavery movement, and abolitionist criticism of conservative Unitarians continued until the Civil War.

Another liberal denomination that balked at adopting religious abolitionist practices was the Universalist church. Orthodox abolitionists regarded Universalists as near-infidels and refused to associate with them in antislavery projects. The Garrisonians were more tolerant, but very few Universalists joined the AASS. Individually and in denominational conventions, however, some northern Universalists spoke out against slavery. For example, over three hundred Universalists signed a public declaration in 1846 that condemned slavery as "an insurmountable barrier to the promulgation of the great truth of Universal Brotherhood. . . ."[35] The denomination, however, rejected any proscriptive action against slaveholders in favor of further appeals to their consciences. Although they acknowledged that many Universalists publicly condemned slavery, abolitionists attacked the denomination's lack of action to hasten emancipation. As one abolitionist sarcastically observed, there was no effective barrier to Universalists' becoming slaveholders except "their pecuniary ability to purchase slaves."[36]

Theological considerations similarly played a major role in the rejection of abolitionism by the Disciples of Christ. The Disciples preached an unusual version of postmillennialism. Unlike most other denominations, they denied that perfectionist standards of social behavior, including the renunciation of slaveholding, could be demanded before the Second Coming of Christ. Adhering to a doctrine of scriptural literalism, the Disciples' leader, Alexander Campbell, had pronounced slaveholding not to be intrinsically sinful. The Disciples' commitment to Christian unity likewise led them to spurn antislavery membership tests and to accept slave owners into the denomination. The Disciples' American Christian Missionary Society even refused aid to any applicant with outspoken antislavery views. Although Disciples infrequently participated in Christian abolitionist projects, antislavery sentiments nevertheless grew inside the denomination, particularly in Ohio and Indiana during the 1850s. Antislavery Disciples launched their own newspaper and college and eventually their own mission society. Despite the action of these radicals, slaveholders remained welcome as members of the Disciples of Christ until the Civil War brought about emancipation.[37]

Although most contemporary and historical accounts describe the almost exclusively northern Congregational church as a strongly antislavery denomination in the 1840s and 1850s, the abolitionists regarded its testimony against slavery as defective. Many churches and local associations of Congregationalists, especially in the Midwest, adopted rules against fellowship with slaveholders, but no power existed to make such a policy binding on the whole denomination. As a result of this traditional deference to local authority, northern churches still occasionally welcomed visiting slaveholders to communion, and a few ministers publicly defended slavery without effective rebuke. Even moderate antislavery Congregationalists cooperated in benevolent projects and corresponded fraternally with denominations known to include slave owners. Nonabolitionist Congregationalists objected to the blanket condemnation of slave owners as sinners, preferring to acknowledge that circumstances could absolve an individual from guilt. Except for a sizable abolitionist minority, Congregational antislavery sentiment usually expressed itself in support for such gradualist programs as colonization and antiextensionism.[38]

Abolitionist efforts to prod Congregationalists to strengthen their antislavery testimony had mixed success. Just as they had during the bitter battles of the 1830s, the New England Congregational clergy in later decades rejected Garrisonian criticism of their denomination's treatment of slavery as the product of infidels.[39] The Christian and political abolitionists' activities attracted far greater support from that denomination. Congregationalists such as Lewis Tappan, Joshua Leavitt, Amos A. Phelps, and Jonathan Blanchard were important figures in the American and Foreign Anti-Slavery Society and in later religious abolitionist projects. Abolitionist comeouters from the New School Presbyterians and from other denominations often joined the Congregationalists and strengthened their antislavery commitment. In interdenominational abolitionist projects, Congregationalists were among the most active members of the Christian Anti-Slavery Conventions and the Church Anti-Slavery Society. Political issues similarly aroused Congregational antislavery sentiments. The higher law position on the Fugitive Slave Law was popular among much of the Congregational ministry. The Kansas-Nebraska Act provoked Congregational state associations to pass resolutions "to sound an alarm to God's holy mountain against the extension of organized and systematized oppression." Although Oberlin graduates imbued with Charles G. Finney's perfectionist doctrines were active in these religious and political antislavery activities, Congregational abolitionist ranks even in the Midwest remained predominantly orthodox in their theology.[40]

Because Congregationalists supplied the preponderance of financial contributions to most of the religous benevolent societies, abolitionists strove to enlist the denomination's support for the antislavery campaign inside those bodies. Moderate antislavery Congregationalists joined abolitionists in protesting the American Tract Society's resistance to publishing even the mildest reproofs of slavery. Congregational moderates, however, refused to support abolitionist-run religious publication bodies and founded their own organization to print less aggressive antislavery tracts. The American Missionary Association's stand against fellowship with slaveholders attracted numerous antislavery Congregationalists as contributors and as missionaries. Many more Congregationalists refused to break from the American Board of Commissioners for Foreign Missions, but their antislavery protests helped convince that society to drop its mission to slaveholding Indians. Antislavery Congregationalists also successfully pressured the American Home Missionary Society to end its aid to southern churches with slaveholding members. Although the established missionary organizations continued to fall short of abolitionist standards, the progress made by those bodies was in significant measure a product of growing antislavery sentiment among the Congregationalists. Despite such advances, the abolitionists continued to warn the moderate antislavery Congregationalists that their support for the benevolent societies remained an indirect means of sanctioning slavery.[41]

The abolitionists also lobbied vigorously to end the Congregationalists' fraternal relations with the New and Old School Presbyterians, who still counted slaveholders among their members. Although the Rhode Island, Vermont, and Ohio Congregational ministerial associations responded positively to these demands, most state associations attempted to silence antislavery dissension by the less drastic step of addressing remonstrances to the Presbyterians that advised discipline of slaveholding members. For example, Connecticut Congregationalists resolved that Presbyterian inaction on slave owning was "painful evidence of delinquincy in respect to principles and sympathies that are essential to the Christian integrity."[42] The Presbyterians reacted in different ways to this campaign. In 1857, Old School Presbyterians ended formal communications with the Congregationalists. In the same year, however, the New School Presbyterians took antislavery actions that caused a southern secession from the church but redeemed the denomination in the estimation of most Congregationalists.

Despite these Congregational antislavery advances, strict abolitionists remained dissatisfied with that denomination's overall position on slavery before the Civil War. Most Congregationalists still contributed to benevolent societies that refused to cast out the slaveholders. As agents of the Church Anti-Slavery Society discovered in the late 1850s, only a minority of Congregationalists would declare slaveholding invariably sinful and automatic grounds for excommunication. In fact, moderate antislavery spokesmen in the denomination, especially Leonard Bacon and Joseph Thompson of the New York *Independent,* harassed Congregational abolitionists such as George B. Cheever as extremists. Despite the Congregationalists' antislavery reputation, the denomination was not fully abolitionized before 1860.[43]

The final and perhaps most difficult denomination to evaluate for antislavery progress in the years 1845–1860 is the Baptist church. Because of the lack of strong unifying machinery among nineteenth-century Baptists, contemporaries debated the thoroughness of the denomination's sectional schism in 1845. According to most northern Baptists, including a few veteran abolitionists such as Nathaniel Colver, their church had gone beyond all other major faiths in cutting ties with slavery. Most abolitionists, and especially the members of the comeouter American Baptist Free Mission Society (ABFMS), disputed this claim. In particular, the abolitionists charged that northern Baptist congregations and missionary and publication societies still maintained cordial relations with southern slaveholding Baptists. Because of these objections, abolitionists continued to lobby northern Baptist institutions for antislavery reforms until the Civil War.

Antislavery agitation among the Baptists was conducted principally by the ABFMS and its non-Baptist abolitionist allies. The nondenominational American and Foreign Anti-Slavery Society and the interdenominational Chicago Christian Anti-Slavery Convention of 1851 endorsed the comeouter mission society as the only genuine antislavery body in the Baptist church. The American Missionary Association supplied the ABFMS with financial assistance. Encouragement and support from Christian abolitionists of other faiths helped the ABFMS wage an unceasing propaganda campaign against the toleration of slavery by the established Baptist missionary and publication bodies.[44]

Abolitionist agitation in the Baptist societies had mixed success. In the years immediately after the southern secession of 1845, northern conservatives led by Francis Wayland, Spencer Cone, and Daniel Sharp blocked abolitionist attempts to add explicit bars against slave owners to the missionary societies' constitutions on the grounds that it would prevent an eventual reunion with southerners. Although contributions from the slave states to the American Baptist Missionary Union tapered off, that body remained on friendly terms with its southern counterpart. The American Baptist Home Mission Society withdrew almost completely from southern fields but stationed missionaries among the slaveholding Choctaw Indians until 1859. Southern Baptists founded their own Bible society in 1851 but continued to support the American Baptist Publication Society until well after the Civil War. Although most northern Baptist benevolent operations greatly reduced their dealings with southerners in the late 1840s and the 1850s, abolitionists concluded that substantial fellowship with slaveholders continued in those bodies.[45]

Besides the behavior of the benevolent societies, the practices of individual Baptist congregations and local associations reveal that many northerners retained some bonds of fellowship with slaveholders. After the Baptists divided in 1845, many northern Baptist associations passed strongly worded antislavery resolutions and ceased fraternizing with slave owners. In the lower Midwest and in some eastern cities, however, some Baptist churches continued to welcome southerners to their pulpits and communion tables even during the Civil War. Among the worst offenders were the anti-mission Baptists in southern Indiana and Illinois, whose aloofness from the denominational benevolent organization had isolated them from most abolitionist agitation. Baptist abolitionists in several areas of the North considered such behavior so objectionable that they seceded and formed their own churches and associations on uncompromising anti-slavery principles.[46]

Political trends after 1845, however, increased antislavery sentiment among northern Baptists. Local congregations and associations spoke out against government measures favoring slavery such as the Fugitive Slave Law of 1850 and the Kansas-Nebraska Act. In the same years, northern Baptist newspapers had an increasingly antislavery bias in their editorials on political events. Even as prominent a conservative spokesman as Wayland joined the antiextensionist Republican party. Nevertheless, abolitionist critics denied that antislavery political behavior satisfied the northern Baptists' moral obligation as church members to treat slave owners as sinners.[47]

Because the denomination lacked a central authority to enforce any uniform policy, including slavery policy, it is difficult to generalize about abolitionists' success or failure among the Baptists. Some northern Baptists had broken all religious ties with slaveholders. Because of their membership in congregations, associations, or benevolent societies that continued to fellowship with slaveholders, a much larger number of Baptists fell short of strict abolitionist standards. Although the political issues of the 1850s helped make the northern Baptists more antislavery than in earlier years, the denomination's practices reveal that the church did not join abolitionist ranks before the Civil War.

v

Although many northern churches made significant antislavery advances in the decade and a half before the Civil War, most failed to meet the strict criteria demanded by the abolitionists. Only the new comeouter sects and some of the historically antislavery denominations enacted the entire abolitionist program by branding slave owners as sinners and subjecting them to church discipline. Southern secession from the New School Presbyterian and Methodist Episcopal churches effectively ended fellowship with slaveholders in those denominations, but these bodies still refrained from formally endorsing abolitionism. Although many northern Unitarians, Universalists, Congregationalists, Baptists, and Disciples of Christ strengthened their antislavery testimony, their denominations continued to fellowship slave owners. The ritualist and old-line Calvinist denominations even refused to acknowledge that slavery was an appropriate subject for church legislation. This complex pattern of northern denominational practices toward slaveholding was the product of a number of closely interrelated theological, institutional, and sociocultural factors.

Theological considerations were crucial in determining the reception of abolitionism within the northern religious community. The abolitionists' evangelically inspired contention that slave owners were sinners who must be expelled from Christian fellowship proved alien to a wide range of denominations. From their own diverse theological perspectives, liberal, ritualist, and strict Calvinist faiths regarded abolitionist religious principles and practices as arbitrary and unwarrantable. Denominations that had traditionally exercised substantial toleration toward the behavior of their members rejected the expulsion of slaveholders as unduly proscriptive. In contrast, abolitionism generally achieved its fullest acceptance in the major evangelical denominations, whose doctrines stressed collective responsibility for the moral behavior of church members and thus barred unrepentant sinners from their communions

The organizational structure of a denomination and the authority of its central governing body or hierarchy had a strong effect on the progress of abolitionism in the churches during the 1840s and 1850s. The decentralized organization of such denominations as the Congregationalists, Baptists, and Unitarians made it impossible for the growing abolitionist element in those bodies to enforce disciplinary rules against the fellowship of slaveholders beyond the local level. From the 1830s on, abolitionists overcame official harassment and censorship in the Methodist, Congregational, and Baptist denominations, but the power of Roman Catholic and Episcopalian bishops effectively suppressed antislavery agitation inside their church councils. It was in denominations such as the Methodists and New School Presbyterians, which had both a federated governing structure and a large measure of open discussion, that abolitionist-related positions received the most thorough debate and finally achieved a form of de facto assent.

The demographic composition of many denominations produced major obstacles to the abolitionist campaign. Whereas the Scottish Presbyterians and a few other small sects of immigrants rapidly conformed to antislavery doctrines, the denominations that embraced the large majority of the

foreign born—the Roman Catholic, Lutheran, German Reformed, and
Dutch Reformed churches—rejected abolitionist tenets as foreign to their
Old World traditions. The surge of nativism and the hardening of eth-
nocultural political lines in the 1840s and 1850s made cooperation between the latter churches and evangelically inspired reformers more difficult than ever to establish. In contrast, the influence of southerners
declined in several denominations, as was dramatically demonstrated by
their resort to secession to protest denominational antislavery pronouncements by the New School Presbyterian and Methodist churches shortly
before the Civil War. Among such churches as the Episcopalians, Disciples of Christ, and Old School Presbyterians, however, slaveholders remained a powerful antiabolitionist bloc until the Civil War. In addition,
southern-born Butternut elements from the lower Midwest added volume
to the conservative voice in the slavery debate inside these and other
denominations, particularly the Methodists and Baptists.

Traditional denominational attitudes toward questions of social ethics,
especially as related to slavery, also influenced the antislavery movement
in the northern churches. After much effort, the abolitionists were able to
overcome the sectarian scruples of the small, traditionally antislavery
churches and to enlist their active assistance. In a similar manner, the
abolitionists generated considerable support among denominations such as
the Methodists and Presbyterians by calling for enforcement of long-
ignored antislavery disciplines. The initial inclination of northern churchmen to steer clear of abolition as a controversial and divisive issue de-
creased, especially after the mid-1850s, in consequence of rising antisouthern sentiment and the willingness of some northern politicians to
portray slavery-related issues in moral terms. Although gradualist antislavery programs retained the support of more conservative members of
the northern religious community, antiextensionism replaced colonization
as the solution most often endorsed by denominational assemblies.

Comparison of the northern churches' position toward slavery in 1860
with their position just two decades earlier leaves no doubt that denominations embracing a large majority of northern churchgoers had strengthened
their antislavery witness. The toleration shown slaveholders by the ritualist, old-line Calvinist, and a few other denominations stood in increasingly sharp contrast to the antislavery opinions of most northern churchmen.
Nevertheless, no major denomination endorsed the abolitionist position
that slave owning was intrinsically sinful and therefore automatic ground
for church discipline. The bitter debate over abolitionist principles in the
1830s had left religious circles polarized. In later decades, moderate
antislavery church leaders refused to concede the letter of the argument to

the abolitionists even as their intensified antislavery professions drove slave owners from their fellowship.[48] Only in the midst of the Civil War would most northern denominations finally issue unqualified moral condemnations of slavery.

VI

Garrisonian abolitionists had a small but important influence on these antislavery developments in the northern churches during the late 1840s and 1850s. The public's image of Garrisonians as infidels handicapped the latters' efforts among orthodox churchmen. Opponents of abolitionism branded Garrisonian criticism of the churches as the product of irreligious, not antislavery, sentiment. The secession of many AASS members from the churches to protest proslavery policies served only to reinforce suspicions about the soundness of Garrisonian religious views. Many Garrisonians, however, remained members of religious bodies and contributed to antislavery advances, especially in the Hicksite Quaker and Unitarian denominations. In addition, Garrisonians opened their platforms and presses to churchmen striving to spur their denominations to stronger antislavery action. Most important, the Garrisonians' extensive propaganda operation aided Christian abolitionists by spreading primarily moral antislavery arguments among northerners. Thus, by both direct and indirect means the Garrisonians contributed to the growing antislavery activism in the northern churches during the years immediately before the Civil War.

The Christian abolitionists had even greater success in provoking antislavery action by the churches. Their propaganda resources were fewer than those of the Garrisonians but concentrated more upon developments in the religious community. Because the orthodoxy of most Christian abolitionist leaders was beyond question, this faction had more success in gaining the cooperation of moderate antislavery church groups. Many of the Christian abolitionists' accomplishments were products of the new church-oriented tactics devised in the 1840s and 1850s. The formation of proabolition comeouter sects influenced many denominations to take stronger antislavery stands in order to prevent further secessions. Interdenominational antislavery conventions and societies attracted invaluable publicity for an uncompromised abolitionist program for the churches. The antislavery reform movements in the voluntary benevolent societies enlisted the participation of antislavery moderates in a large number of denominations. Through these efforts, Christian abolitionists helped guide many northern churches toward more active repudiation of all forms of toleration of slavery.

But the limited success of abolitionist tactics within the religious community revealed the diminishing effectiveness of church-oriented efforts toward ending slavery. As the testimony of northern churchmen against the immorality of slave owning increased, the influence of such censures on southerners dwindled. While far more northerners than ever before denounced slaveholding as a sinful practice, increasing numbers of southern churchmen reacted by defending slavery as a divinely ordained institution. When abolitionist agitation induced several northern denominations to discipline slaveholders, southern members simply seceded and formed their own churches. Ironically, the impact of the growing antislavery sentiment in the churches came to be felt more strongly in secular affairs. As noted in Chapter 8, abolitionist moral principles helped to reinforce and give direction to the antislavery political movement. When the Civil War began, abolitionized northern churches would play a leading role in the eventual acceptance of emancipation as the goal of the North's military effort.

—10—

Abolitionism and the Churches during the Civil War

The election of 1860 touched off the greatest crisis in the nation's history. For the first time, a candidate pledged to the containment of slavery was elected to the presidency. Although neither Abraham Lincoln nor the Republican party was committed to an abolitionist program, eleven southern states chose secession and civil war rather than risk continued union with an unfriendly federal government. The southerners' rebellion, however, placed slavery in extreme jeopardy. As the war to restore the Union dragged on, abolitionist proposals to punish the South and to aid the military effort by ending slavery gained in popularity. With the encouragement of abolitionists, the churches took a leading role in efforts to pressure the Republican administration to adopt emancipation as a war goal.

The Civil War also produced the final showdown on the slavery question in the northern churches. The military conflict increased antislavery and antisouthern feelings among northern churchmen. When southern secession became a reality, the argument of conservative religious leaders that antislavery action threatened both denominational and national harmony became an academic one. Several denominations, hitherto only cautiously antislavery, now reformed their practices by prohibiting slaveholding and racial discrimination. The war also caused unprecedented participation by the churches in the nation's political debates. Conservatives, antislavery moderates, and abolitionists battled in religious councils to shape the churches' position on questions of support for the Union, emancipation for the slaves, and assistance for the freedmen. With a few significant exceptions, northern religious bodies developed into active antislavery agencies by the war's end.

The Civil War also caused considerable alterations in abolitionist strategies. All abolitionist factions realized that southern secession made slavery preeminently a political question. In particular, the abolitionists recognized that the war gave them an unprecedented opportunity to press the federal government to adopt an emancipation policy. Longtime pacifists and disunionists joined veteran political abolitionists in endorsing the war and in calling for decisive antislavery action by the government. When the Republican Congress and administration hesitated to take such a revolutionary step, both Christian and Garrisonian abolitionists attempted to embolden the politicians by producing evidence of the northern public's support for emancipation.

The abolitionists' preoccupation with political questions during the war affected their behavior toward the churches. Support for a federal emancipation policy and for aid to the freedmen replaced calls to break religious fellowship with slaveholders as the abolitionists' chief demands upon northern religious institutions. The bulk of Garrisonian commentary on religious affairs after 1860 shifted from criticism of weak antislavery church disciplines to complaints against denominations that endorsed the war effort while continuing to oppose action against slavery. Christian abolitionists remained convinced of the necessity for consistent antislavery religious practices but converted their immediate goal to enlisting the moral authority of the churches behind the political emancipation drive. Numerous abolitionists echoed William Goodell's description of the war as God's punishment for the toleration of slavery by "Churchianity" and called on religious leaders to endorse emancipation as a sign of their "repentance."[1]

I

The secession of seven slave states during the winter of 1860–61 disturbed and divided northern church leaders. A few abolitionist churchmen welcomed disunion as a means of relieving the North of responsibility for the sin of slavery. All abolitionists, however, opposed northern concessions to the slaveholders in attempts to restore sectional harmony.[2] In contrast, many conservative church leaders and editors blamed abolitionist agitation for the calamities that beset the nation. These men endorsed the various plans of reconciliation that circulated during the secession crisis. But even as they worked to placate southern grievances, conservative northern churchmen announced "that while we offer concession, conciliation, compromise, we are determined that this Federal Union shall be preserved."[3]

When fighting began at Fort Sumter, most northern denominations gave an early and unqualified endorsement to a war to suppress the rebellion. A few strongly antislavery religious bodies also announced their hope that the war would bring an end to slavery. Most churches, however, complied with the scruples of their conservative element and proclaimed support solely for military efforts to maintain the civil government and the Union. The New School Presbyterian General Assembly of 1861, for example, endorsed war against secession but recommended prayer as the proper cure for slavery.[4] A few denominations hesitated even to make a pledge of loyalty to the northern cause. Their reluctance warrants closer scrutiny.

As befitted a heavily border-state denomination, the Disciples of Christ were divided among themselves about the Civil War. Several of the Disciples' leaders, including the influential Alexander Campbell, were committed pacifists and refused to endorse or to take up arms for either side. Many rank-and-file Disciples, however, sided with their section. James A. Garfield, for example, resigned as principal of a Disciples' academy in Ohio to become a Union army officer, and one of Campbell's sons enlisted under the Confederate banner. In October 1861 the American Christian Missionary Society, the denomination's only national agency, refused to adopt a formal pro-Union resolution. Not until 1863 did the society officially declare its opposition to "the attempts of armed traitors to overthrow our government."[5] Because of their quest for an undivided Christianity, Disciples only reluctantly abandoned their neutrality on sectional issues.

The beginning of hostilities produced great trauma among Old School Presbyterians, for it brought the long-dreaded secession of southern members from the denomination. Twenty-six southern presbyteries failed to send delegates to the Old School General Assembly of 1861. At this gathering, the Reverend Gardiner Spring, an antislavery moderate from New York, introduced a resolution "to acknowledge and declare our obligations to promote and perpetuate . . . the integrity of these United States."[6] Spring's motion sparked a lengthy debate in which border-state representatives and many northern conservatives denied the General Assembly's right to express sentiments on political matters. Sixty-six of 222 delegates voted against Spring's resolution. Throughout the military conflict, a strong minority of Old School Presbyterians continued to deny the authority of their denomination's pronouncements on the war and on slavery.[7]

Ritualist denominations also tried to avoid taking sides in the Civil War. Only the Roman Catholic church, however, successfully maintained its neutrality on the issue of preserving the Union. Lutherans postponed their General Synod's meeting from 1861 until 1862 to delay recognition of the southern defection from their denomination. Nevertheless, the General Synod of 1862 condemned secession and asked God to grant speedy victory to the northern armies.[8] The Protestant Episcopal church's General Convention also assembled without southern members for the first time in 1862. Their highly conservative presiding bishop, the Right Reverend John Henry Hopkins of Vermont, opposed any acknowledgment by the convention that secession or war had taken place. The Episcopalians finally adopted a weak statement deploring the evil effect of secession upon the church and the country but containing no condemnation or reproach of the seceders.[9] The hestitation of these denominations even to endorse the Union cause revealed that the conservatives in some churches retained the strength and determination to resist the abolitionist program.

The abolitionists closely monitored the reaction of the northern churches to secession and to the advent of war. Frederick Douglass accused prominent eastern clergymen of preaching proslavery sermons to reassure the wavering border states that the North had not turned abolitionist. Christian abolitionists described the secession of southern church members from the Episcopalian and Old School Presbyterian churches as evidence of the failure of those denominations' traditional policies of appeasing slaveholders. Most of all, abolitionists complained that many larger denominations still hesitated to blame slavery for the great national calamity. Both the Garrisonians and Christian abolitionist presses charged that many northern church leaders had endorsed the war only to avoid falling behind the sentiment of their congregations.[10]

II

Abolitionist agitation for church discipline against slave owning continued vigorously in 1861 and 1862, when the war's impact on slavery was in doubt. Abolitionists believed that any church pronouncements against slavery would encourage politicians to enact an emancipation program. And if slavery managed to survive the war, abolitionists at least hoped to deprive slaveholders of the moral aid and comfort derived from fellowship with northern Christians.[11]

The denominations that had most strongly resisted abolitionist principles before the war continued to oppose disciplinary action against slaveholders. The Roman Catholic hierarchy still maintained that the exclusion of slaveholders ran counter to the church's practice of excommunicating only heretics. The Old School Presbyterians retained their border-state membership and balked at any church legislation that might drive away any more southern communicants. The Episcopalians combined the Catholics' attitude toward church discipline with the Old School Presbyterians' caution against adding to the sectional turmoil and rejected all attempts to expel either secessionist or border-state slaveholders. The loose denominational organization of the Disciples of Christ simply had no machinery or inclination to enforce a fellowship test that would damage Christian unity. All these churches hoped for a quick restoration of fraternal ties as soon as the war was over and opposed any actions that might discourage a return of southerners.[12]

Among northern Methodists, however, the war added impetus to the demand for an uncompromising antislavery discipline. The 1860 General Conference's advisory ruling against slaveholding had satisfied neither abolitionists nor border-state church members. Before the war began, conservative northern Methodists opposed any action that would drive the denomination's border-state remnant into the Methodist Episcopal Church, South. In the midst of the conflict, however, even the conservatives' strongest bastion, the Philadelphia Conference, resolved that it would be best if all ministers infected with "proslaverism or disunionism" were out of the church.[13] By an overwhelming vote of 207 to 9, the 1864 General Conference added "slaveholding" to "buying or selling slaves" as grounds for discipline, and the annual conferences ratified that action during the next year. Thus, not until a full twenty years after the secession of the majority of southern members did the Methodist church finally satisfy abolitionists by placing slaveholding outside the bounds of acceptable Christian behavior.[14]

In the war's early years, abolitionists continued to complain that northern Baptists, New School Presbyterians, and Congregationalists had yet to back up their antislavery professions with action to expel slaveholders. Abolitionists also charged that northern clerical apologists for slavery had received no official censure from their denomination. Even the Reverend Henry Ward Beecher came under abolitionist attack for describing the slaveholder Confederate General Thomas "Stonewall" Jackson as "a rare and eminent Christian."[15] By 1863 proemancipation declarations by these denominations finally quieted most of their abolitionist critics.

The abolitionists similarly complained that the established interdenominational benevolent societies had yet to eliminate the last vestiges of toleration for slavery. The only acknowledged exception was the American Home Missionary Society, which had withdrawn aid from churches admitting slave owners in the late 1850s and issued strong antislavery statements during the war. Abolitionist opposition to the American Board of Commissioners for Foreign Missions was kept alive by statements by that society's senior secretary, the Reverend Rufus Anderson, declaring that abolition would violate the Constitution. The war led the American Tract Society to issue its first criticism of the evils produced by slavery, but the organization's reelection of Nehemiah Adams to its executive committee caused abolitionists to question the extent of that society's reformation. The American Bible Society remained anathema to abolitionists during the war because the organization's managers not only refused to denounce slavery but also continued to supply southerners with the Scriptures. As a result of such unrelenting conservatism, most Christian abolitionists remained loyal to their own benevolent institutions.[16]

III

While still working for the adoption of antislavery practices by the churches and the benevolent societies, abolitionists concentrated a steadily expanding proportion of their energies to converting northern support for the war into advocacy of emancipation. The war nurtured antisouthern sentiment among northern churchmen, and most denominations needed little encouragement from the abolitionists to endorse government action against slavery. Abolitionists labored to guide the newly antislavery churchmen clear of rival programs of gradualism, compensation, and colonization and toward immediate emancipation and recognition of racial equality. Although not all religious bodies adopted the abolitionist program during the war, the churches exerted significant influence for the enactment of antislavery legislation.

When the Civil War broke out, Christian abolitionist groups were among the first to insist that the war to save the Union also be used to eradicate slavery. As early as January 1861, William Goodell resurrected John Quincy Adams's contention that the federal government had the constitutional power to abolish slavery in time of war. The Church Anti-Slavery Society immediately endorsed this view and resolved that the government possessed, "in the case of rebellion or insurrection, the right to suppress rebellion and to abolish slavery, the cause of it."[17] After a few months of fighting, other Christian abolitionist organizations, including the American Missionary Association and the American Reform Tract and Book Society, joined the call for the government to use its war powers to emancipate the slaves. The Garrisonians at first hesitated to disrupt the northern public's support for the war by advancing demands for an antislavery war policy. In the summer of 1861, however, the American Anti-

Slavery Society began its own agitation for government action against slavery.[18]

Christian abolitionists adopted a variety of tactics during the war to promote emancipation's acceptance by the northern public in general and by the religious community in particular. The Church Anti-Slavery Society called for a monthly prayer meeting in every northern congregation on behalf of the slaves. George Cheever, William Goodell, John G. Fee, and many other abolitionist ministers went on lecturing tours to generate popular sentiment for emancipation. Cheever even offered to debate prominent ministers who still held doubts concerning the wisdom and necessity of immediate abolition. Christian abolitionists got their friends in foreign churches to address remonstrances to their American counterparts that counseled the need for emancipation. American abolitionists wrote hundreds of public letters, tracts, and newspaper articles to encourage church support for wartime emancipation. Antislavery groups utilized petition drives and interdenominational conventions to publicize the enlistment of large numbers of ministers and church members in the emancipation drive. The abolitionists' efforts helped create widespread support for an uncompromising antislavery program among northern churchmen.[19]

The churches that responded most promptly to the abolitionists' wartime emancipation campaign were the traditionally antislavery denominations and the comeouter sects. Their periodicals and public meetings pronounced slavery to be the cause of the national calamity. The Reformed Presbyterians were typical of these militantly antislavery churchmen in resolving "that this war is the infliction of the just punishment of an offended God upon our country" for its toleration of slavery.[20] The sentiments of most of these denominations coincided with those in the Free Presbyterians' declaration that "there will be no peace in this country, in either Church or state, until Slavery . . . shall be entirely and forever removed."[21] With the exception of the pacifist Quakers, all these denominations publicly argued that the war should continue until slavery ended. As early as the summer of 1861, these denominations petitioned Lincoln and the Republican Congress for a commitment to emancipation.[22]

Beginning in 1862 other northern denominations also endorsed wartime emancipation. In May of that year the New School Presbyterian General Assembly blamed the rebellion on slavery and concluded that the war must bring about its destruction. The Methodist Episcopal church did not meet in General Conference until 1864, but earlier local conferences and official periodicals announced the denomination's proemancipation bias.

The Detroit Conference in 1861, for example, acknowledged that "liberty or slavery is the real issue of the contest."[23] The American Baptist Missionary Union and most local Baptist associations endorsed emancipation as an essential war measure. The more cautious American Baptist Home Missionary Society waited until 1864 before announcing its "hearty assent to the policy of conquering disunion by uprooting slavery, its cause."[24] Even such spokesmen for the conservative northeastern element of the Congregationalists and Unitarians as Leonard Bacon and Henry Bellows conceded that all southern prerogatives should be restored after the war save the right to hold property in man.[25]

Despite these bold antislavery expressions, sizable antiemancipation minorities existed in many northern denominations throughout the war. As late as the summer of 1862, Christian abolitionists complained that eastern Congregational periodicals contained no endorsement of emancipation. More seriously, several New School Presbyterian editors declared a national emancipation program unconstitutional. One of the latter, the Reverend Amasa Converse, finally moved his newspaper, the *Christian Observer,* from Philadelphia to Richmond, Virginia, to escape harassment by government officials. The conservative editors of the *Methodist* of New York City supported a war against rebellion but argued that so many border-state slaveholders had remained loyal to the Union that the institution of slavery "cannot legally enter into controversy."[26] Discontent with the growing antislavery consensus in their denominations even sparked small secessions in the Midwest from the Baptist, Methodist, and Presbyterian denominations during the war. These seceders protested that northern abolitionists shared the blame with slaveholders for the nation's troubles. Wartime political disputes added to the quarrels in these denominations, with the conservatives opposing their churches' encouragement of Republican emancipation action.[27]

A few northern denominations hesitated or completely refused to endorse emancipation during the war. Still possessing a strong border-state element, the Old School Presbyterian church passed resolutions condemning the rebellion but did not mention slavery. Only in 1864 did the Old School General Assembly resolve that the war had "taken away every motive for [slavery's] further toleration."[28] The Disciples' American Christian Missionary Society showed even more deference to border-state sentiments and never went beyond acknowledging the denomination's allegiance to the Union cause. Among the ritualist sects, only the Lutherans gave official approval to emancipation during the war, and even then they qualified it with a suggestion to compensate slaveholders. Roman Catholics and Episcopalians steadfastly clung to the policy of neutrality toward slavery as a worldly rather than a religious matter. Hoping to win back the loyalty of southern church members, these conservative denominations refused to sanction actions likely to alienate slaveholders.[29]

IV

The abolitionists attempted to use the northern churches' growing support for emancipation as part of their propaganda campaign to lobby the federal government for decisive action against slavery. One method that the abolitionists hoped would demonstrate public support for antislavery action was the emancipation petition addressed to the president and Congress. Christian abolitionists remembered the attention attracted by the clerical remonstrances against the Kansas-Nebraska Act and strove to circulate antislavery petitions among clergymen and church members. As early as May 1861, the Church Anti-Slavery Society sought signatures of northern churchmen for a memorial to Lincoln that demanded emancipation because of "national exigencies" and

because we believe the National neglect of this heaven required duty is rebellion against God; [and] because a nation wielding the war power to suppress a pro-slavery rebellion cannot afford to risk the divine judgments for a single day, by a continuance of rebellion against God, in neglecting to abolish slavery.[30]

This volume of emancipation petitions to Washington officials grew so great that Goodell organized the National Emancipation Association in New York City to serve as a clearinghouse.

The Christian abolitionists had less success in arranging shows of interdenominational support for a federal emancipation program. The Church Anti-Slavery Society proposed "a National Christian Convention" in 1861 and again in 1862 to agitate for emancipation, but its calls failed to attract sufficient numbers to hold the gatherings. The society also unsuccessfully called for a series of regional "Christian Mass Meetings" for July 4, 1863, "to encourage and fortify the National Government" to enact "a universal and immediate abolishment of slavery out of obedience to God."[31] The only significant wartime interdenominational antislavery conventions met in Chicago and New York City in the fall of 1862. Both meetings wrote memorials to the president that expounded moral arguments for emancipation. Veteran Christian abolitionists, including William W. Patton, George Cheever, William Goodell, Simeon S.

Jocelyn, Duncan Dunbar, and Hiram Mattison, were leading figures at these meetings. Delegations from both conventions met with Lincoln but failed to convince him to adopt a stronger antislavery policy.[32]

Individual denominations also lobbied federal officials for emancipation. The editors of a growing number of religious periodicals endorsed the abolitionists' argument that the Constitution empowered the federal government to end slavery in time of war. Several of these editors criticized Lincoln for annulling antislavery proclamations issued by Union commanders in the field. In April 1862 an article in the *Freewill Baptist Quarterly* complained that Lincoln resisted emancipation for fear of offending the border-state "semi-secessionist who is prevented only by his locality and interests from being an active rebel."[33] To overcome this hesitation, most of the smaller abolitionized denominations wrote remonstrances and dispatched delegations to argue the emancipation case to the president and Congress. Even among the previously more moderate antislavery denominations, numerous ministers, laymen, and local judicatories proclaimed their desire for immediate and complete emancipation.[34]

The culmination of the agitation for emancipation came when Lincoln issued his preliminary Emancipation Proclamation in the fall of 1862. Although that measure exempted at least one million slaves from its provisions and was surrounded by an aura of expediency, most antislavery churchmen and many abolitionists responded favorably to Lincoln's action. By 1864 most northern denominations had officially applauded the proclamation and sent delegations to Washington to congratulate Lincoln. The New School Presbyterian General Assembly of 1863, for example, declared that the church recognized the Emancipation Proclamation as a product of "that wonder-working providence of God, by which military necessities become the instruments of justice in breaking the yoke of oppression."[35] Even the archconservative Old School Presbyterians finally enlisted in the antislavery ranks after Lincoln's action, leaving only the Catholics and Episcopalians as denominations that refused to endorse emancipation. Among Christian abolitionists, such stalwarts as Lewis Tappan, John Rankin, and John G. Fee applauded the Emancipation Proclamation as promising the general overthrow of slavery in the near future. In a similar manner, William Lloyd Garrison described the proclamation as "an historic step in the right direction" while he continued to lobby for a constitutional amendment abolishing slavery.[36]

Not all abolitionists and antislavery churchmen were pleased with the Emancipation Proclamation. The old Radical Abolitionist–Church Anti-Slavery Society faction, now led by William Goodell and the Cheever brothers, protested the shortcomings and expedient motives of Lincoln's action. George Cheever denounced the Emancipation Proclamation as "nothing more than a bribe to win back the slaveholding states to loyalty by confirming to them the privilege of tyrannizing over millions of their fellow creatures in perpetual slavery."[37] Cheever, Goodell, and Nathan Brown, a Free Mission Baptist leader, met with Lincoln in December 1862 but failed to convince the president that the federal government possessed sufficient constitutional power to abolish slavery everywhere in the United States. A large group of Garrisonian abolitionists led by Wendell Phillips, Stephen Foster, and Parker Pillsbury similarly complained that Lincoln still shrank from immediate and complete emancipation.[38]

The dissatisfaction of many abolitionists with Lincoln's hesitant emancipation policy resulted in an attempt to block his reelection in 1864. After a short-lived movement in behalf of Secretary of the Treasury Salmon P. Chase, many Republican antislavery radicals turned to John C. Frémont as a candidate with whom to challenge Lincoln's renomination. A number of Christian and Garrisonian abolitionists quickly enlisted in this campaign. Goodell's periodical, the *National Principia,* endorsed Frémont in March 1864. Later that spring, the Church Anti-Slavery Society condemned Lincoln's inclination "to drift with events and wait for 'indispensable necessity' before acting against slavery."[39] At the same time, narrow majorities passed anti-Lincoln resolutions at various Garrisonian conventions. The Frémont movement failed to block the Republicans' renomination of Lincoln in June, but discontent would not die. During July and August the Cheever brothers, Wendell Phillips, and other abolitionists joined radical Republicans in an unsuccessful effort to persuade Lincoln and Frémont to stand aside so that antislavery men could unite behind a new candidate pledged to complete emancipation.[40]

One important reason for the failure of these anti-Lincoln efforts was the inability of discontented abolitionists to gain support from the religious community. The Church Anti-Slavery Society lacked the financial resources to conduct lecturing tours to spread its radical political views. Goodell's *National Principia* was forced to suspend publication when pro-Lincoln Republicans withdrew their financial subsidies. The only religious group that praised the Frémont movement was the American Baptist Free Mission Society, and even it stopped short of an official endorsement. More typical of the sentiment of antislavery northern churchmen was the *Independent'*s statement that the anti-Lincoln campaign had led many "good men into a snare."[41] The New School Presbyterian General Assembly went so far as to order its ministers to "urge all Christians to refrain from weakening the authority of the Administration by ill-timed complaints and unnecessary criticism.''[42] Fear of dividing the antislavery vote and allowing the Democrats to capture the White House caused most proemancipation churchmen to remain loyal to the administration.

After Lincoln's reelection in November, antislavery groups reunited in a movement for a constitutional amendment to abolish slavery nationwide. Garrisonians cooperated closely with the Women's Loyal National League to collect signatures on a petition calling for an emancipation amendment. Although the Church Anti-Slavery Society continued to contend that the president and Congress possessed sufficient power to outlaw slave owning, the group also endorsed a constitutional amendment to prevent any later judicial challenges. With a few exceptions, the editors of the northern religious press observed that the progress of public opinion during the war demanded legislation to end the divisive slavery question once and for all. In response to the unabated antislavery pressure, Congress passed the Thirteenth Amendment outlawing slavery on January 31, 1865, and the necessary three-fourths of the states completed ratification by the end of the year.[43]

V

Ironically, the wartime antislavery advances in religious and political life created a crisis for the Christian abolitionist institutions organized during the 1840s and 1850s. Founded principally to promote abolitionism, the approaching end of slavery forced the comeouter sects to reassess the justification for their independent existence. For example, wartime events accelerated the dissolution of the Free Presbyterian Church, a process that had begun soon after the southern secession from New School Presbyterian ranks in 1857. The war forced the American Missionary Association to drop its assistance to Free Presbyterian congregations in the Northwest in order to finance work with southern freedmen. The small denomination established its own Home Missionary Fund in 1862 but nevertheless had to abandon many struggling congregations. The last recorded meeting of the Free Presbyterians' synod was in 1863. Although a few Free Presbyterian congregations retained their comeouter identity after the war's end, most members and ministers returned to the major Presbyterian denominations. Having lost the rallying point of uncompromising opposition to slavery, the diverse elements in the Free Presbyterian Church lacked sufficient bonds to remain together.[44]

The American Baptist Free Mission Society came to a similar end. During the Civil War, Free Mission Baptists actively lobbied Republican politicians for adoption of a constitutional amendment to abolish slavery. The Free Mission Baptists also launched a vigorous freedmen's aid program in 1862. The society condemned the War Department for turning over control of southern congregations without loyal ministers to the American Baptist Home Mission Society. Abolitionists complained that the larger missionary board had been laggard both in endorsing emancipation and in supplying ministers to the freedmen and therefore merited no government assistance. The Free Mission Society doubted that "the conservative element" of its denomination was yet "ready to treat our colored brother as a man."[45] Not until 1869 would the merger of the American Baptist Free Mission Society with the denomination's established missionary organizations signal the end of the slavery controversy among northern Baptists.

The war and the demise of slavery also threatened the continued existence of the Wesleyan Methodist Connection. The Wesleyans were forced to applaud the Methodist Episcopal church's adoption of an unqualified antislavery discipline in 1864. Such advances led one comeouter leader to confess that the Wesleyans had lost "their influence and progressive power."[46] A large portion of the Wesleyan Methodists returned to their old denominational affiliations soon after the war. The Wesleyans, however, survived these defections because the sect had developed distinctive positions on other moral and theological questions in addition to that of slavery. Though not irreconcilable with the positions of the Methodist Episcopal church, the Wesleyans' perfectionistic stands against alcohol, tobacco, and secret societies were more clearly stated and more rigorously enforced in the smaller church's discipline. The same perfectionism that had added fervor to the Wesleyan Methodist Connection's antislavery activities made the comeouter sect a viable denomination that has survived to the present time.[47]

Wartime events brought different ends to the two smallest comeouter sects, the Franckean Evangelical Lutheran Synod and the Progressive Friends. During the war, southern Lutherans formed their own denomination, and the northern General Synod endorsed a government emancipation program. Although they continued to quarrel over certain doctrinal questions, the Franckeans were satisfied with the antislavery position of other northern Lutherans and returned to the General Synod's jurisdiction in 1864.[48] Among the Friends, a greater toleration of abolitionist activities had healed the schism among orthodox Quakers before the war. No such reunion of Progressive Friends with Hicksite Yearly Meetings ever took place, however. The Progressive Friends' concentration on secular reform issues eventually diluted their Quaker strain. Although the heirs of the original Progressive Friends met annually until 1940 to advocate causes such as racial equality, the group had long before lost the attributes of a religious organization.[49]

The war also created serious problems for the antislavery benevolent institutions: the American Missionary Association (AMA), the American Reform Tract and Book Society (ARTBS), and the American Tract Society, Boston. The function of these organizations was to propagate an antislavery gospel and to protest the established benevolent societies' fellowship with slaveholders. Southern secession produced only limited reform in the policies of most of the older benevolent bodies. As the prospects for emancipation increased during the war, however, the antislavery benevolent associations had to find new justifications for their continued existence. To combat the moral dissoluteness of military life, both antislavery publication societies distributed tracts to Union soldiers. The ARTBS also printed works that championed the principle of racial equality. Most important, the war opened up a new area of effort for the antislavery benevolent societies, that of caring for the freedmen's religious needs. In fact the passing of slavery as a divisive issue allowed these organizations to attract a broader range of support than ever before and to continue to function for many more decades.[50]

VI

Even before the Thirteenth Amendment ended slavery, many abolitionists began work to ensure that freedom would have genuine substance for ex-slaves. Among the most important goals of this later phase of the abolition campaign were to supply education to the freedmen and to erase all legal and social barriers to their equal participation in American life. The Church Anti-Slavery Society disbanded soon after the war's end, but the American Missionary Association and the American Reform Tract and Book Society continued to function in the interests of the blacks. In addition, antislavery churchmen acted through their denominations to aid freedmen and to end racial discrimination. In the last years of the war and thereafter, many northern churches cooperated with abolitionists in efforts to add meaning to emancipation.

Christian abolitionist organizations began to undertake freedmen's aid projects very early in the war. In 1863 the Church Anti-Slavery Society issued a warning that emancipation would throw "a vast burden of responsibility and care for [slavery's] victims" upon religious institutions.[51] The ARTBS began publishing works for the instruction of ex-slaves in

1862. The American Missionary Association launched religious and educational work with black refugees in Union army camps in the fall of 1861. The Garrisonians founded secular freedmen's societies, but the AMA surpassed all other nongovernmental agencies in postwar assistance programs for blacks. Lewis Tappan boasted that the AMA's combination of missionary and educational programs offered "something more" to the ex-slaves than did the secular societies by endeavoring to help them "be free citizens, and good men and women also . . . free from sin as well as free from slavery."[52] Christian abolitionists hoped that the education and religious training of the freedmen would overcome some of the evil effects of slavery and thus win greater acceptance for blacks.

As early as 1862, the veteran antislavery religious bodies began to dispatch missionaries and teachers to southern freedmen. The various Scottish Presbyterian sects, the Freewill Baptists, the American Baptist Free Mission Society, and other abolitionist church groups sent agents into newly liberated Confederate territory. Because of their antislavery heritage, these groups concluded that they had a "special call of Providence to this great work."[53] At the same time, the small black sects, such as the African Methodist denominations, began establishing new congregations in areas of the South secured by Union troops. Within a few years, both black Methodist denominations reported phenomenal gains in membership through their successful proselytizing among freedmen.[54]

The major Protestant denominations—the Baptists, Methodists, New School Presbyterians, and Old School Presbyterians—also began sending missionaries into the South before the war's end. Despite the objections of some of their conservative members, these denominations launched ambitious programs for the education and religious training of the freedmen. At the same time, the most strongly antislavery Methodists, Baptists, and Presbyterians were intent on reuniting their denominations—on northern terms. The American Baptist Home Mission Society, for example, urged northern Christians to oversee an "entire reorganization of the social and religious state of the south."[55] Beginning in 1863, the War Department assisted northern missionaries in taking over the pulpits of "disloyal" (pro-Confederate) ministers. Such close associations of the missionaries with the Union military effort, however, further alienated southern whites from the northern churches and added to the hostility that the freedmen's aid campaign would encounter after the war.[56]

In addition to aiding the ex-slaves, northern churchmen gave support to other abolitionist wartime efforts to guarantee the reality of black freedom. In particular, abolitionists and their allies in the churches battled northern racism which threatened to curtail freedmen's rights. Many northern churchmen, for example, backed abolitionist calls to repeal state and local legislation that barred blacks from the polls in most states and forced their children into racially separate public schools. After the war, abolitionist prodding also led many denominations to campaign publicly for adoption of the Thirteenth and Fourteenth Amendments and for congressional passage of additional civil rights legislation. The *Freewill Baptist Quarterly* expressed the feelings of most Christian abolitionists that the nation's religious institutions were "duty bound to testify against prejudices which deprive [freedmen] of their rights and equality before human law. When they are emancipated the struggle is not over. It is yet a long march to millennium."[57]

To reinforce their attacks on racially discriminatory government policies, antislavery churchmen also attempted to reform their own denominations' practices towards blacks. During the war, the Church Anti-Slavery Society expressed fear that "every other door in the nation would be opened to the negro before the pew door."[58] In most denominations, individual congregations and regional judicatories decided the question of integrating northern churches. The New England and Erie conferences of the Methodist Episcopal church, for example, removed all discriminatory rules against black members. In 1863 white Episcopalians in Philadelphia admitted black delegates to their conventions for the first time. Numerous New England Congregational churches voted to abolish the custom of Negro pews. Although many northern churches continued to discriminate against blacks, these wartime advances helped the abolitionists to combat racial prejudices in other areas of life that threatened to rob emancipation of much of its meaning.[59]

The outcome of all of these ventures lies beyond the scope of this book. Fortunately, several valuable studies have recently documented the efforts of the abolitionists and other northerners to assist the freedmen during and after Reconstruction. Their findings constitute a final chapter to more than a generation of antislavery effort.

In the early years of Reconstruction, the abolitionists and the major northern churches had some initial success in their programs to aid southern blacks. Still directed by veteran Christian abolitionists, the AMA supported hundreds of teachers in schools for the ex-slaves and their children, ranging from rudimentary Sunday schools to four-year collegiate institutions such as Fisk and Straight Universities. Under the leadership of Bishop Gilbert Haven, a recruit to the abolitionist ranks in the 1850s, the northern Methodist Episcopal church founded a system of integrated schools and churches in the South despite opposition from local whites. The reunification of northern New and Old School Presbyterians in 1869 enabled the denominations to merge in support of an active educational program for freedmen that combined religious, academic, and vocational education on all levels. The American Baptist Home Mission Society gave much-needed financial aid to southern black congregations and supported a number of secondary schools for freedmen.[60]

Despite these energetic beginnings, the northern churches' commitment to assisting the freedmen began to falter even before the end of political Reconstruction and had nearly disappeared by the end of the century. For example, northern denominations dropped their endorsements of political programs aimed at protecting black rights, on the grounds that such programs created sectional tensions. The desire of many northern churchmen for denominational reunion with their southern counterparts led them eventually to deemphasize or abandon their support of racial equality. To win greater acceptance for their churches among the southern white religious and social establishment, the major northern denominations segregated their southern institutions. Even the American Missionary Association finally succumbed to a segregation policy for its schools at the behest of northern Congregationalists, who provided most of the society's funds and who desired to shift their missionary efforts to southern whites. Although northern churchmen continued to support many of the schools financially, the segregation of those institutions destroyed their power as examples to the nation of the abolitionists' fundamental premise that black and whites could live, work, and worship together on a basis of equality.[61]

VII

The Civil War produced the culmination of the abolitionist campaign in the churches. Although abolitionists continued to work for stronger church disciplines against slaveholding, most of their wartime activity concentrated upon converting northern churchmen into advocates for emancipation. In the first years of the conflict most denominations resisted abolitionist calls for a strong antislavery declaration. By the war's end, however, only the Catholics and the Episcopalians had failed to condemn slavery and to demand its speedy destruction. Abolitionists used the churches' endorsements of emancipation to reinforce their own pressure on federal officials for decisive antislavery action. Efforts by some abolitionist factions to replace Lincoln with a more decidedly antislavery president, however, attracted little church support. Nevertheless, antislavery churchmen continued to lobby Congress to end slavery until the Thirteenth Amendment was passed.

The northern churches contributed significantly to the abolitionists' success during the Civil War. The end of the war did not end cooperation between abolitionists and the churches to aid blacks. In fact such cooperation increased. Most of the comeouter sects merged with their parent denominations after the Thirteenth Amendment had removed the divisive question of fellowship with slaveholders. The abolitionist benevolent societies shifted their operations from competition with the established institutions to work with the freedmen. The abolitionists' wartime efforts to aid the ex-slaves and to give substance to their freedmen attracted broad support from northern denominations. After the war, northern religious bodies continued to support such projects until the desire to conciliate southern white churchmen caused them to submit to segregation.

The northern churches' unwillingness to stand by the freedmen exposes the abolitionists' failure to convert the religious bodies into thoroughgoing antislavery vehicles. Despite more than three decades of abolitionist lobbying, few denominations ever accepted the principles of the inherent sinfulness of slaveholding and the equality of all races. Although antislavery moderates gained control of many denominations, initiative for the strongest actions against slavery came from other sources. Several northern church groups ceased fellowship with slaveholders not through the adoption of strong antislavery disciplines but through the secession of southern proslavery militants. The northern churches' failure to endorse emancipation before the Civil War reveals acceptance of wartime antisouthern passions rather than of moral arguments for immediate abolition. In both the religious and political spheres, expediency, not antislavery conviction, was the prime motive behind action against slavery. Because of these fragile origins, the churches' commitment to the welfare of blacks proved no better able than that of other northern institutions to weather the storms of Reconstruction.

Although the northern churches never became the preeminent advocates of emancipation and racial equality that the early abolitionists had hoped they would, church-oriented antislavery efforts were not a complete failure. Abolitionists maintained an active and innovative campaign to spread morally based antislavery principles among the northern denominations. Through their wide variety of moral suasion tactics, abolitionists persuaded many churches to adopt at least a moderate antislavery stand. The churches, in turn, made antislavery expressions more respectable in northern circles. That the abolitionists obtained even this limited assistance for their radical programs from such established and conservative institutions as the churches was testimony to the labor of antislavery militants. If the war had not intervened, the abolitionists might eventually have created enough antislavery sentiment among churchmen to bring about a more peaceful and more decisive end to slavery. Although the antislavery movement failed to make the northern churches into firm friends of the blacks, the ultimate responsibility for this failure rests with the churches and the northern public, not with the abolitionists.

Religious Affiliations of the Officers of the Four National Abolition Societies, 1833–1864

Name	Society[1]	Office[2]	Dates in Office	Religion[3]
*Aaron, Samuel	AASS	V.P.	1839–40	Baptist
	AASS/G	Manager	1840–42	
	AFASS	Ex. Com.	1840–43	
Adair, William A.	AASS	Manager	1837–40	?
*Adam, William	AASS/G	Manager	1843–45	Unitarian
*Adams, E. M.	AASS	Manager	1836–37	Methodist
Adams, William	AASS	Manager	1837–40	Quaker
	AASS/G	Manager	1840–42, 1843–46	
Aldis, Asa	AASS	Manager	1835–37	Episcopalian
Allen, Abraham	AASS/G	Manager	1843–52	Hicksite Friend
Allen, James	CASS	V.P.	1861–64	?
Allen, William	AASS	Manager	1833–37	?
*Allen, William T.	AASS	Manager	1834–37	New School Presbyterian
Andrews, Samuel C.	AASS	V.P.	1838–39	?
Aplin, William	AASS/G	Manager	1840–42	Freewill Baptist

*indicates an ordained clergyman who had not publicly renounced that office even though he may not have been currently filling a ministerial position.

1. Standard abbreviations used in the text designate the American Anti-Slavery Society for the period 1833–1840, the American and Foreign Anti-Slavery, and the Church Anti-Slavery Society. AASS/G designates the American Anti-Slavery Society while under Garrisonian control after 1840.

2. The following abbreviations are for the officers of the abolition societies: V.P. designates a vice-president; Ex. Com., a member of the executive committee; Rec. Sec., a recording secretary; and Cor. Sec., a corresponding secretary.

3. As in the text, ABFMS designates the American Baptist Free Mission Society. For officers who changed religion during their tenure, a solidus (/) separates the earlier and later religious affiliations. A question mark indicates that the person's religious affiliation could not be determined.

Appendix (Cont.)

Name	Society[1]	Office[1]	Dates in Office	Religion[3]
Appleton, James	AASS	V.P.	1839–40	?
*Arthur, William	AASS	Manager	1833–36	Congregational
Atkinson, George	AASS/G	Manager	1848–52	Hicksite Friend
		V.P.	1850–54, 1855–62	
*Atkinson, John	AASS/G	Manager	1842–48	Universalist
Atlee, Edwin P.	AASS	V.P.	1833–36	Hicksite Friend
		Manager	1833–37	
Bacon, Joseph N.	CASS	V.P.	1861–64	Congregational
*Bailey, Kiah	AASS	Manager	1837–39	Congregational
Baldwin, Jesse G.	AFASS	Ex. Com.	1840–41	Methodist
*Ballard, Charles	CASS	Ex. Com.	1859	Baptist
Ballard, James	AASS	V.P.	1834–35	Congregational
		Manager	1835–37	
Bancroft, William W.	AASS	Manager	1837–40	Congregational
Barbadoes, James G.	AASS	Manager	1833–36	Quaker
Barber, Edward D.	AASS	Manager	1838–40	Baptist
	AASS/G	Manager	1840–41	
Barbour, John N.	AFASS	Ex. Com.	1853–55	ABFMS
*Barker, Joseph	AASS/G	V.P.	1852–56	Unitarian
*Barnaby, James	AASS	V.P.	1833–40	Baptist
Barstow, Amos C.	CASS	V.P.	1861–64	Congregational
Bartlett, Luther	AASS/G	Manager	1843–53	?
Bascom, Elisha	AASS	Manager	1833–37	Universalist
Bassett, William	AASS	Manager	1839–40	Orthodox Friend/
	AASS/G	Manager	1843–45	Unitarian
*Bates, Merrit	AASS	Manager	1839–40	Methodist
*Beecher, Edward	AASS	Manager	1838–40	New School Presbyterian
	AFASS	Ex. Com.	1840–42	
*Beecher, William H.	CASS	V.P.	1859	Congregational
*Belden, Henry	AFASS	Ex. Com.	1852–55	Congregational
*Beman, Amos G.	AFASS	Ex. Com.	1840–41	Congregational
*Beman, Jehiel C.	AASS	Manager	1837–39	?
	AFASS	Ex. Com.	1841–43	
Benedict, Seth W.	AASS	Manager	1839–40	New School Presbyterian
	AFASS	Ex. Com.	1840–51	
Benson, Edmund L.	AASS/G	Ex. Com.	1842–44	?
Benson, George	AASS	V.P.	1834–35	Hicksite Friend
Benson, George W.	AASS	Manager	1833–40	Hicksite Friend
	AASS/G	Manager	1841–42, 1843–51, 1862–64	
*Benton, Andrew	AASS	Manager	1834–36	New School Presbyterian
Birchard, Matthew W.	AASS	V.P.	1833–35	?
Birge, Luther	AASS/G	Manager	1843–44	Congregational
Birney, James G.	AASS	Manager	1835–36	New School Presbyterian
		V.P.	1835–38	
		Ex. Com.	1838–40	
		Cor. Sec.	1838–40	

Appendix

Name	Society[1]	Office[1]	Dates in Office	Religion[3]
	AFASS	Secretary	1840–41	
		Ex. Com.	1840–42	
*Blain, John	AASS	V.P.	1834–37	Baptist
Blaisdell, James J.	AASS	Manager	1839–40	?
Blaisdell, Timothy K.	AASS	Manager	1838–39	Congregational
	AASS/G	Manager	1840–42	
*Blanchard, Jonathan	CASS	V.P.	1861–64	Congregational
Bleecker, Leonard	AASS	V.P.	1834–35	?
Bloss, William C.	AASS/G	Manager	1843–45	New School Presbyterian
Bolles, William	AASS/G	Manager	1840–42, 1843–46	Swedenborgian
Borden, Nathaniel B.	AASS/G	Manager	1840–42	?
		Ex. Com.	1842–43	
*Bourne, George	AASS	Manager	1833–39	New School Presbyterian
Bowditch, William I.	AASS/G	V.P.	1852–56	Unitarian
		Treasurer	1862–64	
		Ex. Com.	1863–64	
Bown, Benjamin	AASS/G	Manager	1841–42, 1843–53	?
		V.P.	1860–63	
*Boyle, James	AASS/G	Manager	1841–43	Union Church
*Boynton, Charles B.	CASS	V.P.	1861–64	Congregational
Brackett, Josiah	AFASS	Ex. Com.	1841–43	?
Brainerd, Lawrence	AASS	Manager	1839–40	Congregational
Bramhall, Cornelius	AASS/G	V.P.	1856–64	?
Brewster, Henry	AASS	Manager	1837–40	?
*Brisbane, William H.	AFASS	Ex. Com.	1840–43	Baptist
Brockett, Zenas	AASS/G	Manager	1852–53	Comeouter
Brooke, Abram	AASS/G	V.P.	1843–45	Progressive Friend
Brown, Asa B.	AASS/G	Manager	1840–42	New School Presbyterian
Brown, David P.	AASS	V.P.	1834–35	Quaker
Brown, James C.	AASS	Manager	1838–39	?
Brown, John	AASS/G	Manager	1840–46	Congregational
Brown, Moses	AASS	V.P.	1833–34	Quaker
Brown, Samuel F.	AASS/G	Manager	1840–42	?
Brown, Stephen W.	AASS/G	Manager	1844–45	?
*Bruce, Robert	AASS	V.P.	1833–35	Associate Synod Presbyterian
*Buchanan, James M.	AASS	Manager	1837–40	New School Presbyterian
Buffum, Arnold	AASS	Manager	1833–34, 1835–37	Orthodox Friend
		V.P.	1834–36	
	AFASS	Ex. Com.	1846–55	
Buffum, James M.	AASS/G	Manager	1845–53	Hicksite Friend/Comeouter
Buffum, William	AASS	Manager	1837–40	Quaker
	AASS/G	Ex. Com.	1840–41	
Burgess, Daniel	AASS/G	Manager	1840–41	Congregational
	AFASS	Ex. Com.	1841–43	

(continued)

Appendix

Name	Society[1]	Office[1]	Dates in Office	Religion[3]
Burleigh, Charles C.	AASS/G	Cor. Sec.	1840–43, 1859–64	Comeouter
		Manager	1843–44	
Burleigh, William H.	AASS/G	Manager	1840–41	Congregational
Bush, Oren N.	AASS	Manager	1839–40	?
Butler, J.	AASS	Manager	1833–34	?
Buzby, Samuel	AASS	Manager	1839–40	?
Cady, Josiah	AASS	Manager	1833–37	Congregational
		V.P.	1837–38	
Cambell, Amos	AASS	Manager	1833–37	?
Camp, David M.	AASS	Manager	1837–40	Congregational
Campbell, Alfred G.	AASS/G	V.P.	1849–50 1854–64	?
		Manager	1852–53	
*Campbell, David	AASS/G	Manager	1841–42	Baptist
Capron, Effingham, L.	AASS	V.P.	1833–36	Quaker
Carey, George	AASS	Manager	1837–40	?
Carmichael, Daniel	AASS/G	Ex. Com.	1843–44, 1845–46	?
		Manager	1846–51	
Cassey, Joseph	AASS	Manager	1834–37	?
Chace, Elizabeth B.	AASS/G	Manager	1851–53	Comeouter
Chandler, Thomas	AASS/G	Manager	1840–42	Progressive Friend
*Channing, William H.	AASS/G	Ex. Com.	1844–49	Unitarian
Chapin, Josiah	AFASS	Ex. Com.	1840–43	Congregational
Chaplin, William L.	AASS	Manager	1839–40	Congregational
Chapman, Maria W.	AASS/G	Ex. Com.	1840–41, 1844–63	Comeouter
		Cor. Sec.	1843–46	
*Cheever, George B.	AASS	Manager	1835–37	Congregational
*Cheever, Henry T.	CASS	Secretary	1859–64	Congregational
Chester, Elisha W.	AFASS	Ex. Com.	1853–55	Congregational
Child, David L.	AASS	Manager	1833–40	Unitarian
	AASS/G	Manager	1840–42	
		Ex. Com.	1841–43	
Child, Lydia M.	AASS/G	Ex. Com.	1840–41	Unitarian
		Rec. Sec.	1843–44	
Church, Jefferson	AASS/G	Manager	1851–53	?
Church, William	AFASS	Ex. Com.	1840–41	?
*Claflin, Jehiel C.	AASS/G	V.P.	1855–64	Freewill Baptist
Claflin, William H.	CASS	V.P.	1859–62	Methodist
Clark, John G.	AASS	Manager	1836–40	Quaker
Clarke, Augustine	AASS	Manager	1833–36	?
Clarke, Peleg C.	AASS	V.P.	1838–40	?
	AASS/G	V.P.	1840–46	
Cleveland, Charles D.	CASS	V.P.	1861–64	New School Presbyterian
*Cleveland, John P.	AASS	Manager	1837–40	New School Presbyterian
	AFASS	Ex. Com.	1840–43	
Coates, Lindley	AASS	Manager	1833–40	Hicksite Friend
	AASS/G	President	1840–43	

Appendix

Name	Society[1]	Office[1]	Dates in Office	Religion[3]
*Coffin, Joshua	AASS	Manager	1834–37	Congregational
Coffin, Levi	AASS/G	Manager	1840–42	Orthodox Friend
Cogswell, Daniel	AASS/G	Manager	1844–45	?
Collins, Amos M.	AASS	Manager	1835–37	Congregational
Collins, William	AFASS	Ex. Com.	1851–52	?
Comings, Benjamin	AASS/G	Manager	1847–48	?
		V.P.	1848–54	
Conger, Ellison	AASS/G	Manager	1848–53	?
*Cook, James	AASS	Manager	1836–40	Baptist
Cooper, Griffith M.	AASS/G	Manager	1852–53	Comeouter
Copeland, Melvin	AASS	Manager	1837–39	Congregational
*Cornish, Samuel E.	AASS	Manager	1834–37	Old School Presbyterian
	AFASS	Ex. Com.	1840–55	
*Cowles, Henry	AASS	Manager	1834–36	Congregational
Cowles, Horace	AASS	Manager	1833–40	?
	AASS/G	Manager	1840–41	
Cox, Abraham	AASS	Rec. Sec.	1833–36	New School Presbyterian
*Cox, Samuel H.	AASS	Cor. Sec.	1834–35	New School Presbyterian
		Ex. Com.	1834–40	
*Crandall, Phineas	AASS	Manager	1834–36, 1839–40	Methodist
*Crosby, Josiah	AFASS	Ex. Com.	1841–43	Congregational
*Crothers, Samuel	AASS	V.P.	1833–37	Old School Presbyterian
*Crozier, Hiram F.	AFASS	Ex. Com.	1849–51	Union Church
Culver, Erastus D.	AFASS	Ex. Com.	1851–55	?
*Curtis, Jonathan	AFASS	Ex. Com.	1840–41	Congregational
Cushing, Henry	AASS	Manager	1833–40	?
Cushman, John P.	AASS	Manager	1835–37	New School Presbyterian
*Cutler, Calvin	AASS	V.P.	1833–35	New School Presbyterian
		Manager	1835–40	
Davis, Asa	AASS/G	V.P.	1852–54	?
Davis, Edward M.	AASS/G	Ex. Com.	1842–44	Quaker
		V.P.	1848–64	
*Davis, Elnathan	AASS/G	Manager	1840–47	Congregational
*Davis, Gustavus F.	AASS	V.P.	1834–36	Baptist
*Davis, Patten	AASS/G	Manager	1848–52	Disciples of Christ
		V.P.	1849–55	
Davis, Thomas	AASS/G	Manager	1840–46	?
*Day, George T.	CASS	Ex. Com.	1859–64	Freewill Baptist
Dean, James E.	AASS	Manager	1835–37	?
Delavan, Edward C.	AASS	Manager	1837–39	?
Deming, Samuel	AFASS	Ex. Com.	1840–43	?
*Denison, Charles W.	AASS	Manager	1833–40	Baptist
Dennet, Oliver	AASS/G	Manager	1844–45	?
		V.P.	1845–51	
*Dickey, James H.	AASS	Manager	1836–37, 1839–40	New School Presbyterian
*Dickinson, James T.	AASS	Manager	1833–34	Congregational
Dickson, John	AASS	Manager	1835–37	?
Dimond, Isaac M.	AASS	Manager	1833–34	?

(continued)

Appendix (*Cont.*)

Name	Society[1]	Office[1]	Dates in Office	Religion[3]
Dodge, William B.	AASS	Manager	1834–37	Congregational
Dole, Ebenezer	AASS	V.P.	1833–35	Congregational
Dole, S. F.	AASS	Manager	1833–35	?
Donald, Samuel	AASS	Manager	1839–40	?
Donaldson, Thomas	AASS/G	V.P.	1846–64	Comeouter
Donaldson, William	AASS	Manager	1838–40	?
Doten, David	AASS/G	Manager	1840–42	?
Dougherty, Alexander M.	AASS	Manager	1838–40	New School Presbyterian
Doughty, George	AASS/G	Manager	1843–44	?
Douglass, Frederick	AASS/G	Manager	1848–53	African Methodist Episcopal
*Dowling, John	AASS	V.P.	1834–35	Baptist
Dowling, Thomas	AASS	Manager	1834–37	?
Drury, Asa	AASS	Manager	1835–39	?
*Duffield, George	AASS	V.P.	1834–35	New School Presbyterian
Dugdale, Joseph A.	AASS/G	V.P.	1841–43	Progressive Friend
		Manager	1843–51	
*Dunbar, Duncan	AASS	Ex. Com.	1837–40	Baptist
*Eames, James H.	AASS	V.P.	1836–40	Episcopalian
Earle, Thomas	AASS	Manager	1839–40	Hicksite Friend
Eddy, John S.	AFASS	Ex. Com.	1840–43	Baptist
Eells, Oliver J.	AASS	Manager	1835–37, 1838–39	?
	AASS/G	Manager	1840–42	
*Eggleston, Nathaniel	AFASS	Ex. Com.	1853–55	Congregational
Ellis, William H.	AASS/G	Manager	1841–42	Hicksite Friend
Ernest, Sarah O.	AASS/G	V.P.	1857–60	?
Esten, George W.	AASS	Manager	1837–39	?
Evans, Andrew	AASS/G	Manager	1852–53	?
Everard, Andrew	AASS/G	Manager	1850–52	?
*Everest, Asa	AFASS	Ex. Com.	1851–52	Congregational
Fairbanks, Asa	AASS/G	V.P.	1846–64	?
Fairbanks, Dexter	AFASS	Ex. Com.	1841–42	Congregational
Farmer, John	AASS	Manager	1837–39	Congregational
Farnsworth, Amos	AASS	Manager	1837–40	?
	AASS/G	Manager	1840–42, 1843–53	
*Farnsworth, Benjamin	AASS	Manager	1835–36	Baptist
Ferris, Benjamin	AASS	V.P.	1833–34	Quaker
Ferris, Ziba	AASS	V.P.	1838–40	Hicksite Friend
Fessenden, Samuel	AASS	V.P.	1833–39	Congregational
		Manager	1839–40	
	AASS/G	V.P.	1840–44	
*Field, Chester	CASS	Ex. Com.	1859	Methodist
Field, Isaac	AASS	Manager	1839–40	Congregational
*Field, Nathaniel	AASS	V.P.	1835–39	Adventist
*Finley, James B.	AFASS	Ex. Com.	1853–55	Methodist
*Finney, Charles G.	AASS/G	Manager	1840–41	Congregational
Fisk, Lydia M.	AASS/G	Manager	1849–50	?

Appendix (*Cont.*)

Name	Society[1]	Office[1]	Dates in Office	Religion[3]
*Fitch, Eleazer T.	AASS	V.P.	1833–35	Congregational
*Fletcher, Leonard	AASS	Manager	1838–40	Baptist
Fletcher, Ryland	CASS	V.P.	1861–64	Baptist
Folger, Robert H.	AASS/G	Manager	1840–41	Quaker
*Follen, Charles	AASS	V.P.	1834–35 1836–37	Unitarian
		Ex. Com.	1837–38	
Follen, Charles C.	AASS/G	Ex. Com.	1860–63	Unitarian
Follen, Eliza L.	AASS/G	Ex. Com.	1846–60	Unitarian
Forten, James, Sr.	AASS	V.P.	1834–35	Episcopalian
		Manager	1835–40	
Forten, James, Jr.	AASS/G	Manager	1843–44	?
Foster, Newall A.	AASS/G	Manager	1845–53	Spiritualist
Foster, Stephen S.	AASS/G	Manager	1843–45	Comeouter
*Freeman, Amos N.	AFASS	Ex. Com.	1853–55	Congregational
*Frost, Daniel, Jr.	AASS	Manager	1837–39	New School Presbyterian
*Frost, John	AASS	V.P.	1834–35	New School Presbyterian
*Fuller, Aaron	AASS/G	Manager	1840–42	Methodist
Fuller, Cyrus	AASS/G	V.P.	1854–64	?
Fuller, James C.	AASS	Manager	1839–40	Orthodox Friend
	AASS/G	V.P.	1841–44	
Fussell, Bartholomew	AASS	Manager	1833–37	Hicksite Friend
Fussell, Edwin	AASS/G	Manager	1842–64	Hicksite Friend
Galbraith, David L.	AASS/G	Manager	1843–53	?
*Gale, George W.	AASS	Manager	1837–40	New School Presbyterian
*Galusha, Elon	AASS	Manager	1839–40	Baptist
*Gardiner, Charles W.	AASS	Manager	1839–40	New School Presbyterian
Garretson, Jesse	AASS/G	Manager	1843–44	Progressive Friend
		V.P.	1844–45	
Garrett, Thomas	AASS/G	V.P.	1843–64	Hicksite Friend
Garrigues, William A.	AASS/G	Manager	1840–41	Quaker
Garrison, William L.	AASS	Cor. Sec.	1833–34	Comeouter
		Manager	1834–40	
	AASS/G	President	1843–64	
		Ex. Com.	1844–64	
Gay, Sidney H.	AASS/G	Ex. Com.	1844–64	?
		Cor. Sec.	1846–49, 1853–64	
*Gayley, Samuel M.	AASS	Manager	1838–40	Old School Presbyterian
Gazzam, J. P.	AASS	Manager	1837–40	?
Gibbons, Abigail H.	AASS/G	Ex. Com.	1841–44	Hicksite Friend/Comeouter
Gibbons, Henry	AASS	Manager	1839–40	Hicksite Friend
	AASS/G	V.P.	1840–43	
Gibbons, James S.	AASS	Ex. Com.	1839–40	Hicksite Friend/Comeouter
	AASS/G	Ex. Com.	1840–44	
Gibbons, William	AASS	V.P.	1834–37	Hicksite Friend
Gibbs, Leonard	AFASS	Ex. Com.	1841–46	Congregational
Gilchrist, Archibald	AASS/G	Manager	1851–53	?

(*continued*)

Appendix

Name	Society[1]	Office[1]	Dates in Office	Religion[3]
Gildersleeve, William C.	CASS	V.P.	1861–64	?
*Gilleland, James	AASS	Manager	1839–40	Old School Presbyterian
Gillingham, Lucas	AASS/G	Manager	1842–47	?
*Goodell, William	AASS	Manager	1833–39	Congregational/Union Church
*Gordon, George	CASS	V.P.	1861–64	Free Presbyterian
Goss, Roswell	AASS/G	Ex. Com.	1841–43	?
*Graham, Daniel M.	AFASS	Ex. Com.	1853–55	Freewill Baptist
Graham, J. T.	AASS	Manager	1836–37	?
*Graves, Frederick W.	AASS	Manager	1838–39	New School Presbyterian
*Green, Beriah	AASS	V.P.	1833–37	Congregational
		Manager	1837–40	
Green, Caleb	AASS/G	V.P.	1852–64	Comeouter
Green, Samuel A.	AASS/G	Manager	1844–48	?
Green, William, Jr.	AASS	Treasurer	1833–36	?
		Ex. Com.	1834–35	
		Manager	1835–37	
*Greene, Henry K.	AASS	V.P.	1834–35	Baptist
Greene, Martha W.	AASS/G	Ex. Com.	1843–44	?
Greenleaf, Patrick H.	AASS	Manager	1833–36	Episcopalian
Grimes, John	AASS	Manager	1839–40	New School Presbyterian
*Grosvenor, Cyrus P.	AASS	V.P.	1834–35	Baptist
		Manager	1839–40	
	AASS/G	Manager	1840–41	
Gunn, John N.	AASS/G	Manager	1840–42	?
		V.P.	1842–47	
Gunn, Lewis C.	AASS/G	Manager	1842–43	?
Guthrie, Austin A.	AASS/G	V.P.	1840–41	New School Presbyterian
*Hale, Josiah W.	AASS	Manager	1839–40	Methodist
*Halsey, Job F.	AASS	Manager	1833–37	New School Presbyterian
Halstead, C. Stockton	AFASS	Rec. Sec.	1848–50	?
Hanna, A. F.	AASS/G	Manager	1840–41	?
Hanna, Robert	AASS/G	Manager	1840–42, 1843–46	?
Harned, William	AFASS	Rec. Sec.	1846–47	Congregational
*Harrison, Marcus	AASS	Manager	1838–40	New School Presbyterian
Hartt, Henry A.	AASS/G	V.P.	1860–64	Congregational
Haskell, Benjamin F.	AASS/G	Manager	1841–42	?
Hastings, Charles	AASS	Manager	1839–40	New School Presbyterian
	AFASS	Ex. Com.	1840–43	
Hastings, Erotas P.	AASS	V.P.	1833–36	New School Presbyterian
		Manager	1836–37	
Hathaway, Joseph C.	AASS/G	Manager	1840–42	Quaker
		Rec. Sec.	1840–42, 1843–44	
		Ex. Com.	1840–41, 1842–43, 1844–46	
		V.P.	1844–48	

Appendix (*Cont.*)

Name	Society[1]	Office[1]	Dates in Office	Religion[3]
*Hawes, Joel T.	AASS	Manager	1838–39	Congregational
Hawks, John M.	AASS/G	V.P.	1859–64	?
Hawley, Orestes K.	AASS	Manager	1833–37	Congregational
Hearn, William	AASS/G	V.P.	1854–64	?
Higgins, James W.	AASS	Manager	1839–40	?
*Hill, Moses	AASS	Manager	1839–40	Methodist
Hines, Stephen D.	AASS	Manager	1833–36	?
Hoit, Daniel	AASS	Manager	1836–40	Methodist
	AFASS	Ex. Com.	1841–43	
Holcomb, Jedediah	AASS/G	Manager	1841–45	Baptist
Hollister, David S.	AASS	Manager	1837–40	?
Hopkins, William	AASS/G	V.P.	1856–64	?
Hopper, Isaac T.	AASS/G	Ex. Com.	1840–42	Hicksite Friend
		Treasurer	1840–44	
Hovey, Charles F.	AASS/G	Ex. Com.	1848–59	Comeouter
Howells, Henry C.	AASS	Manager	1833–37	Swedenborgian
	AASS/G	Manager	1841–42	
Hudson, James	AASS/G	Ex. Com.	1841–43	?
Hunt, Richard P.	AASS/G	Manager	1840–43	Hicksite Friend
*Hunt, Samuel	CASS	Ex. Com.	1859–64	Congregational
Hussey, Samuel F.	AASS	V.P.	1833–35	Quaker
Hutchins, Isaac T.	CASS	V.P.	1861–64	?
*Hutchins, Samuel	AASS	Manager	1839–40	Freewill Baptist
*Ide, Jacob	AASS	Manager	1833–37	Congregational
	CASS	V.P.	1861–64	
Irish, Lydia C.	AASS/G	Manager	1843–49, 1850–53	Hicksite Friend
Ives, Eli	AASS	V.P.	1833–38	Congregational
Jackson, Edmund	AASS/G	Ex. Com.	1862–64	Unitarian
Jackson, Francis	AASS	V.P.	1837–40	Unitarian
	AASS/G	Ex. Com.	1840–61	
		V.P.	1840–61	
		Treasurer	1844–61	
Jackson, James C.	AASS/G	Ex. Com.	1840–41	Union Church
		Cor. Sec.	1840–42	
*Jackson, William	AASS	V.P.	1833–36	Baptist
	AASS/G	Manager	1840–42	
Jackson, William	AFASS	Ex. Com.	1840–41	Congregational
Janes, D. P.	AASS	Manager	1839–40	Congregational/Comeouter
Janney, Joseph	AASS	V.P.	1834–38	Quaker
Jay, William	AASS	Cor. Sec.	1835–38	Episcopalian
		Ex. Com.	1836–37	
	AFASS	Ex. Com.	1840–55	
		V.P.	1849–55	
Jenckes, John	AASS	Manager	1836–37	?
Jenkins, Huron	AASS	Manager	1838–40	?
Jenkins, Jonathan	AASS	Manager	1837–38	Quaker
Jessup, William	AASS	Manager	1838–40	New School Presbyterian

(*continued*)

Appendix (*Cont.*)

Name	Society[1]	Office[1]	Dates in Office	Religion[3]
*Jocelyn, Simeon S.	AASS	V.P.	1834–35	Congregational
		Manager	1835–40	
		Ex. Com.	1835–40	
	AFASS	Ex. Com.	1840–55	
Johnson, Nathan	AASS	Manager	1839–40	?
	AASS/G	Manager	1841–42	
*Johnson, Nathaniel E.	AASS	Manager	1839–40	Congregational
Johnson, Oliver	AASS/G	Ex. Com.	1841–43	Hicksite Friend/Progres-
		Manager	1852–53	sive Friend
Johnson, Rowland	AASS/G	V.P.	1858–64	Comeouter
Johnson, William	AFASS	Ex. Com.	1843–51	?
Johnson, William H.	AASS/G	Manager	1843–61	Quaker
*Johnston, Nathan R.	AASS/G	V.P.	1863–65	Reformed Presbyterian
Jones, William R.	AASS	V.P.	1834–35	?
*Kanouse, Peter	AASS	Manager	1835–38	New School Presbyterian
Keese, Samuel	AASS/G	Manager	1841–42	Hicksite Friend
Kellogg, Spencer	AASS	V.P.	1834–35	New School Presbyterian
Kennedy, James M.	AASS	V.P.	1836–37	?
Kent, George	AASS	V.P.	1837–40	Congregational
	AASS/G	V.P.	1840–41	
Ketchum, Edgar	CASS	V.P.	1861–64	?
*Kimball, David T.	AASS	Manager	1833–37	Congregational
Kimball, George	AASS	Manager	1837–38	?
King, Leicester	AASS	Manager	1837–39	?
		V.P.	1839–40	
Kingsley, Alpheus	AASS	Manager	1833–37	?
Kirby, Georgiana	AASS/G	V.P.	1853–64	?
Kirkland, William	AASS	Manager	1837–40	Quaker/Unitarian
	AFASS	Ex. Com.	1843–46	
Kittridge, Ingalls	AASS	Manager	1834–37	?
Knapp, Chauncy L.	AASS	Manager	1837–40	?
	AFASS	Ex. Com.	1840–44	
	AASS/G	Manager	1840–41	
Knapp, Isaac	AASS	Manager	1833–37	?
*Lansing, Dirck C.	AASS	V.P.	1833–35	New School Presbyterian
	AFASS	Ex. Com.	1851–55	
*Leavitt, Harvey F.	AASS	Manager	1837–40	Congregational
	AASS/G	Manager	1840–41	
*Leavitt, Joshua	AASS	Manager	1833–37	Congregational
		Ex. Com.	1834–40	
		Rec. Sec.	1838–40	
	AFASS	Ex. Com.	1840–44, 1849–55	
*Lee, Luther	AFASS	Ex. Com.	1846–52	Wesleyan Methodist
*Leeds, Samuel	AFASS	Ex. Com.	1850–51	Congregational
LeMoyne, Francis J.	AASS	Manager	1837–40	New School Presbyterian/
	AASS/G	Manager	1840–41	Union Church
	AFASS	V.P.	1840–55	

Appendix

Name	Society[1]	Office[1]	Dates in Office	Religion[3]
Leonard, Jonathan J.	AASS/G	V.P.	1847–50	Free Thinker
Lewis, Evan	AASS	V.P.	1833–35	Hicksite Friend
*Libby, Peter	AASS/G	V.P.	1851–64	Freewill Baptist
Lillie, William	AFASS	Ex. Com.	1844–51	?
*Lincoln, Sumner	AASS/G	Manager	1844–48	Unitarian
		V.P.	1848–49	
Lines, Charles B.	AASS	Manager	1836–37	?
*Lord, Nathan	AASS	Manager	1833–34	Congregational
Loring, Ellis G.	AASS	Manager	1833–40	Unitarian
	AASS/G	Manager	1840–43	
		Ex. Com.	1843–44	
*Lovejoy, Owen	AASS	Manager	1838–40	Congregational
Lowell, James R.	AASS/G	Ex. Com.	1846–57	Unitarian
Luca, Alexander C.	AASS	Manager	1839–40	Congregational
*Ludlow, Henry G.	AASS	Manager	1834–37	Congregational
Ludlow, James C.	AASS	Manager	1837–40	?
Lundy, Benjamin	AASS	Manager	1833–34, 1837–40	Quaker
		V.P.	1834–35	
*Lyman, Huntington	AASS	Manager	1834–35	Congregational
MacDonald, Alexander	AFASS	Ex. Com.	1849–55	?
*Mack, Enoch	AASS	Manager	1833–37	Freewill Baptist
	AASS/G	V.P.	1841–44	
Magill, Jonathan P.	AASS/G	Manager	1840–42, 1843–52	Quaker
*Mahan, Asa	AASS	V.P.	1834–35	Congregational
Marriott, Charles	AASS	Manager	1834–38	Hicksite Friend
	AASS/G	Ex. Com.	1840–42	
*Mattison, Hiram	CASS	V.P.	1861–64	Independent Methodist
*May, Samuel J.	AASS	V.P.	1833–35	Unitarian
		Manager	1835–40	
	AASS/G	Manager	1840–42, 1843–48	
		V.P.	1848–64	
*May, Samuel, Jr.	AASS/G	Ex. Com.	1849–64	Unitarian
McClintock, Thomas	AASS/G	Manager	1843–48	Progressive Friend
		V.P.	1848–56	
McCormick, Richard S.	AFASS	Ex. Com.	1841–42	Baptist
McCrummell, James	AASS	Manager	1833–37	Quaker
McKim, James M.	AASS/G	Manager	1843–53	New School Presbyterian/ Comeouter
Melendy, Luther	AASS/G	Manager	1841–42, 1845–52	Congregational
		V.P.	1853–64	
Merritt, Joseph	AASS/G	V.P.	1852–64	Progressive Friend
*Middleton, Jonathan	AASS	Manager	1835–37	Baptist
*Millard, David	AASS/G	Manager	1840–41	Disciple of Christ
Miller, Jonathan P.	AASS	Manager	1835–37	?

(continued)

—213—

Appendix (*Cont.*)

Name	Society[1]	Office[1]	Dates in Office	Religion[3]
*Milligan, James	AASS	Manager	1835–37	Reformed Presbyterian
Millisack, Jacob	AASS/G	Manager	1852–53	Wesleyan Methodist
Mitchell, Daniel	AASS/G	Manager	1847–53	Orthodox Friend
*Montieth, John	AASS	Manager	1833–37	New School Presbyterian
Moore, Joseph	AASS/G	V.P.	1857–64	?
Morgan, John	AASS	V.P.	1834–35	Congregational
Morrill, Ruth	AASS/G	Manager	1844–53	?
Morris, Thomas	AFASS	Ex. Com.	1840–44	Baptist
Morrow, James	AASS	V.P.	1839–40	?
*Moses, Theodore P.	AASS/G	Manager	1844–45	Freewill Baptist
		V.P.	1854–59	
Mott, James	AASS	V.P.	1834–35	Hicksite Friend
	AASS/G	Manager	1841–42	
Mott, Lucretia	AASS/G	V.P.	1855–64	Hicksite Friend
Mott, Lydia	AASS/G	Ex. Com.	1840–41	?
		V.P.	1858–64	
Munsell, Luke	AASS	Manager	1835–40	New School Presbyterian
*Murray, Orson, S.	AASS	Manager	1834–40	Baptist
	AASS/G	Manager	1840–44	
*Myrick, Luther	AASS/G	Manager	1841–42	Union Church
Neall, Daniel, Jr.	AASS	Manager	1838–40	Hicksite Friend
Needles, John	AASS	V.P.	1839–40	Hicksite Friend
	AASS/G	V.P.	1840–42	
*Nelson, David	AASS	V.P.	1836–40	New School Presbyterian
	AFASS	Ex. Com.	1840–44	
Nevin, John W.	AASS	Manager	1835–37	German Reformed
*Newcomb, Harvey	AASS	Manager	1836–37	Congregational
*Newton, Calvin	AASS	Manager	1833–40	Baptist
	AFASS	Ex. Com.	1840–44	
Norton, John T.	AASS	V.P.	1838–40	?
	AASS/G	V.P.	1840–41	
	AFASS	V.P.	1840–41	
Oakes, William	AASS	Manager	1834–37	?
*Osgood, Samuel	AASS	Manager	1837–40	Congregational
Page, Simon	CASS	V.P.	1861–64	Congregational
Paine, Armancy	AASS/G	Manager	1844–46	?
*Parker, Charles	AFASS	Ex. Com.	1851–52	Congregational
Parkhurst, Jonathan	AASS	Manager	1833–40	?
Parrish, Isaac	AASS	Manager	1834–37	Hicksite Friend
Parrish, Joseph, Jr.	AASS/G	V.P.	1841–46	Hicksite Friend
Payne, John A.	AFASS	Ex. Com.	1842–44	?
Peirce, John B.	AASS/G	V.P.	1850–52	?
Peloubet, Chabrier	AASS	Manager	1839–40	?
*Pennington, James W.	AFASS	Ex. Com.	1848–55	Congregational
Pennock, Abraham L.	AASS	V.P.	1835–40	Hicksite Friend
	AASS/G	V.P.	1840–42	
Pennypacker, Elijah F.	AASS/G	Manager	1841–42	Hicksite Friend
			1843–53	

Appendix (*Cont.*)

Name	Society[1]	Office[1]	Dates in Office	Religion[3]
*Perkins, Jared	AASS	Manager	1839–40	Methodist
	AFASS	Ex. Com.	1840–41	
*Perry, Gardiner B.	AASS	V.P.	1834–35	Congregational
*Perry, John M.	AASS	Manager	1833–36	Congregational
Pettengill, Moses	AASS	Manager	1834–37	Congregational
*Phelps, Amos A.	AASS	Manager	1834–35	Congregational
		V.P.	1834–35	
		Ex. Com.	1836–38	
		Rec. Sec.	1836–40	
	AFASS	Ex. Com.	1844–47	
		Cor. Sec.	1845–47	
Phillips, Wendell	AASS	Manager	1838–40	Congregational
	AASS/G	Ex. Com.	1842–64	
		Rec. Sec.	1845–64	
Phoenix, Samuel F.	AASS	Manager	1835–37	Baptist
	AFASS	Ex. Com.	1840–44	
Pillsbury, Parker	AASS/G	Manager	1840–42, 1843–44, 1845–53	Comeouter
Platt, Zephaniah	AASS/G	V.P.	1840–50	Congregational
Plumly, Benjamin R.	AASS/G	V.P.	1846–49	Hicksite Friend
*Pomeroy, Swan L.	AASS	V.P.	1834–35	Congregational
		Manager	1836–39	
Pond, Samuel	AASS	Manager	1837–40	?
Porter, Arthur L.	AASS	Manager	1837–40	?
Porter, Benjamin	AASS	Manager	1834–37	?
Porter, Samuel D.	AASS/G	Manager	1843–44	New School Presbyterian
*Post, Albert L.	AASS/G	Manager	1840–41	Baptist/ABFMS
	AFASS	Ex. Com.	1840–44	
Post, Amy K.	AASS/G	V.P.	1855–64	Spiritualist
Post, Isaac L.	AASS/G	Manager	1846–52	Hicksite Friend/Spiritual-
		V.P.	1852–55	ist
Post, Joseph	AASS/G	Ex. Com.	1842–43	Hicksite Friend
		Manager	1843–53	
Potter, Anson	AASS	V.P.	1834–35	Deist
*Potter, Ray	AASS	Manager	1833–37	Freewill Baptist
Powell, William P.	AASS/G	Ex. Com.	1841–44	?
Prentice, John	AASS	Manager	1833–37	Congregational
Preston, Jonas	AASS	V.P.	1833–34	Quaker
Puckett, Clarkson	AASS/G	Manager	1846–52	Quaker
		V.P.	1852–54	
Pugh, Sarah	AASS/G	Manager	1843–44	Hicksite Friend
		Ex. Com.	1844–53	
Purvis, Joseph	AASS/G	Manager	1840–41	?
Purvis, Robert	AASS	Manager	1833–40	?
	AASS/G	Manager	1840–42	
		V.P.	1842–64	
Putnam, George	AFASS	Ex. Com.	1840–41	?

(*continued*)

Appendix (*Cont.*)

Name	Society[1]	Office[1]	Dates in Office	Religion[3]
Quincy, Edmund	AASS	Manager	1838–40	Unitarian
	AASS/G	Manager	1840–42	
		Ex. Com.	1843–64	
		V.P.	1848–64	
		Cor. Sec.	1853–56	
*Rand, Asa	AASS	V.P.	1833–35	Congregational
*Randall, Daniel B.	AASS	Manager	1839–40	Methodist
Rankin, John	AASS	V.P.	1833–35	New School Presbyterian
		Ex. Com.	1834–40	
		Treasurer	1836–40	
*Rankin, John	AASS	Manager	1835–38, 1839–40	New School Presbyterian
*Ray, Charles B.	AFASS	Ex. Com.	1847–51, 1853–55	Congregational
		Rec. Sec.	1849–52	
Reed, George B.	AASS	Manager	1836–37, 1839–40	Baptist
*Reed, Samuel B.	CASS	V.P.	1861–64	?
Reid, William W.	AASS	Manager	1834–37	New School Presbyterian
Remond, Charles L.	AASS/G	Ex. Com.	1843–48	Comeouter
		Manager	1848–53	
Rentoul, William S.	CASS	V.P.	1861–64	?
Richardson, John A.	AASS/G	Manager	1840–46	?
Ritter, Thomas	AFASS	Ex. Com.	1848–55	?
Robbins, Sampson	AASS/G	Manager	1843–44	?
Roberts, Daniel	AASS	Manager	1839–40	?
Robeson, Andrew	AASS/G	Manager	1840–42, 1843–53, 1862–63	Quaker
Robinson, Elizabeth	AASS/G	Manager	1843–46	Hicksite Friend/Comeouter
Robinson, Marius R.	AASS/G	V.P.	1863–65	Comeouter
Robinson, Rowland T.	AASS	V.P.	1835–40	Quaker
	AASS/G	V.P.	1840–43	
Rockwell, Reuben	AASS	Manager	1836–37	Congregational
Rogers, Nathaniel P.	AASS	Manager	1837–40	Congregational/Comeouter
	AASS/G	Manager	1842–44	
Rogers, William C.	AASS/G	Manager	1841–42	Methodist
*Root, David	AASS	Manager	1835–40	Congregational
Ropes, George	AASS/G	Manager	1842–46	Baptist
*Rush, Christopher	AASS	Manager	1834–37	African Methodist Episcopal Zion
	AFASS	Ex. Com.	1841–51	
*Russell, Philemon R.	AASS	Manager	1833–37	Baptist
Safford, Nathaniel	AFASS	Ex. Com.	1841–42	?
*Sailor, John	AASS	Manager	1837–40	New School Presbyterian
*Sanborn, John	AASS/G	Manager	1844–46	Baptist
*Sargent, John T.	AASS/G	Ex. Com.	1862–64	Unitarian
*Sawyer, Leicester A.	AASS	Manager	1837–40	New School Presbyterian

Appendix

Name	Society[1]	Office[1]	Dates in Office	Religion[3]
Scott, James	AASS	Manager	1834–36	Quaker
*Scott, Orange	AASS	Manager	1838–40	Methodist/Wesleyan
	AFASS	Ex. Com.	1840–48	Methodist
Sellers, John, Jr.	AASS/G	Manager	1843–45	Hicksite Friend
*Sewall, Charles	AASS	Manager	1834–37	Unitarian
Sewall, Samuel	AASS	Manager	1833–37	Unitarian
Sexton, Pliny	AASS/G	V.P.	1852–64	Hicksite Friend
Shadd, Abraham D.	AASS	Manager	1833–37	?
Sharp, George	AASS	Manager	1836–37	?
	AASS/G	Manager	1841–53	
Shedd, James A.	AASS/G	V.P.	1854–57	?
*Shepard, George B.	AASS	Manager	1833–37, 1838–40	Congregational
Shipley, Thomas	AASS	Manager	1833–35	Orthodox Friend
Shotwell, William	AFASS	Treasurer	1841–46	?
		Ex. Com.	1846–47	
Simmons, Anthony	AASS/G	V.P.	1840–41	?
Sisson, Joseph, Jr.	AASS/G	Manager	1840–42, 1846–47	?
Slaton, James	AASS/G	Manager	1844–49	?
Sleeper, Reuben	AASS	Manager	1839–40	?
*Sloane, James R.	CASS	V.P.	1861–64	Reformed Presbyterian
Smith, Ezra C.	AASS/G	Manager	1841–45	?
Smith, Gerrit	AASS	V.P.	1836–40	New School Presbyterian/
	AASS/G	V.P.	1840–41	Union Church
	AFASS	Ex. Com.	1840–44	
Smith, Israel	AASS	Manager	1835–36	Congregational
Smith, James M.	AFASS	Rec. Sec.	1852–55	Episcopalian
Smith, James W.	AASS	V.P.	1834–35	?
Smith, Samuel	AASS	V.P.	1837–38	Quaker
*Smith, Stephen	AASS/G	Manager	1842–43	African Methodist Episcopal
Smyth, William	AASS	Manager	1835–37	Congregational
	AFASS	Ex. Com.	1840–44	
Southard, Nathaniel	AASS/G	Ex. Com.	1840–41	Adventist
*Souther, Samuel	CASS	Ex. Com.	1861–64	Congregational
*Southmayd, Daniel S.	AASS	Manager	1833–34	Congregational
Southwick, Edward	AASS	Manager	1839–40	?
Southwick, Joseph	AASS	V.P.	1833–35	Quaker
*Spaulding, Timothy	AASS	Manager	1838–40	Baptist
Spencer, Thomas	AASS	Manager	1834–35	?
Sperry, Croyden S.	AFASS	Rec. Sec.	1847–48	?
Spooner, Bourne	AASS/G	Manager	1845–53	?
		V.P.	1863–64	
Sprague, Seth	AASS/G	Manager	1840–48	Methodist/Wesleyan Methodist
Springstead, Mary	AASS/G	Manager	1843–53	Quaker
Stanley, William H.	AASS/G	Manager	1841–42	?

(continued)

Appendix (*Cont.*)

Name	Society[1]	Office[1]	Dates in Office	Religion[3]
Stanton, Benjamin	AASS	Manager	1837–40	Orthodox Friend
Stanton, Henry B.	AASS	Manager	1837–40	New School Presbyterian
	AFASS	Secretary	1840–41	
		Ex. Com.	1840–44	
Stebbins, Giles B.	AASS/G	V.P.	1850–52	Hicksite Friend
		Manager	1852–53	
Stedman, William	AASS/G	V.P.	1848–56	?
Sterling, John M.	AASS	Manager	1833–40	Disciples of Christ
Stern, Nathaniel	AASS	Manager	1837–40	?
Stewart, Alvan	AASS	V.P.	1834–35	New School Presbyterian
		Manager	1837–40	
	AFASS	Ex. Com.	1844–49	
Stewart, Philo P.	CASS	V.P.	1861–64	Congregational
Stewart, Robert	AASS	Manager	1835–40	?
	AASS/G	V.P.	1840–50	
Stewart, William	AASS	Manager	1837–39	?
Stocking, Samuel	AASS	V.P.	1834–35	?
*Storrs, George	AASS	Manager	1835–36	Methodist
		V.P.	1835–37	
	AFASS	Ex. Com.	1840–41	
Storrs, Nathan	AASS	Manager	1839–40	Congregational
*Stow, Baron	AASS	V.P.	1834–36	Baptist
Strong, Butler	AASS/G	Manager	1841–52	?
Stuart, Charles	CASS	V.P.	1861–64	New School Presbyterian
Stuart, Robert	AASS	V.P.	1839–40	New School Presbyterian
Sugar, Nathan	AASS/G	Manager	1840–41	?
*Sunderland, LaRoy	AASS	Manager	1833–37	Methodist
	AFASS	Ex. Com.	1840–42	
Swaim, Mary A.	AASS/G	Manager	1846–53	Hicksite Friend
Sweet, Samuel N.	AASS	Manager	1834–35	?
Tappan, Arthur	AASS	President	1833–40	Congregational
	AFASS	President	1840–55	
		Ex. Com.	1840–55	
	CASS	V.P.	1861–64	
Tappan, Lewis	AASS	Manager	1833–37	Congregational
		Ex. Com.	1834–40	
	AFASS	Ex. Com.	1840–55	
		Treasurer	1840–42	
		Secretary	1842–44	
		Cor. Sec.	1845–46, 1848–55	
	CASS	Ex. Com.	1859–61	
Tappan, Weare	AASS/G	V.P.	1844–45	?
Tapping, Lewis	AASS	Manager	1839–40	?
*Thatcher, Moses	AASS	Manager	1833–37	Congregational
Thomas, N. P.	AASS	Manager	1838–40	?
Thome, Arthur	AASS	V.P.	1839–40	New School Presbyterian
*Thome, James A.	AASS	V.P.	1839–40	Congregational
	CASS	V.P.	1861–64	

Appendix

Name	Society[1]	Office[1]	Dates in Office	Religion[3]
Thompson, Cyrus	AASS/G	Manager	1843–46	?
Thompson, E. N.	AASS	Manager	1835–36	?
*Thurston, David	AASS	Manager	1833–40	Congregational
*Tilden, William P.	AASS/G	V.P.	1845–48	Unitarian
		Manager	1848–53	
Tomlinson, Carver	AASS/G	V.P.	1858–64	Comeouter
Trevor, Joseph	AASS/G	Manager	1841–42	Baptist
*Turner, Asa, Jr.	AASS	Manager	1837–40	Congregational
Tuttle, Uriel	AASS	Manager	1839–40	Congregational
*Twining, William	AASS	Manager	1837–40	Congregational
	AFASS	Ex. Com.	1840–44	
*Twombley, John H.	CASS	Ex. Com.	1859–61	Methodist
*Tyler, Charles M.	CASS	Ex. Com.	1863–64	Congregational
Van Epps, Abraham	AASS/G	Manager	1843–46	?
Van Rensselaer, Thomas	AASS/G	Ex. Com.	1840–42	?
		Manager	1840–42	
Van Vliet, Peter	AASS	V.P.	1839–40	?
Vashon, John B.	AASS	Manager	1833–37	?
Vose, Richard H.	AASS	Manager	1833–37	?
Walker, Amasa	AASS	Manager	1837–40	Congregational
	AASS/G	Manager	1840–41, 1843–44	
Walker, John	AASS/G	Manager	1840–42	?
Ward, George W.	AASS	Manager	1833–37	?
Warner, James	AFASS	Ex. Com.	1844–55	?
Warren, James	AASS	Manager	1833–34	?
Washburn, Ichabod	CASS	Treasurer	1859–64	Congregational
Waters, Henry	AFASS	Ex. Com.	1853–55	?
*Watkins, William	AASS	V.P.	1834–35	?
Wattles, John O.	AASS/G	Manager	1843–44	Spiritualist
Webb, Samuel	AASS/G	Manager	1840–41	Quaker
*Webster, John C.	CASS	President	1859–64	Congregational
*Weeks, William R.	AASS	V.P.	1834–39	New School Presbyterian
Weld, Theodore	AASS	Manager	1833–35	Congregational
		Cor. Sec.	1839–40	
*Wells, Eleazar M.	AASS	V.P.	1833–35	Episcopalian
*Wells, Samuel	AASS	Manager	1839–40	Congregational
Wells, Woolsey	AASS	Manager	1834–36	?
*Welton, Alonzo	AASS	Manager	1838–39	New School Presbyterian
Wess, Samuel	AASS	Manager	1839–40	?
Weston, Anne W.	AASS/G	Ex. Com.	1843–64	Comeouter
Wetmore, Lauren	AASS/G	Manager	1851–53	?
Whipple, Charles K.	AASS	Manager	1836–37	?/Comeouter
	AASS/G	Ex. Com.	1857–64	
*Whipple, George	AASS	Manager	1839–40	Congregational
	AFASS	Ex. Com.	1846–55	
Whitcomb, James	AASS	Manager	1837–39	?
	AASS/G	Manager	1840–41	
		V.P.	1850–64	

(continued)

Appendix (*Cont.*)

Name	Society[1]	Office[1]	Dates in Office	Religion[3]
White, James	AASS	Manager	1833–40	?
Whiting, William E.	AFASS	Ex. Com.	1844–55	Congregational
		Treasurer	1846–55	
Whitman, Isaac	AASS	Manager	1833–34	?
Whitson, Thomas	AASS	Manager	1833–37	Hicksite Friend
	AASS/G	Manager	1840–42	
		V.P.	1852–64	
Whittier, John G.	AASS	Manager	1833–40	Orthodox Friend
	AFASS	Ex. Com.	1840–41	
Wichell, John	AASS/G	V.P.	1851–57	?
Wilde, Samuel	AFASS	Ex. Com.	1846–49	?
Williams, Austin F.	AFASS	Ex. Com.	1848–51	Congregational
Williams, Herbert	AASS	Manager	1837–40	?
	AASS/G	V.P.	1840–44	
*Williams, Peter	AASS	Manager	1833–36	Episcopalian
		Ex. Com.	1834–35	
Williams, Ransom G.	AFASS	Ex. Com.	1844–49	?
*Williams, Samuel	AASS	Manager	1833–37	Baptist
*Williams, Thomas	AASS	Manager	1833–34	Congregational
Williston, John P.	AFASS	Ex. Com.	1841–44	?
	CASS	V.P.	1861–64	
Wilmarth, Lucinda	AASS/G	Manager	1843–44	Comeouter
*Wilson, Daniel	AASS/G	V.P.	1844–52	Wesleyan Methodist
Wilson, David	AASS/G	Manager	1841–46	?
Wilson, James	AASS	Manager	1833–36	Baptist
Wilson, J. R.	AASS	V.P.	1834–35	?
Winslow, Nathan	AASS	Manager	1834–40	Quaker/Comeouter
	AASS/G	Manager	1840–44	
		V.P.	1844–45	
Wood, Amos	AASS/G	Manager	1845–53	Congregational
*Worth, Edmund	AASS	Manager	1839–40	Baptist
Wright, Elizur, Jr.	AASS	V.P.	1833–35	Congregational
		Secretary	1833–39	
Wright, Francis	AASS/G	Manager	1843–45	?
Wright, Henry C.	AASS/G	Ex. Com.	1859–64	Comeouter
Wright, Peter	AASS	Manager	1837–40	?
Wright, Richard P.	AASS	Manager	1834–40	?
*Wright, Theodore S.	AASS	Manager	1834–40	New School Presbyterian
		Ex. Com.	1834–40	
	AFASS	Ex. Com.	1843–47	
Wright, William	AASS/G	Manager	1840–41	Free Thinker
Wyman, Jonas	AASS/G	Manager	1840–44	?

Abbreviations

AAS MSS	American Abolition Society Letterbooks and Records, Oberlin College Archives
AASS	American Anti-Slavery Society
ABCFM	American Board of Commissioners for Foreign Missions
ABFMS	American Baptist Free Mission Society
ABMC	American Baptist Missionary Convention
AFASS	American and Foreign Anti-Slavery Society
AFAS Reporter	*American and Foreign Anti-Slavery Reporter*
AHMS	American Home Missionary Society
AMA	American Missionary Association
AMA MSS	American Missionary Association Manuscripts, Amistad Research Center, Dillard University
AME	African Methodist Episcopal church
AMEZ	African Methodist Episcopal Zion church
ARTBS	American Reform Tract and Book Society
ATS	American Tract Society
CASS	Church Anti-Slavery Society
CWH	*Civil War History*
Eman.	*Emancipator*
JAH	*Journal of American History*
JSH	*Journal of Southern History*
Lib.	(Boston, Mass.) *Liberator*
MASS	Massachusetts Anti-Slavery Society
MVHR	*Mississippi Valley Historical Review*
NASS	*National Anti-Slavery Standard*
YMCA	Young Men's Christian Association

Notes

Introduction

1. Charles K. Whipple, *The Relations of Anti-Slavery to Religion*, Anti-Slavery Tract 19 (New York, n.d.), 1.

2. Parker Pillsbury, *Acts of the Anti-Slavery Apostles* (Boston, 1884), 283–84; also Wendell Phillips, *The Philosophy of the Abolition Movement* (New York, 1860), 26–28; H. Shelton Smith, *In His Image But . . . : Racism in Southern Religion, 1780–1910* (Durham, N.C., 1972), 128; Ralph A. Keller, "Northern Protestant Churches and the Fugitive Slave Law of 1850" (Ph.D. diss., University of Wisconsin, 1969), 19–22.

3. AASS, *First Annual Report . . . 1834* (New York, 1834), 19; Milton B. Powell, "The Abolitionist Controversy in the Methodist Episcopal Church, 1840–1864" (Ph.D. diss., University of Iowa, 1963), 49–50.

4. John Wesley's description of American slavery, which abolitionists quoted frequently; John Wesley, *The Works of the Rev. John Wesley, A.M.*, 14 vols. (London, 1872), 3:453.

5. Only the most important of these works can be mentioned here. Gilbert H. Barnes, *The Antislavery Impulse, 1830–1844* (New York, 1933), 103; and Dwight L. Dumond, *Antislavery Origins of the Civil War* (Ann Arbor, 1939), 35, and *Antislavery: The Crusade for Freedom in America* (Ann Arbor, 1961), 179, first noted the close ties between organized abolitionism and the churches. Although many subsequent historians have discussed the role of scriptural arguments in the debate over slavery, Adelaide A. Lyons, "Religious Defense of Slavery in the North," *Trinity College Historical Society, Historical Papers* 13 (1919): 5–34, remains the best compendium of the biblical case for slavery. Two denominations that held out from the dominant attitude toward slavery in the early nineteenth-century United States are examined in Thomas Drake, *Quakers and Slavery in America* (New Haven, 1950); and Norman A. Baxter, *History of the Freewill Baptists: A Study in New England Separatism* (Rochester, N.Y., 1957). The best studies of the role of the slavery question in the

important denominational schisms before the Civil War are Donald G. Mathews, *Slavery and Methodism: A Chapter in American Morality, 1780–1845* (Princeton, N.J., 1965); Andrew E. Murray, *Presbyterians and the Negro—A History* (Philadelphia, 1966); and Mary Putnam, *The Baptists and Slavery, 1840–1845* (Ann Arbor, 1913). Two of the many discussions of the sectional breakup of the nation's churches are Avery Craven, *The Coming of the Civil War* (New York, 1942), 201; and James G. Randall and David Donald, *The Civil War and Reconstruction* (2d ed., Lexington, Mass., 1969), 25–26.

6. AASS, *Proceedings of the American Anti-Slavery Society at Its Second Decade* (New York, 1854), 82; Craven, *Coming of the Civil War,* 201; Sydney E. Ahlstrom, *A Religious History of the American People* (New Haven, 1972), 657; Henry H. Simms, *Emotion at High Tide: Abolition as a Controversial Factor, 1830–1845* (Baltimore, 1960), 212; Stanley Elkins, *Slavery: A Problem in American Institutional and Intellectual Life* (Chicago, 1959), 184–85; Chester F. Dunham, *The Attitude of the Northern Clergy toward the South, 1860–1865* (Toledo, Ohio, 1942), 1–2; H. Richard Niebuhr, *The Social Sources of Denominationalism* (New York, 1929), 191–99; Liston Pope, "The Negro and Religion in America," in *The Sociology of Religion: An Anthology,* ed. Richard D. Knudten (New York, 1967), 17–25; William W. Sweet, "Some Religious Aspects of the Kansas Struggle," *Journal of Religion* 7 (October 1927): 578–95. This study has confined itself to examining the relations of abolitionists with Christian denominations. An informative study of American Jewish abolitionists is Jayme A. Sokolow, "Revolution and Reform: The Antebellum Jewish Abolitionists," *Journal of Ethnic Studies* 9 (Spring 1981): 27–41.

7. For many years, most students of the antislavery movement accepted the interpretation of the previously cited landmark works of Barnes and Dumond, which contended that American abolitionism shifted from religious to political channels in the mid-1840s. More recently, Aileen S. Kraditor, *Means and Ends in American Abolitionism: Garrison and His Critics on Strategy and Tactics* (New York, 1967); Gerald Sorin, *Abolitionism: A New Perspective* (New York, 1972); James B. Stewart, *Holy Warriors: The Abolitionists and American Slavery* (New York, 1976); and others have reasserted the importance of the apolitical and secular tactics of moral suasion practiced by Garrisonian abolitionists in the 1840s and 1850s. Although these studies are useful correctives to the anti-Garrisonian biases of earlier works, they ignore the unabated efforts of many abolitionists to convert the churches to antislavery activism that continued down to the Civil War. A few of the historical accounts of abolitionism written in the past two decades, however, give at least a degree of note to the later phase of church-oriented antislavery endeavors. Louis Filler, *The Crusade against Slavery, 1830–1860* (New York, 1960), describes the continuing abolitionist agitation in the interdenominational benevolent societies in the 1850s as an indication of a growing antislavery sentiment in the North in more than political affairs. Carleton Mabee, *Black Freedom: The Nonviolent Abolitionists from 1830 through the Civil War* (London, 1970), accurately describes the dissatisfaction of the abolitionists with the northern churches even after southern members had seceded from several denominations. Merton L. Dillon, *The Abolitionists: The Growth of a Dissenting Minority* (De

Kalb, Ill., 1974), notes an abolitionist revival of interest in nonpolitical methods of agitation but does not trace its impact on the religious denominations of the free states. Bertram Wyatt-Brown, *Lewis Tappan and the Evangelical War against Slavery* (Cleveland, 1969), perhaps undervalues its subject's contribution to awakening much of the northern religious community to the moral case against slavery. Lawrence J. Friedman, *Gregarious Saints: Self and Community in American Abolitionism, 1830–1870* (Cambridge, Mass., 1982), devotes a chapter to the church-oriented activities of a New York City abolitionist circle centered around Lewis Tappan. Two examples of historical works that credit the more moderate mainstream church leaders, rather than the abolitionists, with supplying the North with the ethical arguments to resist the encroachments of the "Slave Power" are Clifford S. Griffin, *Their Brothers' Keepers: Moral Stewardship in the United States, 1800–1865* (New Brunswick, N.J., 1960); and Timothy L. Smith, *Revivalism and Social Reform: American Protestantism on the Eve of the Civil War* (1957; reprint, New York, 1965).

8. Historians have used other labels, such as "Tappanities" and "evangelical," to describe those abolitionists pursuing church-oriented tactics, but I have followed the lead of Clifton H. Johnson and William Gravely in using "Christian." This label should not be interpreted as implying that the religious views of members of the other abolitionist factions were anti-Christian, as some of their contemporaries charged. Clifton H. Johnson, "The American Missionary Association, 1846–1861: A Study of Christian Abolitionism" (Ph.D. diss., University of North Carolina, 1958), 5–11; Mabee, *Black Freedom*, 3–4; Ronald G. Walters, "The Boundaries of Abolitionism," in *Antislavery Reconsidered: New Perspectives on the Abolitionists,* ed. Lewis Perry and Michael Fellman (Baton Rouge, La., 1979), 17; William B. Gravely, "Christian Abolitionism," in *The Social Gospel: Religion and Reform in Changing America,* ed. Ronald C. White, Jr., and C. Howard Hopkins (Philadelphia, 1976), 14–20.

Chapter 1. *No Christian Fellowship with Slaveholders*

1. Whipple, *Relations of Anti-Slavery to Religion,* 1.

2. Eric Foner, *Free Soil, Free Labor, Free Men: The Ideology of the Republican Party before the Civil War* (New York, 1970), 3–5; Charles C. Cole, Jr., *The Social Ideas of the Northern Evangelists, 1826–1860* (New York, 1954), 193; Stanley M. Elkins, "Slavery and Ideology," in *The Debate over Slavery: Stanley Elkins and His Critics,* ed. Ann J. Lane (Urbana, Ill., 1971), 375.

3. David B. Davis, *The Problem of Slavery in the Age of Revolution, 1770–1823* (Ithaca, N.Y., 1975), 42–47, 196–212; Lester B. Scherer, *Slavery and the Churches in Early America, 1619–1819* (Grand Rapids, Mich., 1975), 126–49; Dillon, *The Abolitionists,* 3–12.

4. David B. Davis, "The Emergence of Immediatism in British and American Antislavery Thought," *MVHR* 49 (September 1962): 228; Anne C. Loveland, "Evan-

gelicalism and 'Immediate Emancipation' in American Antislavery Thought," *JSH* 32 (May 1966): 177; Whitney R. Cross, *The Burned-over District: The Social and Intellectual History of Enthusiastic Religion in Western New York, 1800–1850* (New York, 1950), 40–41; Charles R. Keller, *The Second Great Awakening in Connecticut* (New Haven, 1942), 41–42; Seymour M. Lipset, *The First New Nation: The United States in Historical and Comparative Perspective* (New York, 1963), 161–62.

5. Quoted in Barnes, *Antislavery Impulse,* 11; T. Scott Miyakawa, *Protestants and Pioneers: Individualism and Conformity on the American Frontier* (Chicago, 1964), 172, 220–21; M. Leon Perkal, "William Goodell: A Life of Reform" (Ph.D. diss., City University of New York, 1972), 31–32; Cross, *Burned-over District,* 158–60, 165–66, 204, 241–42, 250; Loveland, " 'Immediate Emancipation,' " 178–79.

6. Ronald G. Walters, *American Reformers, 1815–1860* (New York, 1978), 21–37; Cole, *Social Ideas,* 63; Clifford S. Griffin, "Religious Benevolence as Social Control, 1815–1860," *MVHR* 44 (December 1957): 23–26; Gregory H. Singleton, "Protestant Voluntary Organizations and the Shaping of Victorian America," *American Quarterly* 27 (December 1975): 552–58; Loveland, " 'Immediate Emancipation,' " 181–83; Johnson, "American Missionary Association," 31–32.

7. Alice Felt Tyler, *Freedom's Ferment: Phases of American Social History from the Colonial Period to the Outbreak of the Civil War* (Minneapolis, 1944), 184–86; Sidney Lens, *Radicalism in America* (New York, 1966), 98–99; Cross, *Burned-over District,* 238; John L. Thomas, "Romantic Reform in America, 1815–1865," *American Quarterly* 17 (Winter 1965): 195; Powell, "Abolitionist Controversy in the Methodist Episcopal Church," 7–8.

8. James B. Stewart, "Peaceful Hopes and Violent Experiences: The Evolution of Reforming and Radical Abolitionism, 1831–1837," *CWH* 17 (December 1971): 293–309; Powell, "Abolitionist Controversy in the Methodist Episcopal Church," 83–84.

9. George M. Marsden, *The Evangelical Mind and the New School Presbyterian Experience: A Case Study of Thought and Theology in Nineteenth Century America* (New Haven, 1970), 182–96; Smith, *Revivalism and Social Reform,* 225–36.

10. Ohio Anti-Slavery Society, *Proceedings of the Ohio Anti-Slavery Convention, Held at Putnam, on the 22nd, 23rd, and 24th of April, 1835* (New York, n.d.), 7–8 (hereafter cited as *Convention . . . 1835*); also quoted in *Anti-Slavery Record* 1 (July 1836): 75.

11. *Anti-Slavery Record* 1 (January 1836): 10–11; *Lib.,* 20 July 1838; MASS, *Fifth Annual Report . . . 1837* (Boston, 1837), vii; John G. Fee, *An Anti-Slavery Manual: Being an Examination, in the Light of the Bible, and of Facts, into the Moral and Social Wrongs of American Slavery, with a Remedy for the Evil* (Maysville, Ky., 1848), 126–43; Loveland, " 'Immediate Emancipation,' " 181–83, 187; Davis, "Emergence of Immediatism," 224.

12. Jonathan Blanchard, *Sermon on Slaveholding Preached by Appointment before the Synod of Cincinnati at Their Late State Meeting at Mount Pleasant, Ohio, October 20, 1841* (Cincinnati, 1842), 5; Luther Lee, *Slavery Examined in the Light of the Bible* (Syracuse, N.Y., 1855), 12, 20; *Anti-Slavery Record* 1 (June 1837): 69.

13. AASS, *Influence of Slavery upon the White Population, by a Former Resident of Slave States,* Anti-Slavery Tract 9 (New York, n.d.), 11; also AASS, *Third Annual Report . . . 1836* (New York, 1836), 66–75; MASS, *Sixth Annual Report . . . 1838* (Boston, 1838), 53.

14. New England Anti-Slavery Society, *Second Annual Report . . . 1834* (Boston, 1834), 8; also *Anti-Slavery Record* 3 (April 1837): 7 and (October 1837): 113; *Lib.,* 20 July 1835.

15. Luther R. Marsh, ed., *Writings and Speeches of Alvan Stewart on Slavery* (New York, 1860), 187–88.

16. *Anti-Slavery Record* 1 (March 1835): 28–29; Ohio Anti-Slavery Society, *Convention . . . 1835,* 16.

17. James G. Birney to Lewis Tappan, 3 February 1835, in *Letters of James Gillespie Birney, 1831–1857,* ed. Dwight L. Dumond, 2 vols. (New York, 1938), 1:176–80.

18. John G. Fee, *Non-Fellowship with Slaveholders, the Duty of Christians* (New York, 1851), 27.

19. Ibid., 21.

20. *Anti-Slavery Record* 3 (September 1837): 105; also *Lib.,* 28 June 1834.

21. Linda Jeanne Evans, "Abolitionism in the Illinois Churches, 1830–1865" (Ph.D. diss., Northwestern University, 1981), 95, 99.

22. AASS, *The American Anti-Slavery Almanac for 1840* (New York and Boston, n.d.), 21; Jane H. Pease and William H. Pease, *They Who Would Be Free: Blacks' Search for Freedom, 1830–1861* (New York, 1974), 161–63; Leon F. Litwack, *North of Slavery: The Negro in the Free States, 1790–1860* (Chicago, 1961), 187–213; Mabee, *Black Freedom,* 127–38.

23. Russell B. Nye, *The Cultural Life of the New Nation, 1776–1830* (New York, 1960), 219; Edwin S. Gaustad, *Dissent in American Religion* (Chicago, 1973), 152–53; Smith, *Revivalism and Social Reform,* 196–97; Keller, "Churches and the Fugitive Slave Law," 33.

24. Philip Schaff, *America: A Study of Its Political, Social, and Religious Character* (1855; reprint, Cambridge, Mass., 1961), 80.

25. Smith, *Revivalism and Social Reform,* 188–91; Keller, "Churches and the Fugitive Slave Law," 113; Powell, "Abolitionist Controversy in the Methodist Episcopal Church," 95–97; Conrad J. Engelder, "The Churches and Slavery: A Study of the Attitudes toward Slavery of the Major Protestant Denominations" (Ph.D. diss., University of Michigan, 1964), 285–87.

26. David B. Davis, "Slavery and Sin: The Cultural Background," in *The Antislavery Vanguard: New Essays on the Abolitionists,* ed. Martin Duberman (Princeton, N.J., 1965), 30–31; Scherer, *Slavery and the Churches,* 155–56.

27. Mabee, *Black Freedom,* 217–18; Dillon, *The Abolitionists,* 9–10; Cushing Strout, *The New Heavens and New Earth: Political Religion in America* (New York, 1974), 148; Hilary A. Herbert, *The Abolition Crusade and Its Consequences: Four Periods of American History* (New York, 1912), 176; Lyons, "Religious Defense of Slavery," 5; Engelder, "Churches and Slavery," 4, 11.

28. Donald G. Mathews, *Religion in the Old South* (Chicago, 1977), 66–80; Scherer, *Slavery and the Churches,* 137–41; Miyakawa, *Protestants and Pioneers,* 174–75, 196–97; Lewis B. Purifoy, "The Methodist Anti-Slavery Tradition, 1784–1844," *Methodist History* 4 (July 1966): 15–16; and Purifoy, "The Southern Methodist Church and the Pro-Slavery Argument," *JSH* 32 (December 1966): 325.

29. Scherer, *Slavery and the Churches,* 132–35; Murray, *Presbyterians and the Negro,* 16–20; Victor B. Howard, "The Anti-Slavery Movement in the Presbyterian Church, 1835–1861" (Ph.D. diss., Ohio State University, 1961), 3; Engelder, "Churches and Slavery," 186–87.

30. John W. Christie and Dwight L. Dumond, *George Bourne and the Book and Slavery Irreconcilable* (Philadelphia, 1969), 57–64; Murray, *Presbyterians and the Negro,* 26–28.

31. Robert G. Torbet, *A History of the Baptists* (Philadelphia, 1950), 284–86; James D. Essig, *The Bonds of Wickedness: American Evangelicals against Slavery, 1770–1808* (Philadelphia, 1982), 145–48; Miyakawa, *Protestants and Pioneers,* 150–51; Scherer, *Slavery and the Churches,* 135–37; Merton L. Dillon, "John Mason Peck: A Study of Historical Rationalization," *Journal of the Illinois State Historical Society* 50 (Winter 1957): 390; Engelder, "Churches and Slavery," 57–61.

32. Arthur Zilversmit, *The First Emancipation: The Abolition of Slavery in the North* (Chicago, 1967), 153–56; Essig, *Bonds of Wickedness,* 97–114.

33. *Christian Examiner* 24 (July 1838): 287–88, 293; Douglas C. Stange, *Patterns of Antislavery among American Unitarians, 1831–1860* (Rutherford, N.J., 1977), 177–90; Theodore D. Bacon, *Leonard Bacon: A Statesman in the Church* (New Haven, 1931), 59–60; J. Earl Thompson, Jr., "Lyman Beecher's Long Road to Conservative Abolitionism," *Church History* 42 (March 1973): 93; Robert C. Senior, "New England Congregationalists and the Anti-Slavery Movement, 1830–1860" (Ph.D. diss., Yale University, 1954), 27–83; Engelder, "Churches and Slavery," 97–98.

34. Samuel J. May, *Some Recollections of Our Anti-Slavery Conflict* (Boston, 1869), 333–34; Ernest Cassara, *Hosea Ballou: The Challenge to Orthodoxy* (Boston, 1961), 105; Ernest Cassara, ed., *Universalism in America: A Documentary History* (Boston, 1971), 189–90; Cross, *Burned-over District,* 323; Evans, "Abolitionism in Illinois Churches," 244–46.

35. Harold L. Lunger, *The Political Ethics of Alexander Campbell* (St. Louis, 1954), 222; Robert Richardson, *Memoirs of Alexander Campbell* (Cincinnati, 1872), 500–1, 523–24; Winifred E. Garrison and Alfred T. DeGroot, *The Disciples of Christ: A History* (St. Louis, 1948), 323.

36. Paul Kleppner, *The Cross of Culture: A Social Analysis of Midwestern Politics, 1850–1900* (New York, 1970), 73; Richard Jensen, *The Winning of the Midwest: Social and Political Conflict, 1888–1896* (Chicago, 1971), 65–66; L. Richard Bradley, "The Lutheran Church and Slavery," *Concordia Historical Institute Quarterly* 44 (February 1971): 33, 41; Robert J. Murphy, "Catholic Church in the United States during the Civil War Period, 1852–1866," *American Catholic Historical Society of Philadelphia Records* 39 (December 1928): 283–93; Douglas C. Stange, "Com-

passionate Mother to Her Poor Negro Slaves: The Lutheran Church and Negro Slavery in Early America,'' *Phylon* 29 (Fall 1968): 272–81; Lyons, ''Religious Defense of Slavery,'' 8; Engelder, ''Churches and Slavery,'' 193.

37. *Eman.*, 22 May 1840; *Lib.*, 27 March 1840; New England Anti-Slavery Society, *Second Annual Report . . . 1834*, 32; Drake, *Quakers and Slavery*, 5, 48, 68–84, 114–32, 167–222; Dumond, *Antislavery*, 16–20; Dillon, *The Abolitionists*, 7–9.

38. *Eman.*, 28 November 1839; *Freewill Baptist Quarterly* 1 (January 1855): 6–7; Freewill Baptist Connection, *Eighth General Conference* (Byron, N.Y., 1835), 7; AASS, *Fifth Annual Report . . . 1838* (New York, 1838), 49–50; Oliver Johnson, *William Lloyd Garrison and His Times; or, Sketches of the Anti-Slavery Movement in America and of the Man Who Was Its Founder and Moral Leader* (Boston, 1881), 81; John F. Cady, *The Origin and Development of the Missionary Baptist Church in Indiana* (Franklin, Ind., 1942), 222; Baxter, *Freewill Baptists*, 94–95, 99–101; Dumond, *Antislavery*, 349.

39. Quoted in Marion Morrison, ed., *Life of the Reverend David McDill, D.D., Minister of the United Presbyterian Church* (Philadelphia, 1874), 61–62; also AASS, *Fourth Annual Report . . . 1837* (New York, 1837), 42; Murray, *Presbyterians and the Negro*, 9–11; Randolph A. Roth, ''The First Radical Abolitionists: The Reverend James Milligan and the Reformed Presbyterians of Vermont,'' *New England Quarterly* 55 (December 1982): 540–63 (hereafter cited as ''James Milligan''); William L. Fisk, ''The Associate Reformed Church in the Old Northwest: A Chapter in the Acculturation of the Immigrant,'' *Journal of Presbyterian History* 46 (June 1968): 167.

40. Johnson, ''American Missionary Association,'' 11–12, 25–26, has influenced my thinking on these categories of attitudes toward slavery among members of the antebellum northern churches.

41. Arthur C. Cole, *The Irrepressible Conflict, 1850–1865* (New York, 1934), 256; Arthur Y. Lloyd, *The Slavery Controversy, 1831–1860* (Chapel Hill, N.C., 1939), 190–92; Davis, *Problem of Slavery*, 532; Mathews, *Slavery and Methodism*, 228–29; Engelder, ''Churches and Slavery,'' 30–32.

42. Nathan Lord, *A Letter of Inquiry to Ministers of the Gospel, of All Denominations, on Slavery, By a Northern Presbyter*, 4th ed. (Hanover, N.H., 1860), 7; also Lord, *A Northern Presbyterian's Second Letter to Ministers of the Gospel of All Denominations on Slavery* (New York, 1855), 37, 53–61; John H. Hopkins, *A Scriptural, Ecclesiastical, and Historical View of Slavery from the Days of the Patriarch Abraham to the Nineteenth Century* (New York, 1864), 12–13; Richard M. Cameron, *Methodism and Society in Historical Perspective* (New York, 1961), 143; Larry Edward Tise, ''The Interregional Appeal of Proslavery Thought: An Ideological Profile of the Antebellum American Clergy,'' *Plantation Society in the Americas* 1 (February 1979): 63–72; Lyons, ''Religious Defense of Slavery,'' 17.

43. *Christian Examiner* 42 (September 1857): 175; William G. Brownlow and Abram Pryne, *Ought American Slavery to Be Perpetuated? A Debate between Reverend W. G. Brownlow and Reverend A. Pryne, Held at Philadelphia, September 1858*

(Philadelphia, 1858), 119–20 (hereafter cited as *Debate*); Charles Elliott, *The Bible and Slavery.* . . . (Cincinnati, 1857), 354; Lorenzo D. Turner, *Antislavery Sentiment in American Literature prior to 1865* (Washington, D.C., 1926), 76–77; Timothy Williston, "Is American Slavery an Institution Which Christianity Sanctions, and Will Perpetuate? And, in View of This Subject, What Ought American Christians to Do, and Refrain from Doing?" in *Liberty or Slavery: The Great National Question* (Boston, 1857), 110–11.

44. John Rankin, quoted in Engelder, "Churches and Slavery," 49; G. F. Kettell, *Reply of Reverend G. F. Kettell to Reverend Daniel Curry's Review of His Thanksgiving Sermon: Fugitive Slave Law* (Poughkeepsie, N.Y., 1851), 7; Elliott, *Bible and Slavery*, 354; Joseph P. Thompson, *Christianity and Emancipation; or, The Teachings and Influence of the Bible against Slavery* (New York, 1863), 5; Enoch Pond, *Slavery and the Bible* (Boston, n.d.), 3–4, 9–10; Horace T. Love, *Slavery in Its Relation to God: A Review of Reverend Dr. Lord's Thanksgiving Sermon in Favor of Slavery* (Buffalo, 1851), 25.

45. Lord, *Letter of Inquiry*, 5, also 9; Lord, *Second Letter*, 15, 21, 31–32, 35; Hopkins, *View of Slavery*, 18–24; Charles Elliott, *Sinfulness of American Slavery . . . and the Duties of American Citizens in Regard to Slavery* (Cincinnati, 1851), 251; Samuel Seabury, *American Slavery Distinguished from the Slavery of English Theorists and Justified by the Law of Nature* (New York, 1861), 21, 23–24; Theodore T. Munger, *Horace Bushnell: Preacher and Theologian* (Boston, 1899), 297; Lyons, "Religious Defense of Slavery," 28–31.

46. William Graham, *The Contrast; or, The Bible and Abolitionism: An Exegetical Argument* (Cincinnati, 1844), 39–44; also Lord, *Second Letter*, 84–85.

47. Albert Barnes, *The Church and Slavery* (2d ed.; Philadelphia, 1857), 34–35; William W. Patton, *Slavery and Infidelity; or, Slavery in the Church Ensures Infidelity in the World* (Cincinnati, 1856), 9–11, 12–14, 26–29, 44–45, 56–57, 60, 64, 66–68; Ebenezer Hussey, *The Religion of Slavery*, Tract 9 (n.p.: New England Anti-Slavery Tract Association, n.d.), 3; *The Works of John Greenleaf Whittier*, 7 vols. (Boston, 1892), 7:98–99; William Jay, *Reply to Remarks of Rev. Moses Stuart on John Jay and an Examination of His Scriptural Exegesis Contained in His Recent Pamphlet, "Conscience and the Constitution"* (New York, 1850), 20–21; Brownlow and Pryne, *Debate*, 241–42; Joseph Barker, *The Life of Joseph Barker, Written by Himself* (London, 1880), 314.

48. Joseph C. Stiles, *Speech on the Slavery Resolutions, Delivered in the General Assembly Which Met in Detroit in May Last* (Washington, D.C., 1850), 7–10, 30–33; Thomas J. Taylor, *Essay on Slavery as Connected with the Moral and Providential Government of God and as an Element of Church Organization* (New York, 1851), 268; George W. Blagden, *Remarks and a Discourse on Slavery* (Boston, 1854), 16; John Robinson, *The Testimony and Practice of the Presbyterian Church in Reference to American Slavery* (Cincinnati, 1852), 86–87, 100–7; Cortlandt Van Rensselaer, *Presbyterian Views on Slaveholding: Letters and Rejoinders to George D. Armstrong* (Philadelphia, 1858), 6.

49. Elliott, *Sinfulness of American Slavery,* 21–22; also A. C. Baldwin, "Friendly Letters to a Christian Slaveholder," and R. B. Thurston, "The Error and the Duty in Regard to Slavery," in *Liberty or Slavery,* 25–26 and 51–52, respectively.

50. *Eman.,* 19 November 1845; *AFAS Reporter,* October 1845, 65–66; Robert Merideth, *The Politics of the Universe: Edward Beecher, Abolition, and Orthodoxy* (Nashville, 1968), 106–12 (hereafter cited as *Edward Beecher*); L. Wesley Norton, "The Religious Press and the Compromise of 1850: A Study of the Relationship of the Methodist, Baptist, and Presbyterian Press to the Slavery Controversy, 1846–1851" (Ph.D. diss., University of Illinois, 1959), 83–84.

51. Williston, "American Slavery," 127–29; Blagden, *Remarks . . . on Slavery,* 21–23; Robinson, *Testimony and Practice,* 173–74, 197, 214–15; James S. Lamar, *Memoirs of Isaac Errett,* 2 vols. (Cincinnati, 1893), 1:86–87, 217–18; Cross, *Burned-over District,* 258–59; Johnson, "American Missionary Association," 12.

52. Sidney E. Morse, *The Bible and Slavery* (New York, 1855), 2; also Joshua R. Balme, *American States, Churches, and Slavery* (London, 1863), 259–61; David D. Addison, *The Clergy in American Life and Letters* (New York, 1900), 32–33; Arthur S. Hoyt, *The Pulpit and American Life* (New York, 1921), 255–56; A. C. Dickerson, *Anti-Slavery Agitation in the Church Not Authorized* (Philadelphia, 1857), 61; Martin E. Marty, *Righteous Empire: The Protestant Experience in America* (New York, 1970), 58; Keller, "Churches and the Fugitive Slave Law," 13–15; Powell, "Abolitionist Controversy in the Methodist Episcopal Church," 72–73.

53. Balme, *American States,* 352–54; Hoyt, *Pulpit and American Life,* 255–56; John R. Bodo, *The Protestant Clergy and Public Issues, 1812–1848* (Princeton, N.J., 1954), 138–39; Jane H. Pease and William H. Pease, *Bound with Them in Chains: A Biographical History of the Antislavery Movement* (Westport, Conn., 1972), 12–13; James H. Moorhead, "Social Reform and the Divided Conscience of Antebellum Protestantism," *Church History* 48 (December 1979): 424–25; Hugh H. Davis, "The Reform Career of Joshua Leavitt, 1794–1873" (Ph.D. diss., Ohio State University, 1969), 153–54.

54. Robert Baird, *Religion in America; or, An Account of the Origin, Relation to the State, and Present Condition of the Evangelical Churches in the United States* (New York, 1845), 40–41, 337; also Van Rensselaer, *Presbyterian Views,* 43; Taylor, *Essay on Slavery,* 268; Baldwin, "Friendly Letters," 73–74; Mathews, *Slavery and Methodism,* 228–29.

55. Jairus Burt, *The Law of Christian Rebuke: A Plea for Slave-Holders* (Hartford, Conn., 1843), 16–17; George Duffield, *A Sermon on American Slavery: Its Nature and the Duties of Christians in Relation to It* (Detroit, 1840), 30; Nathan Bangs, *Emancipation: Its Necessity and Means of Accomplishment Calmly Submitted to the Citizens of the United States* (New York, 1849), 65–66; Williston, "American Slavery," 123–24.

56. Quoted in Engelder, "Churches and Slavery," 63–64; Thurston, "Error and Duty in Regard to Slavery," 30–33; Morse, *Bible and Slavery,* 1; Bangs, *Emancipation,* 14–17; Van Rensselaer, *Presbyterian Views,* 18; Baldwin, "Friendly Letters," 94–97; Philip J. Staudenraus, *The African Colonization Movement, 1816–1865* (New

York, 1961), 48–58; Friedman, *Gregarious Saints,* 14–15; Marsden, *Evangelical Mind,* 92.

57. William Lloyd Garrison, *Thoughts on African Colonization* (1832; reprint, New York, 1968), 7, 25, 33–38, 57–61; William Jay, *Inquiry into the Character and Tendency of the American Colonization and American Anti-Slavery Societies* (New York, 1838), 61, 96–97; Friedman, *Gregarious Saints,* 21–35; Bruce Rosen, "Abolition and Colonization, the Years of Conflict: 1829–1834," *Phylon* 33 (June 1972): 177–92.

58. Lawrence J. Lesick, *The Lane Rebels: Evangelicalism and Antislavery in Antebellum America* (Metuchen, N.J., 1980), 93–94, 123–25; Thompson, "Lyman Beecher's Long Road," 98–102.

Chapter 2. *Donning the Prophet's Mantle*

1. Zilversmit, *First Emancipation,* 61–93; 162–229; Essig, *Bonds of Wickedness,* 41, 54–55, 62–72; Davis, *Problem of Slavery,* 42–47, 196–212; Scherer, *Slavery and the Churches,* 126–49; Dillon, *The Abolitionists,* 3–12.

2. Essig, *Bonds of Wickedness,* 115–39; Dumond, *Antislavery,* 46–52, 126–32; Filler, *Crusade against Slavery,* 10–27; Stewart, *Holy Warriors,* 11–32; Dillon, *The Abolitionists,* 15–26.

3. Barnes, *The Antislavery Impulse,* 3–37, 44, 55–56; Dillon, *The Abolitionists,* 35–46, 52–58; Dumond, *Antislavery,* 177; Filler, *Crusade against Slavery,* 59–63, 65–67; Stewart, *Holy Warriors,* 50–55.

4. Stewart, *Holy Warriors,* 78–81.

5. These generalizations require some qualification. After studying the socioeconomic backgrounds of signers of antislavery petitions in New York City during the 1830s, John Jentz concludes that "while evangelical professionals provided most of the leadership for abolition they did not provide most of the followers. . . ." Jentz instead argues that abolitionism in New York City drew the majority of its support from local artisans whose antislavery activities were inspired more by Thomas Paine and European secular radicalism than by Charles Finney and evangelical benevolence. This discrepancy with the findings of other studies might be due to the fact that Jentz examined the broader "constituency" who signed antislavery petitions rather than the actual membership of abolition societies. John B. Jentz, "Artisans, Evangelicals, and the City: A Social History of Abolition and Labor Reform in Jacksonian New York" (Ph.D. diss., City University of New York, 1977), 170, 201–23; also AASS, *Third Annual Report . . . 1836,* 76; Gerald Sorin, *The New York Abolitionists: A Case Study of Political Radicalism* (Westport, Conn., 1971), 96–97; Edward O. Schriver, *Go Free: The Antislavery Impulse in Maine, 1833–1855* (Orono, Maine, 1970), 80–86; Hermann R. Muelder, *Fighters for Freedom: History of Anti-Slavery Activities of Men and Women Associated with Knox College* (New York, 1959), 74–83, 129–32, 268–77; Cross, *Burned-over District,* 222–23, 264; Dillon, *The Abolitionists,* 51; Senior, "New England Congregationalists," 248.

6. AASS, *The American Anti-Slavery Almanac for 1838* (Boston, n.d.), 9; also *Anti-Slavery Record* 3 (October 1837): 113; New England Anti-Slavery Society, *Second Annual Report . . . 1834,* 8.

7. The *Liberator* did receive a subsidy from the Massachusetts Anti-Slavery Society in the mid-1830s; Walter M. Merrill, *Against Wind and Tide: A Biography of William Lloyd Garrison* (Cambridge, Mass., 1963), 139; Dumond, *Antislavery* 177–79; Dillon, *The Abolitionists,* 56–57.

8. William L. Garrison to Henry E. Benson, 2 December 1836, in *The Letters of William Lloyd Garrison,* ed. Walter M. Merrill and Louis Ruchames, 6 vols. (Cambridge, Mass., 1971–81) 2:187–88 (hereafter cited as *Garrison Letters*); MASS, *Fourth Annual Report . . . 1836* (Boston, 1836), 4; *Eman.,* 3 October 1839; Dumond, *Antislavery,* 180–89; John L. Myers, ''The Agency System of the Anti-Slavery Movement, 1832–1837, and Its Antecedents in Other Benevolent and Reform Societies'' (Ph.D. diss., University of Michigan, 1961), 401–5.

9. *Eman.,* 31 August 1837; also *Anti-Slavery Record* 3 (October 1837): 169–70; New England Anti-Slavery Society, *Second Annual Report . . . 1834,* 8; Lewis Tappan, Diary, 16 December 1838, Lewis Tappan Papers, Manuscript Division, Library of Congress (hereafter cited as Tappan Diary); Lewis Tappan to Samuel D. Hastings, Lewis Tappan Papers (hereafter cited as Tappan Papers); William L. Garrison to William E. Channing, 20 January 1834, *Garrison Letters,* 1:281.

10. AASS, *Third Annual Report . . . 1836,* 29, and *Second Annual Report . . . 1835* (New York, 1835), 29; also AASS, *The American Anti-Slavery Almanac for 1839* (New York, n.d.), 22–28.

11. *Lib.,* 4 October 1834, 1 November 1839, 3 January and 6 March 1840; *Eman.,* 23 April 1836; MASS, *Fourth Annual Report . . . 1836,* 16–17, and *Seventh Annual Report . . . 1839* (Boston, 1839), 39; Dumond, *Antislavery,* 183; Betty Fladeland, *James G. Birney: Slaveholder to Abolitionist* (Ithaca, N.Y., 1955), 99, 134–35.

12. Gerrit Smith to Elizur Wright, 20 August 1841, Elizur Wright Papers, Manuscript Division, Library of Congress (hereafter cited as Wright Papers); *Eman.,* 19 December 1839, 23 January 1840; AASS, *Second Annual Report . . . 1835,* 29–30; Ohio Anti-Slavery Society, *Convention . . . 1835,* 6.

13. AASS, *Second Annual Report . . . 1835,* 32; *Eman.,* 25 January 1838.

14. Samuel D. Hastings to Lewis Tappan, 7 December 1838, 23 February 1839, 25 March 1840, Tappan Papers; Samuel D. Hastings to Theodore Weld, 12 July 1838, in *Letters of Theodore Dwight Weld, Angeline Grimke Weld, and Sarah Grimke, 1822–1844,* ed. Gilbert H. Barnes and Dwight L. Dumond, 2 vols. (New York, 1934), 2:690–91.

15. Lewis Tappan to Samuel D. Hastings, 30 December 1838, 12 January 1840; Lewis Tappan to ''Rev. Burchard,'' 18 January 1840, all in Tappan Papers; Evangelical Union Anti-Slavery Society, *Address to the Churches of Jesus Christ by the Evangelical Union Anti-Slavery Society of the City of New York . . .* (New York, 1839), 45; Dumond, *Antislavery,* 349; Kraditor, *Means and Ends,* 95–96.

16. MASS, *Fourth Annual Report . . . 1836,* 56–57; Frank Thistlewaite, *The Anglo-American Connection in the Early Nineteenth Century* (Philadelphia, 1959),

114–15; Thomas F. Harwood, "British Evangelical Abolitionism and American Churches in the 1830s," *JSH* 28 (August 1962): 287–306.

17. *Eman.*, 10 June 1844; William L. Garrison to Oliver Johnson, 3 July 1840, *Garrison Letters*, 2:666; Howard R. Temperley, *British Antislavery, 1833–1870* (Columbia, S.C., 1972), 85–92; Betty Fladeland, *Men and Brothers: Anglo-American Antislavery Cooperation* (Urbana, Ill., 1972), 261–70; Douglas H. Maynard, "The World's Anti-Slavery Convention of 1840," *MVHR* 47 (December 1960): 461, 470.

18. Quoted in Evans, "Abolitionism in Illinois Churches," 317; also Freewill Baptist Connection, *Eighth General Conference*, 7; AASS, *Fifth Annual Report . . . 1838*, 49–50; Baxter, *Freewill Baptists*, 94–95.

19. *Eman.*, 28 November 1839. The small Seventh Day Baptist sect held a similar strong antislavery position; see Evans, "Abolitionism in Illinois Churches," 323.

20. AASS, *Fourth Annual Report . . . 1837*, 42; Roth, "James Milligan," 540–63; Fisk, "Associate Reformed Church," 167; Howard, "Antislavery Movement in the Presbyterian Church," 204–5, 369–71; Evans, "Abolitionism in Illinois Churches," 250.

21. *Non-Slaveholder* 4 (October 1849): 227; also Levi Coffin, *Reminiscences of Levi Coffin* (Cincinnati, 1876), 272–74; Levi Coffin to E. D. Coffin, 11 March 1845, Miscellaneous Manuscripts Collection, Manuscript Division, Library of Congress; Drake, *Quakers and Slavery*, 171–72; Robert W. Doherty, *The Hicksite Separation: A Sociological Analysis of Religious Schism in Early Nineteenth Century America* (New Brunswick, N.J., 1967), 28–29; Dumond, *Antislavery*, 350–52.

22. William L. Garrison to Mary Benson, 27 November 1835, *Garrison Letters*, 1:563–64.

23. Quoted in Engelder, "Churches and Slavery," 186–87.

24. *Anti-Slavery Record* 1 (July 1835): 80–84; AASS, *Third Annual Report . . . 1836*, 82–83; Robert H. Abzug, *Passionate Liberator: Theodore Dwight Weld and the Dilemma of Reform* (New York, 1980), 124, 128; Fladeland, *James G. Birney*, 99; Harwood, "British Evangelical Abolitionism and American Churches," 298–302; Engelder, "Churches and Slavery," 190–96.

25. AASS, *Fourth Annual Report . . . 1837*, 64–66; Murray, *Presbyterians and the Negro*, 105.

26. Robert H. Nichols, *Presbyterians in New York State: A History of the Synod and Its Predecessors* (Philadelphia, 1963), 125; Marsden, *Evangelical Mind*, 94, 99–100; Lesick, *The Lane Rebels*, 77–85; Howard, "Antislavery Movement in the Presbyterian Church," 19, 26.

27. Ohio Anti-Slavery Society, *Second Annual Report . . . 1837* (Cincinnati, 1837), 24; AASS, *Fourth Annual Report . . . 1837*, 64–69.

28. Marsden, *Evangelical Mind*, 93–94. Chapter 4 describes the events surrounding the Presbyterian schism.

29. *Lib.*, 16 February 1833; *Eman.*, 23 April 1836; MASS, *Fourth Annual Report . . . 1836*, 16–17; AASS, *Third Annual Report . . . 1836*, 76; Lucius C. Matlack, *The Antislavery Struggle and Triumph in the Methodist Episcopal Church*

(New York, 1881), 86, 91–92; Harwood, "British Evangelical Abolitionism and American Churches," 295.

30. *Eman.*, 19 January 1837; AASS, *Fourth Annual Report . . . 1837*, 64, and *Fifth Annual Report . . . 1838*, 52; Ohio Anti-Slavery Society, *Second Annual Report . . . 1837*, 23; Luther Lee, *Autobiography of the Reverend Luther Lee, D.D.* (New York, 1882), 153–57; Matlack, *Antislavery Struggle*, 83, 86–89; 113–17; Margaret B. MacMillan, *The Methodist Church in Michigan: The Nineteenth Century* (Grand Rapids, Mich., 1967), 130–31, 137; Cameron, *Methodism and Society*, 160–63; Mathews, *Slavery and Methodism*, 137.

31. Mathews, *Slavery and Methodism*, 129–30; Robert D. Clark, *Life of Mathew Simpson* (New York, 1956), 56; Cameron, *Methodism and Society*, 161; Evans, "Abolitionism in Illinois Churches," 345.

32. *Eman.*, 6 September 1838; MASS, *Seventh Annual Report . . . 1839*, 39; Matlack, *Antislavery Struggle*, 121, 125; Cross, *Burned-over District*, 264–65; Mathews, *Slavery and Methodism*, 137; Engelder, "Churches and Slavery," 135–37.

33. William Goodell, *Slavery and Anti-Slavery: A History of the Great Struggle in Both Hemispheres; With a View of the Slavery Question in the United States* (New York, 1852), 183; Engelder, "Churches and Slavery," 57–61.

34. Muelder, *Fighters for Freedom*, 122–23; Evans, "Abolitionism in Illinois Churches," 273–85.

35. *Lib.*, 1 November 1839, also 3 January 1840; Maria Weston Chapman, *Right and Wrong in Massachusetts* (Boston, 1839), 15.

36. *Lib.*, 3 January 1840; MASS, *Fourth Annual Report . . . 1836*, 13–14; Francis Wayland to James Hoby, 2 May 1837, Wayland Papers, Brown University Archives; William L. Garrison to William Goodell, 26 February 1836, *Garrison Letters*, 2:46; Putnam, *Baptists and Slavery*, 8–9; Cady, *Missionary Baptist Church in Indiana*, 198; Cross, *Burned-over District*, 223–24; Robert A. Baker, *The Southern Baptist Convention and Its People, 1607–1972* (Nashville, 1974), 136, 155–57.

37. AASS, *Fourth Annual Report . . . 1837*, 72–73.

38. *Anti-Slavery Record* 1 (January 1836): 6–7; Tappan Diary, 2 February 1840; Bacon, *Leonard Bacon*, 251–53; Henry H. Simms, "A Critical Analysis of Abolition Literature, 1830–1840," *JSH* 6 (August 1940): 376; Senior, "New England Congregationalists," 89–94, 140, 289.

39. Julian M. Sturtevant, *An Autobiography* (New York, 1896), 229–30; Muelder, *Fighters for Freedom*, 272–75; Lesick, *The Lane Rebels*, 116–46, 167–81; Samuel C. Pearson, "From Church to Denomination: American Congregationalism in the Nineteenth Century," *Church History* 38 (March 1969): 73, 82; James D. Essig, "The Lord's Free Man: Charles G. Finney and His Abolitionism," *CWH* 24 (March 1978): 31–32.

40. *Christian Examiner* 22 (March 1837): 25–26, and 24 (July 1838): 293, 397–98; Madeleine H. Rice, *Federal Street Pastor: The Life of William Ellery Channing* (New York, 1961), 216; Stange, *Patterns of Antislavery*, 177–79, 189–90.

41. Cross, *Burned-over District*, 323; Parker Pillsbury, *The Church as It Is; or, The Forlorn Hope of Slavery,* (1847; reprint, Concord, N.H., 1885), 49–50.

42. Lunger, *Political Ethics of Alexander Campbell,* 193–94; Richardson, *Memoirs of Alexander Campbell,* 366–68, 501–02.

43. M. Theophane Geary, *A History of Third Parties in Pennsylvania, 1840–1860* (Washington, D.C., 1938), 34–35; Jane Grey Swisshelm, *Half a Century* (Chicago, 1880), 150–53; Willis D. Weatherford, *American Churches and the Negro: An Historical Study from Early Slave Days to the Present* (Boston, 1957), 154–55, 163; Stange, "Compassionate Mother," 150–51; Robert Fortenbaugh, "American Lutheran Synods and Slavery, 1830–1860," *Journal of Religion* 13 (January 1933): 78–79; Lawrence J. Friedman, " 'Historical Topics Sometimes Run Dry': The State of Abolitionist Studies," *Historian* 43 (February 1981): 188–89; Engelder, "Churches and Slavery," 260–65.

44. Although the secondary works cited in the previous section are of value in explaining the reaction of specific denominations toward early abolitionist appeals, only a few studies have aimed at a comprehensive explanation of the patterns of response along the entire spectrum of northern religious bodies. Some of these exceptions are: Smith, *Revivalism and Social Reform,* 188–98; Engelder, "Churches and Slavery," 280–88; Evans, "Abolitionism in Illinois Churches," 120–33; and Friedman, " 'Historical Topics Sometimes Run Dry,' " 188–91.

45. AASS, *Fourth Annual Report . . . 1837,* 40–43, and *Fifth Annual Report . . . 1838,* 82–83.

Chapter 3. *Garrisonianism, the Churches,
and the Division of the Abolitionist Movement*

1. Quoted in Kraditor, *Means and Ends,* 116; John L. Thomas, *The Liberator: William Lloyd Garrison* (Boston, 1963), 232, 234, 248–49. An excellent recent survey of the antebellum reform movements is Walters, *American Reformers,* especially 88–94, 115–17.

2. Friedman, *Gregarious Saints,* 43–67; Filler, *Crusade against Slavery,* 120–22; Thomas, *The Liberator,* 232–34, 248–49; Kraditor, *Means and Ends,* 102–8; Lewis Perry, *Childhood, Marriage, and Reform: Henry Clarke Wright, 1797–1870* (Chicago, 1980), 20–21, 23, 37–41.

3. Lewis Perry, *Radical Abolitionism: Anarchy and the Government of God in Antislavery Thought* (Ithaca, N.Y., 1973), 55–63; Goodell, *Slavery and Anti-Slavery,* 449–50, 455, 513; Mabee, *Black Freedom,* 67–88; Kraditor, *Means and Ends,* 79–82.

4. Ronald G. Walters, *The Antislavery Appeal: American Abolitionism after 1830* (Baltimore, 1976), 86–89, 104–6; Lois W. Banner, *Elizabeth Cady Stanton: A Radical for Women's Rights* (Boston, 1980), 23–25; Margaret H. Bacon, *Valiant Friend: The Life of Lucretia Mott* (New York, 1980), 72–82; Kraditor, *Means and Ends,* 79.

5. Stewart, *Holy Warriors,* 89–92; Mabee, *Black Freedom,* 13–14; Walters, *Antislavery Appeal,* 48; Perry, *Radical Abolitionism,* 65.

6. Elizur Wright to Amos A. Phelps, 20 August 1834; Elizur Wright to Beriah Green, 19 March 1835, both in Wright Papers; William L. Garrison to Henry E. Benson, 26 January 1836, *Garrison Letters,* 2:22; MASS, *Eighth Annual Report . . . 1840* (Boston, 1840), 5–6; Calvin M. Clark, *American Slavery and Maine Congregationalists: A Chapter in the History of the Development of Anti-Slavery Sentiment in the Protestant Churches of the North* (Bangor, Maine, 1940), 56–65; Thomas, *The Liberator,* 197; Friedman, *Gregarious Saints,* 38–39; Thompson, "Lyman Beecher's Long Road," 99; James R. Stirn, "Urgent Gradualism: The Case of the American Union for the Relief and Improvement of the Colored Race," *CWH* 25 (December 1979): 309–28.

7. William L. Garrison to Thomas Shipley, 17 December 1835, *Garrison Letters,* 1:584–85; MASS, *Fourth Annual Report . . . 1836,* 56; Rice, *Federal Street Pastor,* 34; Thomas, *The Liberator,* 214–15; Patsy S. Ledbetter and Billy D. Ledbetter, "The Agitator and the Intellectuals: William Lloyd Garrison and the New England Transcendentalists," *Mid-America: An Historical Review* 62 (October 1980): 174–77.

8. Quoted in Thomas, *The Liberators,* 244.

9. Filler, *Crusade against Slavery,* 131–32; Dillon, *The Abolitionists,* 117; Simms, *Emotion at High Tide,* 172; Merrill, *Against Wind and Tide,* 135.

10. MASS, *Eighth Annual Report . . . 1840,* 6, 9; also *Anti-Slavery Record* 3 (October 1837): 120; Senior, "New England Congregationalists," 209.

11. Quoted in Dillon, *The Abolitionists,* 118; also Thomas, *The Liberator,* 244; Merrill, *Against Wind and Tide,* 137–38.

12. William Jay to Lewis Tappan, 22 August 1835, Tappan Papers; also Friedman, *Gregarious Saints,* 87–89; J. Mark Stewart, "The Chillicothe Presbytery in Ohio's Antislavery Movement in the 1820s and 1830s" (Master's thesis, Ohio State University, 1971), 41–42.

13. Elizur Wright to Maria W. Chapman, 15 September 1837; Elizur Wright to Beriah Green, 17 October 1837, both in Wright Papers; William L. Garrison to Samuel J. May, 24 April 1838, *Garrison Letters,* 2:347; Thomas, *The Liberator,* 244; Fladeland, *James Gillespie Birney,* 161–62.

14. William L. Garrison to Lewis Tappan, 13 September 1837, *Garrison Letters,* 2:298–300.

15. William L. Garrison to George W. Benson, 23 September 1837, *Garrison Letters,* 2:304.

16. MASS, *Sixth Annual Report . . . 1838,* x, 27–28.

17. Goodell, *Slavery and Anti-Slavery,* 482–89; Kraditor, *Means and Ends,* 124; Thomas, *The Liberator,* 250–51; Stewart, "Peaceful Hopes and Violent Experiences," 298–307.

18. *Lib.,* 8 November 1839, also 4 October 1839; MASS, *Seventh Annual Report . . . 1839,* 31–35; Hazel C. Wolf, *On Freedom's Altar: The Martyr Complex in the Abolition Movement* (Madison, 1952), 83–84.

19. Chapman, *Right and Wrong in Massachusetts,* 94–96, 145–46; William L. Garrison to Mary Benson, 23 December 1835, *Garrison Letters,* 2:407; *Lib.,* 28 February and 12 June 1840.

20. *Lib.,* 17 January 1840.

21. MASS, *Eighth Annual Report . . . 1840,* 10–15; Chapman, *Right and Wrong in Massachusetts,* 35–36.

22. Francis Jackson and William L. Garrison to the Abolitionists of Massachusetts, 17 July 1839, *Garrison Letters,* 2:503.

23. *Lib.,* 7 February 1840; Chapman, *Right and Wrong in Massachusetts,* 145–46; Kraditor, *Means and Ends,* 71, 115; Thomas, *The Liberator,* 279.

24. Lewis Tappan to Samuel D. Hastings, 11 December 1839; Tappan to William McKee, 11 December 1839; Tappan to Gerrit Smith, 24 March 1840; Tappan to Seth Gates, 2 April 1840; Samuel D. Hastings to Lewis Tappan, 25 May 1840, all in Tappan Papers; Tappan Diary, 12 December 1839; Kraditor, *Means and Ends,* 95–97; Merrill, *Against Wind and Tide,* 156–57, 352.

25. William L. Garrison to Nathaniel P. Rogers, 24 April 1840; Francis Jackson and William L. Garrison to the Abolitionists of the United States, 24 April 1840, *Garrison Letters,* 2:586 and 589, respectively.

26. Francis Jackson and William L. Garrison to the Abolitionists of the United States, 28 February 1840; William L. Garrison to the Editor of the *Emancipator,* 31 May 1839, *Garrison Letters,* 2:474 and 564, respectively; AASS, *Fifth Annual Report . . . 1838,* 12; MASS, *Seventh Annual Report . . . 1839,* 28–29.

27. Lydia M. Child to Ellis G. Loring, 17 May 1840, quoted in Kraditor, *Means and Ends,* 69; also *Lib.,* 29 May 1840; Samuel D. Hastings to Lewis Tappan, 25 March 1840, Tappan Papers; Wyatt-Brown, *Lewis Tappan,* 196–97, 226.

28. Filler, *Crusade against Slavery,* 135–36; Kraditor, *Means and Ends,* 69–70.

29. Barnes, *Antislavery Impulse,* 158–60; Dumond, *Antislavery,* 283–85; Thomas, *The Liberator,* 284, 293; Mabee, *Black Freedom,* 24–26; Pease and Pease, *Bound with Them in Chains,* 10–14; Kraditor, *Means and Ends,* 10, 118–20; Walters, *Antislavery Appeal,* 9–18.

30. *Lib.,* 22 May 1840; also AASS, *Seventh Annual Report . . . 1840* (New York, 1840), 16.

31. MASS, *Eighteenth Annual Report . . . 1850* (Boston, 1850), 83, also 88; MASS, *Seventeenth Annual Report . . . 1849* (Boston, 1849), 80–81.

32. Stephen S. Foster, *The Brotherhood of Thieves; or, A True Picture of the American Church and Clergy* (Boston, 1843), 15–20.

33. Ibid., 29–30.

34. Ibid., 6–7; MASS, *Eleventh Annual Report . . . 1843* (Boston, 1843), 23; Pease and Pease, *Bound with Them in Chains,* 192–96.

35. Pillsbury, *Church as It Is,* 3.

36. *New York Observer,* 19 February 1848; *Congregationalist* (Boston), 7 June 1850; *Pennsylvania Freeman* (Philadelphia), 18 May 1854; *Lib.,* 28 March 1856; *Presbyterian Expositor* 1 (December 1857): 19–20; AASS, *Second Decade,* 65–66; Nathaniel P. Rogers, *A Collection from the Newspaper Writings of Nathaniel Peabody Rogers* (Concord, N.H., 1847), 196–97, 208–10, 370–73; Whipple, *Relations of Anti-Slavery to Religion,* 1.

37. *Lib.,* 19 March 1841, 4 February, 31 March 1848, 3 January and 23 November 1849, 10 and 23 June 1853, 15 December 1854, 4 March 1859; William L. Garrison to George W. Benson, 1 November 1840; William L. Garrison to John A. Collins, 1

December 1840, *Garrison Letters,* 2:722 and 724, respectively; Johnson, *William Lloyd Garrison,* 250–55; W. P. Garrison and F. J. Garrison, *William Lloyd Garrison, 1805–1879,* 4 vols. (New York, 1885–89), 1:218–20, 384; Jayme A. Sokolow, "Henry Clarke Wright: Antebellum Crusader," *Essex Institute Historical Collections* 3 (April 1975): 130–32; Lewis E. Atherton, "Daniel Howell Hise, Abolitionist and Reformer," *MVHR* 26 (December 1939): 356–57; Douglas A. Gamble, "Moral Suasion in the West: Garrisonian Abolitionism, 1831–1861" (Ph.D. diss., Ohio State University, 1973), 435–36.

38. *Congregationalist,* 7 June 1850; also *Christian Observer* (Philadelphia), 21 December 1856; *Independent* (New York), 23 June 1859, 26 January and 5 April 1860; George Wells to James B. Finley, 1 May 1850, James B. Finley Papers, United Methodist Archives Center, West Ohio Conference, United Methodist Church, Breghly Library, Ohio Wesleyan University (hereafter cited as Finley Papers); Henry Van Dyke, *The Character and Influence of Abolitionism* (New York, 1860), 29; Nathan L. Rice, *Lectures on Slavery* (Chicago, 1860), 78; Garrison and Garrison, *William Lloyd Garrison,* 3:398–99.

39. William L. Garrison, *The "Infidelity" of Abolitionism,* Anti-Slavery Tract 10 (New York, 1860), 8, also 3–4, 9–11; *Lib.,* 4 December 1846, 24 May 1850, 19 September 1851, 23 December 1853, 8 February and 28 March 1856; MASS, *Thirteenth Annual Report . . . 1845* (Boston, 1845), 51–52; AASS, *Second Decade,* 65–66, 139; Whipple, *Relations of Anti-Slavery to Religion,* 2–3; Garrison and Garrison, *William Lloyd Garrison,* 2:221; Pillsbury, *Acts of the Anti-Slavery Apostles,* 22–23.

40. Foster, *Brotherhood of Thieves,* 51; Dillon, *The Abolitionists,* 156–59; Lewis Perry, "Versions of Anarchism in the Antislavery Movement," *American Quarterly* 20 (Winter 1968): 775–76.

41. *Lib.,* 22 December 1843; Henry C. Wright, *Duty of Abolitionists to Rebuke Proslavery Ministers and Churches* (Concord, N.H., 1841), 3; Pease and Pease, *Bound with Them in Chains,* 192–93; Mabee, *Black Freedom,* 222; Dillon, *The Abolitionists,* 156–59; Louis Filler, "Parker Pillsbury: An Anti-Slavery Apostle," *New England Quarterly* 19 (September 1946): 320–21; Jane H. Pease and William H. Pease, "Confrontation and Abolition in the 1850s," *JAH* 58 (March 1972): 923; James B. Stewart, "The Aims and Impact of Garrisonian Abolitionism, 1840–1860," *CWH* 15 (September 1969): 197–99.

42. Wright, *Duty of Abolitionists,* 3.

43. Quoted in Pease and Pease, *Bound with Them in Chains,* 192–93; also Filler, "Parker Pillsbury," 320–21.

44. Lydia M. Child, *Isaac T. Hopper: A True Life* (Boston, 1853), 394; Drake, *Quakers and Slavery,* 158–60; Herbert Aptheker, "The Quakers and Negro Slavery," *Journal of Negro History* 25 (July 1940): 360–61.

45. Pillsbury, *Acts of the Anti-Slavery Apostles,* 445; *NASS* 4 April 1844; Dillon, *The Abolitionists,* 156–59; Dumond, *Antislavery,* 285; Cross, *Burned-over District,* 242–43; Lawrence Lader, *The Bold Brahmins: New England's War against Slavery, 1831–1863* (New York, 1961), 125.

46. *Lib.*, 5 October 1841.

47. *Lib.*, 1 October 1844, also 23 February and 3 November 1844; *NASS*, 23 November 1843, 23 May 1844; Friedman, *Gregarious Saints*, 59–61; Kraditor, *Means and Ends*, 33, 106; Thomas, *The Liberator*, 320, 343; Merrill, *Against Wind and Tide*, 213, 223–25.

48. *Lib.*, 15 October and 24 March 1844, also 4 June 1841, 23 February 1844; MASS, *Ninth Annual Report . . . 1841* (Boston, 1841), 7–9; Pillsbury, *Acts of the Anti-Slavery Apostles*, 288–89; Friedman, *Gregarious Saints*, 257–58.

49. *Lib.*, 17 July 1840, 4 June 1841, 23 February and 1 March 1844; William L. Garrison to J. B. Yerrington, 7 May 1844, *Garrison Letters*, 2:256–57; Pillsbury, *Acts of the Anti-Slavery Apostles*, 97–99, 116–17, 172.

50. MASS, *Eleventh Annual Report . . . 1843*, 95.

51. *Lib.*, 24 May 1844; *NASS*, 16 and 23 May 1844; Kraditor, *Means and Ends*, 200; Merrill, *Against Wind and Tide*, 205.

52. *Lib.*, 6 June 1840, 9 January 1841; *NASS*, 14 September 1843, 23 March and 20 April 1844; MASS, *Eighth Annual Report . . . 1840*, xxviii–xxx, and *Tenth Annual Report . . . 1842* (Boston, 1842), 7; Pennsylvania Anti-Slavery Society, *Thirteenth Annual Report, Presented to the Pennsylvania State Anti-Slavery Society, by Its Executive Committee, October 15, 1850* (Philadelphia, 1850), 49–50; Kraditor, *Means and Ends*, 16, 108; Thomas, *The Liberator*, 318–23; Gamble, "Moral Suasion in the West," 137–38.

53. The negative assessment of Garrisonian effectiveness is most strongly stated in Barnes, *Antislavery Impulse*, 92, 173–75; Dumond, *Antislavery*, 283–85; Thomas, *The Liberator*, 232; Mabee, *Black Freedom*, 222; Pease and Pease, *Bound with Them in Chains*, 26–27; Thomas, "Romantic Reform in America," 673. The more positive appraisal of the post-1840 political activities of the AASS can be found in Kraditor, *Means and Ends*, 7–16, 78–79, 102–6; Sorin, *Abolitionism*, 73–76, 89; Stewart, *Holy Warriors*, 107–8, 112–13; Walters, *Antislavery Appeal*, 130–43.

54. *Lib.*, 6 July 1849, 21 April 1854; AASS, *Annual Report . . . 1855* (New York, 1855), 143–44, and *Second Decade*, 31–32; MASS, *Thirteenth Annual Report . . . 1845*, 57–58; May, *Some Recollections*, 335–37; Stange, *Patterns of Antislavery*, 46–59; Gamble, "Moral Suasion in the West," 359–60, 368–69, 396.

55. *Lib.*, 20 May 1853, 6 October 1854, 9 March 1855; MASS, *Fourteenth Annual Report . . . 1846* (Boston, 1846), 39, 73–74, *Twentieth Annual Report . . . 1852* (Boston, 1852), 49–50; and *Twenty-fourth Annual Report . . . 1856* (Boston, 1856), 59; William L. Garrison to Helen E. Garrison, 13 May 1857, 12 May 1859, *Garrison Letters*, 4:438–39 and 625, respectively; Pillsbury, *Acts of the Anti-Slavery Apostles*, 2–4.

56. *Lib.*, 21 May 1847; Frederick Douglass to the Editor of the *Belfast Protestant Journal*, 23 July 1846; Frederick Douglass to William L. Garrison, 18 April 1846, both in Frederick Douglass Papers, Manuscript Divison, Library of Congress (hereafter cited as Douglass Papers); Fladeland, *Men and Brothers*, 296–301.

Chapter 4. *Church-Oriented Abolitionism and the Sectional Schism in the American Churches*

1. Examples of such historical accounts are: Craven, *Coming of the Civil War*, 201; Randall and Donald, *Civil War and Reconstruction*, 25–26; Ahlstrom, *Religious History of the American People*, 657; Simms, *Emotion at High Tide*, 212; Elkins, *Slavery*, 184–85; Dunham, *Attitude of Northern Clergy*, 1–2; H. Shelton Smith, Robert T. Handy, and Lefferts A. Loetscher, *American Christianity*, 2 vols. (New York, 1963), 2:178; Donald G. Jones, *The Sectional Crisis and Northern Methodism: A Study in Piety, Political Ethics, and Civil Religion* (Metuchen, N.J., 1979), 30–33; Niebuhr, *Social Sources of Denominationalism*, 191–99; Pope, "Negro and Religion in America," 17–25; Sweet, "Kansas Struggle," 578–81; Donald G. Mathews, "The Methodist Schism of 1844 and the Popularization of Antislavery Sentiment," *Mid-America: An Historical Review* 51 (January 1968): 17–19.

2. Pillsbury, *Church as It Is*, 46.

3. AFASS, *Thirteenth Annual Report . . . 1853* (New York, 1853), 97.

4. Wyatt-Brown, *Lewis Tappan*, 198, 248–49; Richard H. Sewell, *Ballots for Freedom: Antislavery Politics in the United States, 1837–1860* (New York, 1976), 108; Walters, *Antislavery Appeal*, 3, 7.

5. Barnes, *Antislavery Impulse*, 176; Dumond, *Antislavery*, 265–86.

6. Kraditor, *Means and Ends*, 16–18, 78; Dumond, *Antislavery*, 287.

7. Kraditor, *Means and Ends*, 107–8; Wyatt-Brown, *Lewis Tappan*, 193; Dillon, *The Abolitionists*, 125–26.

8. *Herald and Philanthropist* (Cincinnati), 23 June 1841 (hereafter cited as *Philanthropist*); Wyatt-Brown, *Lewis Tappan*, 248–49; Barnes, *Antislavery Impulse*, 169–70; Abzug, *Passionate Liberator*, 217–19; Perkal, "William Goodell," 182; Maurice D. Ndukwu, "Antislavery in Michigan: A Study of Its Origin, Development, and Expansion from Territorial Period to 1860" (Ph.D. diss., Michigan State University, 1979), 47–48; Evans, "Abolitionism in Illinois Churches," 59–62.

9. *Eman.*, 18 February 1841; also Fladeland, *James G. Birney*, 175; Barnes, *Antislavery Impulse*, 176.

10. Lewis Tappan to William Jay, 9 September 1843, Tappan Papers; Friedman, *Gregarious Saints*, 90–93.

11. *Eman.*, 20 May and 16 December 1841, 10 February 1842; Tappan Diary, 9 June 1841; Lewis Tappan to Gerrit Smith, 9 September 1843, Tappan Papers; Friedman, *Gregarious Saints*, 89–94; Phyllis M. Bannan, "Arthur and Lewis Tappan: A Study of Religious and Reform Movements in New York City" (Ph.D. diss., Columbia University, 1950), 142.

12. *AFAS Reporter*, September 1841, 31–32; June 1841, n.p.; September 1842, 6–7; November 1844, n.p.; July 1845, 46; AFASS, *Eighth Annual Report . . . 1848* (New York, 1848), 10–15; Friedman, *Gregarious Saints*, 89–93.

13. Pease and Pease, *They Who Would Be Free*, 81–82; Mabee, *Black Freedom*, 104, 106.

14. *Eman.*, 20 March 1841, 9 June 1842; *AFAS Reporter*, June 1840, 1–4; July 1840, 9; June 1842, 53; July 1845, 45–47; Samuel D. Hastings to Lewis Tappan, 25

May 1840, Tappan Papers; Tappan Diary, 17 May 1840; Joshua Leavitt to "Dear Brother," 1 July 1840, Leavitt Family Papers, Manuscript Division, Library of Congress; Executive Committee of the American and Foreign Anti-Slavery Society, printed circular, November 1845, American Missionary Association Manuscripts, Amistad Research Center (hereafter cited as AMA MSS).

15. Three positive appraisals of Lewis Tappan's abolitionist career are: Wyatt-Brown, *Lewis Tappan;* Bannon, "Arthur and Lewis Tappan"; and Friedman, *Gregarious Saints*, 68–95.

16. *Eman.,* 25 February 1841; *Lib.,* 12 June 1840; also *AFAS Reporter,* November 1844, 13; Amos A. Phelps to Lewis Tappan, 1 April 1841, Tappan Papers; William L. Garrison to Elizabeth Pease, 1 March 1841, *Garrison Letters,* 3:16–17.

17. Lewis Tappan to Samuel D. Hastings, 28 May 1840, Tappan Papers; also Lewis Tappan to Charles G. Finney, 24 December 1843, Robert S. Fletcher Collection, Oberlin College Archives (hereafter cited as Fletcher Collection).

18. Lewis Tappan to Mrs. L. E. Sturge, 10 July 1855, Tappan Papers; also *Eman.,* 3 June 1846; *American Jubilee* 1 (February 1855): 75; *NASS,* 21 May 1855, 26 May 1859; *Lib.,* 15 June 1860; William Jay, *Miscellaneous Writings on Slavery* (Boston, 1853), 634; Goodell, *Slavery and Anti-Slavery,* 514–16, 553, 557–58; Lewis Tappan to F. J. LeMoyne, 26 December 1849, Carter G. Woodson Collection, Manuscript Division, Library of Congress (hereafter cited as Woodson Collection); William Jay to Lewis Tappan, 8 February 1847, Tappan Papers; Bayard Tuckerman, *William Jay and the Constitutional Movement for the Abolition of Slavery* (1893; reprint, New York, 1969), 147–48.

19. *Lib.,* 2 July 1852; *National Era* (Washington, D.C.), 10 June 1852; Lewis Tappan to Salmon P. Chase, 23 June 1847, Salmon P. Chase Papers, Historical Society of Pennsylvania, Philadelphia (hereafter cited as Chase Papers); John G. Whittier to H. I. Bowditch, 26 August 1846, John G. Whittier Papers, Manuscript Division, Library of Congress (hereafter cited as Whittier Papers); Arthur S. Bolster, Jr., *James Freeman Clarke: Disciple to Advancing Truth* (Boston, 1954), 233–34.

20. AFASS, *An Address to the Anti-Slavery Christians of the United States* (New York, 1852), 15; Lewis Tappan to John Tappan, 13 September 1843; Amos A. Phelps to Lewis Tappan, 9 October 1843, both in Tappan Papers; Pease and Pease, *Bound with Them in Chains,* 237–38.

21. *Church Review and Ecclesiastical Register* 5 (October 1852): 471–72; *Presbyterian Expositor* 1 (December 1857): 19–20; *New York Observer,* 12 May 1849; *Congregationalist,* 21 June 1850; *Zion's Herald* (Boston), 1 June 1859.

22. *AFAS Reporter,* July 1841, 6; also March 1843, 133.

23. *Philanthropist,* 15 June 1842; also *AFAS Reporter,* June 1842, 52–53; August 1845, n.p.; September 1841, 31; *Liberty Almanac for 1849* (New York, 1848), 18.

24. *Eman.,* 20 May 1841; *AFAS Reporter,* July 1841, 8–9; also July 1845, 45–47.

25. AFASS, *Tenth Annual Report . . . 1850* (New York, 1850), 11; *Twelfth Annual Report . . . 1852* (New York, 1852), 19; *Thirteenth Annual Report . . . 1853,* 180–81; *Liberty Almanac for 1849,* 18; Lewis Tappan to Mrs. L. T. Phelps, 31 December 1854; Lewis Tappan to Richard H. Storrs, 23 April 1852, both in Tappan Papers; Tuckerman, *William Jay,* 145–46; Mabee, *Black Freedom,* 127.

26. *AFAS Reporter*, May 1846, 8; *Eman.*, 18 November 1846; *Liberty Almanac for 1848* (New York, 1847), n.p.; *Union Missionary* 1 (May 1844): 8; AFASS, *Tenth Annual Report . . . 1850*, 22; *Twelfth Annual Report . . . 1852*, 9; and *Address to the Anti-Slavery Christians*, 10–11; Jay, *Miscellaneous Writings*, 426–27, 635; Lewis Tappan to Joseph Soule, 30 April 1844; Horace Bushnell to Lewis Tappan, 9 August 1850; John Scoble to Lewis Tappan, 6 June 1851; William Jay to Lewis Tappan, 1 October 1851, all in Tappan Papers; Lewis Tappan to Scoble, 14 November 1847, in Annie Heloise Abel and Frank J. Klingberg, eds., *A Side-Light on Anglo-American Relations, 1839–1858* (Lancaster, Pa., 1927), 226–28; Wyatt-Brown, *Lewis Tappan*, 315–17; Schriver, *Go Free*, 40–41; Bannan, "Arthur and Lewis Tappan," 150.

27. AFASS, *Address to the Anti-Slavery Christians*, 10–11; Abel and Klingberg, *Side-Light on Anglo-American Relations*, 262–64; Wyatt-Brown, *Lewis Tappan*, 199, 315; Fladeland, *Men and Brothers*, 285–86; Bannan, "Arthur and Lewis Tappan," 151–52.

28. *AFAS Reporter*, September 1840, 28; also *Anti-Slavery Record* 3 (April 1837): 105 and (September 1837): 9–10; *Friend of Man* (Utica, N.Y.), 23 September 1840; *Christian Investigator* February 1842, n.p.

29. C. Bruce Staiger, "Abolitionism and the Presbyterian Schism of 1837–1838," *MVHR* 36 (December 1949): 402, 405, 408–9. This interpretation is accepted by Dillon, *The Abolitionists*, 60; Filler, *Crusade against Slavery*, 185–86; Smith, *Revivalism and Social Reform*, 185–86; James E. Johnson, "Charles G. Finney and a Theology of Revivalism," *Church History* 38 (September 1969): 338–58; Engelder, "Churches and Slavery," 339–40.

30. Murray, *Presbyterians and the Negro*, 109; Christie and Dumond, *George Bourne*, 57–64.

31. *Biblical Repository and Princeton Review* 21 (October 1845): 586, 606; also AASS, *Sixth Annual Report . . . 1839* (New York, 1839), 69–70; Goodell, *Slavery and Anti-Slavery*, 156; Murray, *Presbyterians and the Negro*, 106–11; Edward B. Welsh, ed., *Buckeye Presbyterianism* (n.p., 1968), 128–29; Howard, "Anti-Slavery Movement in the Presbyterian Church," 129–33.

32. *AFAS Reporter*, September 1841, 25; November 1844, 14; and July 1845, 44; *Eman.*, 28 July 1842; *Philanthropist*, 23 June 1841; *Lib.*, 30 May 1845; Engelder, "Churches and Slavery," 236–39; Howard, "Anti-Slavery Movement in the Presbyterian Church," 59; Stewart, "Chillicothe Presbytery," 54–56.

33. Quoted in Howard, "Anti-Slavery Movement in the Presbyterian Church," 134; also Robinson, *Testimony and Practice*, 34–39; B. M. Palmer, *The Life and Letters of James Henley Thornwell, D.D.* (Richmond, Va., 1875), 286.

34. *AFAS Reporter*, July 1840, 14–15; December 1840, 77; September 1841, 31; and November 1844, 11; *Eman.*, 6 September 1838; *Friend of Man*, 11 November 1840; *New York Observer*, 13 June 1846; MASS, *Twelfth Annual Report . . . 1844* (Boston, 1844), 58; Jonathan Blanchard to Henry Cowles, 3 September 1840, Henry Cowles Papers, Oberlin College Archives (hereafter cited as Cowles Papers); Samuel D. Hastings to Lewis Tappan, 26 May 1840, Tappan Papers; Muelder, *Fighters for Freedom*, 282; Engelder, "Churches and Slavery," 216–22; Howard, "Anti-Slavery Movement in the Presbyterian Church," 83–106.

35. *New York Observer*, 4 July 1846.

36. *NASS*, 13 July 1843; Goodell, *Slavery and Anti-Slavery*, 152–55; Pillsbury, *Church as It Is*, 23.

37. Quoted in Goodell, *Slavery and Anti-Slavery*, 144–50.

38. Engelder, "Churches and Slavery," 113–36.

39. *Watchman and Wesleyan Observer* (New York), 10 October 1840; *AFAS Reporter*, September 1840, 36; October 1840, n.p.; and January 1843, 119; *Friend of Man*, 8 April 1840, 28 September 1841; *Eman.*, 5 August 1841, 7 October 1841; *Philanthropist*, 30 June 1841, 27 October 1841; William G. Lewis, *Biography of Samuel Lewis* (Cincinnati, 1857), 306–307; Mathews, *Slavery and Methodism*, 217–18; Donald G. Mathews, "The Abolitionists on Slavery: The Critique behind the Social Movement," *JSH* 33 (May 1967): 172–73.

40. *AFAS Reporter*, June 1840, 8; July 1840, 13; September 1840, 36; November 1840, 69; and January 1843, 119; *Eman.*, 7 October 1841; *Friend of Man*, 4 December 1839, 28 September 1841; James G. Birney Diary, 22 April 1842, James G. Birney Papers, Manuscript Division, Library of Congress; Lewis, *Samuel Lewis*, 306–307, 338–39, 356–58.

41. Lucius C. Matlack, *The Life of Reverend Orange Scott* (New York, 1847), 213; also *Lib.*, 17 July 1840; *Eman.*, 29 July 1841; Lucius C. Matlack, *Narrative of the Anti-Slavery Experience of a Minister in the Methodist Episcopal Church . . . Deprived of License to Preach for Being an Abolitionist* (Philadelphia, 1845), 22–23; Mathews, *Slavery and Methodism*, 229.

42. *True Wesleyan* (New York), 13 January 1844, also 20 January and 25 May 1844; *Friend of Man*, 26 August 1840, 1 June and 6 July 1841; LaRoy Sunderland to Francis Wright, 2 October 1843, Miscellaneous Manuscripts Collection, Library of Congress; Goodell, *Slavery and Anti-Slavery*, 490; Smith, *In His Image But . . .*, 107; J. R. Jacob, "LaRoy Sunderland: The Alienation of an Abolitionist," *Journal of American Studies* 6 (April 1972): 1–9; Engelder, "Churches and Slavery," 142–43; Ndukwu, "Antislavery in Michigan," 159–62.

43. *True Wesleyan*, 24 February and 2 March 1844.

44. *Christian Witness and Western Reserve Advocate* (Cuyahoga Falls, Ohio), 7 September and 28 December 1843.

45. Ibid., 9 January and 30 April 1844; Lee, *Autobiography*, 251–52; Cameron, *Methodism and Society*, 170–71; Mathews, *Slavery and Methodism*, 263.

46. Thomas B. Neely, *American Methodism: Its Divisions and Unification* (New York, 1915), 69–70; Lyons, "Religious Defense of Slavery," 16–17; John N. Norwood, "The Schism in the Methodist Episcopal Church, 1844: A Study of Slavery and Ecclesiastical Politics" (Ph.D. diss., Cornell University, 1915), 130–31.

47. Hiram Mattison, *The Impending Crisis of 1860; or, The Present Connection of the Methodist Episcopal Church with Slavery, and Our Duty in Regard to It* (New York, 1859), 40–42; Powell, "Abolitionist Controversy in the Methodist Episcopal Church," 171–76. For a different assessment of these events see Mathews, "Methodist Schism of 1844," 17–19, and *Slavery and Methodism*, 269–70.

48. *True Wesleyan*, 15 June, and 4 May, 22 June, 27 July, and 3 August 1844; Mathews, *Slavery and Methodism*, 269–70.

49. MASS, *Fourteenth Annual Report . . . 1846*, 68; also *Thirteenth Annual Report . . . 1845*, 52–53; *Lib.*, 21 June 1844, 15 August 1845; Pillsbury *Church as It Is*, 130.

50. *Liberty Standard* (Hallowell, Maine), n.d., quoted in *True Wesleyan*, 29 June 1844; also Lewis Tappan to William Jay, 14 June 1844, Tappan Papers.

51. *Friend of Man*, 24 August 1841; also *Eman.*, 27 February and 12 March 1840, 9 December 1841, 19 May and 30 June 1842; *Baptist Anti-Slavery Correspondent* 1 (March 1841): 46; Andrew T. Foss and Edward Mathews, *Facts for Baptist Churches, Collected, Arranged and Received by A. T. Foss, of New Hampshire, and E. Mathews, of Wisconsin* (Utica, N.Y., 1850), 44–49.

52. *AFAS Reporter*, June 1840, 2, 8; December 1840, 79; May 1841, 169; September 1841, 30–31; and June 1842, 56; *Friend of Man*, 20 April, 20 July, 24 August, and 7 September 1841; *Eman.*, 13 May and 9 December 1841, 30 June 1842; *Lib.*, 28 May and 22 October 1841; Lewis Tappan to William H. Brisbane, 17 December 1842, Tappan Papers; Edwin R. Warren, *Free Missionary Principle; or, Bible Missions: A Plea for Separate Missionary Action from Slaveholders*, 2d ed. (Boston, 1847), 10; Foster, *Brotherhood of Thieves*, 52–55.

53. *American Baptist Memorial* 3 (June 1844): 185; also *Christian Reflector* (Boston), 14 May 1844, 25 June 1846; Putnam, *Baptists and Slavery*, 55–59.

54. *Baptist Memorial and Monthly Record* 4 (May 1845): 157.

55. American Baptist Home Missionary Society, *Thirteenth Annual Report . . . 1845* (New York, 1845), 7; also *Twelfth Annual Report . . . 1844* (New York, 1844), 5–6; *American Baptist Memorial* 3 (June 1844): 173–76.

56. Francis Wayland to James Hoby, 17 December 1845, Wayland Papers; also *Baptist Missionary Magazine* 25 (July 1845): 150; *Christian Secretary* (Hartford), 28 November 1845; Goodell, *Slavery and Anti-Slavery*, 503–5.

57. American Baptist Home Missionary Society, *Thirteenth Annual Report . . . 1845*, 7; *American Baptist Memorial* 3 (June 1844): 173–76; *Christian Reflector*, 8 May 1845; Putnam, *Baptists and Slavery*, 38–42, 48–51.

58. American Baptist Home Missionary Society, *Fourteenth Annual Report . . . 1846* (New York, 1846), 6; *Fifteenth Annual Report . . . 1847* (New York, 1847), 38; and *Sixteenth Annual Report . . . 1848* (New York, 1848), 4; Foss and Mathews, *Facts for Baptist Churches*, 171–80.

59. Quoted in Cyrus Pitt Grosvenor, *A Review of the Correspondence of Messrs. Fuller and Wayland on the Subject of American Slavery* (Utica, N.Y., 1847), 134–35; *Christian Watchman* (Boston), 14 November 1845, 19 June 1846; *Cross and Journal* (Cincinnati), n.d., quoted in *Christian Reflector*, 26 June 1848; *Christian Secretary*, 5 December 1845; *Eman.*, 14 January 1846; Goodell, *Slavery and Anti-Slavery*, 507; Torbet, *History of the Baptists*, 284–86; Justin A. Smith, *A History of the Baptists in the Western States East of the Mississippi* (Philadelphia, 1896), 334–35; Rufus Babcock, *Memoir of John Mason Peck, D.D.* (Philadelphia, 1864), lxvi–lxvii.

60. *AFAS Reporter*, July 1845, 42; also *Lib.*, 12 May and 16 June 1843, 31 May and 27 September 1844; *Christian Reflector*, 27 November 1845; ABFMS, *Report . . . 1847* (Utica, N.Y., 1847), 28; Justin A. Smith, *Memoir of Reverend*

Nathaniel Colver (Boston, 1875), 195–200; Warren, *Free Missionary Principle*, 11–12; Putnam, *Baptists and Slavery*, 57.

61. AFASS, *Thirteenth Annual Report . . . 1853*, 97; *AFAS Reporter*, September 1844, 5–6, and July 1845, 42; Amos A. Phelps to Lewis Tappan, 2 September 1844, Tappan Papers; Goodell, *Slavery and Anti-Slavery*, 503–8.

62. *Lib.*, 17 May 1844, 15 August 1845; MASS, *Fourteenth Annual Report . . . 1846*, 70–71; Foster, *Brotherhood of Thieves*, 52.

63. *Western Christian Advocate* (Cincinnati), 13 September, 4 and 11 October 1844; *Christian Watchman*, 14 November 1845, 19 June 1846; *Christian Reflector*, 20 November and 11 December 1845, 2 January and 28 May 1846; *Christian Secretary*, 5 December 1846; [Methodist Episcopal Church], *Journal of the General Conference of the Methodist Episcopal Church* (New York, 1844), 199–222; George Peck, *Slavery and Episcopacy: Being an Examination of Dr. Bascom's Review* (New York, 1845), 111; Mathews, *Slavery and Methodism*, 263–68; Friedman, " 'Historical Topics Sometimes Run Dry,' " 188–91.

64. "Oberlin Congregational Church Records," 22 April and 12 August 1846, Typescript in Fletcher Collection; MASS, *Fourteenth Annual Report . . . 1846*, 72–73; Muelder, *Fighters for Freedom*, 273; Matthew Spinka, ed., *A History of Illinois Congregational and Christian Churches* (Chicago, 1944), 147; Irving H. Bartlett, *Wendell Phillips: Brahmin Radical* (Boston, 1961), 96; Pearson, "From Church to Denomination," 74.

65. MASS, *Fourteenth Annual Report . . . 1846*, 69; *Lib.*, 15 August 1845; William L. Garrison to Samuel J. May, 13 January 1850, *Garrison Letters*, 4:3–5.

Chapter 5. *Abolitionists and the Comeouter Sects*

1. Revelations 18:4; also *Christian Investigator* 3 (March 1843): 12; Fee, *Non-Fellowship with Slaveholders*, 37–38.

2. *Lib.*, 5 February and 26 March 1847, 18 June 1852, 2 February and 9 March 1855; *NASS*, 22 May 1845; *Pennsylvania Freeman*, 30 October 1851; AASS, *Annual Report . . . 1859–60* (Boston, 1861), 278–80; MASS, *Twenty-first Annual Report . . . 1853* (Boston, 1853), 89; Pennsylvania Anti-Slavery Society, *Thirteenth Annual Report . . . 1850*, 45–50; Phillips, *Philosophy of the Abolition Movement*, 22–23; Perry, *Radical Abolitionism*, 106–8.

3. *True Wesleyan*, 26 October 1844; *Free Presbyterian* (Mercer, Pa., Albany and Yellow Springs, Ohio) 7 September 1853, 5 November 1856.

4. AFASS, *Ninth Annual Report . . . 1849* (New York, 1849), 84, and *Address to the Anti-Slavery Christians*, 10; *AFAS Reporter*, September 1840, 28.

5. Mabee, *Black Freedom*, 226–27; Tuckerman, *William Jay*, 147–48; Evans, "Abolitionism in Illinois Churches," 78–79.

6. Matlack, *Antislavery Struggle*, 140–45; Murray, *Presbyterians and the Negro*, 118–21; Evans, "Abolitionism in Illinois Churches," 57, 65.

7. A contemporary religious movement that should not be confused with antislavery comeouterism was the founding of "Free Churches" in East Coast cities in the 1830s. Though "free" in the sense of having a more democratic form of local church government, these congregations affiliated with neighboring Presbyterians. Although such abolitionists as Arthur and Lewis Tappan hoped to make the Free Church models of nondiscriminatory and antislavery religious practices, these bodies attracted membership primarily because they introduced evangelical preaching styles into conservative eastern Presbyterianism and Congregationalism. Ironically, these progressive ventures became so resistant to antislavery reforms that abolitionists eventually abandoned them. Wyatt-Brown, *Lewis Tappan,* 178–79; Bannan, "Arthur and Lewis Tappan," 175–76.

8. *Lib.,* 17 July 1840; *Christian Investigator* 3 (March 1843): 15–16 and (October 1843): 72; 6 (March 1846): 306; A. H. Plumb to William Goodell, 5 January 1847; William Goodell to Clarissa Goodell, 25 January 1845, both in William Goodell Papers, Oberlin College Archives (hereafter cited as Goodell Papers); Goodell, *Slavery and Anti-Slavery,* 454; Friedman, *Gregarious Saints,* 107–9; Cross, *Burned-over District,* 278–81; Perkal, "William Goodell," 167–68, 188.

9. Lewis Tappan to William Goodell, 30 October 1843; also Lewis Tappan to Gerrit Smith, 13 January 1844; Lewis Tappan to John Morgan, 25 March 1840, all in Tappan Papers; *Lib.,* 31 July and 16 October 1840; *Eman.,* 18 February 1841; *Christian Investigator* 6 (March 1846): 306; Friedman, *Gregarious Saints,* 108–9; Perkal, "William Goodell," 167–68, 172–73; Alan Morton Kraut, "The Liberty Men of New York: Political Abolitionism in New York State, 1840–1848" (Ph.D. diss., Cornell University, 1975), 286–87, 380.

10. *True Wesleyan,* 25 May 1844, 5 July 1851; *National Principia* (New York), 23 June 1860; Ira Ford McLeister and Roy Nicholson, *History of the Wesleyan Methodist Church in America,* 3d ed. (Marion, Ind., 1959), 41; Jacobs, "LaRoy Sunderland," 1–2; Evans, "Abolitionism in Illinois Churches," 351–52; Engelder, "Churches and Slavery," 142–43.

11. *True Wesleyan,* 24 February 1844, 30 November 1849; *American Missionary Magazine* 3 (June 1859): 132; Timothy Stow to S. S. Jocelyn, 4 September 1855; S. N. Foster to Lewis Tappan, 13 June 1854; Luther Lee to S. S. Jocelyn, 20 March 1857; John Lowry to S. S. Jocelyn, 17 April 1857; P. Scewiner to George Whipple, 10 June 1857; James Dayton to Lewis Tappan, 17 May 1858; R. Bandriff to [AMA], 1 January 1860; John Johnson to [AMA], 1 February 1860; W. R. J. Clemens to Lucius Matlack, 15 May 1860; Lucius Matlack to S. S. Jocelyn, 11 October 1860, all in AMA MSS; Daniel Dorchester, *Christianity in the United States* (New York, 1888), 480–81; Ronald P. Formisano, *The Birth of Mass Political Parties: Michigan, 1827–1861* (Princeton, N.J., 1971), 170; Johnson, "American Missionary Association," 234–35.

12. *National Principia,* 7 April 1860, also 23 June 1860; *True Wesleyan,* 2 August and 8 November 1845; Orange Scott, *The Grounds of Secession from the M. E. Church; or, Book for the Times: Being an Examination of Her Connection with Slavery and Also of Her Form of Government* (New York, 1848), 65–66.

13. Lucius Matlack, *The History of American Slavery and Methodism from 1780 to 1849; and History of the Wesleyan Methodist Connection of America* (New York, 1849), 367–68; *Wesleyan* (Syracuse, N.Y.), 3 March and 1 September 1853, 7 October 1857, 28 March 1860; John P. Betker, *The M. E. Church and Slavery, as Described by Revs. H. Mattison, W. Hosmer, E. Bowen, D.D., D. DeVinne, and J. D. Long, with a Bible View of the Whole Subject* (Syracuse, N.Y., 1859), 31–32.

14. *Wesleyan,* 15 August 1860; also *True Wesleyan,* 4 May, 15 and 22 June, 27 July, and 3 August 1844; Lee, *Autobiography,* 170–71; Mathews, *Slavery and Methodism,* 269–70.

15. *True Wesleyan,* 24 February and 25 May 1844, 5 July 1851; *National Principia,* 23 June 1860; *American Missionary Magazine* 3 (June 1859): 132; McLeister and Nicholson, *Wesleyan Methodist Church in America,* 41; John L. Peters, *Christian Perfection and American Methodism* (New York, 1956), 125–27.

16. Scott, *Grounds of Secession,* n.p.; also Luther Lee, *Wesleyan Manual: A Defense of the Organization of the Wesleyan Methodist Connection* (Syracuse, N.Y., 1862), 125–26.

17. *True Wesleyan,* 21 December 1844; *Wesleyan,* 15 August 1860; *National Principia,* 7 April 1860; *Lib.* 23 February 1855; Matlack, *American Slavery and Methodism,* 367–68; Lee, *Autobiography,* 242–49, 272; McLeister and Nicholson, *Wesleyan Methodist Church,* 13–19. Clifton H. Johnson, "Abolitionist Missionary Activities in North Carolina," *North Carolina Historical Review* 40 (July 1963): 295–320.

18. *True Wesleyan,* 26 October 1844.

19. *NASS,* 22 May 1845; also Mathews, *Slavery and Methodism,* 232–33.

20. *Lib.,* 5 February and 26 March 1847, 18 June and 16 July 1852, 2 February 1855; Lee, *Autobiography,* 281; Merrill and Ruchames, *Garrison Letters,* 4:271–76; Gamble, "Moral Suasion in the West," 337–38.

21. *True Wesleyan,* 3 February 1844.

22. Ibid., 13 and 27 April 1844, 24 March, 7 July, and 10 November 1853; *American Jubilee* 1 (February 1855): 73–74; Scott, *Grounds of Secession,* 92–93; Lee, *Autobiography,* 218–30, 281; Matlack, *Narrative of Anti-Slavery Experience,* 17.

23. Applying a strict definition to the term *sect,* some historians have viewed the ABFMS as simply a denominational abolitionist society. See Evans, "Abolitionism in Illinois Churches," 301–5; and Kenneth R. Short, "New York Central College: A Baptist Experiment in Integrated Higher Education, 1848–1861," *Foundations* 5 (July 1962): 254–56.

24. *Christian Contributor* (Utica, N.Y.), 8 September and 17 November 1847; *American Baptist* (Utica, N.Y.), 7 July and 25 September 1851, 31 July 1856; *Free Mission Record* 1 (August 1857): 1; *Free Mission Tract* 1 (January 1853): 4; American Baptist Publication Society, *The Baptist Almanac for the Year of Our Lord, 1852* (Philadelphia, 1852), 43; Curtis Marshall, "Eleutherian College," *Indiana History Bulletin* 25 (November 1948): 201–2; Short, "New York Central College," 251–55; Litwack, *North of Slavery,* 141–42.

25. *Christian Contributor,* 30 December 1846; 9 June and 15 December 1847; 5 January, 14 June, and 6 December 1848; *American Baptist,* 1 August 1850, 29 May

and 27 November 1860; ABFMS, *Annual Reports: 1847*, 7; *1848*, 25; *1849*, 29–39; *1856*, 25; *1858*, 10; (Utica, N.Y.; dates vary); Foss and Mathews, *Facts for Baptist Churches*, 201–16, 308, 340–44; Warren, *Free Missionary Principle*, 19–21.

26. Warren, *Free Missionary Principle*, 47, also 25–37; *American Missionary* 3 (August 1849): 87.

27. *Christian Contributor*, 2 April 1846, 21 April 1847, 19 January, 15 March and 21 August 1848; ABFMS, *Annual Reports: 1853*, n.p.; *1847*, 5; *1850*, 30; *1852*, 17; *1859*, 6; *1860*, 18; Grosvenor, *Review of Correspondence of Fuller and Wayland*, 130–31, 134–35, 143–44; Samuel Aaron, *His Life, Sermons, Correspondence, Etc.* (Norristown, Pa., 1890), 31, 233; Foss and Mathews, *Facts for Baptist Churches*, 10.

28. *American Baptist*, 13 March 1851; ABFMS, *Annual Reports: 1848*, 25; *1850*, 20–21; and *1851*, 5–11; Edward Mathews, *The Autobiography of the Rev. E. Mathews, the "Father Dickson" of Mrs. Stowe's "Dred"* (1866; reprint, Miami, 1969), 332–430.

29. ABFMS, *Annual Report . . . 1857*, 2; also *American Missionary Magazine* 1 (September 1857): 213; William Goodell to J. J. Linton, 7 November 1856, American Abolition Society Letterbook and Records, Oberlin College Library (hereafter cited as AAS MSS).

30. *Lib.*, 9 March 1855; Merrill and Ruchames, *Garrison Letters*, 4:317.

31. Goodell, *Slavery and Anti-Slavery*, 508.

32. *American Missionary* 3 (August 1849): 87; also *Christian Contributor*, 28 October 1846, 10 February 1847, 10 May and 13 September 1848; *American Baptist*, 21 August and 16 October 1851, 12 February 1852, 14 June 1859, 30 October 1860; *National Era*, 22 April 1847; *Weekly Chronotype* (Boston), 3 June 1848; *Non-Slaveholder* 5 (August 1850): 175; *North Star* (Rochester, N.Y.), 28 January 1848; ABFMS, *Annual Reports: 1847*, 6–7, 19–20; *1860*, 12; AFASS, *Tenth Annual Report . . . 1850*, 60; *Eleventh Annual Report . . . 1851* (New York, 1851), 73; *Thirteenth Annual Report . . . 1853*, 123.

33. Gaius J. Slosser, ed., *They Seek a Country: The American Presbyterians* (New York, 1955), 221–22; Welsh, *Buckeye Presbyterianism*, 180–81.

34. *Free Presbyterian*, 18 and 25 February, 4 March 1857; AFASS, *Tenth Annual Report . . . 1850*, 42–43; *National Era*, 29 July and 30 December 1847; Free Presbyterian Board, *The Life and Writings of Reverend Joseph Gordon* (Cincinnati, 1860), 35–37.

35. *Free Presbyterian*, 10 August 1853, 17 May 1854, 23 April 1856, 29 April and 20 May 1857; *Free Church Portfolio* (New Castle, Pa.), 26 January, 6 September, and 13 December 1860; *Christian Press* (Cincinnati), 10 December 1852; *National Era*, 16 August 1849; A. L. Rankin to [AMA], 11 February 1858; William Perkins to S. S. Jocelyn, 2 February 1860, both in AMA MSS; John R. McKivigan, "Prisoner of Conscience: George Gordon and the Fugitive Slave Law," *Journal of Presbyterian History* 60 (Winter 1982), 339–40 (hereafter cited as "George Gordon"); Larry Gene Willey, "The Reverend John Rankin: Early Ohio Antislavery Leader" (Ph.D. diss., University of Iowa, 1976), 280–82; Evans, "Abolitionism in Illinois Churches," 224–30.

36. *Lib.*, 13 December 1861; also Murray, *Presbyterians and the Negro*, 125–26; McKivigan, "George Gordon," 336–54.

37. AFASS, *Tenth Annual Report . . . 1850*, 42–43; also *Free Presbyterian*, 11 February 1857; *National Era*, 7 September 1848; *Distinctive Principles of the Free Presbyterian Church of the United States* (Mercer, Pa., 1851), 4–5.

38. *Free Presbyterian*, 10 August and 19 October 1853, 17 May 1854, 18 February 1857; *Free Church Portfolio* 1 (December 1859): 382; 19 January 1860; *National Era*, 7 September 1848; George Gordon, *Secession from a Pro-Slavery Church a Christian Duty* (Mercer, Pa., 1850), 6–7, 27–31; Free Presbyterian Board, *Joseph Gordon*, 46–54, 99–100, 215–16, 257–61; *Distinctive Principles of Free Presbyterian Church*, 3–8, 15–16.

39. *Free Church Portfolio* 1 (December 1859): 359, 362; also Thomas Merrill to George Whipple, 4 August 1850, AMA MSS; AFASS, *Tenth Annual Report . . . 1850*, 31.

40. *Free Presbyterian*, 29 April 1857, also 11 February 1857, 27 June 1855; Slosser, *They Seek a Country*, 226–27, 251.

41. *Free Church Portfolio* 1 (December 1859): 372; J. H. Byrd to George Whipple, 30 July 1851; James Robertson to S. S. Jocelyn, 11 November 1856, both in AMA MSS; Edward B. Welsh, "Notes and Extracts on the Free Presbyterian Church," 3 vols. (Typescript, Presbyterian Historical Society, n.d.), 2:222, 230, 265; Howard E. Johnson, "The Free Presbyterian Church: A History of an Abolitionist Sect" (Senior independent study, Wooster College, 1970), 50–57.

42. AASS, *Annual Report . . . 1859–1860*, 278–80, 331; *Pennsylvania Freeman*, 30 October 1851; *Radical Abolitionist* 1 (March 1856): 59.

43. *Lib.*, 8 April 1853; also *Free Presbyterian*, 7 September 1853, 5 November 1856; Free Presbyterian Board, *Joseph Gordon*, 307; Slosser, *They Seek a Country*, 229–30; Paul R. Grim, "The Reverend John Rankin, Early Abolitionist," *Ohio State Archaeological and Historical Quarterly* 46 (May 1937): 223–24.

44. *Lib.*, 8 April, 28 October 1853; Gamble, "Moral Suasion in the West," 316–17.

45. *National Era*, 3 January and 2 May 1850, 10 July 1851; *Non-Slaveholder* 5 (August 1850): 12; *Free Presbyterian*, 10 and 24 August 1853; *The Liberty Almanac for 1852* (New York, 1851), 25; Willey, "John Rankin," 262–72.

46. Quoted in Abdel R. Wentz, *A Basic History of Lutheranism in America* (Philadelphia, 1955), 163, also 125, 141; *AFAS Reporter*, July 1840, 16; Nicholas Van Alstine to [AMA], 25 June 1853 and 22 November 1860, AMA MSS; Douglas C. Stange, *Radicalism for Humanity: A Study of Lutheran Abolitionism* (St. Louis, 1970), 5–6, 12–14, 32–33; Fortenbaugh, "American Lutheran Synods and Slavery," 73–76, 81–82, 90–91.

47. Coffin, *Reminiscences*, 231–36; Walter Edgerton, *A History of the Separation in the Indiana Yearly Meeting of Friends, Which Took Place in the Winter of 1842 and 1843 on the Anti-Slavery Question* (Cincinnati, 1856), 47–74; Louis T. Jones, *The Quakers of Iowa* (Iowa City, 1914), 136, 144–45; Drake, *Quakers and Slavery*, 165;

John W. Buys, "An Ante-Bellum History of the Indiana Yearly Meeting of Friends" (Master's thesis, Purdue University, 1968), 65–66.

48. Edgerton, *Separation in Indiana*, 98, also 77–78, 99, 201–2.

49. *NASS*, 27 October 1842; AFASS, *Thirteenth Annual Report* . . . *1853*, 103–4; Lewis Tappan to Joseph Sturge, 31 March 1846, Tappan Papers; Coffin, *Reminiscences*, 232–33; Goodell, *Slavery and Anti-Slavery*, 491; Mabee, *Black Freedom*, 225; Drake, *Quakers and Slavery*, 167–68; Aptheker, "Quakers and Negro Slavery," 361; Buys, "Indiana Yearly Meeting of Friends," 67–80.

50. Joseph A. Dugdale, *Extemporaneous Discourses* (Poughkeepsie, N.Y., 1850), 21; also *National Era*, 25 May 1857; Oliver Johnson to Theodore Parker, 4 April 1857, Theodore Parker Papers, Manuscript Division, Library of Congress (hereafter cited as Parker Papers); Child, *Isaac T. Hopper*, 392–96; Drake, *Quakers and Slavery*, 160, 174–76; Buys, "Indiana Yearly Meeting of Friends," 65; Gamble, "Moral Suasion in the West," 359–60.

51. William L. Garrison to J. Miller McKim, 11 September 1858, *Garrison Letters*, 4:553; also *Lib.*, 21 April 1854, 1 June 1855; AASS, *Second Decade*, 31–32; S. S. Foster to A. K. Foster, 14 September 1855, Abigail Kelley Foster and Stephen S. Foster Papers, American Antiquarian Society, Worcester, Mass.

52. E. Franklin Frazier, *The Negro Church in America* (New York, 1964), 1–19; Litwack, *North of Slavery*, 194–95; Sorin, *Abolitionism*, 101–3; Scherer, *Slavery and the Churches*, 144–49; Vincent Harding, "Religion and Resistance among Antebellum Negroes, 1800–1860," in *The Making of Black America*, ed. August Meier and Elliot Rudwick (New York, 1969), 179–97; Carol V. R. George, "Widening the Circle: The Black Church and the Abolitionist Crusade, 1830–1860," in *Antislavery Reconsidered: New Perspectives on the Abolitionists*, ed. Lewis Perry and Michael Fellman (Baton Rouge, 1979), 75–95.

53. Daniel A. Payne, *History of the African Methodist Episcopal Church* (Nashville, 1891), 334–45; William J. Walls, *The African Methodist Episcopal Zion Church: Reality of the Black Church* (Charlotte, N.C., 1974), 138–71; Carol V. R. George, *Segregated Sabbaths: Richard Allen and the Emergence of Independent Black Churches, 1760–1840* (New York, 1973), 135–40, 144–59; George, "Widening the Circle," 86–90, 93–95.

54. ABMC, *Thirteenth Annual Report* . . . *1853* (Boston, 1853), 9; also *Ninth Annual Report* . . . *1849* (Boston, 1849), 5; *Fourteenth Annual Report* . . . *1854* (Boston, 1854), 15; *Seventeenth Annual Report* . . . *1857* (Boston, 1857), 13; *Nineteenth Annual Report* . . . *1859* (Boston, 1859), n.p.; *Twentieth Annual Report* . . . *1860* (Boston, 1860), 14; Mechal Sobel, *Trabelin' On: The Slave Journey to an Afro-Baptist Faith* (Westport, Conn., 1979), 191, 217, 364–66; Lewis G. Jordan, *Negro Baptist History, U.S.A., 1750–1930* (Nashville, 1930), 66–87; Litwack, *North of Slavery*, 195; Gravely, "Christian Abolitionism," 18.

55. Pease and Pease, *They Who Would Be Free*, 81–82, 183; idem, *Bound with Them in Chains*, 142, 152–53; Benjamin Quarles, *Black Abolitionists* (New York, 1969), 69–70; Murray, *Presbyterians and the Negro*, 39–40; George, "Widening the Circle," 81–83.

56. Lewis Tappan to Richard S. Storrs, 13 February 1857, Tappan Papers; ABMC, *Twentieth Annual Report . . . 1860*, 14; Pease and Pease, *Bound with Them in Chains*, 157–58; idem, *They Who Would Be Free*, 81–82; Wyatt-Brown, *Lewis Tappan*, 292.

57. Bryan Wilson, *Religious Sects: A Sociological Study* (New York, 1970), 15, 36–46, 167; Strout, *New Heavens and New Earth*, 150–51, 162–63; J. Milton Yinger, "The Present Status of the Sociology of Religion," in *The Sociology of Religion: An Anthology*, ed. Richard D. Knudten (New York, 1967), 30–31.

58. Murray, *Presbyterians and the Negro*, 126; Evans, "Abolitionism in Illinois Churches," 60, 89.

Chapter 6. *Abolitionism and the Benevolent Empire*

1. Griffin, *Their Brothers' Keepers*, vi–vii; Griffin, "The Abolitionists and the Benevolent Societies, 1831–1861," *Journal of Negro History* 44 (1959): 195–96; Thomas, "Romantic Reform in America," 657–59; Lois W. Banner, "Religious Benevolence as Social Control: A Critique of an Interpretation," *JAH* 60 (June 1973): 35–39; James L. McElroy, "Social Control and Romantic Reform in Antebellum America: The Case of Rochester, New York," *New York History* 58 (January 1977): 17–19; Singleton, "Protestant Voluntary Organizations," 550, 552–54.

2. Lewis Tappan to the Editor of the *British and Foreign Anti-Slavery Reporter*, in Abel and Klingberg, *Side-Light on Anglo-American Relations*, 320–21; *Union Missionary* 1 (August 1844): 19; *AFAS Reporter*, May 1845, 39; *American Missionary Magazine* 3 (January 1859): 313; AASS, *Annual Report . . . 1855*, 137–38; William Jay to Theodore Frelinghuysen, 10 October 1849, Tappan Papers; Gerrit Smith to Lewis Tappan, 27 February 1853; Pierpont Edwards to Lewis Tappan, 2 September 1861, both in AMA MSS; Cole, *Irrepressible Conflict*, 259; Griffin, "Abolitionists and the Benevolent Societies," 196–97.

3. Griffin, *Their Brothers' Keepers*, 162–63, 177–80; Ahlstrom, *Religious History of the American People*, 423, 451, 465–67, 859; Howard, "Anti-Slavery Movement in the Presbyterian Church," 63–66.

4. Quoted in Griffin, "Abolitionists and the Benevolent Societies," 203–5; also Johnson, "American Missionary Association," 41–42.

5. Lewis Tappan to John Scoble, 31 July 1844, in Abel and Klingberg, *Side-Light on Anglo-American Relations*, 187–88; Griffin, "Abolitionists and the Benevolent Societies," 204; Evans, "Abolitionism in Illinois Churches," 214.

6. *AFAS Reporter*, November 1842, 97; also July 1840, 12; October 1840, 53; December 1840, 79–80; October 1841, 43; January 1842, 52; September 1842, 81; "Extra," May 1843, 10–15; "Extra," April 1844, 2, 5; *Friend of Man*, 1 December 1840; *Eman.*, 12 August and 23 December 1841, 17 February 1842; Charles K. Whipple, *Relation of the American Board of Commissioners for Foreign Missions to Slavery* (Boston, 1861), 16–17, 19–24, 32; Thomas Lafon, *The Great Obstruction to the Conversion of Souls at Home and Abroad* (New York, 1843), 12–20; A. A. Phelps

to Henry Cowles, 4 November 1842, Cowles Papers; Lewis Tappan to John Tappan, 9 June 1845, Tappan Papers; Joshua Leavitt to editor of the *British and Foreign Anti-Slavery Reporter*, 1 April 1843, in Abel and Klingberg, *Side-Light on Anglo-American Relations*, 130.

7. Phelps was also the editor of the *AFAS Reporter*. *AFAS Reporter*, August 1845, 49–53, 56; *Union Missionary* 2 (October 1845): 25–28; Whipple, *American Board*, 32.

8. *AFAS Reporter*, October 1845, 65–66; January 1845, 92; *Eman.*, 19 November 1845; MASS, *Fourteenth Annual Report . . . 1846*, 74–75; Whipple, *American Board*, 45–47; Goodell, *Slavery and Anti-Slavery*, 207–8; Bacon, *Leonard Bacon*, 260–61; Robert T. Lewit, "Indian Missions and Antislavery Sentiment: A Conflict of Evangelical and Humanitarian Ideals," *MVHR* 50 (June 1963): 46–47.

9. MASS, *Fifteenth Annual Report . . . 1847* (Boston, 1847), 77; also *Fourteenth Annual Report . . . 1846*, 74–75, 94–95; *AFAS Reporter*, January 1846, 90–92; *Christian Investigator* January 1846, 290; *Eman.*, 10 October and 19 November 1845.

10. *AFAS Reporter*, January 1846, 89–92, 96; April 1846, 118; May 1846, 6; *New York Observer*, 5 September 1846; Ovid Miner to Thomas Lafon, 27 August 1846, AMA MSS; Lewis Tappan to G. W. Perkins, 8 August 1846; A. A. Phelps to Lewis Tappan, 27 February 1845, both in Tappan Papers; Whipple, *American Board*, 56; Perkal, "William Goodell," 174–75.

11. S. D. Hastings to Lewis Tappan, 21 May 1841, Tappan Papers; Wyatt-Brown, *Lewis Tappan*, 209, 212, 218–20.

12. *AFAS Reporter*, September 1842, 82, and November 1842, 98; *Union Missionary* 1 (October 1844): 29–30 and 3 (August 1846): 20; Tappan Diary, 27 May 1840; Wyatt-Brown, *Lewis Tappan*, 205–25; Pease and Pease, *They Who Would Be Free*, 81–82.

13. *Union Missionary* 1 (October 1844): 31; *NASS*, 23 June 1843; *American Missionary* 3 (June 1848): 66; West Indian Missionary Committee, *Quarterly Report*, February 1845, 17; Lewis Tappan to John Scoble, 31 July 1844, in Abel and Klingberg, *Side-Light on Anglo-American Relations*, 187–88; Lewis Tappan to R. R. Gillett, 27 September 1843, Tappan Papers; J. P. Bardwell to George Whipple, 1 September 1847; J. A. Thome to George Whipple, 16 May 1848, both in AMA MSS; Wyatt-Brown, *Lewis Tappan*, 292–93; Johnson, "American Missionary Association," 59–63.

14. Quoted in Bannan, "Arthur and Lewis Tappan," 181–83; also *Christian Investigator*, January 1846, 295–96 and September 1846: 359; *American Missionary* 2 (January 1848): 21; *American Missionary Magazine* 1 (July 1857): 149; George B. Cheever, *The Commission from God of the Missionary Enterprise against the Sin of Slavery, and the Responsibility on the Church and the Ministry for Its Fulfillment* (New York, 1858), 186; Henry Belden to George Whipple, 9 August 1850, AMA MSS; George L. Cady, *The American Missionary Association and the Churches of the Midwest before 1861* (n.p., 1936), 3; Johnson, "American Missionary Association," 81–96, 184–85; Perkal, "William Goodell," 177–82.

15. *American Missionary Magazine* 1 (November 1857): 1, 17–19 and 2 (November 1858): 5–8; *National Era*, 1 and 8 December 1859; AFASS, *Eleventh Annual*

Report . . . 1851, 64, and *Thirteenth Annual Report . . . 1853*, 122–23; *Liberty Almanac for 1851* (New York, 1850), 33; Andrew Benton to George Whipple, 11 June 1850; C. B. Boynton to George Whipple, 7 January 1851, and 19 August 1859; William Jay to William Harned, 4 September 1851; C. B. Boynton to Jonathan Blanchard, 22 December 1852; Lewis Tappan to Andrew Benton, 21 September 1853; E. M. Bartlett to [AMA], 18 November 1854; Gerrit Smith to George Whipple, 20 November 1855, all in AMA MSS; Augustus F. Beard, *A Crusade for Brotherhood: A History of the American Missionary Association* (Boston, 1909), 115–16; Wyatt-Brown, *Lewis Tappan*, 292–97; Johnson, "American Missionary Association," 99–114, 245–90; Lloyd V. Hennings, "The American Missionary Association: A Christian Antislavery Society" (Master's thesis, Oberlin College, 1933), 59–60.

16. Johnson, "American Missionary Association," 169–83, 203.

17. AFASS, *Seventh Annual Report . . . 1847* (New York, 1847), 24; George Whipple to F. J. LeMoyne, 14 September 1850, Woodson Collection; Tappan Diary, 21 November 1855; Lewis Tappan to J. S. Green, 28 November 1854; Lewis Tappan to William Allinson, 2 January 1855, both in Tappan Papers; Cheever, *Commission from God*, 185; William Goodell, *American Slavery a Formidable Obstacle to the Conversion of the World* (New York, 1854), 2.

18. *American Missionary* 2 (April 1847): 41; 3 (November 1848): 7; 4 (March 1849): 44 and (April 1849): 52; *American Missionary Magazine* 1 (May 1857): 109; 2 (January 1858): 13–14; 3 (September 1859): 208–9 and (October 1859): 227; 4 (March 1860): 60; *National Era*, 16 December 1858; John Rankin to George Whipple, 5 March 1853; E. E. Willis to S. S. Jocelyn, 29 September 1854; J. B. Walker to S. S. Jocelyn, 26 June 1856; J. P. Bardwell to Lewis Tappan, 2 September 1858; Theodore Tilton to Lewis Tappan, 20 December 1860; Henry Cowles to George Whipple, 16 November 1861; J. P. Bardwell to George Whipple, 2 December 1861, all in AMA MSS; Friedman, *Gregarious Saints*, 30; Fletcher M. Green, "Northern Missionary Activities in the South, 1846–1861," *JSH* 21 (May 1955): 161; Evans, "Abolitionism in Illinois Churches," 214.

19. L. H. Allen to Lewis Tappan, 29 November 1858; Amos Kingsbury to Lewis Tappan, 22 February 1859, both in AMA MSS; Johnson, "American Missionary Association," 279, 433–39.

20. *American Missionary* 2 (August 1847): 76–77 and 6 (August 1851): 78; *American Missionary Magazine* 1 (December 1857): 276 and 3 (October 1859): 225; *Oberlin Evangelist*, 3 July 1850; *Congregationalist*, 10 October 1851; *Church Review and Ecclesiastical Register* 13 (October 1860): 402–3; J. R. Johnson to George Whipple, 2 February 1852; E. D. Taylor to George Whipple, 30 August 1852; Joseph Hurlbut to S. S. Jocelyn, 7 May 1855; J. P. Bardwell to S. S. Jocelyn, 25 January 1856; T. R. Stackpole to Lewis Tappan, 25 July 1858, J. T. Addams to [AMA], 11 September 1858; James Underhill to J. G. Fee, 29 September 1858; A. A. Whitmore to S. S. Jocelyn, 7 February 1857; Edward Evans to Lewis Tappan, 27 August and 1 November 1858, all in AMA MSS; Edgar F. Raines, Jr., "The American Missionary Association in Southern Illinois, 1856–1862: A Case History in the Abolition Movement," *Journal of the Illinois State Historical Society* 65 (Autumn 1972): 246–68; Johnson,

"American Missionary Association," 32–35, 282–83, 433–39; Hennings, "American Missionary Association," 20–21; Evans, "Abolitionism in Illinois Churches," 214–15.

21. *American Missionary Magazine* 1 (November 1857): 3; also Johnson, "American Missionary Association," 565–66.

22. Ovid Miner to George Whipple, 26 January 1850; C. H. Thompson to S. S. Jocelyn, 3 September 1857; Benjamin Fern to S. S. Jocelyn, 21 May 1858; H. H. Garnet to S. S. Jocelyn, 14 September 1859, all in AMA MSS; Lewis Tappan to S. C. Pomeroy, 11 September 1858, Tappan Papers; Lawrence R. Murphy, *Antislavery in The Southwest: William G. Kephart's Mission to New Mexico, 1850–53* (El Paso, 1978), 5–50; Johnson, "American Missionary Association," 565–66; Bannan, "Arthur and Lewis Tappan," 184–85; Hennings, "American Missionary Association," 111–19, 127–28.

23. John G. Fee returned to Berea with the Union army in 1861, revived his church and school, and continued to battle for racial equality until his death in 1901. *American Missionary Magazine*, 4 (March 1860): 58; also 1 (March 1857): 66 and 1 (July 1857): 148; 4 (April 1860): 80–81, and (May 1860): 106, 108; J. A. R. Rogers to S. S. Jocelyn, 12 January 1860; J. G. Fee to S. S. Jocelyn, 31 July 1861, both in AMA MSS; Elizabeth S. Peck, *Berea's First Century, 1855–1955* (Lexington, Ky., 1955), 2–6; Todd Armstrong Reynolds, "The American Missionary Association's Antislavery Campaign in Kentucky, 1848 to 1860" (Ph.D. diss., Ohio State University, 1979), 42–58, 83–85, 166–78; Johnson, "American Missionary Association," 125–31.

24. *Lib.*, 13 March 1846 and 5 October 1849; AASS, *Annual Report . . . 1855*, 137–38; *Annual Report . . . 1856* (New York, 1856), 67; Whipple, *Relations of Anti-Slavery to Religion*, 5–6.

25. *Weekly Chronotype*, 3 December 1846; *Free Presbyterian*, 3 October 1855; W. B. Brown to George Whipple, 29 November 1847; M. E. Strieby to George Whipple, 22 February 1848, both in AMA MSS; Tappan Diary, 18 and 19 May 1854; MASS, *Nineteenth Annual Report . . . 1851* (Boston, 1851), 65–66.

26. *New York Observer*, 8 September 1849; *Presbyterian of the West* (Cincinnati), 8 October 1848, 12 July 1850; *Christian Watchman*, 9 March 1854; William Jay to Lewis Tappan, 18 March 1853, AMA MSS; Lewis Tappan to G. B. Cheever, 24 February 1856, Tappan Papers; William S. Kennedy, *The Plan of Union; or, A History of the Presbyterian and Congregational Churches in the Western Reserve* (Hudson, Ohio, 1856), 261–62; Muelder, *Fighters for Freedom*, 290–91.

27. *National Principia*, 4 February 1860; *American Missionary Magazine* 4 (March 1860): 60; AASS, *Nineteenth Annual Report . . . 1855*, 138; Lewis Tappan to W. W. Patton, 19 October 1854; Lewis Tappan to the Editor of the *Non-Conformist*, 23 November 1854, both in Tappan Papers; Lewis Tappan to L. A. Chamerovzov, 20 March 1855, in Abel and Klingberg, *Side-Light on Anglo-American Relations*, 355; Balme, *American States*, 319–20; Bacon, *Leonard Bacon*, 400; Filler, *Crusade against Slavery*, 197; Wyatt-Brown, *Lewis Tappan*, 313–14; Lewit, "Indian Missions," 43, 46, 52; Johnson, "American Missionary Association," 11–14.

28. Quoted in Whipple, *American Board*, 130, also 55–66, 84–85, 125–26, 143; *Eman.*, 3 November 1847; *New York Observer*, 14 August and 18 September 1847, 16 September 1848, 3 March and 16 September 1849; *New York Evangelist*, 6, 20, and 27 September 1849; *Presbyterian of the West*, 5 October 1848, 1 February 1849; MASS, *Seventeenth Annual Report . . . 1849*, 69–70; Muelder, *Fighters for Freedom*, 290–91; Lewit, "Indian Missions," 43.

29. *National Era*, 14 August 1851; AFASS, *Tenth Annual Report . . . 1850*, 51, 53; AASS, *Second Decade*, 107; MASS, *Seventeenth Annual Report . . . 1849*, 68–69, and *Eighteenth Annual Report . . . 1850*, 76–77; Lewis Tappan to Charles D. Cleveland, 26 October 1849, Tappan Papers; Whipple, *American Board*, 147–52.

30. Quoted in Whipple, *American Board*, 180; *American Missionary Magazine* 4 (March 1860): 60; *Lib.*, 22 September 1854 and 21 August 1857; AASS, *Annual Report . . . 1854* (New York, 1854), 281–85; *Annual Report . . . 1855*, 83–92; and *Annual Report . . . 1856*, 20–21; Lewis Tappan to W. W. Patton, 19 October 1854; Tappan to C. Cushing, 8 November 1854; Tappan to S. D. Hastings, 27 November 1854; Tappan to the Editors of the *Congregationalist Herald*, 9 December 1854; Tappan to C. B. Boynton, 15 December 1854; Tappan to J. H. Cooke, 8 September 1855; Tappan to George Bush, 7 October 1855, all in Tappan Papers; Theodore Tilton to Lewis Tappan, 20 December 1860, AMA MSS; Lewis Tappan to L. A. Chamerovzov, 20 March 1855, in Abel and Klingberg, *Side-Light on Anglo-American Relations*, 355; Whipple, *American Board*, 156–61, 185; Bacon, *Leonard Bacon*, 40; Wyatt-Brown, *Lewis Tappan*, 314; Filler, *Crusade against Slavery*, 197; Lewit, "Indian Missions," 52.

31. *American Missionary Magazine* 2 (November 1858): 279.

32. Ibid., 3 (December 1859): 271; *National Principia*, 17 December 1859 and 10 November 1860; *Lib.*, 12 November and 24 December 1858, 21 October 1859, 12 October 1860; *NASS*, 22 October 1859; *Independent*, 22 March 1860; J. P. Bardwell to Lewis Tappan, 2 September 1858, AMA MSS; Lewis Tappan to the Editors of the *Congregationalist Herald*, 11 January 1858, Tappan Papers; Tappan Diary, 3 October 1857; AASS, *Annual Report . . . 1859–60*, 288–93; Whipple, *American Board*, 188–89, 215–16, 233; Pillsbury, *Acts of the Anti-Slavery Apostles*, 405; Theodore Tilton, *The American Board and American Slavery* (New York, 1860), 16–17; Charles K. Whipple, *Slavery and the American Board of Commissioners for Foreign Missions* (New York, 1859), 18–24.

33. *American Missionary* 4 (March 1849): 44; *Congregationalist*, 11 July 1851; AFASS, *Eleventh Annual Report . . . 1851*, 64; Free Presbyterian Board, *Joseph Gordon*, 196; Griffin, "Abolitionists and the Benevolent Societies," 203–5; Green, "Northern Missionary Activities," 161.

34. Lewis Tappan to the Editor of the *British and Foreign Anti-Slavery Reporter*, 26 October 1852, in Abel and Klingberg, *Side-Light on Anglo-American Relations*, 290–99; Wyatt-Brown, *Lewis Tappan*, 320–21; Muelder, *Fighters for Freedom*, 295–300; Griffin, "Abolitionists and the Benevolent Societies," 205–8; Engelder, "Churches and Slavery," 113–14; Evans, "Abolitionism in Illinois Churches," 128.

35. Quoted in Congregational Home Mission Society, *Home Missions and Slavery* (New York, 1857), 3; Mabee, *Black Freedom*, 234–37; Colin B. Goodykoontz, *Home Missions on the American Frontier* (Caldwell, Idaho, 1939), 291–92; Griffin, "Abolitionists and the Benevolent Societies," 209.

36. *American Missionary Magazine* 1 (May 1857): 104–10; Congregational Home Missionary Society, *Home Missions and Slavery*, 3–4, 26–27, 46; C. B. Boynton to George Whipple, 1 January 1859; Henry Cowles to George Whipple, 16 November 1861, both in AMA MSS; Goodykoontz, *Home Missions*, 292; Evans, "Abolitionism in Illinois Churches," 128, 214–15; 292; Griffin, "Abolitionists and the Benevolent Societies," 209–11.

37. *Presbyterian Magazine* 4 (January 1854): 44–45; *Oberlin Evangelist*, 27 November 1854; *Lib.*, 20 November 1857; *Independent*, 26 May and 14 July 1859; *Presbyter* (Cincinnati), 9 February 1860; *American Missionary Magazine* 4 (July 1860): 157; AASS, *Annual Report . . . 1855*, 82; Henry M. Baird, *Life of Reverend Robert Baird, D.D.* (New York, 1860), 300; William Jay to Charles Lowell, 8 December 1854, Miscellaneous Manuscripts Collection, Manuscript Division, Library of Congress; Green, "Northern Missionary Activities," 161–72; Howard, "Antislavery Movement in the Presbyterian Church," 239–40; Johnson, "American Missionary Association," 569–71.

38. Griffin, *Their Brothers' Keepers*, 66–67.

39. Ibid., 31, 66, 191; Tyler, *Freedom's Ferment*, 32; Wyatt-Brown, *Lewis Tappan*, 156–57.

40. *Free Presbyterian*, 10 March 1852; also AASS, *Annual Report . . . 1855*, 93; Fourth Congregational Church of Hartford, Connecticut, *The Unanimous Remonstrance of the Fourth Congregational Church, Hartford, Connecticut, against the Policy of the American Tract Society on the Subject of Slavery* (Hartford, 1855), 9; Goodell, *Slavery and Anti-Slavery*, 213–14; A. A. Phelps to Lewis Tappan, 4 May 1844; S. C. Stevens to Lewis Tappan, 20 July 1854, both in Tappan Papers; Dumond, *Antislavery*, 156–57.

41. *Free Missionary* 2 (January 1852): 9, 12; also C. B. Boynton to George Whipple, 31 January 1852, AMA MSS; John Rankin, "Life of Reverend John Rankin Written by Himself in His Eightieth Year" (Typescript, Ohio Historical Center, n.d.), 56–57; Willey, "John Rankin," 269–71; Grim, "John Rankin," 55–56.

42. This information on the leadership of the American Reform Tract and Book Society comes from abbreviated reports on the society's activities printed on the last page of its tracts and from occasional printed circulars. For examples see: Jonathan Cable to William Harned, 13 February 1852; G. L. Weed to Henry Belden, 18 June 1856, both in AMA MSS; Patton, *Slavery and Infidelity*, n.p.; Charles K. Whipple, *The Family Relation as Affected by Slavery*, Tract 40 (Cincinnati, n.d.), n.p.; Johnson, "American Missionary Association," 296–97, incorrectly lists some of the society's officers. Also see AFASS, *Thirteenth Annual Report . . . 1853*, 126–27; *American Missionary Magazine* 1 (December 1857): 258 and 2 (December 1858): 296–97; Andrew Ritchie, *The Soldier, the Battle, and the Victory: Being a Brief Account of the Work of Reverend John Rankin in the Antislavery Cause* (Cincinnati, 1868), 27, 76 (hereafter cited as *John Rankin*).

43. *Christian Press,* 10 and 24 December 1852; *National Era,* 20 January and 18 August 1853; *American Missionary Magazine* 1 (December 1857): 258; American Reform Tract and Book Society circulars, January 1857, November 1857, October 1859; Andrew Benton to George Whipple, 7 May 1852; G. L. Weed to Lewis Tappan, 4 April 1857; G. L. Weed to S. S. Jocelyn, 14 October 1857, all in AMA MSS; C. B. Boynton to Henry Cowles, 8 January 1853, Cowles Papers; ARTBS, *Hebrew Servitude and American Slavery,* Tract 2; *A Tract for Sabbath Schools,* Tract 7; *Colonization: The Present Scheme of Colonization—Wrong, Delusive, and Retards Emancipation,* Tract 14; *Fellowship with Slavery; Report Republished from the Minutes of the Evangelical Consociation, Rhode Island,* Tract 15; *A Tract for the Free States; Let Every One Read and Consider Before He Condemns: A Safe and Generous Proposition for Abolishing Slavery,* Tract 20 (Cincinnati, n.d.); Patton, *Slavery and Infidelity,* 72; Raines, "American Missionary Association in Southern Illinois," 255; Johnson, "American Missionary Association," 450–53.

44. *Christian Press,* 10 and 24 December 1852; *National Era,* 20 January 1853; *Frederick Douglass' Paper* (Rochester, N.Y.), 23 July 1852; *Radical Abolitionist* 2 (June 1857): 98; *Oberlin Evangelist,* 9 November 1859; ARTBS, *Duty of Voting for Righteous Men for Office,* Tract 10 (Cincinnati, n.d.); *Tract for the Free States,* 2–3; and *Colonization,* 47–48; S. D. Lewis to Lewis Tappan, 15 December 1852; G. L. Weed to S. S. Jocelyn, 24 November 1857, both in AMA MSS.

45. Griffin, *Their Brothers' Keepers,* 191–92; Smith, *Revivalism and Social Reform,* 193–94.

46. *Radical Abolitionist* 3 (August 1857): 6, and 4 (April 1858): 66; *American Missionary Magazine* 1 (June 1857): 132, (September 1857): 203–4, and (October 1857): 224; *Lib.,* 18 December 1857; *Christian Watchman,* 24 September 1857; *Presbyterian Expositor* 1 (May 1858): 335–36 and (June 1858): 376–78; Griffin, *Their Brothers' Keepers,* 194–95; Smith, *Revivalism and Social Reform,* 193–94.

47. *National Era,* 26 November 1857 and 20 May 1858; *Radical Abolitionist* 3 (May 1858): 76; William Jay to Lewis Tappan, 11 May 1858, Tappan Papers; Tappan Diary, 18 May 1858.

48. *Lib.,* 21 May 1858; also *Radical Abolitionist* 3 (May 1858): 78; *American Missionary Magazine* 2 (June 1858): n.p.; *Presbyterian Expositor* 1 (June 1858): 376–78; Tappan Diary, 16 May 1858; Seth Bliss, *Letters to the Members, Patrons, and Friends of the Branch American Tract Society in Boston, Instituted 1814, and to Those of the National Society in New York, Instituted 1825 By the Secretary of the Boston Society* (Boston, 1858), 92–94; Griffin, *Their Brothers' Keepers,* 195–96.

49. *Independent,* 3 March 1859, also 24 February 1859; *Lib.,* 28 May and 10 December 1858; *NASS,* 21 May 1859; *American Missionary Magazine* 3 (June 1859): 128 and (December 1859): 33; *Church Review and Ecclesiastical Register* 12 (July 1859): 357; AASS, *Annual Report . . . 1859–60,* 301; Charles K. Whipple, *The American Tract Society, Boston* (Boston, 1859), 11; Griffin, *Their Brothers' Keepers,* 197.

50. Whipple, *American Tract Society, Boston,* 23–24; AASS, *Annual Report . . . 1859–60,* 301–3.

51. ARTBS circular, 15 March 1859, quoted in *National Era*, 26 May 1859; also *Oberlin Evangelist*, 13 April, 26 May, 26 October, and 9 November 1859; J. H. Byrd to George Whipple, 8 May 1859; G. L. Weed to S. S. Jocelyn, 24 November 1857; G. L. Weed to Lewis Tappan, 30 June 1858, all in AMA MSS.

52. *American Missionary Magazine* 3 (October 1859): 226, (November 1859): 250, and (December 1859): 279; *Oberlin Evangelist*, 26 October and 9 November 1859; *Independent*, 27 October 1859; *National Principia*, 17 March 1860; *Presbyter*, 4 October 1860, G. L. Weed to George Whipple, 8 July 1859; G. L. Weed to Lewis Tappan, 13 March 1860, both in AMA MSS; Spinka, *Illinois Congregational and Christian Churches*, 150; Engelder, "Churches and Slavery," 109–10.

53. *Church Review and Ecclesiastical Register* 12 (July 1859): 357; *Presbyterian Expositor* 1 (June 1857): 335–36; *Presbyter*, 19 January 1860; *Independent*, 24 May 1860; Henry Cowles to S. S. Jocelyn, 3 July 1858, AMA MSS; Bliss, *Letters to Branch American Tract Society in Boston*, 111–12; Hartford, Connecticut, City Tract Society, *The Tract Society and Slavery: Speeches of Chief Justice Williams, Judge Parsons, and Ex-Governor Ellsworth* (Hartford, 1859), 17–18.

54. AASS, *Second Annual Report . . . 1835*, 29–30; Ohio Anti-Slavery Society, *Convention . . . 1835*, 6; Goodell, *Slavery and Anti-Slavery*, 211; Wyatt-Brown, *Lewis Tappan*, 314–15; Griffin, "Abolitionists and the Benevolent Societies," 199–201.

55. *Lib.*, 21 May 1847; *Eman.*, 16 September 1846 and 20 October 1847; *North Star*, 18 May 1849; AFASS, *Tenth Annual Report . . . 1850*, 14; AFASS, *Shall We Give the Bible to Three Millions of American Slaves?*, Tract 1 (n.p., n.d.), 8; Henry Bibb to the Executive Committee of the American Missionary Association, 14 February 1849, AMA MSS; Wyatt-Brown, *Lewis Tappan*, 314–15; Griffin, "Abolitionists and the Benevolent Societies," 200; John R. McKivigan, " 'The Gospel Will Burst the Bonds of the Slaves': The Abolitionists' Bibles for Slaves Campaign," *Negro History Bulletin* 45 (July–September 1982): 62–64, 77; A similar agitation against fellowship with slaveholders occurred in denominational Bible societies.

56. *American Missionary* 2 (March 1848): 37 and (April 1848): 47; *New York Evangelist*, 19 and 26 July 1849; *Lib.*, 27 February 1857 and 14 May 1858; *American Missionary Magazine* 1 (February 1857): 36; *Liberty Almanac for 1849*, 38; Lewis Tappan to Joshua Leavitt, 8 January 1848; William Jay to Lewis Tappan, 11 September 1851 and 28 February 1857, all in Tappan Papers; James Gregg to A. M. Rose, 26 March 1851, AMA MSS; William Goodell to S. Cole, 6 December 1856, AAS MSS; Griffin, "Abolitionists and the Benevolent Societies," 200–1.

57. *Weekly Chronotype*, 3 June 1848; William Jay to Lewis Tappan, 14 March 1849; Lewis Tappan to the Members of the Congregation of the Pilgrims, 19 December 1858, both in Tappan Papers; Filler, *Crusade against Slavery*, 260–61; Engelder, "Churches and Slavery," 110–11.

58. Wyatt-Brown, *Lewis Tappan*, 316; Ernest R. Sandeen, "The Distinctiveness of American Denominationalism: A Case Study of the 1846 Evangelical Alliance," *Church History* 45 (June 1976): 234.

59. Thomas Smyth, *Autobiographical Notes, Letters, and Reflections* (Charleston, S.C., 1914), 361–63.

60. *National Era*, 11 February 1847; *Lib.*, 25 September 1846; *Weekly Chronotype*, 24 September 1846; AFASS, *Seventh Annual Report . . . 1847*, 7–8; MASS, *Sixteenth Annual Report . . . 1848* (Boston, 1848), 65–66; Pillsbury, *Church as It Is*, 24–25; Lyman Beecher, *Autobiography, Correspondence, Etc., of Lyman Beecher*, ed. Charles Beecher, 2 vols. (New York, 1865), 2:519, 522; Baird, *Robert Baird*, 233–35; George Peck, *The Life and Times of Reverend George Peck* (New York, 1874), 285–87; AFASS, *Remonstrance against the Course Pursued by the Evangelical Alliance on the Subject of American Slavery* (New York, 1847), 7–8; J. F. Maclear, "The Evangelical Alliance and the Antislavery Crusade," *Huntington Library Quarterly* 42 (Spring 1979): 141–64.

61. AFASS, *Remonstrance*, 12, also 2–3, 78; *National Era*, 11 February 1847; *Eman.*, 3 March 1847; *Weekly Chronotype*, 25 September 1846; *Lib.*, 25 September 1846; AFASS, *Seventh Annual Report . . . 1847*, 20–21; MASS, *Fifteenth Annual Report . . . 1847*, 51–52; Henry C. Wright, *Christian Communion with Slave-Holders: Will the Alliance Sanction It? Letters to Reverend John Angell James, D.D., and Reverend Ralph Wardlaw, D.D., Showing Their Position in the Alliance* (Rochdale, England, 1846), 4–5, 9; Lewis Tappan to Joseph Sturge, 7 October 1846, Tappan Papers; Lewis Tappan to John Scoble, 1 February 1847, in Abel and Klingberg, *Side-Light on Anglo-American Relations*, 213; William L. Garrison to Richard Webb, 19 August 1846, *Garrison Letters*, 4:83–84, also 418–20.

62. Quoted in MASS, *Sixteenth Annual Report . . . 1848*, 65–66; and in AFASS, *Seventh Annual Report . . . 1847*, 7–8; also *Weekly Chronotype*, 20 May 1847; Lewis Tappan to A. A. Phelps, 5 February 1847, Tappan Papers.

63. *Lib.*, 21 May 1847; *Weekly Chronotype*, 24 December 1846; *Oberlin Evangelist*, 22 October 1851; AFASS, *Seventh Annual Report . . . 1847*, 28, 45; Stephen Olin, *The Life and Letters of Stephen Olin, D.D., Late President of the Wesleyan University*, 2 vols. (New York, 1853), 2:325–26, 370; Robert Baird, *The Progress and Prospects of Christianity in the United States of America, with Remarks on the Subject of Slavery in America and on the Intercourse between British and American Churches* (London, 1851), 59; Wyatt-Brown, *Lewis Tappan*, 316; Smith, *Revivalism and Social Reform*, 193.

64. *Lib.*, 13 March 1857; Charles H. Hopkins, *History of the Y.M.C.A. in North America* (New York, 1951), 59–60, 64; Smith, *Revivalism and Social Reform*, 76, 193.

Chapter 7. *Interdenominational Antislavery Endeavors*

1. *NASS*, 20 August 1859, also AASS, *Annual Report . . . 1859–60*, 274; Whipple, *Relations of Anti-Slavery to Religion*, 3–4; William L. Garrison to James M. McKim, 14 October 1856, *Garrison Letters*, 4:405; AASS, *Second Decade*, 146.

2. AASS, *The American Anti-Slavery Almanac for 1838*, 9; S. D. Hastings to Lewis Tappan, 7 December 1838, 23 February 1839, and 25 March 1840, all in Tappan Papers; William Goodell to Clarissa Goodell, 25 January 1843, Goodell

Papers; Evangelical Union Anti-Slavery Society, *Address to the Churches,* 45; Perkal, "William Goodell," 157–61, 172–73; Dumond, *Antislavery,* 349.

3. *Eman.,* 18 February 1842; 25 January 1844; 21 January, 11 February, 4 March, 13 and 20 May, 3 June, and 26 August 1846; 10 and 17 February 1847; *Christian Freeman* (Hartford), 26 October 1843; *Liberty Standard* (Hallowell, Maine), 4 and 18 January 1844, 6 February 1845, 15 January 1846, 4 and 11 February 1847, and 2 March 1848; *Christian Investigator,* August 1845, 255, and April 1846, 315–16; *Lib.,* 4 July 1845, 6 March and 3 April 1846; *Weekly Chronotype,* 28 May 1846; *The Declaration and Pledge against Slavery Adopted by the Religious Anti-Slavery Convention, Held at Marlboro Chapel, Boston, February 26, 1846* (Boston, 1846), 6–8; Austin Willey, *The History of the Anti-Slavery Cause in State and Nation* (Portland, Maine, 1886), 236–38; William Gravely, *Gilbert Haven, Methodist Abolitionist: A Study in Race, Religion, and Reform, 1850–1880* (Nashville, 1973), 25–26.

4. *National Era,* 10 January 1850; also *Non-Slaveholder* 4 (April 1850): 89; *Oberlin Evangelist,* 10 April 1850; Christian Anti-Slavery Convention, *The Minutes of the Christian Anti-Slavery Convention Assembled April 17th–20th, 1850 at Cincinnati, Ohio* (Cincinnati, 1850), 3; Dillon, *The Abolitionists,* 199.

5. Edward Goodman to Henry Cowles, 9 February 1850, Cowles Papers; Christian Anti-Slavery Convention, *Minutes . . . April 17th–20th 1850,* 3.

6. Committee on Invitations to F. J. LeMoyne, 20 March 1850, Woodson Collection; *North Star,* 27 June 1850; C. D. Cleveland to Lewis Tappan, 12 June 1850, Tappan Papers; Christian Anti-Slavery Convention, *Minutes . . . April 17th–20th, 1850,* 47–84.

7. *Anti-Slavery Bugle* (New Lisbon, Ohio), 4 and 18 May 1850; *National Era,* 2 and 9 May 1850; *Journal and Messenger* (Cincinnati), 26 April 1850; also Lewis Tappan to F. D. Parrish, 13 April 1850, Tappan Papers; Quarles, *Black Abolitionists,* 81; Dillon, *The Abolitionists,* 158; Engelder, "Churches and Slavery," 33.

8. *Anti-Slavery Bugle,* 6 April, 4 and 18 May 1850; *Pennsylvania Freeman,* 9 May 1850; *North Star,* 27 June 1850; AFASS, *Tenth Annual Report . . . 1850,* 49–50; *Liberty Almanac for 1851,* 32; Goodell, *Slavery and Anti-Slavery,* 492.

9. *True Wesleyan,* 4 May 1850, also 11 May 1850.

10. Quoted in *Non-Slaveholder* 4 (June 1850): 137–38.

11. *Presbyterian of the West,* 2 May 1850; also *Journal and Messenger,* 26 April 1850; *Christian Observer,* 4 May 1850; more favorable comments are found in *Congregationalist,* 15 February 1850; *Oberlin Evangelist,* 8 May 1850; *New York Evangelist,* 2 May 1850.

12. Peter Cartwright, *Autobiography of Peter Cartwright: The Backwoods Preacher* (Cincinnati, 1856), 431–33.

13. *Oberlin Evangelist,* 19 June 1850; *National Era,* 10 July 1850, 15 May 1851; *NASS,* 21 April 1851; *Anti-Slavery Bugle,* 25 May 1850, 12 July 1851; AFASS, *Tenth Annual Report . . . 1850,* 50; and *Eleventh Annual Report . . . 1851,* 69–70.

14. *National Era,* 22 May and 12 June 1851; *North Star,* 10 April 1851; Jonathan Cable to George Whipple, 10 May 1850 and 1 July 1851; C. B. Boynton to George Whipple, 7 January 1851; Jonathan Cable to William Harned, 23 May 1851; C. B.

Boynton to George Whipple, 9 June 1851, all in AMA MSS; Muelder, *Fighters for Freedom*, 223–24.

15. *National Era*, 10 July and 14 August 1851; *Frederick Douglass' Paper*, 2 October 1851; *American Missionary* 6 (August 1851): 76; C. B. Boynton to Henry Cowles, 13 June 1851, Cowles Papers; Goodell, *Slavery and Anti-Slavery*, 492; Clyde S. Kilby, *Minority of One: The Biography of Jonathan Blanchard* (Grand Rapids, Mich., 1959), 152–53; Evans, "Abolitionism in Illinois Churches," 213.

16. *National Era*, 7 August 1851.

17. Ibid., 31 July 1851, also 14 August 1851; *True Wesleyan*, 27 September 1851; *Watchman of the Prairie* (Chicago), 8 July 1851; *American Baptist*, 14 August 1851; Frederick I. Kuhns, *The Home Missionary Society and the Anti-Slavery Controversy in the Old Northwest* (Billings, Mont., 1959), 29–31; Kilby, *Minority of One*, 117–18.

18. *Watchman of the Prairie*, 8 July 1851, also 15 and 29 July 1851; *American Baptist*, 24 and 31 July, 7 and 14 August 1851.

19. *Oberlin Evangelist*, 27 August 1851; *New York Evangelist*, 14 August 1851; *Independent*, n.d., quoted in *True Wesleyan*, 16 August 1851; *American Missionary* 6 (August 1851): 76; Engelder, "Churches and Slavery," 423–24.

20. *True Wesleyan*, 16 August 1851; also *Oberlin Evangelist*, 27 August 1851.

21. Rankin, "John Rankin," 56–57; C. B. Boynton to George Whipple, 18 July 1851, AMA MSS; Kuhns, *Home Missionary Society*, 29.

22. *Anti-Slavery Bugle*, 9 August 1851.

23. Ibid., 9 August 1851, also 19 and 26 July, 30 August 1851; *Lib.*, 8 August 1851; *NASS*, 7 August 1851.

24. *Free Presbyterian*, 19 November 1851, 10 and 24 August 1853; *National Era*, 1 April and 6 May 1852, 13 October 1853; *Oberlin Evangelist*, 23 June 1852, 22 November 1854; *True Wesleyan*, 6 December 1851; *American Baptist*, 29 January 1852; J. B. Walker to George Whipple, 4 February and 13 December 1852, AMA MSS; AFASS, *Thirteenth Annual Report . . . 1853*, 127–28; Evans, "Abolitionism in Illinois Churches," 83–85.

25. *Lib.*, 30 January 1852, also 27 February 1852; AFASS, *Thirteenth Annual Report . . . 1853*, 127–28; Wyatt-Brown, *Lewis Tappan*, 178; Willey, *Anti-Slavery Cause*, 385–87.

26. *Lib.*, 5 June 1857; Tappan Diary, 6 June 1857.

27. *National Era*, 13 March, 1 and 15 May 1851; 22 January, 6 and 13 May 1852; 12 and 19 May 1853; 27 April 1854; *Journal and Messenger*, 14 March and 18 April 1851, 7 May 1852; *Anti-Slavery Bugle*, 3, 10, and 31 May 1851; *Lib.*, 9 May 1851, 27 February 1852; *Frederick Douglass' Paper*, 22 January and 13 May 1852, 6 May 1853, 28 April 1854; *American Baptist*, 15 April 1852; *Daily Cincinnati Gazette*, 20, 28, and 29 April 1852; AASS, *Second Decade*, 146; Patrick Riddleberger, *George Washington Julian: Radical Republican* (Indianapolis, 1966), 84–85; Dillon, *The Abolitionists*, 202–4; Willey, "John Rankin," 271–77.

28. Ohio State Christian Anti-Slavery Convention, *Proceedings of the Ohio State Christian Anti-Slavery Convention, Held in Columbus, August 10 and 11, 1859* (Columbus, 1859), 21, also 1–2, 4–12, 16–18, 20–26; *National Era*, 4 August 1859;

Ohio State Journal (Columbus), 11 and 12 August 1859; *Oberlin Evangelist*, 17 August 1859; E. H. Fairchild to George Whipple, 28 July 1858; S. S. Jocelyn to Lewis Tappan, 5 August 1859, both in AMA MSS; Dillon, *The Abolitionists*, 237–39.

29. Ohio State Christian Anti-Slavery Convention, *Proceedings*, 19, 25–28; *Ohio State Journal*, 11 and 13 August 1859; *National Era*, 18 August 1859; *NASS*, 20 August 1859; AASS, *Annual Report . . . 1859–60*, 286–87; *National Principia*, 19 November 1859; James Thorpe to Lewis Tappan, 3 September 1859, AMA MSS.

30. *Oberlin Evangelist*, 9 November 1859; also *American Missionary Magazine* 3 (November 1859): 251; *Ohio State Journal*, 20 October 1859; Circular, "Call of Northwestern Christian Anti-Slavery Convention," 1 October 1859, Cowles Papers.

31. *Oberlin Evangelist*, 9 November 1859; also Dillon, *The Abolitionists*, 240–41.

32. Salmon P. Chase to James Monroe, 13 October 1859, James Monroe Papers, Oberlin College Archives (hereafter cited as Monroe Papers); also Ohio State Christian Anti-Slavery Convention, *Proceedings*, 10–11; Dillon, *The Abolitionists*, 199–202.

33. *Oberlin Evangelist*, 9 November 1859; Cole, *Irrepressible Conflict*, 260; Dillon, *The Abolitionists*, 240–41.

34. Robert M. York, *George B. Cheever: Religious and Social Reformer, 1807–1890* (Orono, Maine, 1955), v–vii, 84–87, 100, 115; George I. Rockwood, "George Barrell Cheever, Protagonist of Abolition: Religious Emotionalism the Underlying Factor in the Cause of the Civil War," *American Antiquarian Society Proceedings* 46 (1936): 96–113.

35. *NASS*, 21 May, 2 July and 3 December 1859; *National Principia*, 3 November 1860; George B. Cheever, *The Guilt of Slavery and the Crime of Slaveholding Demonstrated from the Hebrew and Greek Scriptures* (Boston, 1860), v, xvii–xix, 25, 57–58, 235–36, 322–33, 466–67; George B. Cheever, *God against Slavery, and the Freedom and Duty of the Pulpit to Rebuke It* (New York, 1857), 51–52, 55–56, 93–94, 251–52, 259–60; Cheever, *Commission from God*, 176, 178, 180; Henry T. Cheever, *A Tract for the Times on the Question, Is It Right to Withhold Fellowship of Churches from Individuals That Tolerate or Practice Slavery?* (New York, 1859), 5–8, 13–17, 19–20, 22–23; G. B. Cheever to H. T. Cheever, 27 September 1856 and 23 August 1857; G. B. Cheever to Elizabeth Cheever, 18 April 1859 and 22 September 1860; J. A. Thome to G. B. Cheever, 16 December 1859; Joseph P. Thompson to G. B. Cheever, 6 September 1860, all in Cheever Family Papers, American Antiquarian Society (hereafter cited as Cheever Papers); Davis, *Problem of Slavery*, 523–25; York, *George B. Cheever*, 142–59.

36. *Lib.*, 25 March 1859; H. T. Cheever to G. B. Cheever, 29 December 1859, Cheever Papers; William Goodell to J. C. Webster, 29 January 1859, AAS MSS; York, *George B. Cheever*, 164.

37. Church Anti-Slavery Society, *Proceedings of the Convention Which Met at Worcester, Massachusetts, March 1, 1859* (New York, 1859), 3–10, 27–28; *American Missionary Magazine* 3 (April 1859): 77–79; *Lib.*, 18 March 1859.

38. Church Anti-Slavery Society, *Proceedings . . . 1859*, 9–16; *Lib.*, 25 March and 22 April 1859; *NASS*, 13 August 1859; *American Missionary Magazine* 4 (June 1860): 133; *National Principia*, 6 October 1860; Church Anti-Slavery Society, *Circular—Declaration of Principles and Constitution* (Worcester, Mass., 1859), 3–5; Ohio

State Christian Anti-Slavery Convention, *Proceedings*, 26; James M. McPherson, *The Struggle for Equality: Abolitionists and the Negro in the Civil War and Reconstruction* (Princeton, N.J., 1964), 5.

39. *American Jubilee*, 1 (April 1855): 95; *National Era*, 7 April 1859; *National Principia*, 7 April 1860; G. B. Cheever to H. T. Cheever, 24 June 1859; H. T. Cheever to Elizabeth Washburn, 3 January 1860, both in Cheevers Papers; S. S. Jocelyn to Lewis Tappan, 29 July 1859, AMA MSS; McPherson, *Struggle for Equality*, 5; York, *George B. Cheever*, 164.

40. *National Era*, 7 April 1859; *Zion's Herald*, 1 June 1859; *American Missionary Magazine* 3 (June 1859): 128–29 and (August 1859): 181; 4 (April 1860): 91; *National Principia*, 14 January, 12 May, and 2, 9, and 16 June 1860; *Wesleyan*, 21 March 1860; Church Anti-Slavery Society, *Circular—Declaration of Principles*, 3; Circular, "Letter to the Churches," n.p., AMA MSS; H. T. Cheever to G. B. Cheever, 23 April 1860; G. B. Cheever to H. T. Cheever, 29 April 1860, both in Cheever Papers; Gravely, *Gilbert Haven*, 2, 46; McPherson, *Struggle for Equality*, 5.

41. *National Era*, 7 April 1859; *Lib.*, 7 October 1859, 16 November 1860; *National Principia*, 2 January, 7 April, 2 June, 25 August, and 13 October 1860; *American Missionary Magazine* 4 (February 1860): 45; *Douglass' Monthly* 3 (August 1860): 305; Ohio State Christian Anti-Slavery Society, *Proceedings*, 27–28; G. B. Cheever to H. T. Cheever, 25 October 1859; H. T. Cheever to Elizabeth Washburn, 3 January and 21 February 1860, all in Cheever Papers.

42. *NASS*, 28 May 1859; *American Missionary Magazine* 3 (June 1859): 128–29; and 4 (February 1860): 45; *National Principia*, 14 January, 2 and 23 June 1860; *Wesleyan*, 21 March and 10 October 1860; *American Baptist*, 12 June 1860; *Free Church Portfolio*, 9 February 1860; Church Anti-Slavery Society, *Circular—Declaration of Principles*, 4; Ohio State Christian Anti-Slavery Convention, *Proceedings*, 27–28; S. S. Jocelyn to Lewis Tappan, 29 July 1859, AMA MSS; G. B. Cheever to H. T. Cheever, 25 October 1859, Cheever Papers.

43. *National Principia*, 31 December 1859; 7 April, 2 and 23 June 1860; *Douglass' Monthly* 3 (October 1860): 338; Church Anti-Slavery Society, *Proceedings . . . 1859*, 9–10; and *Circular—Declaration of Principles*, 6–7; "Church Anti-Slavery Society Records," 24 May 1859, Cheever Papers; William Goodell to Gerrit Smith, 4 May 1858; William Goodell to J. C. Webster, 29 January 1859; William Goodell to William Burwick, 8 March 1859, all in AAS MSS; S. S. Jocelyn to Lewis Tappan, 29 July and 2 August 1859, AMA MSS; Michael F. Holt, *Forging a Majority: The Formation of the Republican Party before the Civil War* (New Haven, 1969), 301; Dillon, *The Abolitionists*, 237; McPherson, *Struggle for Equality*, 5.

44. *NASS*, 21 and 28 May, 13 August 1859; *Lib.*, 22 April 1859.

45. *Lib.*, 25 March, 1 and 22 April, 7 and 14 October 1859; *NASS*, 28 May and 13 August 1859; AASS, *Annual Report . . . 1859–60*, 285–86; H. T. Cheever to Elizabeth Cheever, 12 March 1859, Cheever Papers; York, *George B. Cheever*, 165–67.

46. *Lib.*, 16 November 1860.

47. *Lib.*, 2 July 1852; *National Era*, 10 June 1852; Ellis Gray Loring to Joshua Leavitt, 28 December 1840; Ellis Gray Loring to Lewis Tappan, 22 October 1840; Ellis Gray Loring to Lydia Maria Child, 29 April 1841; all in Ellis Gray Loring Papers,

Houghton Library, Harvard University; Lewis Tappan to Salmon P. Chase, 23 June 1847, Chase Papers; John G. Whittier to H. I. Bowditch, 26 August 1846, Whittier Papers; Bolster, *James Freeman Clarke*, 233–34; Friedman, *Gregarious Saints*, 257–58; Pease and Pease, *Bound with Them in Chains*, 293–94, 300.

48. Maria Weston Chapman to Samuel E. Sewall, 9 August 1857, Robie-Sewall Papers, Massachusetts Historical Society; Wyatt-Brown, *Lewis Tappan*, 310–31; Walters, *Antislavery Appeal*, 13, 17, 45; Friedman, *Gregarious Saints*, 257–58.

49. *Lib.*, 22 and 29 May 1857, 4 June 1858, 20 May 1859, 25 May 1860; *NASS*, 22 May 1858; York, *George B. Cheever*, 173.

Chapter 8. *Vote as You Pray and Pray as You Vote: Church-Oriented Abolitionism and Antislavery Politics*

1. Sewell, *Ballots for Freedom*, 6–15; Kraditor, *Means and Ends*, 119; Dillon, *The Abolitionists*, 127–28; Stewart, *Holy Warriors*, 81–82.

2. Sewell, *Ballots for Freedom*, 6–15; Kraditor, *Means and Ends*, 119–20; Dillon, *The Abolitionists*, 121; Stewart, *Holy Warriors*, 81–83.

3. Lewis Tappan to William Jay, 9 September 1843, Tappan Papers; *Eman.*, 20 May and 16 December 1841; AASS, *American Anti-Slavery Almanac for 1847* (Boston, 1847), n.p.; Friedman, *Gregarious Saints*, 89–94.

4. Formisano, *Birth of Mass Political Parties*, 104, 120, 164, 178; Jensen, *Winning of the Midwest*, 58–59; Lee Benson, *The Concept of Jacksonian Democracy: New York as a Test Case* (Princeton, N.J., 1961), 209–13; John L. Hammond, *The Politics of Benevolence: Revival Religion and American Voting Behavior* (Norwood, N.J., 1979), 189–94; Michael F. Holt, *The Political Crisis of the 1850s* (New York, 1978), 34, 44–45; John F. McFaul, "Expediency vs. Morality: Jacksonian Politics and Slavery," *JAH* 62 (June 1975): 38.

5. *Anti-Slavery Lecturer* 1 (December 1839): n.p., quoted in Perkal, "William Goodell," 121–22; also *Christian Freeman*, 13 November 1845; Stewart, *Holy Warriors*, 97, 104–5; Dillon, *The Abolitionists*, 141–44; Sewell, *Ballots for Freedom*, 81–82, 95–96; Hugh H. Davis, "The Failure of Political Abolitionism," *Connecticut Review* 6 (April 1973): 77–78.

6. Donald Brue, comp., *National Party Platforms*, 2 vols. (Urbana, Ill., 1978), 1:256–57; Kraditor, *Means and Ends*, 167–68; Reinhard O. Johnson, "The Liberty Party in Massachusetts, 1840–1848: Antislavery Third Party Politics in the Bay State," *CWH* 28 (September 1982): 256–57.

7. Goodell, *Slavery and Anti-Slavery*, 523; also W. L. Garrison to J. S. Yerrington, 7 May 1844, *Garrison Letters*, 3:256–57.

8. *Christian Freeman*, 9 January 1845; Goodell, *Slavery and Anti-Slavery*, 472–73; Joseph G. Rayback, *Free Soil: The Election of 1848* (Lexington, Ky., 1970), 102; Stewart, *Holy Warriors*, 99–100; Johnson, "Liberty Party in Massachusetts," 257.

9. Jonathan Blanchard to Henry Cowles, 4 August 1840, Cowles Papers; also Gerrit Smith to John Rankin, in *Philanthropist*, 28 August 1840, 6 January 1841; *Lib.*, 17 July 1840; Willey, "John Rankin," 226–66.

10. *Indiana Democrat and Freeman*, n.d., quoted in *Clarion of Freedom* (New Concord, Ohio), 24 March 1848; also *AFAS Reporter*, November 1842, n.p.; *Western Citizen* (Chicago), 24 October 1844; *Signal of Liberty* (Ann Arbor, Mich.), 3 July 1847.

11. *Eman.*, 10 February 1842; also *Weekly Chronotype*, 25 March 1847; *Western Citizen*, 1 February 1844; Goodell, *Slavery and Anti-Slavery*, 188–89.

12. *Western Citizen*, 2 November 1843, also 31 October and 7 November 1844; *Liberty Press* (Utica, N.Y.), 14 June and 16 August 1845, 19 November 1846; *Friend of Man*, 20 April 1841; *Liberty Standard*, 26 July and 15 September 1841; 8 June, 16 November, and 21 December 1842; 17 May and 14 June 1843; 20 June 1844; *Charter Oak*, n.d., quoted in *Eman.*, 7 December 1841; *Signal of Liberty*, 29 December 1841; 19 January, 27 June, and 7 November 1842; 13 November 1843.

13. *Friend of Man*, 20 July and 24 August 1841; *Christian Freeman*, 23 October 1845; *Western Citizen*, 30 June 1846; *Proceedings of the Great Convention of Friends of Freedom in the Eastern and Middle States, Held in Boston, Oct. 1, 2, & 3, 1845* (Lowell, Mass., 1845), 5–6; Lewis, *Samuel Lewis*, 306–7; Fladeland, *James G. Birney*, 202–3, 256–57; Edward Magdol, *Owen Lovejoy: Abolitionist in Congress* (New Brunswick, N.J., 1967), 60–65, 69–89; Willey, *Anti-Slavery Cause*, 158–59, 224–26, 267.

14. *Liberty Press*, 19 July 1845; also *Eman.*, 17 February 1842; *Christian Investigator* August 1845, 255; and April 1846, 315–16.

15. *Eman.*, 25 January 1844; 21 January, 11 February, 4 March, 13 and 20 May, 3 June, and 26 August 1846; 17 February 1847; *Lib.*, 6 March and 3 April 1846; *Weekly Chronotype*, 26 May 1846; *Declaration and Pledge against Slavery, Adopted by the Religious Anti-Slavery Convention, Held at Marlboro Chapel, Boston, February 26, 1846*, 6–8.

16. *Lib.*, 31 July and 16 October 1840; *Christian Investigator* 6 (March 1846): 306; Perry, *Radical Abolitionism*, 65; Sewell, *Ballots for Freedom*, 76; Kraut, "Liberty Men of New York," 286–87, 380.

17. Quoted in *National Era*, 21 June 1849; also AFASS, *Tenth Annual Report . . . 1850*, 43–44, 64–65; Ritchie, *John Rankin*, 92–94.

18. *True Wesleyan*, 3 February, 11 May, 3 August, 7 September, and 2 November 1844; *Christian Investigator*, June 1845, 288; *American Baptist*, 23 October 1856, 30 October 1860; *Free Church Portfolio*, 19 January and 28 June 1860; Free Presbyterian Board, *Joseph Gordon*, 203–5; Lee, *Autobiography*, 281; AFASS, *Tenth Annual Report . . . 1850*, 64–65; ABFMS, *Annual Report . . . 1857*, 7; Samuel Lewis to Salmon P. Chase, 27 December 1845, Chase Papers; Sewell, *Ballots for Freedom*, 67; Formisano, *Birth of Mass Political Parties*, 45–51; Reinhard O. Johnson, "The Liberty Party in Vermont, 1840–1848: The Forgotten Abolitionists," *Vermont History* 47 (Fall 1979): 269.

19. William R. Brock, *Parties and Political Conscience: American Dilemmas, 1840–1850* (Millwood, N.Y., 1979), 51; Formisano, *Birth of Mass Political Parties,* 120, 192; Hammond, *Politics of Benevolence,* 88–91; Sorin, *New York Abolitionists,* 106–7; Kraut, "Liberty Men of New York," 390. Reinhard O. Johnson has found evidence that in New England after the mid-1840s the Liberty party attracted increasing support from Democratic sources; see Johnson, "Liberty Party in Massachusetts," 252–53.

20. *NASS,* 27 October 1842, 23 March 1843; *AFAS Reporter,* March 1843, 142–43; *Lib.,* 17 November 1843; Edgerton, *Separation in Indiana,* 205; Goodell, *Slavery and Anti-Slavery,* 196–98, 551–52; Drake, *Quakers and Slavery,* 144–47, 164–65; Baxter, *Freewill Baptists,* 98–100; Spinka, *Illinois Congregational and Christian Churches,* 152–53; Clayton S. Ellsworth, "Oberlin and the Anti-Slavery Movement up to the Civil War" (Ph.D. diss., Cornell University, 1930), 107–8.

21. Frederick J. Blue, *The Free Soilers: Third Party Politics, 1848–1854* (Urbana, Ill., 1974), 8–9; Kraditor, *Means and Ends,* 153–54, 182, 190–91; Sewell, *Ballots for Freedom,* 117–21, 131–69; Stewart, *Holy Warriors,* 119–20.

22. After the creation of the Free Soil party, the Liberty League renamed itself the National Liberty party. To avoid confusion when making comparisons with the pre-1848 Liberty party, I retain the designation Liberty League in my discussion. Goodell, *Slavery and Anti-Slavery,* 475; Wyatt-Brown, *Lewis Tappan,* 332–34; Blue, *Free Soilers,* 2, 103, 233–34, 243–47; Friedman, *Gregarious Saints,* 117–20; Johnson, "Liberty Party in Massachusetts," 258–61.

23. Goodell, *Slavery and Anti-Slavery,* 571–72; also Gerrit Smith, "Circular: 'The Liberty Party,'" 28 November 1850, AMA MSS; *Political Abolitionist* (Bryan, Ohio), 10 September 1857; *Radical Abolitionist* 2 (January 1857): 56; Edward Van Horn to Gamaliel Bailey, 13 December 1848, in *National Era,* 25 January 1849; William M. Wiecek, *The Sources of Antislavery Constitutionalism in America, 1760–1848* (Ithaca, N.Y., 1977), 258–75.

24. George Julian to F. W. Bird et al., 29 April 1853, Joshua R. Giddings–George W. Julian Papers, Manuscript Division, Library of Congress; also Foner, *Free Soil,* 109–15; Grace Julian Clarke, *George W. Julian* (Indianapolis, 1923), 433–34; Dillon, *The Abolitionists,* 165, 168.

25. Brue, *National Party Platforms,* 1:18.

26. *National Era,* 31 May 1849; 10 January, 7 February, 25 April, 23 May, 26 September, 31 October, and 11 November 1850; 2 September 1852; *Lib.,* 14 November 1851; *Anti-Slavery Bugle,* 26 April and 16 August 1851; *Clarion of Freedom,* 24 March 1848; *Weekly Chronotype,* 30 December 1848; *North Star,* 2 June 1848, 9 June 1849; Lewis, *Samuel Lewis,* 317–18, 371–72, 423–24; Clarke, *George W. Julian,* 317–18; Martin Duberman, *Charles Francis Adams* (Boston, 1961), 105–6; Stanley C. Harrold, Jr., "Gamaliel Bailey, Abolitionist and Free Soiler" (Ph.D. diss., Kent State University, 1975), 178–80, 237–40.

27. *American Jubilee* 1 (December 1854): 63; also *Christian Investigator* 6 December 1846, 382–83; Goodell, *American Slavery,* 17–18; idem, *Slavery and Anti-Slavery,* 545.

28. *True Wesleyan*, 6 July 1850; *Radical Abolitionist* 1 (October 1855): 18–19; *Political Abolitionist*, 18 December 1856; Ralph V. Harlow, *Gerrit Smith, Philanthropist and Reformer* (New York, 1939), 196–97.

29. Sewell, *Ballots for Freedom*, 167–69, 249–51; Perkal, "William Goodell," 236–38.

30. Gerrit Smith to Lewis Tappan, 28 December 1848; S. S. Sheldon to Lewis Tappan, 29 December 1848; Ovid Miner to George Whipple, 5 March 1848, all in AMA MSS; AFASS, *Eighth Annual Report . . . 1848*, 7, 10–15; Harlow, *Gerrit Smith*, 216; Johnson, "American Missionary Association," 210–19.

31. *National Era*, 31 July, 7 and 14 August 1851; 20 January 1853; *New York Evangelist*, 14 August 1851; *Oberlin Evangelist*, 27 August 1851; *American Missionary* 5 (August 1851): 76; *Christian Press*, 10 and 24 December 1852; C. B. Boynton to Henry Cowles, 8 January 1853, Cowles Papers; Christian Anti-Slavery Convention, *Minutes . . . April 17th–20th, 1850*, 1—20; *Minutes of the Christian Anti-Slavery Convention Held July 3rd, 4th, and 5th, 1851 at Chicago, Illinois* (Chicago, 1851), n.p.; Evans, "Abolitionism in Illinois Churches," 84–87.

32. *Christian Contributor*, 16 August 1848, also 13 and 20 September 1848; *Eman.*, 8 February 1848; *Non-Slaveholder* 3 (October 1848): 220; *True Wesleyan*, 8 July 1850, 4 October 1851; *Wesleyan*, 7 April 1853; *Free Presbyterian*, 7 September 1853; *Christian Reformer* (Hamilton, N.Y.), 28 July 1847; *American Jubilee* 1 (October 1854): 48; William Goodell to W. M. Stewart, 6 October 1857, AAS MSS; Goodell, *Slavery and Anti-Slavery*, 543; Formisano, *Birth of Mass Political Parties*, 150–51.

33. *Northern Advocate* (Auburn, N.Y.), 19 August 1846, 17 March 1847; *Western Christian Advocate*, 10 December 1846, 22 February 1847; *Watchman of the Valley* (Cincinnati), 25 February 1847, 29 August and 2 November 1848; *Zion's Herald*, 3 and 10 March 1847, 12 July 1848; *North Star*, 21 July 1848; *National Era*, 17 August and 2 November 1848; *Watchman of the Prairie*, 29 August 1848; *Congregationalist*, 23 January and 1 October 1852; John W. Chadwick, *Theodore Parker, Preacher and Reformer* (Boston, 1900), 248; Ellsworth, "Oberlin," 113–14.

34. Deut. 23:15–16; Nathaniel Colver, *The Fugitive Slave Bill; or, God's Laws Paramount to the Laws of Men* (Boston, 1850), 13–14; Joseph P. Thompson, *The Fugitive Slave Law, Tried by the Old and New Testaments* (New York, 1850), 34–35; Keller, "Churches and the Fugitive Slave Law," 103–7, 160–61; Norton, "Religious Press and the Compromise of 1850," 270–71.

35. George Carter has documented that the abolitionists utilized the concept of a higher law long before the debate on the Fugitive Slave Law of 1850; see George E. Carter, "The Use of the Doctrine of Higher Law in the American Anti-Slavery Crusade, 1830–1860" (Ph.D. diss., University of Oregon, 1970), especially pp. 379–85; also *Congregationalist*, 8 February, 5 April, and 6 December 1850; *New York Evangelist*, 17 October 1850; *National Era*, 4 December 1851; Charles Beecher, *The Duty of Disobedience to Wicked Laws: A Sermon on the Fugitive Slave Law* (New York, 1851), 16–17, 21; Jacob G. Forman, *The Fugitive Slave Law* (Boston, 1850), 29; L. H. Sheldon, *The Moral Responsibility of the Citizen and Nation in Respect to*

the Fugitive Slave Bill (Andover, Mass., 1851), 12–14, 18–19; George W. Perkins, *Professor Stuart and Slave Catching: Remarks on Mr. Stuart's Book "Conscience and the Constitution"* (West Meriden, Conn., 1850), 20–21; Gilbert Haven, *National Sermons: Sermons, Speeches, and Letters on Slavery and Its War, from the Passage of the Fugitive Slave Bill to the Election of President Grant* (Boston, 1868), 15; William Hosmer, *The Higher Law* (Auburn, N.Y., 1852), 28–29; Rufus W. Clark, *Conscience and Law* (Boston, 1851), 3–5, 16; William L. Roberts, *The Higher Law; or, the Law of the Most High* (Auburn, N.Y., 1851), 30–31; Love, *Slavery in Its Relation to God,* 12–14, 18–19; Lee, *Autobiography,* 335–36; *Distinctive Principles of Free Presbyterian Church,* 9–11; ABFMS, *Annual Report . . . 1851* (Utica, N.Y., 1851), 6–7; Brock, *Parties and Political Conscience,* 328–29; Dunham, *Attitude of the Northern Clergy,* 36; Senior, "New England Congregationalists," 360–61; Norton, "Religious Press and the Compromise of 1850," 263–76; Keller, "Churches and the Fugitive Slave Law," 103–7, 160–61.

36. *Church Review and Ecclesiastical Register* 4 (April 1851): 111; *Christian Observer,* 11 May, 1 June, and 9 November 1850; *Journal of Commerce* (New York), 29 March 1851, 17 January 1852; *Watchman of the Prairie,* 31 December 1850, 2 July 1851; *Zion's Herald,* 15 January 1851; N. S. Wheaton, *Discourse on St. Paul's Epistle to Philemon, Exhibiting the Duty of Citizens of the Northern States in Regard to the Institution of Slavery* (Hartford, 1851), 5–6, 22–23; L. Smith, *The Higher Law; or, Christ and His Law Supreme* (Ravenna, Ohio, 1852), 24; Moses Stuart, *Conscience and the Constitution* (Boston, 1850), 7–8, 33, 45–46, 71–72; Samuel T. Spear, *The Law-Abiding Conscience and the Higher Law Conscience, with Remarks on the Fugitive Slave Question* (New York, 1850), 32; Charles W. Shields, *A Discourse on Christian Politics* (Philadelphia, 1851), 30; Henry A. Boardman, *The American Union* (Philadelphia, 1851), 32–33, 54; Robert L. Stanton, *Civil Government of God: Obedience a Duty* (Cincinnati, 1860), 27–33; George F. Kettell, *A Sermon on the Duty of Citizens, with Respect to the Fugitive Slave Law* (White Plains, N.Y., 1851), 13–14; Kettell, *Reply to Curry's Review,* 13–14; Stiles, *Speech on the Slavery Resolutions,* 54–55; Lorman Ratner, "Northern Concern for Social Order as a Cause for Rejecting Anti-Slavery," *Historian* 27 (November 1965): 5–6; Norton, "Religious Press and the Compromise of 1850," 201–2, 280–83; Senior, "New England Congregationalists," 351–60; Keller, "Churches and the Fugitive Slave Law," 117–22, 184–97, 233–41, 259–61.

37. Keller, "Churches and the Fugitive Slave Law," 239–40, 259–60, 385, 388.

38. Love, *Slavery in Its Relation to God,* 7–8; AFASS, *Address to the Anti-Slavery Christians,* 1–2; MASS, *Twenty-fifth Annual Report . . . 1857* (Boston, 1857), 59; Moncure D. Conway, *Autobiography: Memories and Experiences of Moncure Daniel Conway,* 2 vols. (Boston, 1904), 1:175; Peck, *George Peck,* 327–28; Bolster, *James Freeman Clarke,* 236–37; Stanley W. Campbell, *The Slave Catchers: Enforcement of the Fugitive Slave Law, 1850–1860* (Chapel Hill, N.C., 1968), 55; York, *George B. Cheever,* 135–36; Jayme A. Sokolow, "The Jerry McHenry Rescue and the Growth of Northern Antislavery Sentiment during the 1850s," *Journal of American Studies* 16 (December 1982): 432–37; Keller, "Churches and the Fugitive Slave Law,"

199–200, 290–93, 332; Senior, "New England Congregationalists," 339–40, 370–71.

39. *Lib.*, n.d., quoted in Garrison and Garrison, *William Lloyd Garrison*, 3:404; *Frederick Douglass' Paper*, 3 March 1854; *Lib.*, 17 and 31 March, 21 April 1854; *National Era*, 23 March and 6 April 1854; *Christian Watchman*, 19 January, 8 and 29 June 1854; Freewill Baptist Home Mission Society, *Twentieth Annual Report . . . 1854* (Dover, N.H., 1855), n.p.; Charles H. Bulkley, *Removal of Ancient Landmarks; or, The Causes and Consequences of Slavery Extension* (Hartford, 1854), 21–22; Caleb S. Henry, *Plain Reasons for the Great Republican Movement* (Geneva, N.Y., 1856), 14–15; Charles Beecher, *A Sermon on the Nebraska Bill* (Newark, N.J., 1854), 12–14; Joseph P. Thompson, *No Slavery in Nebraska: The Voice of God against National Crime* (New York, 1854), 27–28; Joshua R. Giddings, *History of the Rebellion: Its Authors and Causes* (New York, 1864), 367–70; Sidney E. Mead, *Nathaniel William Taylor, 1786–1858: A Connecticut Liberal* (Chicago, 1942), 236–38; Gravely, *Gilbert Haven*, 62–63; York, *George B. Cheever*, 139; Meridith, *Edward Beecher*, 598–99; Victor B. Howard, "The 1856 Election in Ohio: Moral Issues in Politics," *Ohio History* 80 (Winter 1971): 25–26, 30–31; Charles R. Denton, "The Unitarian Church and 'Kansas Territory,' 1854–1861," *Kansas Historical Quarterly* 30 (Autumn 1964): 310–11; Sweet, "Kansas Struggle," 582–83, 586–87; Ronald D. Rietveld, "The Moral Issue of Slavery in American Politics, 1854–1860" (Ph.D. diss., University of Illinois, 1967), 40; Senior, "New England Congregationalists," 375–83.

40. Quoted in Rietveld, "Moral Issue of Slavery," 43.

41. *Christian Watchman*, 30 March 1854; also *Protestant Episcopal Quarterly and Church Register* 5 (July 1858): 388; *Methodist Quarterly Review* 39 (October 1859): 541; *Freewill Baptist Quarterly* 6 (June 1858): 76; MASS, *Twenty-third Annual Report . . . 1855* (Boston, 1855), 29, 32–33; David Christy, *Pulpit Politics; or, Ecclesiastical Legislation on Slavery, in Its Disturbing Influences on the American Union* (Cincinnati, 1862), iv, 426–29; John Lawrence, *The Slavery Question* (Dayton, Ohio, 1854), 191; Henry C. Fish, *Freedom or Despotism, the Voice of Our Brother's Blood: Its Sources and Its Summons* (Newark, N.J., 1856), 20; Eden B. Foster, *A North-Side View of Slavery: A Sermon on the Crime against Freedom in Kansas and Washington* (Concord, N.H., 1856), 4–6; Love, *Slavery in Its Relation to God*, 19–20; Lord, *Letter of Inquiry*, 13–14; Lord, *Second Letter*, 34; Clifford E. Clark, Jr., "The Changing Nature of Protestantism in Mid-nineteenth Century America: Henry Ward Beecher's *Seven Lectures to Young Men*," *JAH* 57 (March 1971): 815; Rietveld, "Moral Issue of Slavery," 43.

42. *National Era*, 18 November 1848, 2 March 1854, 17 September and 2 November 1857; *Lib.*, 7 April 1854; *Political Abolitionist*, 8 January 1857; *American Missionary Magazine* 1 (March 1857): 62; South Middlesex Conference of Churches, *The Political Duties of Christians* (Boston, 1848), 7–8, 30–31; Sewell, *Ballots for Freedom*, 254–65; Rietveld, "Moral Issue of Slavery," 40; Howard, "The 1856 Election in Ohio," 40.

43. *Free Church Portfolio*, 7 January 1861; Luther Lee, *The Supremacy of the*

Divine Law (n.p., 1846), 4; Roberts, *The Higher Law*, 30–31; Conway, *Autobiography*, 1:75–76; Murray, *Presbyterians and the Negro*, 125–26; Drake, *Quakers and Slavery*, 180–81; McKivigan, "George Gordon," 345–47; Senior, "New England Congregationalists," 339–40, 365–71; Norton, "Religious Press and the Compromise of 1850," 271.

44. *Lib.*, 14 March 1856; *Christian Watchman*, 2 April 1857; *Wesleyan*, 16 December 1857; *Western Christian Advocate*, 10 February 1858; Bacon, *Leonard Bacon*, 426; Paxton Hibben, *Henry Ward Beecher: An American Portrait* (New York, 1927), 159.

45. Haven, *National Sermons*, 154; also *Zion's Herald*, 23 November 1859; *Independent*, 8 December 1859; *American Baptist*, 25 October 1859; *Oberlin Evangelist*, 21 December 1859; *Free Church Portfolio* 1 (December 1859): 354; Luther Lee, *Dying to the Glory of God* (Syracuse, N.Y., 1860), 5; James Freeman Clarke, *Anti-Slavery Days: A Sketch of the Struggle Which Ended in the Abolition of Slavery* (New York, 1884), 237; Conway, *Autobiography*, 299–300; Amory D. Mayo, *Herod, John, and Jesus; or, American Slavery and Its Christian Cure* (Albany, N.Y., 1860), 28–29; James P. Pilkington, *The Methodist Publishing House: A History* (Nashville, 1968), 392; Bolster, *James Freeman Clarke*, 250; York, *George B. Cheever*, 170; Gravely, *Gilbert Haven*, 76; Dunham, *Attitude of the Northern Clergy*, 67–68; Senior, "New England Congregationalists," 401–5.

46. *Douglass' Monthly* 2 (December 1859): 178; *Lib.*, 6 April 1860; Lewis Tappan to Frederick Douglass, 19 December 1860, Douglass Papers; Pease and Pease, *Bound with Them in Chains*, 17, 317–19; Stewart, *Holy Warriors*, 163–64; Pease and Pease, "Confrontation and Abolition in the 1850s," 925; Michael Fellman, "Theodore Parker and the Abolitionist Role in the 1850s," *JAH* 61 (December 1974): 666–67.

47. Foner, *Free Soil*, 110–39; Sewell, *Ballots for Freedom*, 254, 265–79, 292–95; Holt, *Political Crisis of the 1850s*, 119–30, 146–55.

48. Sewell, *Ballots for Freedom*, 292, 295, 306, 308, 343; Foner, *Free Soil*, 110–13; Dillon, *The Abolitionists*, 239–40; Stewart, *Holy Warriors*, 174–76; Friedman, *Gregarious Saints*, 227–41; Howard, "The 1856 Election in Ohio," 28, 31; Rietveld, "Moral Issue of Slavery," 2.

49. Salmon P. Chase, "Lectures on Slavery," undated, also Salmon P. Chase to G. B. Cheever, 29 November 1858, Chase Papers; *National Era*, 20 May 1858, 6 October and 1 December 1859; *Facts for the People* 1 (August 1855): 60–61; Henry Wilson, *History of the Rise and Fall of the Slave Power in America*, 3 vols. (Boston, 1877), 3:559–60, 720–21; James B. Stewart, *Joshua Giddings and the Tactics of Radical Politics, 1795–1864* (Cleveland, 1969), 208–11, 252–53; Foner, *Free Soil*, 78–79, 109–10.

50. "Constitution of the American Abolition Society, Adopted at Boston, October 1855," AAS MSS and *Radical Abolitionist* 1 (December 1855): 35, also 1 (August 1855): 5–6; 3 (May 1858): 76–77; and 4 (October 1858): 19; *American Jubilee* 1 (April 1855): 89; *National Era*, 18 October and 1 November 1855; Goodell, *Slavery and Anti-Slavery*, 475; Wyatt-Brown, *Lewis Tappan*, 332–34; Blue, *Free Soilers*, 2, 103, 233–34, 243–47; M. Leon Perkal, "American Abolition Society: A Viable

Alternative to the Republican Party," *Journal of Negro History* 65 (Winter 1980): 58–60, 66.

51. *Radical Abolitionist* 3 (August 1857): 2; also *American Jubilee* 1 (March 1854): 14 and 1 (September 1854): 37; William Goodell to Joseph Plumb, 23 August 1856, AAS MSS; Perkal, "American Abolition Society," 59–60.

52. Swisshelm, *Half a Century,* 199–200.

53. 20 May 1858.

54. *Wesleyan,* n.d., quoted in *Radical Abolitionist* 1 (June 1856): 83–84; also *American Baptist,* 23 October 1856, 30 October 1860; *Radical Abolitionist* 2 (October 1856): 24; ABFMS, *Annual Report . . . 1858,* 8.

55. William H. Brisbane to Salmon P. Chase, 22 June 1859, Chase Papers.

56. *Free Church Portfolio,* 11 October 1860; *American Baptist,* 3 July 1856, 18 and 25 September 1860; *National Era,* 7 August 1856; *Freewill Baptist Quarterly* 2 (July 1854): 350–52; *Wesleyan,* 22 December 1853, 11 March 1857; *Political Abolitionist,* 15 January 1857; McPherson, *Struggle for Equality,* 22–23; Stewart, *Holy Warriors,* 171; Howard, "The 1856 Election in Ohio," 29; Richard H. Watkins, "The Baptists of the North and Slavery, 1856–1860," *Foundations* 13 (October–December 1970): 323.

57. George B. Cheever to Elizabeth Cheever, 22 September 1860, Cheever Papers; also *American Missionary Magazine* 3 (December 1859): 271–72; *National Principia,* 31 December 1859, 2 and 23 June and 3 November 1860; American Reform Tract and Book Society, *Duty of Voting for Righteous Men for Office,* 7–8; Johnson, "American Missionary Association," 209–15.

58. William Goodell to W. M. Stewart, 6 October 1857, AAS MSS; also Harlow, *Gerrit Smith,* 385–89.

59. Resolution of the Northwestern Christian Anti-Slavery Convention, quoted in *Oberlin Evangelist,* 9 November 1859; also Ohio State Christian Anti-Slavery Convention, *Proceedings,* 10–11.

60. Salmon P. Chase to James Monroe, 15 October 1859, Monroe Papers; also Ohio State Christian Anti-Slavery Convention, *Proceedings,* 10–11; Dillon, *The Abolitionists,* 199–202.

61. *Wesleyan,* 22 December 1853; *Freewill Baptist Quarterly* 2 (July 1854): 350–51; *Free Presbyterian,* 13 December 1854; *Facts for the People* 1 (July 1855): 18; Haven, *National Sermons,* 111–12; Amory Battles to Israel Washburn, 8 February 1854, in Galliard Hunt, *Israel, Elihu, and Cadwallader Washburn: A Chapter in American Biography* (New York, 1925), 62–64; C. D. Cleveland to Gamaliel Bailey, n.d., in *National Era,* 18 January 1855; W. H. Brisbane to Salmon P. Chase, 22 June 1859, Chase Papers.

62. *National Principia,* 29 September 1860, also 6 and 27 October, 3 November 1860; *National Era,* 24 July and 11 December 1856; *American Baptist,* 2 October 1860; *Radical Abolitionist* 2 (March 1857): 66; Friedman, *Gregarious Saints,* 90–93; Ellsworth, "Oberlin," 123–24; Perkal, "William Goodell," 292–97; Perkal, "American Abolition Society," 60–61.

63. *Independent,* 24 May 1860; Haven, *National Sermons,* 111–12, 120–21, 199; Henry W. Bellows to Cyrus A. Bartol, 7 November 1860, Henry W. Bellows Papers, Massachusetts Historical Society; Francis Wayland to Reverend Nott, 4 January 1859, Wayland Papers; Oliver Johnson to Theodore Parker, 15 August 1856, Parker Papers; Robert C. Albrecht, *Theodore Parker* (New York, 1971), 119; Gardiner Spring, *Personal Reminiscences of the Life and Times of Gardiner Spring,* 2 vols. (New York, 1866), 2:186; Kleppner, *Cross of Culture,* 104–5; Foner, *Free Soil,* 109; L. Wesley Norton, "The Methodist Episcopal Church in Michigan and the Politics of Slavery, 1850–1860," *Michigan History* 48 (September 1964): 209–13; Howard, "The 1856 Election in Ohio," 29–30, 35–36, 44.

Chapter 9. *Abolitionism and the Advance of Religious Antislavery Practices, 1845–1860*

1. *NASS,* 12 June 1851, *Lib.,* 30 May 1851, 12 January 1856; *Frederick Douglass' Paper,* 19 November 1852; Fladeland, *Men and Brothers,* 364–68; Smith, *Revivalism and Social Reform,* 204; Griffin, *Their Brothers' Keepers,* 151, 217–19, 224.

2. *Douglass' Monthly* 1 (February 1859): 17; *American Missionary Magazine* 2 (April 1858): 82–83; *Lib.,* 20 August 1858; William Goodell to W. B. Burwick, 8 March 1859; William Goodell to John Smith, 18 April 1859, both in AAS MSS; William Jay to Lewis Tappan, 31 March 1857, Tappan Papers; Lewis Tappan to George Whipple, 11 March 1858; John Lowry to S. S. Jocelyn, 25 April 1858, both in AMA MSS; Smith, *Revivalism and Social Reform,* 204; Carl L. Spicer, "The Great Awakening of 1857 and 1858" (Ph.D. diss., Ohio State University, 1935), 228–29.

3. MASS, *Seventeenth Annual Report . . . 1849,* 65; also *Eman.,* 9 February 1848; *Lib.,* 24 March 1848; *Freewill Baptist Quarterly* 1 (October 1853): 415, and 2 (January 1854): 44–45; *National Principia,* 14 January 1860; AFASS, *Eighth Annual Report . . . 1848,* 142–43; Freewill Baptist Anti-Slavery Society, *Third Annual Report . . . 1849* (Dover, N.H., 1849), 4; Freewill Baptist Home Missionary Society, *Nineteenth Annual Report . . . 1853* (Dover, N.H., 1854), 18; Foster, *Brotherhood of Thieves,* 61–62; Johnson, *William Lloyd Garrison,* 81; Baxter, *Freewill Baptists,* 98–100; Jason Howard Silverman, "Unwelcome Guests: American Fugitive Slaves in Canada, 1830–1860" (Ph.D. diss., University of Kentucky, 1981), 104.

4. *Journal and Messenger,* 26 April 1850; *National Era,* 19 December 1850, 3 July and 7 August 1856; Murray, *Presbyterians and the Negro,* 127–29; Morrison, *David McDill,* 61–62, 188–89; Fisk, "Associate Reformed Church," 167; Howard, "Antislavery Movement in the Presbyterian Church," 204–5, 369–71.

5. *Covenanter,* n.d., quoted in *Lib.,* 4 December 1846; also *National Era,* 30 August 1849.

6. AASS, *Annual Report . . . 1855,* 143–44; also *Lib.,* 6 July 1849.

7. *Non-Slaveholder* 3 (October 1848): 220; MASS, *Eighteenth Annual Report . . . 1850,* 80–81; Pennsylvania Anti-Slavery Society, *Thirteenth Annual Report . . . 1850,* 31, 34; Drake, *Quakers and Slavery,* 165–68, 173, 176–77; Aptheker, "Quakers and Negro Slavery," 361.

8. AASS, *Annual Report . . . 1856*, 66; *Wesleyan*, 31 March 1853; *Lib.*, 23 October 1853; AFASS, *Thirteenth Annual Report . . . 1853*, 87–112; George Thompson to George Whipple, 7 October 1856; C. W. von Coellin to Lewis Tappan, 22 December 1860, both in AMA MSS; Raymond W. Albright, *History of the Evangelical Church* (Harrisburg, Pa., 1942), 299.

9. *Boston Catholic Observer*, n.d., quoted in *Lib.*, 24 August 1849; also *Lib.*, 10 August 1849, 17 May 1850; *North Star*, 24 August 1849; AFASS, *Tenth Annual Report . . . 1850*, 68; W. L. Garrison to Samuel May, Jr., 28 July 1849, *Garrison Letters*, 3:644; Lewis Tappan to Mrs. Nicholson, 20 July 1849, Tappan Papers; Frederick Douglass to Theobald Mathew, n.d., Douglass Papers; Jay P. Dolan, *The Immigrant Church: New York's Irish and German Catholics, 1815–1865* (Baltimore, 1975), 24–25, 121–29; Filler, *Crusade against Slavery*, 148–49; Bartlett, *Wendell Phillips*, 93; Murphy, "Catholic Church," 283, 293–95.

10. *Church Review and Ecclesiastical Register* 7 (October 1854): 437, also 430; 4 (October 1851): 382; and 9 (January 1857): 617; Samuel D. McConnell, *History of the American Episcopal Church from the Planting of the Colonies to the End of the Civil War*, 6th ed. (New York, 1890), 361–63; Ronald Levy, "Bishop Hopkins and the Dilemma of Slavery," *Pennsylvania Magazine of History and Biography* 91 (January 1967): 56–62; Lyons, "Religious Defense of Slavery," 8; Evans, "Abolitionism in Illinois Churches," 150–53; Engelder, "Churches and Slavery," 261–62.

11. Some moderate antislavery sentiment existed among northern evangelical (Low Church) Episcopalians but they hesitated to express their views from fear of losing southern evangelical support in the contest with ritualist (High Church) elements for control of the denomination. Friedman, " 'Historical Topics Sometimes Run Dry,' " 188–89; Engelder, "Churches and Slavery," 260–63, 268–70; *Church Review and Ecclesiastical Register* 5 (October 1852): 471–72; and 9 (October 1856): 353; *Eman.*, 22 July 1846; *Lib.*, 22 August 1850; AASS, *Second Decade*, 106–7; *Annual Report . . . 1855*, 83; and *Annual Report . . . 1859–60*, 281; MASS, *Twentieth Annual Report . . . 1852*, 63; Pillsbury, *Church as It Is*, 46–47; Foster, *Brotherhood of Thieves*, 58; Goodell, *Slavery and Anti-Slavery*, 191–94; Samuel Ringgold Ward, *Autobiography of a Fugitive Negro* (London, 1855), 282–83; Tuckerman, *William Jay*, 132–33.

12. *Lib.*, 13 July 1855; *American Missionary Magazine* 1 (August 1857): 175; *Presbyterian of the West*, 12 July 1850; S. S. Jocelyn to George Whipple, 13 April 1853, AMA MSS; Ralph L. Moellering, *Christian Conscience and Negro Emancipation* (Philadelphia, 1965), 84–86; Wentz, *Lutheranism in America*, 163, 173; Fortenbaugh, "American Lutheran Synods and Slavery," 73–76, 86–91; David Christiano, "Synod and Slavery, 1855," *New Jersey History* 90 (Spring 1972): 27–42.

13. *Presbyterian Magazine* 3 (July 1853): 349; and 7 (September 1857): 423; *Presbyterian of the West*, 18 November 1847; 29 January, 8 March, and 31 May 1849; 16 May and 8 August 1850; Rice, *Lectures on Slavery*, 14–21, 24, 34, 64–65, 72–75; Van Dyke, *Character and Influence of Abolitionism*, 29, 33; Robinson, *Testimony and Practice*, 116–17; Smith, *Revivalism and Social Reform*, 187; Murray, *Presbyterians and the Negro*, 106–11; Walter B. Posey, "The Slavery Question in the Presbyterian Church in the Old Southwest," *JSH* 15 (August 1949): 321–24; Spicer, "Great

Awakening of 1857 and 1858," 240–42; Engelder, "Churches and Slavery," 239–42; Howard, "Antislavery Movement in the Presbyterian Church," 134.

14. *Presbyterian of the West*, 30 September 1847, 5 October 1848, 1 February and 27 September 1849, 2 May 1850, 25 June 1856; *Presbyterian Expositor* 1 (October 1858): 585–89, (May 1858): 335–36, and (June 1858): 378; *Presbyter*, 16 January, 9 and 23 February 1860; *Presbyterian Magazine* 4 (January 1854): 44–45; AFASS, *Tenth Annual Report . . . 1850*, 34; AASS, *Annual Report . . . 1858* (New York, 1858), 160–61; and *Annual Report . . . 1859–60*, 295; Boardman, *American Union*, 32–33, 54–55; Stanton, *Civil Government of God*, 27–33; Baird, *Robert Baird*, 235; R. C. Galbraith, *The History of the Chillicothe Presbytery, from Its Organization in 1799 to 1889* (Chillicothe, Ohio, 1889), 15; Stewart, "Chillicothe Presbytery," 46–47; Norton, "Religious Press and the Compromise of 1850," 54–56, 280–83; Howard, "Antislavery Movement in the Presbyterian Church," 78–79; Keller, "Churches and the Fugitive Slave Law," 239.

15. *Presbyterian of the West*, 20 July and 10 August 1848; Rice, *Lectures on Slavery*, 47; AFASS, *Tenth Annual Report . . . 1850*, 37; MASS, *Seventeenth Annual Report . . . 1849*, 66; Senior, "New England Congregationalists," 255–56, 282–84, 294–301; Engelder, "Churches and Slavery," 101–4, 248–49.

16. Alfred A. Thomas, ed., *Correspondence of Thomas Ebenezer Thomas, Mainly Relating to the Antislavery Conflict in Ohio, Especially in the Presbyterian Church* (Dayton, Ohio, 1909), 107, also 91–100, 109; *Presbyter*, 22 September 1859; 12 January, 22 March, and 26 July 1860; *Presbyterian of the West*, 7 March 1850; *Presbyterian Expositor* 1 (January 1858): 95 and (November 1858): 664; James Patterson, *The Old School Presbyterian Church on Slavery* (New Wilmington, Ohio, 1857), 3–5, 9, 35; J. R. Gibson to S. S. Jocelyn, 1 July 1859, AMA MSS; T. D. Baird to S. J Baird, 31 October 1856, Samuel J. Baird Papers, Manuscript Division, Library of Congress; Leroy J. Halsey, *History of McCormick Theological Seminary of the Presbyterian Church* (Chicago, 1893), 100, 150–51; Lyons, "Religious Defense of Slavery," 76–77; Irving S. Kull, "Presbyterian Attitudes toward Slavery," *Church History* 7 (June 1938): 109–10; Galbraith, *Chillicothe Presbytery*, 222; William E. Dodd, "The Fight for the Northwest, 1860," *American Historical Review* 16 (July 1911): 781–82; Lester H. Cook, "Anti-Slavery Sentiment in the Culture of Chicago, 1844–1858" (Ph.D. diss., University of Chicago, 1952), 47–48, 140–42; Evans, "Abolitionism in Illinois Churches," 174–76.

17. *Christian Observer*, 8 June 1850; 8 February, 1 March, 5 and 19 April 1851; *New York Observer*, 11 September 1847, 3 February 1849, 8 February 1850; Frederick A. Ross, *Position of the Southern Church in Relation to Slavery* (New York, 1857), 22–23; Frederick A. Ross, *Slavery Ordained of God* (Philadelphia, 1857), 70–71, 75–76, 95–96, 112–13.

18. Albert Barnes, *An Inquiry into the Scriptural Views on Slavery* (Philadelphia, 1846), 78, 381–84; Barnes, *Church and Slavery*, 110–12; Murray, *Presbyterians and the Negro*, 115–19; Marsden, *Evangelical Mind*, 89–90, 102; Howard, "Antislavery Movement in the Presbyterian Church," 123, 153–56; Evans, "Abolitionism in Illinois Churches," 201; Engelder, "Churches and Slavery," 223–36.

19. AASS, *Annual Report . . . 1855*, 80–81; also *Eman.*, 14 January 1846, 30 June 1847; *AFAS Reporter*, April 1846, 110; May 1846, 5; and June 1846, 10–12; *New York Observer*, 7 December 1847, 23 September 1848, 1 June 1850; *Lib.*, 15 June 1849; *Christian Observer*, 4 and 11 May, 9 November 1850; and 20 September 1851; *New York Evangelist*, 17 October 1850; 12 June, 7 and 14 August 1851; *Prairie Herald*, n.d., quoted in *Watchman of the Prairie*, 22 July 1851; AFASS, *Eleventh Annual Report . . . 1851*, 60–61; and *Thirteenth Annual Report . . . 1853*, 72–73, 84; AASS, *Annual Report . . . 1855*, 80–81; Pillsbury, *Church as It Is*, 75; Goodell, *Slavery and Anti-Slavery*, 162; Lewis Tappan to Albert Barnes, 24 December 1849, 18 February 1850, Albert Barnes Papers, Presbyterian Historical Society, Philadelphia; Victor B. Howard, "Presbyterians, the Kansas-Nebraska Act, and the Election of 1856," *Journal of Presbyterian History* 49 (Summer 1971): 135, 143, 148, 153; Howard, "Antislavery Movement in the Presbyterian Church," 179, 200, 206.

20. *Christian Observer*, 24 November 1849, 20 September 1851; *New York Observer*, 1 July 1848; *New York Evangelist*, 22 November 1849, 24 May 1850; *Oberlin Evangelist*, 8 May 1850; AFASS, *Tenth Annual Report . . . 1850*, 40–42; and *Thirteenth Annual Report . . . 1853*, 86–87; Muelder, *Fighters for Freedom*, 285–86; Arthur C. Cole, *Era of the Civil War, 1848–1870* (Springfield, Ill., 1919), 222–23; Marsden, *Evangelical Mind*, 125; Nichols, *Presbyterians in New York State*, 156; Welsh, *Buckeye Presbyterianism*, 101; Frederick Kuhns, "Slavery and Missions in the Old Northwest," *Journal of the Presbyterian Historical Society* 24 (December 1946): 206; Senior, "New England Congregationalists," 287–88; Howard, "Antislavery Movement in the Presbyterian Church," 102–4, 115–19, 183–84; Cook, "Anti-Slavery Sentiment in Chicago," 36–37.

21. Quoted in Engelder, "Churches and Slavery," 225, also 220–28; Marsden, *Evangelical Mind*, 89–90; Howard, "Antislavery Movement in the Presbyterian Church," 153–56, 223–25.

22. *New York Evangelist*, 6 June 1860; *Presbyterian Magazine* 7 (October 1857): 439; *Political Abolitionist*, 12 March 1857; *American Missionary Magazine* 1 (October 1857): 222–23; Barnes, *Church and Slavery*, 18–19, 44–45, 110–12, 118–19, 166, 174–78; A. C. Crist, *The History of Marion Presbytery: Its Churches, Elders, Ministers, Missionary Societies, Etc.* (n.p., 1908), 38–39; Kuhns, *Home Missionary Society*, 14; Lyons, "Religious Defense of Slavery," 11–12; Howard, "Antislavery Movement in the Presbyterian Church," 127–29, 181–92, 219–33; Engelder, "Churches and Slavery," 224–33. The predominantly southern Cumberland Presbyterians also suffered a partial sectional schism in the late 1850s when at least five midwestern ministers, led by the Reverend T. B. McCormick, seceded in protest to their church's instructions not to preach against slavery; *American Missionary Magazine* 1 (March 1857): 67; *Radical Abolitionist* 1 (October 1855): 17–19; *National Era*, 22 November 1855; *Political Abolitionist*, 17 September 1856.

23. *Lib.*, 26 June 1857; *National Principia*, 28 April 1860; *Radical Abolitionist*, 2 (July 1857): 105; *Political Abolitionist*, 18 June 1857; *American Missionary Magazine* 1 (July 1857): 157; AASS, *Annual Report . . . 1859–60*, 280; Free Presbyterian Board, *Joseph Gordon*, 226–27; Joseph Wilson, ed., *The Presbyterian Historical*

Almanac and Annual Rembrancer of the Church for 1858–1859 (Philadelphia, 1859), 58–59, 228; Engelder, "Churches and Slavery," 234–35; Johnson, "Free Presbyterian Church," 64–65.

24. Quoted in Powell, "Abolitionist Controversy in the Methodist Episcopal Church," 150, also 116, 152–69; *Methodist Quarterly Review* 34 (July 1852): 380–82; *Methodist* (New York), 3 November 1860; *Zion's Herald*, 15 January 1851; Peck, *Slavery and Episcopacy*, 8–9, 31–32, 107–8; Olin, *Stephen Olin*, 246–47; Abel Stevens, *The Life and Times of Reverend Nathan Bangs* (New York, 1863), 340; Daniel Curry, *Life-Story of Davis Wasgatt Clark, D.D., Bishop of the Methodist Episcopal Church* (New York, 1874), 9–11; Emory S. Bucke, ed., *The History of American Methodism*, 3 vols. (New York, 1964), 1:167; William W. Sweet, *Methodism in American History* (Nashville, 1954), 254–56; Wallace G. Smeltzer, *Methodism on the Headwaters of the Ohio: The History of the Pittsburgh Conference of the Methodist Church, 1772–1950* (Nashville, 1951), 161–68; Smith, *In His Image But . . .* , 114; Sweet, "Kansas Struggle," 578–95; Norwood, "Schism in the Methodist Church," 138–39.

25. Charles K. Whipple, *The Methodist Church and Slavery* (New York, 1859), 30–31; also *Eman.*, 25 February 1846; MASS, *Fifteenth Annual Report . . . 1847*, 74; AFASS, *Eleventh Annual Report . . . 1851*, 41; and *Thirteenth Annual Report . . . 1853*, 93–99; J. G. Fee to Frederick Merrick, 1 August 1849, Frederick Merrick Papers (United Methodist Archives Center, West Ohio Conference, United Methodist Church, Ohio Wesleyan University).

26. *Zion's Herald*, 18 June 1851, 4 March 1857; *Methodist Quarterly Review* 39 (July 1857): 458–59; Mattison, *Impending Crisis*, 114–15; Abel Stevens, *A Compendious History of American Methodism* (New York, 1868), 525; Haven, *National Sermons*, 39, 45; Scott, *Grounds of Secession*, 168–69; L. L. Hamline to J. B. Finley, 14 September 1844, Finley Papers; Gravely, *Gilbert Haven*, 25, 34–35; Mathews, "Methodist Schism of 1844," 19–21; Norton, "Religious Press and the Compromise of 1850," 56; Powell, "Abolitionist Controversy in the Methodist Episcopal Church," 187–89.

27. *Zion's Herald*, 15 January 1851; John D. Long, *Pictures of Slavery in Church and State* (Philadelphia, 1857), 32–33, 41, 155–56; J. Mayland M'Carter, *Border Methodism and Border Slavery* (Philadelphia, 1858), 4–5, 16–18; J. S. Lame, *Maryland Slavery and Maryland Chivalry* (Philadelphia, 1858), 19–20, 38–39; Samuel Huffman, *A Vindication of Border Methodism* (St. Louis, 1858), 46; William H. Pullen, *The Blast of a Trumpet in Zion* (London, 1860), 23–24, 32–33; Cartwright, *Autobiography*, 427–31; Mattison, *Impending Crisis*, 40–42; Whipple, *Methodist Church and Slavery*, 17–19; Samuel Brooks, *Slavery and the Slaveholders' Religion as Opposed to Christianity* (Cincinnati, 1846), 52, 65–68; Haven, *National Sermon*, vii–ix; William Hosmer, *Slavery and the Church* (Auburn, N.Y., 1853), 36–37, 74–76, 83–84, 98–99, 142; Matlack, *Antislavery Struggle*, 306–10; Bucke, *American Methodism*, 1:188–89; Henry B. Ridgaway, *Life of Alfred Cookman* (New York, 1874), 217–19; Norton, "Methodist Episcopal Church in Michigan," 200–1; Powell, "Abolitionist Controversy in the Methodist Episcopal Church," 171–76, 180–82,

185–86; Norton, "Religious Press and the Compromise of 1850," 47; Cook, "Anti-Slavery Sentiment in Chicago," 34–35.

28. *Methodist*, 14 July 1860; *National Era*, 19 October 1854, 1 November 1855; *Zion's Herald*, 16 January 1856; 25 February, 29 April, 5 August, 16 September, 16 December 1857; 17 November 1858; 9 March, 8 June, 19 October, 21 and 28 December 1859; *Methodist Quarterly Review* 38 (April 1856): 319; and 39 (July 1857): 457–64; *Western Christian Advocate*, 14 April, 22 September, and 10 November 1858; *Independent*, 26 April 1860; *National Principia*, 16 June 1860; Daniel De-Vinne, *The Methodist Episcopal Church and Slavery* (New York, 1857), 96; Elias Bowen, *Slavery in the Methodist Episcopal Church* (Auburn, N.Y., 1859), iv–vi, 77–78, 124–25, 175–76, 189–200, 296–97; William Logan Harris, *The Constitutional Powers of the General Conference, with a Special Application to the Subject of Slave Holding* (Cincinnati, 1860), 134–35; Methodist Anti-Slavery Union, *Proceedings of the Anti-Slavery Convention of the Black River Conference* (New York, 1858), 1–4; Mattison, *Impending Crisis*, 94–124; Cartwright, *Autobiography*, 503; Peck, *George Peck*, 353–54, 367–69; Matlack, *Antislavery Struggle*, 310–22; M'Carter, *Border Methodism*, 87–88; Christy, *Pulpit Politics*, 419; Pullen, *Blast of a Trumpet*, 38, 44–46; Curry, *Davis Wasgatt Clark*, 170–71; Bucke, *American Methodism*, 1:199–262, 500–505; J. Jeffrey Auer, ed., *Antislavery and Disunion, 1858–1861: Studies in the Rhetoric of Compromise and Conflict* (New York, 1963), 154–55; Lewis M. Hagood, *The Colored Man in the Methodist Episcopal Church* (Cincinnati, 1890), 99–100; Gravely, *Gilbert Haven*, 57–59; Marie S. White, "The Methodist Antislavery Struggle in the Land of Lincoln," *Methodist History* 10 (July 1972): 45–51; Powell, "Abolitionist Controversy in the Methodist Episcopal Church," 226–27; Engelder, "Churches and Slavery," 154–62.

29. *Northern Independent*, n.d., quoted in *National Principia*, 16 June 1860; George Crooks, ed., *Sermons of Bishop Matthew Simpson* (New York, 1885), 363, 369; Wilson T. Hogue, *History of the Free Methodist Church of North America*, 2 vols. (Chicago, 1915), 1:22–23; Gravely, *Gilbert Haven*, 60; Cross, *Burned-over District*, 354; William B. Gravely, "Methodist Preachers, Slavery, and Caste: Types of Social Concern in Antebellum America," *Duke Divinity School Review* 34 (Autumn 1969): 224–25; Powell, "Abolitionist Controversy in the Methodist Episcopal Church," 210–19, 226–27, 231–32. In 1858 a similar controversy over the fellowship of slaveholders led northern Methodist Protestant annual conferences to secede from their denomination; see George Brown, *Recollections of Itinerant Life, Including Early Reminiscences* (Cincinnati, 1866), 356–66; Ancel H. Bassett, *A Concise History of the Methodist Protestant Church from Its Origin* (Pittsburgh, 1887), 167–221; Pilkington, *Methodist Publishing House*, 393–95.

30. *National Principia*, 16 June 1860; also *Lib.*, 15 July 1859; AASS, *Annual Report . . . 1857* (New York, 1857), 86–89; and *Annual Report . . . 1859–60*, 276–77, 305; Brownlow and Pryne, *Debate*, 224.

31. *Christian Examiner* September 1854, 235, also 228–30, 242–44; and July 1849, 70–71; George W. Cooke, *Unitarianism in America* (Boston, 1902), 353; Daniel W. Howe, *The Unitarian Conscience: Harvard Moral Philosophy, 1805–1861*

(Cambridge, 1970), 274–79; Bartlett, *Wendell Phillips*, 95; Rice, *William Ellery Channing*, 267–68; Stange, *Patterns of Antislavery*, 77–84, 182–86.

32. AFASS, *Thirteenth Annual Report . . . 1853*, 105–6; MASS, *Thirteenth Annual Report . . . 1845*, 57–58; Conway, *Autobiography*, 185–86; Clarke, *Anti-Slavery Days*, 131; May, *Some Recollections*, 335–37; Rice, *Federal Street Pastor*, 263–68; Cooke, *Unitarianism in America*, 353–58; Conrad Wright, *Liberal Christians* (Boston, 1970), 64–68; Bartlett, *Wendell Phillips*, 95; Henry Steele Commager, *Theodore Parker* (Boston, 1936), 202, 213; Stange, *Patterns of Antislavery*, 98, 174–75, 200–201, 209–10; Ledbetter and Ledbetter, "Agitator and Intellectuals," 178–83; Fellman, "Theodore Parker," 668–69.

33. *Christian Examiner* 47 (November 1849): 471; *NASS*, 5 June 1851; AFASS, *Thirteenth Annual Report . . . 1853*, 105–6; AASS, *Annual Report . . . 1857*, 83; May, *Some Recollections*, 367–69; James Freeman Clarke, *The Rendition of Anthony Burns: Its Causes and Consequences* (Boston, 1854), 17–18; Albrecht, *Theodore Parker*, 202; Chadwick, *Theodore Parker*, 236, 243; Bolster, *James Freeman Clarke*, 175–76, 236–37; Commager, *Theodore Parker*, 207–9; Wright, *Liberal Christians*, 64–65; Dunham, *Attitude of the Northern Clergy*, 33; Stange, *Patterns of Antislavery*, 137–41, 211–17; Denton, "Unitarian Church and 'Kansas Territory,'" 310–11.

34. Quoted in *National Era*, 4 June 1857; also *NASS*, 15 June 1843, 24 July 1851; *Lib.*, 4 April 1845, 24 November 1854, 5 June 1857; MASS, *Fourteenth Annual Report . . . 1846*, 72–73; AFASS, *Thirteenth Annual Report . . . 1853*, 105–6; May, *Some Recollections*, 338–44, 369–72; Oliver Johnson to Theodore Parker, 6 May 1858, Parker Papers; Robert E. Collins, ed., *Theodore Parker, American Transcendentalist: A Critical Essay and a Collection of His Writings* (Metchuen, N.J., 1973), 4; Commager, *Theodore Parker*, 202, 213; Stange, *Patterns of Antislavery*, 218–27; John W. Chadwick, "Samuel May of Leicester," *New England Magazine* 10 (April 1899): 211; Fellman, "Theodore Parker," 668–71; Evans, "Abolitionism in Illinois Churches," 236–39.

35. Quoted in *Lib.*, 24 April 1846, also 30 April 1841; *National Era*, 8 November 1849; *NASS*, 3 November 1842; Cassara, *Hosea Ballou*, 105; Cassara, *Universalism in America*, 189–90.

36. *Lib.*, 8 May 1846, also 24 June 1859; May, *Some Recollections*, 333–34; Pillsbury, *Church as It Is*, 49–50; Cross, *Burned-over District*, 323.

37. *National Era*, 10 November 1853; Pillsbury, *Church as It Is*, 52–54; Brooks, *Slaveholders' Religion*, 23–24; Henry J. Brown and Frederick D. Williams, eds., *The Diary of James A. Garfield*, 3 vols. (East Lansing, Mich., 1967–71), 1:248; Richardson, *Alexander Campbell*, 500–1, 532–34; Lamar, *Isaac Errett*, 1:214–16; William E. Tucker and Lester C. McAllister, *Journey in Faith: A History of the Christian Church (Disciples of Christ)* (St. Louis, 1975), 198–200; Frank S. Mead, *Handbook of Denominations in the United States*, 4th ed. (Nashville, 1965), 66–68; Lunger, *Alexander Campbell*, 222; Garrison and DeGroot, *Disciples of Christ*, 330; David E. Harrell, "The Sectional Origins of the Churches of Christ," *JSH* 30 (August 1964): 265–66; Evans, "Abolitionism in Illinois Churches," 330–33.

38. *Congregationalist*, 14 June 1850; *Independent*, 19 January 1860; *Congregationalist Quarterly* 40 (October 1962): 341–42; *Oberlin Evangelist*, 23 June and 21

July 1852; *American Missionary* 2 (August 1848): 74–75; Leonard Bacon, *The Jugglers Detected* (New Haven, 1861), 13; Congregational Ministers of Massachusetts, *Report of the Committee on Slavery, to the Convention of Congregational Ministers of Massachusetts, Presented May 30, 1849* (Boston, 1849), 87–88; Mark D. Howe, *The Garden and the Wilderness: Religion and Government in American Constitutional History* (Chicago, 1965), 66–67; Muelder, *Fighters for Freedom,* 150–51; Hibben, *Henry Ward Beecher,* 133–34; Dumond, *Antislavery;* 346; James Conner, "The Antislavery Movement in Iowa," *Annals of Iowa* 40 (Summer 1970): 361; Lyons, "Religious Defense of Slavery," 8–9; Senior, "New England Congregationalists," 96–98, 209–13, 331–32, 389–98, 405, 410.

39. *Independent,* 24 January 1856; also 23 June 1859, 25 January and 5 April 1860; *Congregationalist,* 7 June 1850; *Lib.,* 21 September 1849; 13 April, 11 May, and 12 October 1860; *NASS,* 16 July 1859; *Anti-Slavery Bugle,* 27 July 1850; MASS, *Twelfth Annual Report . . . 1844,* 60; and *Eighteenth Annual Report . . . 1850,* 79–80; AASS, *Annual Report . . . 1855,* 37; *Annual Report . . . 1857,* 83; and *Annual Report . . . 1859–60,* 282–83, 328–29; Pillsbury, *Acts of the Anti-Slavery Apostles,* 114–15; Senior, "New England Congregationalists," 66–67, 79.

40. Connecticut General Association of Congregational Ministers, *Minutes . . . 1854,* quoted in Senior, "New England Congregationalists," 382, also 351–63, 375–86; *Congregationalist,* 15 February, 5 April, and 21 June 1850; *Independent,* 5 May 1859; *Oberlin Evangelist,* 30 September 1846, 27 August 1851, 23 June 1852; Horace T. Bushnell, *Slavery in Its Relation to God: A Review of Reverend Dr. Lord's Thanksgiving Sermon in Favor of Domestic Slavery* (Buffalo, 1851), 8–9, 21–22; Leonard Bacon, *The Higher Law* (New Haven, 1851), 14–15; Stuart, *Conscience and the Constitution,* 71–72; Goodell, *Slavery and Anti-Slavery,* 168–71; Beecher, *Duty of Disobedience,* 16–17, 21; Thompson, *Fugitive Slave Law,* 34–35; Beecher, *Sermon on Nebraska Bill,* 12–14; Thompson, *No Slavery in Nebraska,* 27–28; Robert S. Fletcher, *A History of Oberlin College from Its Foundation through the Civil War,* 2 vols. (Chicago, 1943), 1:265–70; Lesick, *The Lane Rebels,* 181–99; Cross, *Burned-over District,* 256–57; Spinka, *Illinois Congregational and Christian Churches,* 147–48; Howard, "The 1856 Election in Ohio," 30–31; Evans, "Abolitionism in Illinois Churches," 182–85, 200–201, 212–13; Ellsworth, "Oberlin," 119–21.

41. *Independent,* 24 February, 3 March, and 14 July 1859; 22 March and 24 May 1860; *Congregationalist,* 27 August 1852; *Oberlin Evangelist,* 20 June 1849, 13 July 1859; *National Principia,* 17 March 1860; *American Missionary Magazine* 1 (December 1857): 276; Henry Cowles to S. S. Jocelyn, 3 January 1858, AMA MSS; Kennedy, *Plan of Union,* 261–62; Muelder, *Fighters for Freedom,* 292, 300; Fletcher, *Oberlin College,* 1:263–64; Spinka, *Illinois Congregational and Christian Churches,* 150; Wyatt-Brown, *Lewis Tappan,* 320–21; Filler, *Crusade against Slavery,* 197; Griffin, "Abolitionists and the Benevolent Societies," 205–9; Engelder, "Churches and Slavery," 109–14; Johnson, "American Missionary Association," 34–35.

42. Connecticut General Association of Congregational Ministers, *Minutes . . . 1854,* quoted in Senior, "New England Congregationalists," 294, also 255–56, 269, 282–87, 292–97, 300–301; *New York Observer,* 1 July 1848; *Congregationalist,* 1 October 1852; AFASS, *Thirteenth Annual Report . . . 1853,* 100; AASS, *Annual*

Report . . . 1859–60, 282–84; Wyatt-Brown, *Lewis Tappan,* 320; Spinka, *Illinois Congregational and Christian Churches,* 125; Pearson, "From Church to Denomination," 82–84; Engelder, "Churches and Slavery," 101–9.

43. *National Principia,* 13 October and 10 November 1860; *Douglass' Monthly* 3 (September 1860): 321; *NASS,* 2 July and 3 December 1859; *Independent,* 19 January 1860; AASS, *Annual Report . . . 1859–60,* 282–84; G. B. Cheever to H. T. Cheever, 23 August 1857; G. B. Cheever to Elizabeth Cheever, 18 April 1859; George Thompson to G. B. Cheever, 6 September 1860, all in Cheever Papers; Wyatt-Brown, *Lewis Tappan,* 319; York, *George B. Cheever,* 142–43, 154; Louis Filler, "Liberalism, Anti-Slavery, and the Founders of the *Independent,*" *New England Quarterly* 27 (September 1954): 306; Senior, "New England Congregationalists," 405–10.

44. *Eman.,* 14 January 1840; *Christian Contributor,* 9 June and 15 December 1847, 14 June and 6 December 1848; *American Baptist,* 1 August 1850, 14 August 1851, 12 February 1852; *Baptist Missionary Magazine* 25 (July 1845): 150; and 38 (July 1858): 219; *Watchman of the Prairie,* 8, 15, and 29 July 1851; *Free Mission Record* 1 (August 1857): 1; *Christian Watchman,* 24 September and 1 October 1857; AFASS, *Tenth Annual Report . . . 1850,* 60; and *Thirteenth Annual Report . . . 1853,* 97, 123; American Baptist Missionary Union, *Twenty-fourth Annual Report . . . 1848* (New York, 1848), 50; ABFMS, *Annual Report . . . 1848,* 21–25; and *Annual Report . . . 1849,* 5; American Baptist Home Mission Society, *Fourteenth Annual Report . . . 1846,* 6; *Fifteenth Annual Report . . . 1847,* 4–5; and *Sixteenth Annual Report . . . 1848,* 4; AASS, *Annual Report . . . 1859–60,* 281–82; *Proceedings of the American Anti-Slavery Society at Its Third Decade* (New York, 1863), 91; Warren, *Free Missionary Principle,* 29–30; Foss and Mathews, *Facts for Baptist Churches,* 308–10; Aaron, *Life, Sermons, Correspondence,* 151–57; Baker, *Southern Baptist Convention,* 197, 203, 206–7; Donnell R. Harris, "The Gradual Separation of Southern and Northern Baptists, 1845–1907," *Foundations* 7 (April 1964): 130–31, 136, 139; Engelder, "Churches and Slavery," 79–81.

45. *Watchman of the Prairie,* 18 June 1850; *Lib.,* 1 October 1852; *Free Mission Record* 1 (June 1857): 1; *Baptist Missionary Magazine* 36 (July 1856): 201, and 41 (July 1861): 272; American Baptist Home Mission Society, *Seventeenth Annual Report . . . 1849* (New York, 1849), 2, 6; and *Twentieth Annual Report . . . 1852* (New York, 1852), 26, 82–83; ABFMS, *Annual Report . . . 1858,* 10; AFASS, *Ninth Annual Report . . . 1849,* 80–81; AASS, *Annual Report . . . 1855,* 144–45; Foss and Mathews, *Facts for Baptist Churches,* 238–68; William Goodell to J. J. Linton, 26 June 1856, AAS MSS; Francis Wayland to James Hoby, 17 December 1845, Wayland Papers; Baker, *Southern Baptist Convention,* 197–98, 203, 206–7; John R. McKivigan, "The American Baptist Free Mission Society: Abolitionist Reaction to the 1845 Baptist Schism," *Foundations* 21 (October–December 1978): 350–51; Harris, "Gradual Separation," 130–32, 136–37, 139; Engelder, "Churches and Slavery," 79–81.

46. *American Missionary Magazine* 1 (September 1857): 213; ABFMS, *Annual Report . . . 1857,* 2; William Goodell to J. J. Linton, 7 November 1856, AAS MSS; Torbet, *History of the Baptists,* 294; Cady, *Missionary Baptist Church in Indiana,*

199–202; Smith, *Baptists in the Western States,* 334–35; Harris, "Gradual Separation," 130; Dodd, "Fight for the Northwest," 783; C. Allyn Russell, "Rhode Island Baptists, 1825–1931," *Rhode Island History* 28 (May 1969): 40–41; Cook, "Anti-Slavery Sentiment in Chicago," 33; Engelder, "Churches and Slavery," 68–69, 81–82; Evans, "Abolitionism in Illinois Churches," 287, 306.

47. *Christian Watchman,* 8 June 1854; *National Era,* 6 April 1854; Francis Wayland to Reverend Dr. Nott, 4 January 1859, Wayland Papers; Howard, "The 1856 Election in Ohio," 29; Watkins, "Baptists of the North and Slavery," 328–29; Wesley, "Religious Press and the Compromise of 1850," 156; Engelder, "Churches and Slavery," 81–84.

48. Evans, "Abolitionism in Illinois Churches," 103–5.

Chapter 10. *Abolitionism and the Churches during the Civil War*

1. *National Principia,* 16 July 1863, also 26 April and 2 November 1861, 5 June 1862, 29 October and 31 December 1863, 16 June 1864; *Lib.,* 4 October and 1 November 1861; 31 January and 3 October 1862; 20 May, 3 and 10 June 1864; *Baptist Missionary Magazine* 46 (July 1866): 207; Wilson, *Presbyterian Historical Almanac . . . of 1863* (Philadelphia, 1863), 417; McPherson, *Struggle for Equality,* 34–36, 39, 56–60, 67–68, 77, 104–6, 111–12, 118, 125–26, 169–74, 179, 242–43, 261, 268–69, 278; Dillon, *The Abolitionists,* 247–66; Richard B. Drake, "Freedmen's Aid Societies and Sectional Compromise," *JSH* 29 (May 1963): 176–77; Perkal, "William Goodell," 292.

2. *Free Church Portfolio,* 17 January 1861; *American Baptist,* 18 December 1861; *Wesleyan,* 14 November 1860; *National Principia,* 26 January 1861; *Presbyter,* 22 November 1860; George W. Bassett, *A Northern Plea for the Right of Secession* (Ottawa, Ill., 1861), 22–24; James Freeman Clarke, *Secession, Concession, or Self-Possession: Which?* (Boston, 1861), 13; Fletcher, *Oberlin College,* 2:844; McPherson, *Struggle for Equality,* 32–39; Dillon, *The Abolitionists,* 247–50; Bannan, "Arthur and Lewis Tappan," 186–87; Keller, "Churches and the Fugitive Slave Law," 352–57, 366–67.

3. *Methodist,* 22 December 1860, also 10 November 1860, 2 and 16 February 1861; *Western Christian Advocate,* 30 January 1861; *Protestant Episcopal Quarterly and Church Review* 8 (January 1861): 245; *Princeton Review,* n.d., quoted in *Free Church Portfolio,* 17 January 1861; J. C. Rankin to the Editors of the *New York Observer,* 26 January 1861; James H. Moorhead, *American Apocalypse: Yankee Protestants and the Civil War, 1860–1869* (New Haven, 1978), 28–30; Tucker and McAllister, *Journey in Faith,* 200–208; Keller, "Churches and the Fugitive Slave Bill," 355–59.

4. Quoted in Engelder, "Churches and Slavery," 234; *Western Christian Advocate,* 22 May 1861; *Methodist,* 20 April 1861; *American Wesleyan* (Syracuse, N.Y.), 1 May and 21 August 1861; *Lib.,* 1 November 1861; Ohio Baptist Annual Convention, *Thirty-sixth Anniversary . . . 1861* (Mansfield, Ohio, 1861), n.p.; Lewis G. Vander

Velde, *The Presbyterian Churches and the Federal Union, 1861–1869* (Cambridge, Mass., 1932), 344–46; Dunham, *Attitude of the Northern Clergy*, 239; Mathews, "Methodist Schism of 1844," 22; Watkins, "Baptists of the North and Slavery," 331.

5. Quoted in Tucker and McAllister, *Journey and Faith*, 207, also 200–208; Winifred E. Garrison, *Religion Follows the Frontier: A History of the Disciples of Christ* (New York, 1931), 330.

6. Spring, *Reminiscences*, 2:186–87, 190–91.

7. Ibid., 186–87, 191; Christy, *Pulpit Politics*, 349–50; Vander Velde, *Presbyterian Churches*, 109–19; Engelder, "Churches and Slavery," 249–57.

8. Charles W. Heathcote, *The Lutheran Church and the Civil War* (New York, 1919), 64–66, 71–76; Wentz, *Lutheranism in America*, 167–74.

9. *Church Review and Ecclesiastical Register* 14 (April 1861): 153–63, and 16 (April 1863): 109–13; John Jay, *Correspondence between John Jay, Esq., and the Vestry of St. Matthew's Church, Bedford, New York* (Bedford, N.Y., 1862), 15; Mark Mohler, "The Episcopal Church and National Reconciliation, 1865," *Political Science Quarterly* 41 (December 1926): 572–73; Engelder, "Churches and Slavery," 273–76.

10. *Lib.*, 1 November 1861; also *National Principia*, 1 and 8 June, 26 October, and 14 December 1861; *Douglass' Monthly* 3 (March 1861): 418; (April 1861): 445; and (June 1861): 471; *Free Church Portfolio*, 17 January 1861.

11. *National Principia*, 11 May and 1 June 1861; *Lib.*, 7 June and 1 November 1861; Samuel Wolcott, *Separation from Slavery: Being a Consideration of the Inquiry, "How Shall Christians and Christian Churches Best Absolve Themselves from All Responsible Connection with Slavery?"* (Boston, n.d.), 41–42.

12. *Church Review and Ecclesiastical Register* 14 (April 1861): 163, and 17 (October 1865): 455; *British and Foreign Anti-Slavery Reporter* 11 (February 1863): 46–47; Garrison and DeGroot, *Disciples of Christ*, 330; Engelder, "Churches and Slavery," 256, 274–76.

13. *Minutes of the Philadelphia Annual Conference, 1864*, quoted in Engelder, "Churches and Slavery," 163–64; also *Lib.*, 15 April and 5 December 1861; *Methodist*, 23 February 1861; *Western Christian Advocate*, 13 February 1861; *British and Foreign Anti-Slavery Reporter* 10 (January 1862): 8–9.

14. *National Principia*, 2 June 1864; *Lib.*, 17 June 1864; *British and Foreign Anti-Slavery Reporter* 12 (July 1864): 164; Engelder, "Churches and Slavery," 164–65.

15. Gerrit Smith, *Gerrit Smith on Religion* (New York, 1863), 19; also *Lib.*, 17 May, 28 June, and 1 November 1861; Wolcott, *Separation from Slavery*, 41–42; Lewis Tappan to Joseph N. Bacon, 9 July 1863, Tappan Papers.

16. *Lib.*, 7 June and 4 October 1861; 31 January, 11 April, 30 May, and 13 June 1862; *National Principia*, 14 September and 9 November 1861, 15 May and 12 June 1862, 21 May 1863; *Free Church Portfolio* 4 (June 1862): 112; Griffin, *Their Brothers' Keepers*, 240, 258–59, 262–63; Robert H. Bremner, *American Philanthropy* (Chicago, 1960), 79.

17. *National Principia,* 26 January 1861; also 13 April and 1 June 1861, 8 June 1863; Wiecek, *Sources of Antislavery Constitutionalism,* 271; McPherson, *Struggle for Equality,* 39; Perkal, "William Goodell," 300–301.

18. *National Principia,* 9 November 1861; *Douglass' Monthly* 4 (July 1861): 492–93 and (February 1862): 603; A. L. Stone, *Emancipation,* Occasional Tract 8 (Cincinnati, n.d.), 2–3, 10; G. B. Cheever to Frederick Douglass, 3 April 1862, Douglass Papers; C. B. Boynton to George Whipple, 13 December 1861; J. G. Fee to S. S. Jocelyn, 25 December 1861, both in AMA MSS; Tappan Diary, 12 September 1861; McPherson, *Struggle for Equality,* 55–61, 67–68.

19. *National Principia,* 1 June 1861, 30 May and 17 December 1862, 31 December 1863; *Douglass' Monthly* 4 (February 1862): 603; *British and Foreign Anti-Slavery Reporter* 9 (May 1861): 111, and 12 (September 1864): 214–17; J. G. Fee to S. S. Jocelyn, 26 March 1863, AMA MSS: Frederick Douglass to G. B. Cheever, 5 April 1862, Cheever Papers; Tappan Diary, 12 September 1861; Wyatt-Brown, *Lewis Tappan,* 336.

20. Quoted in Christy, *Pulpit Politics,* 368–69, also 374–75; *Free Church Portfolio* 3 (April 1861): 54; *American Wesleyan,* 1 May 1861, 22 January 1862; *Freewill Baptist Quarterly* 10 (April 1862): 152–53; ABFMS, *Annual Report . . . 1862* (Utica, N.Y., 1862), 14.

21. *Free Church Portfolio* 3 (May 1861): 72–73; also *American Wesleyan,* 22 January 1862; *Freewill Baptist Quarterly* 10 (April 1862): 152; ABFMS, *Annual Report . . . 1862,* 14.

22. *Free Church Portfolio* 3 (May 1861): 66, 72–73; *American Wesleyan,* 1 May 1861, 22 January 1862; *National Principia,* 26 June 1862; *Freewill Baptist Quarterly* 9 (April 1861): 168–70, and 10 (April 1862): 154; ABFMS, *Annual Report . . . 1862,* 7; Christy, *Pulpit Politics,* 373–74; Drake, *Quakers and Slavery,* 195–97.

23. Quoted in Engelder, "Churches and Slavery," 164, also 234–35; *Methodist Quarterly Review* 43 (April 1861): 321–22; *Western Christian Advocate,* 2 October 1861; Haven, *National Sermons,* 284–85; Jones, *Sectional Crisis and Northern Methodism,* 42–49; *Presbyterian Reunion: A Memorial Volume, 1837–1871* (New York, 1927), 88; Ralph Morrow, *Northern Methodism and Reconstruction* (East Lansing, Mich., 1956), 14–15; Vander Velde, *Presbyterian Churches,* 347–49.

24. American Baptist Home Mission Society, *Thirty-second Annual Report . . . 1864* (New York, 1864), 44–45, also *Thirtieth Annual Report . . . 1862* (New York, 1862), 32–33, 36; *Baptist Missionary Magazine* 42 (July 1862): 214; and 43 (July 1863): n.p.; Ohio Baptist Annual Convention, *Thirty-seventh Anniversary . . . 1862* (Mansfield, Ohio, 1863), 12; Francis Wayland and H. L. Wayland, *A Memoir of the Life and Labours of Francis Wayland,* 2 vols. (New York, 1868), 2:263; Moorhead, *American Apocalypse,* 97, 101–2; Engelder, "Churches and Slavery," 87–88.

25. Leonard Bacon, *Conciliation* (New Haven, 1862), 18–19; James Freeman Clarke, *Discourse on the Aspects of the War* (Boston, 1863), 13–14; William Henry Furness, *A Discourse Delivered on the Occasion of the National Fast, September 26th* (Philadelphia, 1861), 20; Thompson, *Christianity and Emancipation,* 69, 85–86;

Christy, *Pulpit Politics*, 422–25; McPherson, *Struggle for Equality*, 87–88; Fletcher, *Oberlin College*, 2:878–80; Moorhead, *American Apocalypse*, 180–81; Engelder, "Churches and Slavery," 114–15.

26. *Methodist*, 7 September 1861; also *National Principia*, 10 July 1862; *Presbyterian Quarterly Review* 11 (January 1862): 487–88; Vander Velde, *Presbyterian Churches*, 370–71.

27. Cameron, *Methodism and Society*, 171–72; Morrow, *Methodism and Reconstruction*, 18; Cady, *Missionary Baptist Church in Indiana*, 204–5; Welsh, *Buckeye Presbyterianism*, 181–82; Raines, "American Missionary Association in Southern Illinois," 264; Evans, "Abolitionism in Illinois Churches," 176.

28. Quoted in *National Principia*, 21 June 1864; also A. T. McGill, *The Hand of God with the Black Race* (Philadelphia, 1862), 10; Vander Velde, *Presbyterian Churches*, 112–17, 123–28; Engelder, "Churches and Slavery," 256–57.

29. *Church Review and Ecclesiastical Register* 14 (April 1861): 163 and (July 1861): 390; 16 (January 1864): 543–44, 558, 573–75; and 17 (October 1865): 455; *British and Foreign Anti-Slavery Reporter* 11 (February 1863): 46–47; Mark A. Howe, *Memoirs of the Life and Services of the Right Reverend Alonzo Potter, D.D., L.L.D., Bishop of the Protestant Episcopal Church in the Diocese of Pennsylvania* (Philadelphia, 1871), 239–40; Heathcote, *Lutheran Church and Civil War*, 79–82; Garrison and DeGroot, *Disciples of Christ*, 330; Tucker and McAllister, *Journey in Faith*, 206–7; Engelder, "Churches and Slavery," 256, 274–76.

30. Quoted in *National Principia*, 25 May 1861; also 15 June, 9 and 30 November, 28 December 1861, 9 June 1864; *Douglass' Monthly* 4 (July 1861): 492; J. C. Webster to H. T. Cheever, 19 September 1862, Cheever Papers; McPherson, *Struggle for Equality*, 80, 93, 110–11; Perkal, "William Goodell," 381.

31. *National Principia*, 25 June 1863; also 28 December 1861, 10 April and 30 May 1862; *Lib.*, 30 May 1862.

32. *Lib.*, 19 September and 3 October 1862; *National Principia*, 25 December 1862, 8 January 1863; Evans, "Abolitionism in Illinois Churches," 434–35; Perkal, "William Goodell," 306–8.

33. *Freewill Baptist Quarterly* 10 (April 1862): 159–61; also *American Wesleyan*, 18 September 1861; *Western Christian Advocate*, 2 October 1861.

34. *National Principia*, 26 June 1862; ABFMS, *Annual Report . . . 1862*, 7; Christy, *Pulpit Politics*, 374–75; R. H. Evans to [AMA], 1 January 1862, AMA MSS; McPherson, *Struggle for Equality*, 110; Fletcher, *Oberlin College*, 2:870; Engelder, "Churches and Slavery," 114–15.

35. Quoted in Vander Velde, *Presbyterian Churches*, 350, also 127; *National Principia*, 2 June 1864; *American Wesleyan*, 1 October 1862; *Freewill Baptist Quarterly* 11 (January 1863): 102–3; *British and Foreign Anti-Slavery Reporter* 11 (November 1863): 246–47; AASS, *Third Decade*, 15; American Baptist Home Mission Society, *Thirty-second Annual Report . . . 1864*, 44–45; George B. Ide, *The Freedmen of the War* (Philadelphia, 1864), 109–10; Joseph Wilson, ed., *Presbyterian Historical Almanac and Annual Remembrancer of the Church for 1864* (Philadelphia, 1864), 370–71; V. Jacque Voegeli, *Free But Not Equal: The Midwest and the Negro during the Civil War* (Chicago, 1967), 59.

36. Quoted in McPherson, *Struggle for Equality*, 119; AASS, *Third Decade*, 15; J. G. Fee to S. S. Jocelyn, 26 March 1863, AMA MSS; Wyatt-Brown, *Lewis Tappan*, 337–38.

37. G. B. Cheever to Elizabeth Washburn, 29 September 1862, quoted in McPherson, *Struggle for Equality*, 118.

38. *National Principia*, 1 and 8 January 1863; McPherson, *Struggle for Equality*, 118–22, 133; Dillon, *The Abolitionists*, 257–58; Perkal, "William Goodell," 306–8.

39. *National Principia*, 24 March 1864, also 21 April and 16 June 1864; Salmon P. Chase to J. G. Fee, 5 February 1863, AMA MSS; Perkal, "William Goodell," 320–22.

40. *Lib.*, 20 May 1864; H. T. Cheever to G. B. Cheever, 8 June 1864; Henry Wilson to H. T. Cheever, 27 July 1864; Henry Winter Davis to H. T. Cheever, 21 and 31 July 1864; J. A. Stearns to H. T. Cheever, 25 August 1864; Amasa Walker to H. T. Cheever, 26 August 1864; G. B. Cheever to Elizabeth Washburn, 10 and 22 September 1864, all in Cheever Papers; McPherson, *Struggle for Equality*, 261, 268–69, 274–75, 278, 280–81.

41. *Independent*, 23 June 1864, quoted in Perkal, "William Goodell," 325; *National Principia*, 12 May 1864; Aaron, *Life, Sermons, Correspondence*, 195; "Report of the Sixth Annual Business Meeting of the Church Anti-Slavery Society, Adopted May 27th, 1864," Cheever Papers; Perkal, "William Goodell," 326–27.

42. Quoted in Vander Velde, *Presbyterian Churches*, 351; Voegeli, *Free But Not Equal*, 122–23; McPherson, *Struggle for Equality*, 281–84; Moorhead, *American Apocalypse*, 155–59.

43. *Freewill Baptist Quarterly* 13 (January 1865): 80; *Church Review and Ecclesiastical Register* 16 (January 1864): 574–75; *Congregationalist*, 28 April 1865; *National Principia*, 16 June 1864; Thompson, *Christianity and Emancipation*, 85–86; McPherson, *Struggle for Equality*, 125–26, 132–33, 286; Dillon, *The Abolitionists*, 259–60.

44. *Free Church Portfolio* 17 January 1861; (April 1861): 49, 54; (May 1861): 65, 72–73, 91; (November 1861): 263; and 4 (June 1862): 104; *National Principia*, 29 October 1863; AASS, *Third Decade*, 15; Robert E. Thompson, *History of the Presbyterian Churches in the United States* (New York, 1907), 137; Vander Velde, *Presbyterian Churches*, 11; Slosser, *They Seek a Country*, 232; Willey, "John Rankin," 285–90.

45. ABFMS, *Annual Report . . . 1863* (Utica, N.Y., 1863), n.p.; also *Annual Report . . . 1862*, 7, 14–15; and *Annual Report . . . 1864* (Utica, N.Y., 1864), 3; *National Principia*, 12 May 1864; *Baptist Missionary Magazine* 46 (July 1866): 204; Samuel Aaron to C. B. Bates, 10 June 1864, in Aaron, *Life, Sermons, Correspondence*, 195.

46. Lee, *Autobiography*, 299, also 303, 310.

47. *American Wesleyan*, 16 January, 1 May, and 21 August 1861; 22 January, 14 May, and 1 October 1862; Lee, *Wesleyan Manual*, 135–40.

48. *Congregational Quarterly* 4 (April 1862): 174; Wentz, *Lutheranism in America*, 141, 147–50, 161; Heathcote, *Lutheran Church and Civil War*, 76–78; Stange, *Radicalism for Humanity*, 42.

49. *National Principia*, 26 June 1862; McPherson, *Struggle for Equality*, 110; Drake, *Quakers and Slavery*, 176.

50. The American Tract Society, Boston, merged with the American Tract Society in 1878. Both the American Missionary Association and the American Reform Tract and Book Society remained active until the early twentieth century. *National Principia*, 9 November 1861, 15 May 1862, 21 May and 29 October 1863; *Christian Press* 13 (December 1863): 498–99; George Weed to Lewis Tappan, 15 May 1861 and 13 June 1862, both in AMA MSS; McPherson, *Struggle for Equality*, 168–69; Drake, "Freedmen's Aid Societies," 176.

51. Quoted in *National Principia*, 4 June 1863; also *Lib.*, 29 May 1863; Stephen Tabor et al. to G. B. Cheever, 27 October 1864, Cheever Papers.

52. Lewis Tappan to J. P. Warren, 23 December 1864, Tappan Papers; also *Christian Press* 13 (December 1863): 498–99; *National Principia*, 9 November 1861, 19 June 1862, and 29 October 1863; G. L. Weed to Lewis Tappan, 13 June 1862; John Laurence to S. S. Jocelyn, 24 December 1862, both in AMA MSS; McPherson, *Struggle for Equality*, 179, 387, 393, 401–3; Joe M. Richardson, "The Failure of the American Missionary Association to Expand Congregationalism among Southern Blacks," *Southern Studies* 18 (Spring 1979): 52–54; Drake, "Freedmen's Aid Societies," 176–78.

53. ABFMS, *Annual Report . . . 1862*, 15; also *National Principia*, 3 March 1863; *Congregational Quarterly* 3 (July 1862): 292; *Freewill Baptist Quarterly* 13 (July 1865): 306–7; Drake, *Quakers and Slavery*, 199–200; Willie Lee Rose, *Rehearsal for Reconstruction: The Port Royal Experiment* (Indianapolis, 1964), 219; Vander Velde, *Presbyterian Churches*, 453–55.

54. James M. McPherson, *The Negro's Civil War: How American Negroes Felt and Acted during the War for the Union* (New York, 1965), 123, 139; Wesley J. Gaines, *African Methodism in the South; or, Twenty-five Years of Freedom* (1890; reprint, Chicago, 1969), 4–5; Payne, *African Methodist Episcopal Church*, 465–74; Walls, *African Methodist Episcopal Zion Church*, 187–99.

55. American Baptist Home Mission Society, *Thirtieth Annual Report . . . 1862*, 50–51; also *Thirty-second Annual Report . . . 1864*, 14, 20; Haven, *National Sermons*, 283–88; Vander Velde, *Presbyterian Churches*, 128, 196–97, 440–48; Murray, *Presbyterians and the Negro*, 162–64, 170–71; Jones, *Sectional Crisis and Northern Methodism*, 248–49; Oliver S. Heckman, "The Presbyterian Church in the United States of America in Southern Reconstruction, 1860–1880," *North Carolina Historical Review* 20 (July 1943): 223–25.

56. American Baptist Home Mission Society, *Thirty-second Annual Report . . . 1864*, 31, 42–43; Ohio Baptist Annual Convention, *Annual Report . . . 1865* (Mansfield, Ohio, 1865), n.p.; Baker, *Southern Baptist Convention*, 229–30; Vander Velde, *Presbyterian Churches*, 59–62; Morrow, *Methodism and Reconstruction*, 33–40; Heckman, "Presbyterian Church in Southern Reconstruction," 220–21; Drake, "Freedmen's Aid Societies," 181.

57. *Freewill Baptist Quarterly* 13 (January 1865): 65; also McGill, *Hand of God,* 9–10, 18–19; "Report of the Seventh Annual Meeting of the Church Anti-Slavery Society, Adopted May 31st, 1865," Cheever Papers; Frederick Starr, Jr., *What Shall Be Done with the People of Color?* (Albany, N.Y., 1862), 27–29; Richard Lowitt, *A Merchant Prince of the Nineteenth Century: William E. Dodge* (New York, 1954), 196–97; Jones, *Sectional Crisis and Northern Methodism,* 292–95; Ahlstrom, *Religious History of the American People,* 690–97; McPherson, *Struggle for Equality,* 155–56, 223–26, 234; Ena L. Farley, "Methodists and Baptists on the Issue of Black Equality in New York, 1865 to 1868," *Journal of Negro History* 61 (October 1976): 377; Richardson, "Failure of American Missionary Association," 53.

58. *National Principia,* 4 June 1863.

59. Ibid., 11 June 1864; *Lib.,* 7 June 1864; McPherson, *Struggle for Equality,* 226–27; Jones, *Sectional Crisis and Northern Methodism,* 285–88; Engelder, "Churches and Slavery," 164–66, 278–79.

60. James M. McPherson, *The Abolitionist Legacy: From Reconstruction to the NAACP* (Princeton, N.J., 1975), 143–60; Jones, *Sectional Crisis and Northern Methodism,* 285–90, 313; Murray, *Presbyterians and the Negro,* 170–77; Rose, *Rehearsal for Reconstruction,* 180–81; Harris, "Gradual Separation," 135–37; Heckman, "Presbyterian Church in Southern Reconstruction," 230–33.

61. McPherson, *Abolitionist Legacy,* 224–61; Jones, *Sectional Crisis and Northern Methodism,* 313; Murray, *Presbyterians and the Negro,* 190–202; James C. Klotter, "The Black South and White America," *JAH* 66 (March 1980): 844–48; Richardson, "Failure of American Missionary Association," 56–73; Farley, "Methodists and Baptists," 378–82.

Bibliography

The bibliography is divided into sections as follows:

PRIMARY SOURCES

Manuscript Collections

American Antiquarian Society, Worcester, Mass.
  Cheever Family Papers.
  Abigail Kelley Foster and Stephen S. Foster Papers.
Amistad Research Center, Dillard University, New Orleans, La.
  American Missionary Association Manuscripts.
Brown University Archives, Providence, R.I.
  Francis Wayland Papers.
Historical Society of Pennsylvania, Philadelphia, Pa.
  Salmon P. Chase Papers.
Houghton Library, Harvard University, Cambridge, Mass.
  Ellis Gray Loring Papers.

Manuscript Division, Library of Congress, Washington, D.C.
  Samuel J. Baird Papers.
  James G. Birney Papers.
  Frederick Douglass Papers.
  Joshua R. Giddings–George W. Julian Papers.
  Leavitt Family Papers.
  Miscellaneous Manuscripts Collection.
  Theodore Parker Papers.
  Lewis Tappan Papers.
  John G. Whittier Papers.
  Carter G. Woodson Collection.
  Elizur Wright Papers.
Massachusetts Historical Society, Boston, Mass.
  Henry W. Bellows Papers.
  Robie-Sewall Papers.
Oberlin College Archives, Oberlin, Ohio.
  Henry Cowles Papers.
  Robert S. Fletcher Collection.
  William Goodell Papers.
  James Monroe Papers.
Oberlin College Library, Oberlin, Ohio.
  American Abolition Society Letterbooks and Records.
Ohio Historical Center, Columbus, Ohio.
  John Rankin. "Life of the Reverend John Rankin Written in His Eightieth Year."
  Typescript. n.d.
Presbyterian Historical Society, Philadelphia, Pa.
  Albert Barnes Papers.
United Methodist Archives Center, West Ohio Conference, United Methodist Church,
  Bieghly Library, Ohio Wesleyan University, Delaware, Ohio.
  James B. Finley Papers.
  Frederick Merrick Papers.

Published Documents, Autobiographies, Correspondence, Diaries, and Collected Works

Aaron, Samuel. *His Life, Sermons, Correspondence, Etc.* Norristown, Pa.: M. R. Wills, 1890.

Abel, Annie Heloise, and Klingberg, Frank J., eds. *A Side-Light on Anglo-American Relations, 1839–1858.* Lancaster, Pa.: Association for the Study of Negro Life and History, 1927.

Barker, Joseph. *The Life of Joseph Barker, Written by Himself.* London: Hodder & Stoughton, 1880.

Bibliography

Barnes, Gilbert H., and Dumond, Dwight L., eds. *Letters of Theodore Weld, Angelina Grimke Weld, and Sarah Grimke, 1822–1844*. 2 vols. New York: Appleton-Century, 1934.

Beecher, Lyman. *Autobiography, Correspondence, Etc., of Lyman Beecher*. edited by Charles Beecher. 2 vols. New York: Harper, 1865.

Brown, George. *Recollections of Itinerant Life, Including Early Reminiscences*. Cincinnati: R. W. Carroll, 1866.

Brown, Henry J., and Williams, Frederick D., eds. *The Diary of James A. Garfield*. 3 vols. East Lansing: Michigan State University Press, 1967–71.

Cartwright, Peter. *Autobiography of Peter Cartwright: The Backwoods Preacher*. Cincinnati: Cranston & Curtis, 1856.

Coffin, Levi. *Reminiscences of Levi Coffin*. Cincinnati: Western Tract Society, 1876.

Collins, Robert E., ed. *Theodore Parker, American Transcendentalist: A Critical Essay and a Collection of His Writings*. Metuchen, N.J.: Scarecrow Press, 1973.

Conway, Moncure Daniel. *Autobiography, Memoirs, and Experiences of Moncure Daniel Conway*. 2 vols. Boston: Houghton Mifflin, 1904.

Crooks, George, ed. *Sermon of Bishop Matthew Simpson*. New York: Harper, 1885.

Dumond, Dwight L., ed. *Letters of James Gillespie Birney, 1831–1857*. 2 vols. New York: Appleton-Century, 1938.

Free Presbyterian Board. *The Life and Writings of Reverend Joseph Gordon*. Cincinnati: Free Presbyterian Board, 1860.

Haven, Gilbert. *National Sermons: Sermons, Speeches, and Letters on Slavery and Its War, from the Passage of the Fugitive Slave Bill to the Election of President Grant*. Boston: Lee & Shepard, 1868.

Jay, William. *Miscellaneous Writings on Slavery*. Boston: J. P. Jewett, 1853.

Lee, Luther. *Autobiography of the Reverend Luther Lee*. New York: Phillips & Hunt, 1882.

Marsh, Luther R., ed. *Writings and Speeches of Alvan Stewart on Slavery*. New York: A. B. Burdick, 1860.

Mathews, Edward. *The Autobiography of the Rev. E. Mathews, the "Father Dickson" of Mrs. Stowe's "Dred."* 1866. Reprint. Miami: Mnemosyne, 1969.

Matlack, Lucius C. *Narrative of the Anti-Slavery Experience of a Minister in the Methodist Episcopal Church, Who Was Twice Rejected by the Philadelphia Annual Conference and Finally Deprived of License to Preach for Being an Abolitionist*. Philadelphia: Merrihew & Thompson, 1845.

May, Samuel Joseph. *Some Recollections of Our Anti-Slavery Conflict*. Boston: Fields, Osgood, 1869.

Merrill, Walter M., and Ruchames, Louis, eds. *The Letters of William Lloyd Garrison*. 6 vols. Cambridge: Harvard University Press, 1971–81.

Monroe, James. *Oberlin Thursday Lectures, Addresses, and Essays*. Oberlin, Ohio: Edward J. Goodrich, 1897.

Olin, Stephen. *The Life and Letters of Stephen Olin, D.D., Late President of Wesleyan University*. 2 vols. New York: Harper, 1853.

Peck, George. *The Life and Times of Reverend George Peck*. New York: Nelson & Phillips, 1874.

Bibliography

Rogers, Nathaniel P. *A Collection from the Newspaper Writings of Nathaniel Peabody Rogers.* Concord, N.H.: John R. French, 1847.

Smyth, Thomas. *Autobiographical Notes, Letters, and Reflections.* Charleston, S.C.: Walker, Evans, & Cogswell, 1914.

Spring, Gardiner. *Personal Reminiscences of the Life and Times of Gardiner Spring.* 2 vols. New York: Scribner, 1866.

Sturtevant, Julian M. *An Autobiography.* New York: Fleming H. Revell, 1896.

Swisshelm, Jane Grey. *Half a Century.* Chicago: Jansen, McClurg, 1880.

Thomas, Alfred A., ed. *Correspondence of Thomas Ebenezer Thomas, Mainly Relating to the Antislavery Conflict in Ohio, Especially in the Presbyterian Church.* Dayton: A. A. Thomas, 1909.

Ward, Samuel Ringgold. *Autobiography of a Fugitive Negro: His Anti-Slavery Labours in the United States, Canada, and England.* London: John Snow, 1855.

Wesley, John. *The Works of the Rev. John Wesley, A.M.* 14 vols. London: Wesleyan Conference Office, 1872–78.

Whittier, John G. *The Works of John Greenleaf Whittier.* 7 vols. Boston: Houghton Mifflin, 1892.

Newspapers

American Baptist (Utica, N.Y.)
American Wesleyan (Syracuse, N.Y.)
Anti-Slavery Bugle (New Lisbon, Ohio)
Christian Contributor (Utica, N.Y.)
Christian Freeman (Hartford)
Christian Observer (Philadelphia)
Christian Press (Cincinnati)
Christian Reflector (Boston)
Christian Reformer (Hamilton, N.Y.)
Christian Secretary (Hartford)
Christian Watchman (Boston)
Christian Witness and Western Reserve Advocate (Cuyahoga Falls, Ohio)
Clarion of Freedom (New Concord, Ohio)
Congregationalist (Boston)
Cross and Journal (Cincinnati)
Daily Cincinnati Gazette
Emancipator (New York and Boston)
Frederick Douglass' Paper (Rochester, N.Y.)
Free Church Portfolio (New Castle, Pa.)
Free Presbyterian (Mercer, Pa.; Albany, Ohio; and Yellow Springs, Ohio)
Friend of Man (Utica, N.Y.)
Herald and Philanthropist (Cincinnati)
Independent (New York)
Journal and Messenger (Cincinnati)

Bibliography

Journal of Commerce (New York)
Liberator (Boston)
Liberty Press (Utica, N.Y.)
Liberty Standard (Hallowell, Maine)
Methodist (New York)
National Anti-Slavery Standard (New York)
National Era (Washington, D.C.)
National Principia (New York)
New York Evangelist
New York Observer
Northern Advocate (Auburn, N.Y.)
North Star (Rochester, N.Y.)
Oberlin Evangelist
Ohio State Journal (Columbus, Ohio)
Pennsylvania Freeman (Philadelphia)
Political Abolitionist (Bryan, Ohio)
Presbyter (Cincinnati)
Presbyterian of the West (Cincinnati)
Signal of Liberty (Ann Arbor, Mich.)
True Wesleyan (New York)
Watchman and Wesleyan Observer (New York)
Watchman of the Prairie (Chicago)
Watchman of the Valley (Cincinnati)
Weekly Chronotype (Boston)
Wesleyan (Syracuse, N.Y.)
Western Christian Advocate (Cincinnati)
Western Citizen (Chicago)
Zion's Herald (Boston)

Books and Pamphlets

American and Foreign Anti-Slavery Society. *An Address to the Anti-Slavery Christians of the United States.* New York: John A. Gray, 1852.
_____. *Annual Report.* New York, 1847–53.
_____. *Remonstrance against the Course Pursued by the Evangelical Alliance on the Subject of American Slavery.* New York: William Harned, 1847.
_____. *Shall We Give the Bible to Three Millions of American Slaves?* Tract 1. New York, 1847.
American Anti-Slavery Society. *American Anti-Slavery Almanac,* New York and Boston, 1838–40, 1847.
_____. *Annual Report.* New York, 1834–40, 1854–61.
_____. *Influence of Slavery upon the White Population, by a Former Resident of Slave States.* Anti-Slavery Tract 9. New York, n.d.

Bibliography

_____. *Proceedings of the American Anti-Slavery Society at Its Second Decade.* New York, 1854.

_____. *Proceedings of the American Anti-Slavery Society at Its Third Decade.* New York, 1863.

American Baptist Free Mission Society. *Annual Report.* Utica, N.Y., 1847–64.

American Baptist Home Missionary Society. *Annual Report.* New York, 1844–49, 1852, 1862–64.

American Baptist Missionary Convention. *Annual Report.* Boston, 1849–59.

American Baptist Missionary Union. *Twenty-Fourth Annual Report.* New York, 1848.

American Baptist Publication Society. *The Baptist Almanac for the Year of Our Lord, 1852.* Philadelphia, 1851.

American Reform Tract and Book Society. *Colonization: The Present Scheme of Colonization—Wrong, Delusive, and Retards Emancipation.* Tract 14. Cincinnati, n.d.

_____. *Duty of Voting for Righteous Men for Office.* Tract 10. Cincinnati, n.d.

_____. *Fellowship with Slavery; Report Republished from the Minutes of the Evangelical Consociation, Rhode Island.* Tract 15. Cincinnati, n.d.

_____. *Hebrew Servitude and American Slavery.* Tract 2. Cincinnati, n.d.

_____. *Slavery in Rebellion—An Outlaw: How to Deal With It.* Occasional Tract 5. Cincinnati, n.d.

_____. *A Tract for the Free States; Let Everyone Read and Consider Before He Condemns: A Safe and Generous Proposition for Abolishing Slavery.* Tract 20. Cincinnati, n.d.

_____. *A Tract for Sabbath Schools.* Tract 7. Cincinnati, n.d.

Bacon, Leonard. *Conciliation.* New Haven: Peck, White & Peck, 1862.

_____. *The Higher Law.* New Haven: B. L. Hamlen, 1851.

_____. *The Jugglers Detected.* New Haven: Thomas H. Pease, 1861.

Baird, Robert. *The Progress and Prospects of Christianity in the United States of America; with Remarks on the Subject of Slavery in America and on the Intercourse between British and American Churches.* London: Partridge & Oakey, 1851.

_____. *Religion in America; or, An Account of the Origin, Relation to the State, and Present Condition of the Evangelical Churches in the United States.* New York: Harper, 1845.

Baldwin, A. C. "Friendly Letters to a Christian Slaveholder." In *Liberty or Slavery: The Great National Question.* Boston: Congregational Board of Publications, 1857.

Balme, Joshua R. *American States, Churches, and Slavery.* London: Hamilton, Adams, 1863.

Bangs, Nathan. *Emancipation: Its Necessity and Means of Accomplishment Calmly Submitted to the Citizens of the United States.* New York: Lane & Scott, 1849.

Barnes, Albert. *The Church and Slavery.* 2d ed. Philadelphia: Parry & McMillan, 1857.

_____. *An Inquiry into the Scriptural Views on Slavery.* Philadelphia: Perkins & Purves, 1846.

Bassett, George W. *A Northern Plea for the Right of Secession.* Ottawa, Ill.: Free Trader, 1861.

Bibliography

Beecher, Charles. *The Duty of Disobedience to Wicked Laws: A Sermon on the Fugitive Slave Law.* New York: John A. Gray, 1851.

———. *A Sermon on the Nebraska Bill.* Newark, N.J.: Oliver & Brothers, 1854.

Betker, John P. *The M. E. Church and Slavery, as Described by Reverends H. Mattison, W. Hosmer, E. Bowen, D. DeVinne, and J. D. Long, with a Bible View of the Whole Subject.* Syracuse, N.Y.: S. Lee, 1859.

Birney, James Gillespie. *The American Churches: The Bulwarks of American Slavery.* 3d ed. Concord, N.H.: P. Pillsbury, 1885.

Blagden, George W. *Remarks and a Discourse on Slavery.* Boston: Ticknor, Reed, & Fields, 1854.

Blanchard, Jonathan. *Sermon on Slaveholding Preached by Appointment before the Synod of Cincinnati at Their Late Meeting at Mount Pleasant, Ohio, October 20, 1841.* Cincinnati: n.p., 1842.

Bliss, Seth. *Letters to the Members, Patrons, and Friends of the Branch American Tract Society in Boston, Instituted 1814; and to Those of the National Society in New York, Instituted 1825 By the Secretary of the Boston Society.* Boston: Crocker & Brewster, 1858.

Boardman, Henry A. *The American Union.* Philadelphia: Lippincott, Grambo, 1851.

Bowen, Elias. *Slavery in the Methodist Episcopal Church.* Auburn, N.Y.: William J. Moses, 1859.

Brooks, Samuel. *Slavery and the Slaveholders' Religion as Opposed to Christianity.* Cincinnati: Privately printed, 1846.

Brownlow, William G., and Pryne, Abram. *Ought American Slavery to Be Perpetuated? A Debate between Reverend W. G. Brownlow and Reverend A. Pryne, Held at Philadelphia, September 1858.* Philadelphia: Lippincott, 1858.

Buckley, Charles H. *Removal of Ancient Landmarks; or, The Causes and Consequences of Slavery Extension.* Hartford: Case, Tiffany, 1854.

Burt, Jairus. *The Law of Christian Rebuke; A Plea for Slave-Holders.* Hartford: N. W. Goodrich, 1843.

Bushnell, Horace T. *Slavery in Its Relation to God: A Review of Reverend Dr. Lord's Thanksgiving Sermon in Favor of Domestic Slavery.* Buffalo: A. M. Clapp, 1851.

Chapman, Maria Weston. *Right and Wrong in Massachusetts.* Boston: Dow & Jackson Anti-Slavery Press, 1839.

Cheever, George B. *The Commission from God of the Missionary Enterprise against the Sin of Slavery, and the Responsibility on the Church and the Ministry for Its Fulfillment.* New York: American Missionary Supplement, 1858.

———. *God against Slavery; and the Freedom and Duty of the Pulpit to Rebuke It.* Cincinnati: American Reform Tract and Book Society, 1857.

———. *The Guilt of Slavery and the Crime of Slaveholding Demonstrated from the Hebrew and Greek Scriptures.* Boston: John Jewett, 1860.

Cheever, Henry T. *A Tract for the Times on the Question, Is It Right to Withhold Fellowship of Churches from Individuals That Tolerate or Practice Slavery?* New York: John A. Gray, 1859.

Christian Anti-Slavery Convention. *Minutes of the Christian Anti-Slavery Convention Assembled April 17th–20th, 1850 at Cincinnati, Ohio.* Cincinnati: Franklin Book and Job Room, 1850.

——. *Minutes of the Christian Anti-Slavery Convention Held July 3rd, 4th, and 5th, 1851 at Chicago, Illinois.* Chicago: Western Citizen, 1851.

Christy, David. *Pulpit Politics; or, Ecclesiastical Legislation on Slavery, in Its Disturbing Influences on the American Union.* Cincinnati: Faran & McLean, 1862.

Church Anti-Slavery Society. *Circular—Declaration of Principles and Constitution.* Worcester, Mass., 1859.

——. *Proceedings of the Convention Which Met at Worcester, Massachusetts, March 1, 1859.* New York: John F. Trow, 1859.

Clark, Rufus W. *Conscience and Law.* Boston: Tappan & Whittemore, 1851.

Clarke, James Freeman. *Discourse on the Aspects of the War.* Boston: Walker, Wise, 1863.

——. *The Rendition of Anthony Burns: Its Causes and Consequences.* Boston: Crosby, Nichols, 1854.

——. *Secession, Concession, or Self-Possession: Which?* Boston: Walker, Wise, 1861.

Colver, Nathaniel. *The Fugitive Slave Bill; or, God's Laws Paramount to the Laws of Men.* Boston: J. M. Hewes, 1850.

Congregational Home Mission Society. *Home Missions and Slavery.* New York: John A. Gray, 1857.

Congregational Ministers of Massachusetts. *Report of the Committee on Slavery, to the Convention of Congregational Ministers of Massachusetts, Presented May 30, 1849.* Boston: T. R. Marvin, 1849.

The Declaration and Pledge against Slavery Adopted by the Religious Anti-Slavery Convention, Held at Marlboro Chapel, Boston, February 26, 1846. Boston: Devereaux & Seamen, 1846.

DeVinne, Daniel. *The Methodist Episcopal Church and Slavery: A Historical Survey of the Relation of the Early Methodists to Slavery.* New York: Francis Hart, 1857.

Dickerson, A. C. *Anti-Slavery Agitation in the Church Not Authorized.* Philadelphia: King & Baird, 1857.

Distinctive Principles of the Free Presbyterian Church of the United States. Mercer: William F. Clark, 1851.

Duffield, George. *A Sermon on American Slavery: Its Nature and the Duties of Christians in Relation to It.* Detroit: J. S. & S. A. Bragg, 1840.

Dugdale, Joseph A. *Extemporaneous Discourses.* Poughkeepsie, N.Y.: Platt & Schian, 1850.

Edgerton, Walter. *A History of the Separation in the Indiana Yearly Meeting of Friends, Which Took Place in the Winter of 1842 and 1843 on the Anti-Slavery Question.* Cincinnati: A. Pugh, 1856.

Elliott, Charles. *The Bible and Slavery.* Cincinnati: L. Swormstedt and A. Poe, 1857.

——. *Sinfulness of American Slavery.* 2 vols. Cincinnati: L. Swormstedt and A. Poe, 1851.

Bibliography

Evangelical Union Anti-Slavery Society. *Address to the Churches of Jesus Christ.* New York: S. W. Benedict, 1839.

Fee, John G. *An Anti-Slavery Manual: Being an Examination, in the Light of the Bible, and of Facts, into the Moral and Social Wrongs of American Slavery, with a Remedy for the Evil.* Maysville, Ky.: Maysville Herald Office, 1848.

_____. *Non-Fellowship with Slaveholders, the Duty of Christians.* New York: John A. Gray, 1851.

Fish, Henry C. *Freedom or Despotism, the Voice of Our Brother's Blood: Its Sources and Its Summons.* Newark, N.J.: Douglass & Starbuck, 1856.

Forman, Jacob G. *The Fugitive Slave Law.* Boston: William Crosby & H. P. Nichols, 1850.

Foss, Andrew T., and Mathews, E. *Facts for Baptist Churches, Collected, Arranged, and Received by A. T. Foss, of New Hampshire, and E. Mathews, of Wisconsin.* Utica, N.Y.: American Baptist Free Mission Society, 1850.

Foster, Eden B. *A North-Side View of Slavery: A Sermon on the Crime against Freedom in Kansas and Washington.* Concord, N.H.: Jones & Cogswell, 1856.

Foster, Stephen S. *The Brotherhood of Thieves; or, A True Picture of the American Church and Clergy.* Boston: Anti-Slavery Office, 1843.

Fourth Congregational Church of Hartford, Connecticut. *The Unanimous Remonstrance of the Fourth Congregational Church, Hartford, Connecticut, against the Policy of the American Tract Society on the Subject of Slavery.* Hartford: Silas Andrus, 1855.

Freewill Baptist Anti-Slavery Society. *Annual Report.* Dover, N.H., 1849, 1852–53.

Freewill Baptist Connection. *Eighth General Conference.* Byron, N.Y., 1835.

Freewill Baptist Home Mission Society. *Annual Report.* Dover, N.H., 1854–55.

Furness, William Henry. *A Discourse Delivered on the Occasion of the National Fast, September 26th.* Philadelphia: T. B. Pugh, 1861.

Garrison, William Lloyd. *The "Infidelity" of Abolitionism.* Anti-Slavery Tract 10. New York: American Anti-Slavery Society, 1860.

_____. *Thoughts on African Colonization.* 1832. Reprint. New York: Arno, 1968.

Giddings, Joshua R. *History of the Rebellion: Its Authors and Causes.* New York: Follett, Foster, 1864.

Goodell, William. *American Slavery a Formidable Obstacle to the Conversion of the World.* New York: American and Foreign Anti-Slavery Society, 1854.

_____. *Slavery and Anti-Slavery: A History of the Great Struggle in Both Hemispheres, with a View of the Slavery Question in the United States.* New York: William Harned, 1852.

Gordon, George. *Secession from a Pro-Slavery Church a Christian Duty.* Mercer, Pa.: William F. Clark, 1850.

Graham, William. *The Contrast; or, The Bible and Abolitionism: An Exegetical Argument.* Cincinnati: Daily Cincinnati Atlas Office, 1844.

Grosvenor, Cyrus Pitt. *A Review of the Correspondence of Messrs. Fuller and Wayland on the Subject of American Slavery.* Utica, N.Y.: H. H. Curtis, 1847.

Bibliography

Harris, William Logan. *The Constitutional Powers of the General Conference, with a Special Application to the Subject of Slave Holding.* Cincinnati: Methodist Book Concern, 1860.

Hartford, Connecticut, City Tract Society. *The Tract Society and Slavery: Speeches of Chief Justice Williams, Judge Parsons, and Ex-Governor Ellsworth.* Hartford: Elihu Geer, 1859.

Henry, Caleb S. *Plain Reasons for the Great Republican Movement.* Geneva, N.Y.: Dix, Edwards, 1856.

Hopkins, John Henry. *A Scriptural, Ecclesiastical, and Historical View of Slavery from the Days of the Patriarch Abraham to the Nineteenth Century.* New York: W. I. Pooley, 1864.

Hosmer, William. *The Higher Law.* Auburn, N.Y.: Derby and Miller, 1852.

———. *Slavery and the Church.* Auburn, N.Y.: W. J. Moses, 1853.

Huffman, Samuel. *A Vindication of Border Methodism.* St. Louis: R. P. Studley, 1858.

Hussey, Ebenezer. *The Religion of Slavery.* Tract 9. N.p.: New England Anti-Slavery Tract Association, n.d.

Ide, George B. *The Freedmen of the War.* Philadelphia: American Baptist Publication Society, 1864.

Jay, John. *Correspondence between John Jay, Esq., and the Vestry of St. Matthew's Church, Bedford, New York.* Bedford, N.Y.: n.p., 1862.

Jay, William. *Inquiry into the Character and Tendency of the American Colonization and American Anti-Slavery Societies.* 6th ed. New York: R. G. Williams, 1838.

———. *Letters Respecting the American Board of Commissioners for Foreign Missions and American Tract Society.* New York: Lewis J. Bates, 1853.

———. *Reply to Remarks of Rev. Moses Stuart on John Jay and on Examination of His Scriptural Exegesis Contained in His Recent Pamphlet, "Conscience and the Constitution."* New York: John A. Gray, 1850.

Kennedy, William S. *The Plan of Union; or, A History of the Presbyterian and Congregational Churches in the Western Reserve.* Hudson, Ohio: Pentagon Press, 1856.

Kettell, George F. *Reply of Reverend G. F. Kettell to Reverend Daniel Curry's Review of His Thanksgiving Sermon: Fugitive Slave Law.* Poughkeepsie, N.Y.: American Printing Establishment, 1851.

———. *A Sermon on the Duty of Citizens with Respect to the Fugitive Slave Law.* White Plains, N.Y.: Eastern State Journal, 1851.

Lafon, Thomas. *The Great Obstruction to the Conversion of Souls at Home and Abroad.* New York: Union Missionary Society, 1843.

Lame, J. S. *Maryland Slavery and Maryland Chivalry.* Philadelphia: Collins, 1858.

Lawrence, John. *The Slavery Question.* Dayton, Ohio: Conference Printing Establishment of the United Brethren, 1854.

Lee, Luther. *Dying to the Glory of God: A Sermon Preached on the Occasion of the Execution of Captain John Brown.* Syracuse, N.Y.: Samuel Lee, 1860.

____. *Slavery Examined in the Light of the Bible*. Syracuse, N.Y.: Wesleyan Methodist Book Room, 1855.

____. *The Supremacy of the Divine Law: A Sermon Preached on the Occasion of the Death of Reverend Charles Turner Torrey*. N.p., 1846.

____. *Wesleyan Manual: A Defense of the Organization of the Wesleyan Methodist Connection*. Syracuse, N.Y.: S. Lee, 1862.

The Liberty Almanac. New York: William Harned, 1847–52.

Liberty or Slavery: The Great National Question. Boston: Congregational Board of Publications, 1857.

Long, John D. *Pictures of Slavery in Church and State*. Philadelphia: Privately printed, 1857.

Lord, Nathan. *A Letter of Inquiry to Ministers of the Gospel, of All Denominations, on Slavery, By a Northern Presbyter*. 4th ed. Hanover, N.H.: Dartmouth Press, 1860.

____. *A Northern Presbyterian's Second Letter to Ministers of the Gospel of All Denominations on Slavery*. New York: D. Appleton, 1855.

Love, Horace T. *Slavery in Its Relation to God: A Review of Reverend Dr. Lord's Thanksgiving Sermon in Favor of Slavery*. Buffalo: A. M. Clapp, 1851.

M'Carter, J. Mayland. *Border Methodism and Border Slavery*. Philadelphia: Collins, 1858.

McGill, A. T. *The Hand of God with the Black Race*. Philadelphia: William F. Geddes, 1862.

Massachusetts Anti-Slavery Society. *Annual Report*. Boston, 1836–57.

Matlack, Lucius C. *The History of American Slavery and Methodism from 1780 to 1849; and History of the Wesleyan Methodist Connection of America*. New York: Privately printed, 1849.

Mattison, Hiram. *The Impending Crisis of 1860; or, The Present Connection of the Methodist Episcopal Church with Slavery, and Our Duty in Regard to It*. New York: Mason Brothers, 1859.

Mayo, Amory D. *Herod, John, and Jesus; or, American Slavery and Its Christian Cure*. Albany, N.Y.: Weed, Parsons, 1860.

Methodist Anti-Slavery Union. Proceedings of the Anti-Slavery Convention of the Black River Conference. New York, 1858.

Methodist Episcopal Church. *Journal of the General Conference of the Methodist Episcopal Church*. New York, 1844.

Morse, Sidney E. *The Bible and Slavery*. New York: n.p., 1855.

New England Anti-Slavery Society. *Second Annual Report . . . 1834*. Boston, 1834.

Ohio Anti-Slavery Society. *Proceedings of the Ohio Anti-Slavery Convention, Held at Putnam, on the 22nd, 23rd, and 24th of April, 1835*. New York: American Anti-Slavery Society, n.d.

____. *Report of the Second Anniversary*. Cincinnati, 1837.

Ohio Baptist Annual Convention. *Annual Report*. Mansfield, Ohio: George T. Myers, 1861–62, 1865.

Ohio State Christian Anti-Slavery Convention. *Proceedings of the Ohio State Christian Anti-Slavery Convention, Held in Columbus, August 10 and 11, 1859*. Columbus, 1859.

Bibliography

Patterson, James. *The Old School Presbyterian Church on Slavery.* New Wilmington, Ohio: Vincent Ferguson, 1857.

Patton, William W. *Slavery and Infidelity; or, Slavery in the Church Ensures Infidelity in the World.* Cincinnati: American Reform Tract and Book Society, 1856.

Peck, George. *Slavery and Episcopacy: Being an Examination of Dr. Bascom's Review.* New York: Lane & Tippett, 1845.

Pennsylvania State Anti-Slavery Society. *Thirteenth Annual Report, Presented to the Pennsylvania State Anti-Slavery Society, by Its Executive Committee, October 15,1850.* Philadelphia: Anti-Slavery Office, 1850.

Perkins, George W. *Professor Stuart and Slave Catching: Remarks on Mr. Stuart's Book "Conscience and the Constitution."* West Meriden, Conn.: Hinman's Print, 1850.

Phillips, Wendell. *The Philosophy of the Abolition Movement.* New York: American Anti-Slavery Society, 1860.

Pillsbury, Parker. *The Church as It Is; or, The Forlorn Hope of Slavery.* 1847. Reprint. Concord, N.H.: Privately printed, 1885.

Pond, Enoch. *Slavery and the Bible.* Boston: American Tract Society, Boston, n.d.

Proceedings of the Great Convention of Friends of Freedom in the Eastern and Middle States, Held in Boston, Oct. 1, 2, & 3, 1845. Lowell, Mass.: Lowell, Pillsbury & Knapp, 1845.

Pullen, William H. *The Blast of a Trumpet in Zion Calling upon Every Son and Daughter of Wesley in Great Britain and Ireland to Aid Their Brethren in America in Purifying Their American Zion from Slavery.* London: Webb, Millington, 1860.

Rice, Nathan L. *Lectures on Slavery.* Chicago: Daily Democrat Print, 1860.

Roberts, William L. *The Higher Law; or, The Law of the Most High.* Auburn, N.Y.: T. W. Brown, 1851.

Robinson, John. *The Testimony and Practice of the Presbyterian Church in Reference to American Slavery.* Cincinnati: John D. Thorpe, 1852.

Ross, Frederick A. *Position of the Southern Church in Relation to Slavery.* New York: John A. Gray, 1857.

––––. *Slavery Ordained of God.* Philadelphia: Lippincott, 1857.

Scott, Orange. *The Grounds of Secession from the M. E. Church; or, Book for the Times: Being an Examination of Her Connection with Slavery and Also of Her Form of Government.* New York: C. Prindle, 1848.

Seabury, Samuel. *American Slavery Distinguished from the Slavery of English Theorists and Justified by the Law of Nature.* New York: Mason, 1861.

Sheldon, L. H. *The Moral Responsibility of the Citizen and Nation in Respect to the Fugitive Slave Bill.* Andover, Mass.: John H. Flagg, 1851.

Shields, Charles W. *A Discourse on Christian Politics.* Philadelphia: Deacon & Peterson, 1851.

Smith, Gerrit. *Gerrit Smith on Religion.* New York: Sinclair Tousey, 1863.

Smith, L. *The Higher Law; or, Christ and His Law Supreme.* Ravenna, Ohio: Star Print, 1852.

South Middlesex Conferences of Churches. *The Political Duties of Christians.* Boston: Andrews & Prentiss, 1848.

Spear, Samuel T. *The Law-Abiding Conscience and the Higher Law Conscience, with Remarks on the Fugitive Slave Question.* New York: Lambert & Lane, 1850.

Stanton, Robert L. *Civil Government of God: Obedience a Duty.* Cincinnati: J. D. Thorpe, 1860.

Starr, Frederick, Jr. *What Shall Be Done with the People of Color?* Albany, N.Y.: Weed, Parsons, 1862.

Stiles, Joseph C. *Speech on the Slavery Resolutions Delivered in the General Assembly Which Met in Detroit in May Last.* Washington, D.C.: Jonathan T. Towers, 1850.

Stone, A. L. *Emancipation.* Occasional Tract 8. Cincinnati: American Reform Tract and Book Society, n.d.

Stuart, Moses. *Conscience and the Constitution.* Boston: Crocker & Brewster, 1850.

Sunderland, LaRoy. *The Testimony of God against Slavery.* Boston: Webster & Southard, 1835.

Taylor, Thomas J. *Essay on Slavery as Connected with the Moral and Providential Government of God and as an Element of Church Organization.* New York: Privately printed, 1851.

Thompson, Joseph P. *Christianity and Emancipation; or, The Teachings and Influence of the Bible against Slavery.* New York: A. D. F. Randolph, 1863.

_____. *The Fugitive Slave Law, Tried by the Old and New Testaments.* New York: William Harned, 1850.

_____. *No Slavery in Nebraska: The Voice of God against National Crime.* New York: Ivison & Phinney, 1854.

Thurston, R. B. "The Error and the Duty in Regard to Slavery." In *Liberty or Slavery: The Great National Question.* Boston: Congregational Board of Publications, 1857.

Tilton, Theodore. *The American Board and American Slavery.* New York: John A. Gray, 1860.

Van Dyke, Henry. *The Character and Influence of Abolitionism.* New York: D. Appleton, 1860.

Van Rensselaer, Cortlandt. *Presbyterian Views on Slaveholding: Letters and Rejoinders to George D. Armstrong.* Philadelphia: J. M. Milson, 1858.

Wadsworth, Charles. *Politics in Religion.* Philadelphia: T. B. Peterson, 1854.

Warren, Edwin T. *Free Missionary Principle; or, Bible Missions: A Plea for Separate Missionary Action from Slaveholders.* 2d ed. Boston: J. Howe, 1846.

Wheaton, N. S. *Discourse on St. Paul's Epistle to Philemon, Exhibiting the Duty of Citizens of the Northern States in Regard to the Institution of Slavery.* Hartford: Case, Tiffany, 1851.

Whipple, Charles K. *The American Tract Society, Boston.* Boston: Massachusetts Anti-Slavery Society, 1859.

_____. *The Family Relation as Affected by Slavery.* Tract 40. Cincinnati: American Reform Tract and Book Society, n.d.

_____. *The Methodist Church and Slavery.* New York: American Anti-Slavery Society, 1859.

_____. *Relation of the American Board of Commissioners for Foreign Missions to Slavery.* Boston: R. F. Wallcut, 1861.

——. *The Relations of Anti-Slavery to Religion.* Anti-Slavery Tract 19. New York: American Anti-Slavery Society, n.d.

——. *Slavery and the American Board of Commissioners for Foreign Missions.* New York: American Anti-Slavery Society, 1859.

Williston, Timothy. "Is American Slavery an Institution Which Christianity Sanctions, and Will Perpetuate? And, in View of This Subject, What Ought American Christians to Do, and Refrain from Doing?" In *Liberty or Slavery: The Great National Question.* Boston: Congregational Board of Publications, 1857.

Wilson, Joseph, ed. *The Presbyterian Historical Almanac and Annual Remembrancer of the Church.* Philadelphia: J. M. Wilson, 1859–64.

Wolcott, Samuel. *Separation from Slavery: Being a Consideration of the Inquiry, "How Shall Christians and Christian Churches Best Absolve Themselves from All Responsible Connection with Slavery?"* Boston: American Tract Society, n.d.

Wright, Henry C. *Christian Commission with Slave-Holders: Will the Alliance Sanction It? Letters to Reverend John Angell Adams, D.D., and Reverend Ralph Wardlaw, D.D., Showing Their Position in the Alliance.* Rochdale, England: Jesse Hall, 1846.

——. *Duty of Abolitionists to Rebuke Proslavery Ministers.* Concord, N.H.: John R. French, 1841.

SECONDARY SOURCES

Books

Abzug, Robert H. *Passionate Liberator: Theodore Dwight Weld and the Dilemma of Reform.* New York: Oxford University Press, 1980.

Addison, Daniel D. *The Clergy in American Life and Letters.* New York: Macmillan, 1900.

Ahlstrom, Sydney E. *A Religious History of the American People.* New Haven: Yale University Press, 1972.

Albrecht, Robert C. *Theodore Parker.* New York: Twayne, 1971.

Albright, Raymond W. *History of the Evangelical Church.* Harrisburg, Pa.: Evangelical Press, 1942.

Auer, J. Jeffrey, ed. *Antislavery and Disunion, 1858–1861: Studies in the Rhetoric of Compromise and Conflict.* New York: Harper & Row, 1963.

Babcock, Rufus. *Memoir of John Mason Peck, D.D.* Philadelphia: American Baptist Publication Society, 1864.

Bacon, Margaret H. *Valiant Friend: The Life of Lucretia Mott.* New York: Walker, 1980.

Bacon, Theodore D. *Leonard Bacon: A Statesman in the Church.* New Haven: Yale University Press, 1931.

Baird, Henry M. *Life of Reverend Robert Baird, D.D.* New York: A. D. F. Randolph, 1860.

Bibliography

Baker, Robert A. *The Southern Baptist Convention and Its People, 1607–1972*. Nashville. Broadman Press, 1974.

Banner, Lois W. *Elizabeth Cady Stanton: A Radical for Women's Rights*. Boston: Little Brown, 1980.

Barnes, Gilbert H. *The Antislavery Impulse, 1830–1844*. New York: Appleton-Century-Crofts, 1933.

Bartlett, Irving H. *Wendell Phillips: Brahmin Radical*. Boston: Beacon Press, 1961.

Bassett, Ancel H. *A Concise History of the Methodist Protestant Church from Its Origin*. Pittsburgh: William McCracken, Jr., 1887.

Baxter, Norman A. *History of the Freewill Baptists: A Study in New England Separatism*. Rochester, N.Y.: American Baptist Historical Society, 1957.

Beard, Augustus F. *A Crusade for Brotherhood: A History of the American Missionary Association*. Boston: Pilgrim Press, 1909.

Benson, Lee. *The Concept of Jacksonian Democracy: New York as a Test Case*. Princeton: Princeton University Press, 1961.

Blue, Frederick J. *The Free Soilers: Third Party Politics, 1848–54*. Urbana: University of Illinois Press, 1974.

Bodo, John R. *The Protestant Clergy and Public Issues, 1812–1848*. Princeton: Princeton University Press, 1954.

Bolster, Arthur S., Jr. *James Freeman Clarke: Disciple to Advancing Truth*. Boston: Beacon Press, 1954.

Bremner, Robert H. *American Philanthropy*. Chicago: University of Chicago Press, 1960.

Brock, William R. *Parties and Political Conscience: American Dilemmas, 1840–1850*. Millwood, N.Y.: Kto Press, 1979.

Brue, Donald, comp. *National Party Platforms*. 2 vols. Urbana: University of Illinois Press, 1978.

Bucke, Emory S., ed. *The History of American Methodism*. 3 vols. New York: Abingdon Press, 1964.

Cady, George L. *The American Missionary Association and the Churches of the Midwest before 1861*. N.p.: American Missionary Association, 1936.

Cady, John F. *The Origin and Development of the Missionary Baptist Church in Indiana*. Franklin, Ind.: Franklin College Press, 1942.

Cameron, Richard M. *Methodism and Society in Historical Perspective*. New York: Abingdon Press, 1961.

Campbell, Stanley W. *The Slave Catchers: Enforcement of the Fugitive Slave Law, 1850–1860*. Chapel Hill: University of North Carolina Press, 1968.

Cassara, Ernest. *Hosea Ballou: The Challenge to Orthodoxy*. Boston: Beacon Press, 1961.

———, ed. *Universalism in America: A Documentary History*. Boston: Beacon Press, 1971.

Chadwick, John W. *Theodore Parker, Preacher and Reformer*. Boston: Houghton Mifflin, 1900.

Child, Lydia Maria. *Isaac T. Hopper: A True Life*. Boston: J. P. Jewett, 1853.

Christie, John W., and Dumond, Dwight L. *George Bourne and the Book and Slavery Irreconcilable*. Philadelphia: Presbyterian Historical Society, 1969.

Clark, Calvin M. *American Slavery and Maine Congregationalists: A Chapter in the History of the Development of Anti-Slavery Sentiment in the Protestant Churches of the North*. Bangor, Maine: Privately printed, 1940.

Clark, Robert D. *Life of Matthew Simpson*. New York: Macmillan, 1956.

Clarke, Grace Julian. *George W. Julian*. Indianapolis: Indiana Historical Commission, 1923.

Clarke, James Freeman. *Anti-Slavery Days: A Sketch of the Struggle Which Ended in the Abolition of Slavery*. New York: Worthington, 1884.

Cole, Arthur C. *Era of the Civil War, 1848–1870*. Springfield, Ill.: Illinois Centennial Commission, 1919.

———. *The Irrepressible Conflict, 1850–1865*. New York: Macmillan, 1934.

Cole, Charles C., Jr. *The Social Ideas of the Northern Evangelists, 1826–1860*. New York: Columbia University Press, 1954.

Commager, Henry Steele. *Theodore Parker*. Boston: Little, Brown, 1936.

Cooke, George W. *Unitarianism in America*. Boston: American Unitarian Association, 1902.

Craven, Avery. *The Coming of the Civil War*. New York: Scribner, 1942.

Crist, A. C. *The History of Marion Presbytery: Its Churches, Elders, Ministers, Missionary Societies, Etc.* N.p., 1908.

Cross, Whitney R. *The Burned-over District: The Social and Intellectual History of Enthusiastic Religion in Western New York, 1800–1850*. New York: Harper & Row, 1950.

Curry, Daniel. *Life-Story of Davis Wasgatt Clark, D.D., Bishop of the Methodist Episcopal Church*. New York: Nelson & Phillips, 1874.

Davis, David B. *The Problem of Slavery in the Age of Revolution, 1770–1823*. Ithaca: Cornell University Press, 1975.

Dillon, Merton L. *The Abolitionists: The Growth of a Dissenting Minority*. De Kalb: Northern Illinois University Press, 1974.

Doherty, Robert W. *The Hicksite Separation: A Sociological Analysis of Religious Schism in Early Nineteenth Century America*. New Brunswick: Rutgers University Press, 1967.

Dolan, Jay P. *The Immigrant Church: New York's Irish and German Catholics, 1815–1865*. Baltimore: Johns Hopkins University Press, 1975.

Dorchester, Daniel. *Christianity in the United States*. New York: Phillips & Hunt, 1888.

Drake, Thomas. *Quakers and Slavery in America*. New Haven: Yale University Press, 1950.

Duberman, Martin. *Charles Francis Adams*. Boston: Houghton Mifflin, 1961.

Dumond, Dwight L. *Antislavery: The Crusade for Freedom in America*. Ann Arbor: University of Michigan Press, 1961.

———. *Antislavery Origins of the Civil War*. Ann Arbor: University of Michigan Press, 1939.

Bibliography

Dunham, Chester F. *The Attitude of the Northern Clergy toward the South, 1860–1865.* Toledo, Ohio: Gray, 1942.

Elkins, Stanley. *Slavery: A Problem in American Institutional and Intellectual Life.* Chicago: University of Chicago Press, 1959.

Essig, James D. *The Bonds of Wickedness: American Evangelicals against Slavery, 1770–1808.* Philadelphia: Temple University Press, 1982.

Filler, Louis. *The Crusade against Slavery, 1830–1860.* New York: Harper & Row, 1960.

Fladeland, Betty. *James G. Birney: Slaveholder to Abolitionist.* Ithaca: Cornell University Press, 1955.

_____. *Men and Brothers: Anglo-American Antislavery Cooperation.* Urbana: University of Illinois Press, 1972.

Fletcher, Robert S. *A History of Oberlin College from Its Foundation through the Civil War.* 2 vols. Oberlin, Ohio: R. R. Donnelly, 1943.

Foner, Eric. *Free Soil, Free Labor, Free Men: The Ideology of the Republican Party before the Civil War.* New York: Oxford University Press, 1970.

Formisano, Ronald P. *The Birth of Mass Political Parties: Michigan, 1827–1861.* Princeton: Princeton University Press, 1971.

Frazier, E. Franklin. *The Negro Church in America.* New York: Schocken Books, 1964.

Friedman, Lawrence J. *Gregarious Saints: Self and Community in American Abolitionism, 1830–1870.* Cambridge, Mass.: Cambridge University Press, 1982.

Gaines, Wesley J. *African Methodism in the South; or, Twenty-Five Years of Freedom.* 1890. Reprint. Chicago: Afro-Am Press, 1969.

Galbraith, R. C. *The History of the Chillicothe Presbytery, from Its Organization in 1799 to 1889.* Chillicothe, Ohio: Chillicothe Presbytery, 1889.

Garrison, Winifred E. *Religion Follows the Fronter: A History of the Disciples of Christ.* New York: Harper, 1931.

_____., and DeGroot, Alfred T. *The Disciples of Christ: A History.* St. Louis: Bethany Press, 1948.

Garrison, W. P., and Garrison, F. J. *William Lloyd Garrison, 1805–1879.* 4 vols. New York: Century, 1885–89.

Gaustad, Edwin S. *Dissent in American Religion.* Chicago: University of Chicago Press, 1973.

Geary, M. Theophane. *A History of Third Parties in Pennsylvania, 1840–1860.* Washington: Catholic University of America, 1938.

George, Carol V. R. *Segregated Sabbaths: Richard Allen and the Emergence of Independent Black Churches, 1760–1840.* New York: Oxford University Press, 1973.

Goodykoontz, Colin B. *Home Missions on the American Frontier.* Caldwell, Idaho: Caxton, 1939.

Gravely, William. *Gilbert Haven, Methodist Abolitionist: A Study in Race, Religion, and Reform, 1850–1880.* Nashville: Abingdon Press, 1973.

Bibliography

Griffin, Clifford S. *Their Brothers' Keepers: Moral Stewardship in the United States, 1800–1865.* New Brunswick: Rutgers University Press, 1960.

Hagood, Lewis M. *The Colored Man in the Methodist Episcopal Church.* Cincinnati: Cranston & Stowe, 1890.

Halsey, Leroy J. *History of McCormick Theological Seminary of the Presbyterian Church.* Chicago: McCormick Theological Seminary, 1893.

Hammond, John L. *The Politics of Benevolence: Revival Religion and American Voting Behavior.* Norwood, N.J.: Ablex, 1979.

Harlow, Ralph V. *Gerrit Smith, Philanthropist and Reformer.* New York: Holt, 1939.

Heathcote, Charles W. *The Lutheran Church and the Civil War.* New York: Fleming H. Revell, 1919.

Herbert, Hilary A. *The Abolition Crusade and Its Consequences: Four Periods of American History.* New York: Scribner, 1912.

Hibben, Paxton. *Henry Ward Beecher: An American Portrait.* New York: George H. Doran, 1927.

Hogue, Wilson T. *History of the Free Methodist Church of North America.* 2 vols. Chicago: Free Methodist Publishing House, 1915.

Holt, Michael F. *Forging a Majority: The Formation of the Republican Party before the Civil War.* New Haven: Yale University Press, 1969.

_____. *The Political Crisis of the 1850s.* New York: Wiley, 1978

Hopkins, Charles H. *History of the Y.M.C.A. in North America.* New York: Association Press, 1951.

Howe, Daniel W. *The Unitarian Conscience: Harvard Moral Philosophy, 1805–1861.* Cambridge, Mass.: Harvard University Press, 1970.

Howe, Mark A. *Memoirs of the Life and Services of the Right Reverend Alonzo Potter, D.D., LL.D., Bishop of the Protestant Episcopal Church in the Diocese of Pennsylvania.* Philadelphia: Lippincott, 1871.

Howe, Mark D. *The Garden and the Wilderness: Religion and Government in American Constitutional History.* Chicago: University of Chicago Press, 1965.

Hoyt, Arthur S. *The Pulpit and American Life.* New York: Macmillan, 1921.

Hunt, Galliard. *Israel, Elihu, and Cadwallader Washburn: A Chapter in American Biography.* New York: Macmillan, 1925.

Jensen, Richard. *The Winning of the Midwest: Social and Political Conflict, 1888–1896.* Chicago: University of Chicago Press, 1971.

Johnson, Oliver. *William Lloyd Garrison and His Times; or, Sketches of the Anti-Slavery Movement in America and of the Man Who Was Its Founder and Moral Leader.* Boston: Houghton Mifflin, 1881.

Jones, Donald G. *The Sectional Crisis and Northern Methodism: A Study in Piety, Political Ethics, and Civil Religion.* Metuchen, N.J.: Scarecrow Press, 1979.

Jones, Louis T. *The Quakers of Iowa.* Iowa City: State Historical Society of Iowa, 1914.

Jordan, Lewis G. *Negro Baptist History, U.S.A., 1750–1930.* Nashville: Sunday School Publishing Board, N.B.C., 1930.

Keller, Charles R. *The Second Great Awakening in Connecticut.* New Haven: Yale University Press, 1942.

Kennedy, William S. *The Plan of Union; or, A History of the Presbyterian and Congregational Churches in the Western Reserve.* Hudson, Ohio: Pentagon Steam Press, 1856.

Kilby, Clyde S. *Minority of One: The Biography of Jonathan Blanchard.* Grand Rapids, Mich.: William B. Eerdmans, 1959.

Kleppner, Paul. *The Cross of Culture: A Social Analysis of Midwestern Politics, 1850–1900.* New York: Free Press, 1970.

Kraditor, Aileen. *Means and Ends in American Abolitionism: Garrison and His Critics on Strategy and Tactics.* New York: Pantheon, 1967.

Kuhns, Frederick I. *The Home Missionary Society and the Anti-Slavery Controversy in the Old Northwest.* Billings, Mont.: Privately printed, 1959.

Lader, Lawrence. *The Bold Brahmins: New England's War against Slavery, 1831–1863.* New York: Dutton, 1961.

Lamar, James S. *Memoirs of Isaac Errett.* 2 vols. Cincinnati: Standard, 1893.

Lane, Ann J., ed. *The Debate over Slavery: Stanley Elkins and His Critics.* Urbana: University of Illinois Press, 1971.

Lens, Sidney. *Radicalism in America.* New York: Thomas Y. Crowell, 1966.

Lesick, Lawrence T. *The Lane Rebels: Evangelicalism and Antislavery in Antebellum America.* Metuchen, N.J.: Scarecrow Press, 1980.

Lewis, William G. *Biography of Samuel Lewis.* Cincinnati: Methodist Book Concern, 1857.

Lipset, Seymour M. *The First New Nation: The United States in Historical and Comparative Perspective.* New York: Basic Books, 1963.

Litwack, Leon F. *North of Slavery: The Negro in the Free States, 1790–1860.* Chicago: University of Chicago Press, 1961.

Lloyd, Arthur Y. *The Slavery Controversy, 1831–1860.* Chapel Hill: University of North Carolina Press, 1939.

Lowitt, Richard. *A Merchant Prince of the Nineteenth Century: William E. Dodge.* New York: Columbia University Press, 1954.

Lunger, Harold L. *The Political Ethics of Alexander Campbell.* St. Louis: Bethany Press, 1954.

Mabee, Carleton. *Black Freedom: The Nonviolent Abolitionists from 1830 through the Civil War.* London: Macmillan, 1970.

McConnell, Samuel D. *History of the American Episcopal Church from the Planting of the Colonies to the End of the Civil War.* 6th ed. New York: T. Whittaker, 1890.

McLeister, Ira Ford, and Nicholson, Roy. *History of the Wesleyan Methodist Church in America.* 3d ed. Marion, Ind.: Wesley Press, 1959.

MacMillan, Margaret B. *The Methodist Church in Michigan: The Nineteenth Century.* Grand Rapids, Mich.: William B. Eerdmans, 1967.

McPherson, James M. *The Abolitionist Legacy: From Reconstruction to the NAACP.* Princeton: Princeton University Press, 1975.

————. *The Negro's Civil War: How American Negroes Felt and Acted during the War for the Union.* New York: Pantheon, 1965.

————. *The Struggle for Equality: Abolitionists and the Negro in the Civil War and Reconstruction.* Princeton: Princeton University Press, 1964.

Magdol, Edward. *Owen Lovejoy: Abolitionist in Congress.* New Brunswick: Rutgers University Press, 1967.

Marsden, George M. *The Evangelical Mind and the New School Presbyterian Experience: A Case Study of Thought and Theology in Nineteenth Century America.* New Haven: Yale University Press, 1970.

Marty, Martin E. *Righteous Empire: The Protestant Experience in America.* New York: Dial Press, 1970.

Mathews, Donald G. *Religion in the Old South.* Chicago: University of Chicago Press, 1977.

————. *Slavery and Methodism: A Chapter in American Morality, 1780–1845.* Princeton: Princeton University Press, 1965.

Matlack, Lucius C. *The Antislavery Struggle and Triumph in the Methodist Episcopal Church.* New York: Phillips & Hunt, 1881.

————. *The Life of Reverend Orange Scott.* New York: Wesleyan Methodist Book Room, 1847.

Mead, Frank S. *Handbook of Denominations in the United States.* 4th ed. Nashville: Abingdon Press, 1965.

Mead, Sidney E. *Nathaniel William Taylor, 1786–1858: A Connecticut Liberal.* Chicago: University of Chicago Press, 1942.

Merideth, Robert. *The Politics of the Universe: Edward Beecher, Abolition, and Orthodoxy.* Nashville: Vanderbilt University Press, 1968.

Merrill, Walter M. *Against Wind and Tide: A Biography of William Lloyd Garrison.* Cambridge, Mass.: Harvard University Press, 1963.

Miyakawa, T. Scott. *Protestants and Pioneers: Individualism and Conformity on the American Frontier.* Chicago: University of Chicago Press, 1964.

Moellering, Ralph L. *Christian Conscience and Negro Emancipation.* Philadelphia: Fortress Press, 1965.

Moorhead, James H. *American Apocalypse: Yankee Protestants and the Civil War, 1860–1869.* New Haven: Yale University Press, 1978.

Morrison, Marion. *Life of the Reverend David McDill, D.D., Minister of the United Presbyterian Church.* Philadelphia: Privately printed, 1874.

Morrow, Ralph. *Northern Methodism and Reconstruction.* East Lansing: Michigan State University Press, 1956.

Muelder, Hermann R. *Fighters for Freedom: History of Anti-Slavery Activities of Men and Women Associated with Knox College.* New York: Columbia University Press, 1959.

Munger, Theodore T. *Horace Bushnell: Preacher and Theologian.* Boston: Houghton Mifflin, 1899.

Murphy, Lawrence R. *Antislavery in the Southwest: William G. Kephart's Mission to New Mexico, 1850–53.* El Paso: Texas Western Press, 1978.

Murray, Andrew E. *Presbyterians and the Negro—A History*. Philadelphia: Presbyterian Historical Society, 1966.

Neely, Thomas B. *American Methodism: Its Divisions and Unification*. New York: Fleming H. Revell, 1915.

Nichols, Robert H. *Presbyterians in New York State: A History of the Synod and Its Predecessors*. Philadelphia: Presbyterian Historical Society, 1963.

Niebuhr, H. Richard. *The Social Sources of Denominationalism*. New York: Holt, 1929.

Nye, Russell B. *The Cultural Life of the New Nation, 1776–1830*. New York: Harper & Row, 1960.

Palmer, B. M. *The Life and Letters of James Henley Thornwell, D.D.* Richmond, Va.: Whittet & Shepperson, 1875.

Payne, Daniel A. *History of the African Methodist Episcopal Church*. Nashville: A.M.E. Sunday-School Union, 1891.

Pease, Jane H., and Pease, William H. *Bound with Them in Chains: A Biographical History of the Antislavery Movement*. Westport, Conn.: Greenwood Press, 1972.

——. *They Who Would Be Free: Blacks' Search for Freedom, 1830–1861*. New York: Atheneum, 1974.

Peck, Elizabeth S. *Berea's First Century, 1855–1955*. Lexington: University of Kentucky Press, 1955.

Perry, Lewis. *Childhood, Marriage, and Reform: Henry Clarke Wright, 1797–1870*. Chicago: University of Chicago Press, 1980.

——. *Radical Abolitionism: Anarchy and the Government of God in Antislavery Thought*. Ithaca: Cornell University Press, 1973.

Peters, John L. *Christian Perfection and American Methodism*. New York: n.p., 1956.

Pilkington, James P. *The Methodist Publishing House: A History*. Nashville: Abingdon Press, 1968.

Pillsbury, Parker. *Acts of the Anti-Slavery Apostles*. Boston: Cupples, Upham, 1884.

Presbyterian Reunion: A Memorial Volume, 1837–1871. New York: DeWitt C. Lent, 1927.

Putnam, Mary. *The Baptists and Slavery, 1840–1845*. Ann Arbor: George Wahr, 1913.

Quarles, Benjamin. *Black Abolitionists*. New York: Oxford University Press, 1969.

Randall, James G., and Donald, David. *The Civil War and Reconstruction*. 2d ed. Lexington, Mass.: D. C. Heath, 1969.

Rayback, Joseph G. *Free Soil: The Election of 1848*. Lexington: University of Kentucky Press, 1970.

Rice, Madeleine H. *Federal Street Pastor: The Life of William Ellery Channing*. New York: Bookman, 1961.

Richardson, Robert. *Memoirs of Alexander Campbell*. Cincinnati: R. W. Carrol, 1872.

Riddleberger, Patrick. *George Washington Julian: Radical Republican*. Indianapolis: Indiana Historical Bureau, 1966.

Ridgaway, Henry B. *Life of Alfred Cookman.* New York: Harper, 1874.

Ritchie, Andrew. *The Soldier, the Battle, and the Victory: Being a Brief Account of the Work of Reverend John Rankin in the Antislavery Cause.* Cincinnati: Western Tract and Book Society, 1868.

Rose, Willie Lee. *Rehearsal for Reconstruction: The Port Royal Experiment.* Indianapolis: Bobbs-Merrill, 1964.

Schaff, Philip. *America: A Study of Its Political, Social, and Religious Character.* 1855. Reprint. Cambridge, Mass.: Harvard University Press, Belknap Press, 1961.

Scherer, Lester B. *Slavery and the Churches in Early America, 1619–1819.* Grand Rapids, Mich.: William B. Eerdmans, 1975.

Schriver, Edward O. *Go Free: The Antislavery Impulse in Maine, 1833–1855.* Orono: University of Main Press, 1971.

Sewell, Richard H. *Ballots for Freedom: Antislavery Politics in the United States, 1837–1860.* New York: Oxford University Press, 1976.

Simms, Henry H. *Emotion at High Tide: Abolition as a Controversial Factor, 1830–1845.* Baltimore: Privately printed, 1960.

Slosser, Gaius J., ed. *They Seek a Country: The American Presbyterians.* New York: Macmillan, 1955.

Smeltzer, Wallace G. *Methodism on the Headwaters of the Ohio: The History of the Pittsburgh Conference of the Methodist Church, 1772–1950.* Nashville: Parthenon Press, 1951.

Smith, H. Shelton. *In His Image But . . . . : Racism in Southern Religion, 1780–1910.* Durham, N.C.: Duke University Press, 1972.

Smith, H. Shelton; Handy, Robert T.; and Loetscher, Lefferts A. *American Christianity.* 2 vols. New York: Scribner, 1963.

Smith, Justin A. *A History of the Baptists in the Western States East of the Mississippi.* Philadelphia: American Baptist Publication Society, 1896.

———. *Memoir of Reverend Nathaniel Colver.* Boston: George A. Foxcraft, 1875.

Smith, Timothy L. *Revivalism and Social Reform: American Protestantism on the Eve of the Civil War.* 1957. Reprint. New York: Harper & Row, 1965.

Sobel, Mechal. *Trabelin' On: The Slave Journey to an Afro-Baptist Faith.* Westport, Conn.: Greenwood Press, 1979.

Sorin, Gerald. *Abolitionism: A New Perspective.* New York: Praeger, 1972.

———. *The New York Abolitionists: A Case Study of Political Radicalism.* Westport, Conn.: Greenwood Press, 1971.

Spinka, Matthew, ed. *A History of Illinois Congregational and Christian Churches.* Chicago: Congregational and Christian Conference of Illinois, 1944.

Stange, Douglas C. *Patterns of Antislavery among American Unitarians, 1831–1860.* Rutherford, N.J.: Fairleigh Dickinson University Press, 1977.

———. *Radicalism for Humanity: A Study of Lutheran Abolitionism.* St. Louis: O. Slave, 1970.

Staudenraus, Philip J. *The African Colonization Movement, 1816–1865.* New York: Columbia University Press, 1961.

Stevens, Abel. *A Compendious History of American Methodism.* New York: Carlton & Porter, 1868.

———. *The Life and Times of Reverend Nathan Bangs.* New York: Carlton & Porter, 1863.

Stewart, James B. *Holy Warriors: The Abolitionists and American Slavery.* New York: Hill & Wang, 1976.

———. *Joshua Giddings and the Tactics of Radical Politics, 1795–1864.* Cleveland: Press of Case Western Reserve University, 1969.

Strout, Cushing. *The New Heavens and New Earth: Political Religion in America.* New York: Harper & Row, 1974.

Sweet, William W. *Methodism in American History.* Nashville: Abingdon Press, 1954.

Temperley, Howard R. *British Antislavery, 1833–1870.* Columbia: University of South Carolina Press, 1972.

Thistlewaite, Frank. *The Anglo-American Connection in the Early Nineteenth Century.* Philadelphia: University of Pennsylvania Press, 1959.

Thomas, John L. *The Liberator: William Lloyd Garrison.* Boston: Little, Brown, 1963.

Thompson, Robert E. *History of the Presbyterian Churches in United States.* New York: Scribner, 1907.

Torbet, Robert G. *A History of the Baptists.* Philadelphia: Judson Press, 1950.

Tucker, William E., and McAllister, Lester G. *Journey in Faith: A History of the Christian Church (Disciples of Christ).* St. Louis: Bethany Press, 1975.

Tuckerman, Bayard. *William Jay and the Constitutional Movement for the Abolition of Slavery.* 1893. Reprint. New York: Negro University Press, 1969.

Turner, Lorenzo D. *Antislavery Sentiment in American Literature Prior to 1865.* Washington, D.C.: Association for the Study of Negro Life and History, 1926.

Tyler, Alice F. *Freedom's Ferment: Phases of American Social History from the Colonial Period to the Outbreak of the Civil War.* Minneapolis: University of Minnesota Press, 1944.

Vander Velde, Lewis G. *The Presbyterian Churches and the Federal Union, 1861–1869.* Cambridge, Mass.: Harvard University Press, 1932.

Voegeli, V. Jacque. *Free But Not Equal: The Midwest and the Negro during The Civil War.* Chicago: University of Chicago Press, 1967.

Walls, William J. *The African Methodist Episcopal Zion Church: Reality of the Black Church.* Charlotte, N.C.: A.M.E. Zion Publishing House, 1974.

Walters, Ronald G. *American Reformers, 1815–1860.* New York: Hill and Wang, 1978.

———. *The Antislavery Appeal: American Abolitionism after 1830.* Baltimore: Johns Hopkins University Press, 1976.

Wayland, Francis, and Wayland, H. L. *A Memoir of the Life and Labours of Francis Wayland.* 2 vols. New York: Sheldon, 1868.

Weatherford, Willis D. *American Churches and the Negro: An Historical Account from Early Slave Days to the Present.* Boston: Christopher, 1957.

Bibliography

Welsh, Edward B., ed. *Buckeye Presbyterianism*. N.p.: Presbyterian Synod of Ohio, 1968.

Wentz, Abdel R. *A Basic History of Lutheranism in America*. Philadelphia: Muhlenberg Press, 1955.

Wiecek, William M. *The Sources of Antislavery Constitutionalism in America, 1760–1848*. Ithaca: Cornell University Press, 1977.

Willey, Austin. *The History of the Anti-Slavery Cause in State and Nation*. Portland, Maine: Brown, Thurston, & Hoyt; Fogg & Dunham, 1886.

Wilson, Bryan. *Religious Sects: A Sociological Study*. New York: McGraw-Hill, 1970.

Wilson, Henry. *History of the Rise and Fall of the Slave Power in America*. 3 vols. Boston: James R. Osgood, 1877.

Wolf, Hazel C. *On Freedom's Altar: The Martyr Complex in the Abolition Movement*. Madison: University of Wisconsin, 1952.

Wright, Conrad. *Liberal Christians*. Boston: Beacon Press, 1970.

Wyatt-Brown, Bertram. *Lewis Tappan and the Evangelical War against Slavery*. Cleveland: Press of Case Western Reserve University, 1969.

York, Robert M. *George B. Cheever: Religious and Social Reformer, 1807–1890*. Orono: University of Maine Press, 1955.

Zilversmit, Arthur. *The First Emancipation: The Abolition of Slavery in the North*. Chicago: University of Chicago Press, 1967.

Articles

Aptheker, Herbert. "The Quakers and Negro Slavery." *Journal of Negro History* 25 (July 1940): 331–62.

Atherton, Lewis E. "Daniel Howell Hise, Abolitionist and Reformer." *MVHR* 26 (December 1939): 343–58.

Banner, Lois W. "Religious Benevolence as Social Control: A Critique of an Interpretation." *JAH* 60 (June 1973): 23–41.

Bradley, L. Richard. "The Lutheran Church and Slavery." *Concordia Historical Institute Quarterly* 44 (February 1971): 32–41.

Chadwick, John W. "Samuel May of Leicester." *New England Magazine* 10 (April 1899): 200–14.

Christiano, David. "Synod and Slavery, 1855." *New Jersey History* 90 (Spring 1972): 27–42.

Clark, Clifford E., Jr. "The Changing Nature of Protestantism in Mid-nineteenth Century America: Henry Ward Beecher's *Seven Lectures to Young Men*." *JAH* 57 (March 1971): 832–46.

Conner, James. "The Antislavery Movement in Iowa." *Annals of Iowa* 40 (Summer 1970): 343–76 and (Fall 1970): 450–79.

Davis, David B. "The Emergence of Immediatism in British and American Antislavery Thought." *MVHR* 49 (September 1962): 209–30.

Bibliography

_____. "Slavery and Sin: The Cultural Background." In *The Antislavery Vanguard: New Essays on the Abolitionists*, edited by Martin Duberman. Princeton: Princeton University Press, 1965.

Davis, Hugh H. "The Failure of Political Abolitionism." *Connecticut Review* 6 (April 1973): 76–86.

Denton, Charles R. "The Unitarian Church and 'Kansas Territory,' 1854–1861." *Kansas Historical Quarterly* 30 (Autumn 1964): 307–38.

Dillon, Merton L. "John Mason Peck: A Study of Historical Rationalization." *Journal of the Illinois State Historical Society* 50 (Winter 1957): 385–90.

Dodd, William E. "The Fight for the Northwest, 1860." *American Historical Review* 16 (July 1911): 774–88.

Drake, Richard B. "Freedmen's Aid Societies and Sectional Compromise." *JSH* 29 (May 1963): 175–86.

Eddy, Richard. "History of Universalism." *American Church History Series* 10 (1894): 251–493.

Essig, James D. "The Lord's Free Man: Charles G. Finney and His Abolitionism." *CWH* 24 (March 1978): 25–45.

Farley, Ena L. "Methodists and Baptists on the Issue of Black Equality in New York, 1865 to 1858." *Journal of Negro History* 61 (October 1976): 374–92.

Fellman, Michael. "Theodore Parker and the Abolitionist Role in the 1850s." *JAH* 61 (December 1974): 666–84.

Filler, Louis. "Liberalism, Anti-Slavery, and the Founders of the *Independent*." *New England Quarterly* 27 (September 1954): 291–306.

_____. "Parker Pillsbury: An Anti-Slavery Apostle." *New England Quarterly* 19 (September 1946): 315–37.

Fisk, William L. "The Associate Reformed Church in the Old Northwest: A Chapter in the Acculturation of the Immigrant." *Journal of Presbyterian History* 46 (June 1968): 157–74.

Fortenbaugh, Robert. "American Lutheran Synods and Slavery, 1830–1860." *Journal of Religion* 13 (January 1933): 72–92.

Friedman, Lawrence J. " 'Historical Topics Sometimes Run Dry': The State of Abolitionist Studies." *Historian* 43 (February 1981): 177–94.

George, Carol V. R. "Widening the Circle: The Black Church and the Abolitionist Crusade, 1830–1860." In *Antislavery Reconsidered: New Perspectives on the Abolitionists*, edited by Lewis Perry and Michael Fellman. Baton Rouge: Louisiana State University Press, 1979.

Gravely, William B. "Christian Abolitionism." In *The Social Gospel: Religion and Reform in Changing America*, edited by Ronald C. White, Jr., and C. Howard Hopkins. Philadelphia: Temple University Press, 1976.

_____. "Methodist Preachers, Slavery, and Caste: Types of Social Concern in Antebellum America." *Duke Divinity School Review* 34 (Autumn 1969): 209–29.

Green, Fletcher M. "Northern Missionary Activities in the South, 1846–1861." *JSH* 21 (May 1955): 147–72.

Griffin, Clifford S. "The Abolitionists and the Benevolent Societies, 1831–1861." *Journal of Negro History* 44 (1959): 195–216.

Bibliography

_____. "Religious Benevolence as Social Control, 1815–1860." *MVHR* 44 (December 1957): 195–216.

Grim, Paul R. "The Reverend John Rankin, Early Abolitionist." *Ohio State Archaeological and Historical Quarterly* 46 (May 1937): 215–56.

Harding, Vincent. "Religion and Resistance among Antebellum Negroes, 1800–1860." In *The Making of Black America,* edited by August Meier and Elliot Rudwick. New York: Athenum, 1969.

Harrell, David E., Jr. "The Sectional Origins of the Churches of Christ." *JSH* 30 (August 1964): 261–77.

Harris, Donnell R. "The Gradual Separation of Southern and Northern Baptists, 1845–1907." *Foundations* 7 (April 1964): 130–44.

Harwood, Thomas F. "British Evangelical Abolitionism and American Churches in the 1830s." *JSH* 28 (August 1962): 287–306.

Heckman, Oliver S. "The Presbyterian Church in the United States of America in Southern Reconstruction, 1860–1880." *North Carolina Historical Review* 20 (July 1943): 219–37.

Howard, Victor B. "The 1856 Election in Ohio: Moral Issues in Politics." *Ohio History* 80 (Winter 1971): 24–44.

_____. "Presbyterians, the Kansas-Nebraska Act, and the Election of 1856." *Journal of Presbyterian History* 49 (Summer 1971): 133–57.

Jacob, J. R. "LaRoy Sunderland: The Alienation of an Abolitionist." *Journal of American Studies* 6 (April 1972): 1–17.

Johnson, Clifton H. "Abolitionist Missionary Activities in North Carolina." *North Carolina Historical Review* 40 (July 1963): 295–320.

Johnson, James E. "Charles G. Finney and a Theology of Revivalism." *Church History* 38 (September 1969): 338–58.

Johnson, Reinhard O. "The Liberty Party in Massachusetts, 1840–1848: Antislavery Third Party Politics in the Bay State." *CWH* 28 (September 1982): 237–65.

_____. "The Liberty Party in Vermont, 1840–1848: The Forgotten Abolitionists." *Vermont History* 47 (Fall 1979): 258–75.

Klotter, James C. "The Black South and White America." *JAH* 66 (March 1980): 832–49.

Kuhns, Frederick. "Slavery and Missions in the Old Northwest." *Journal of the Presbyterian Historical Society* 24 (December 1946): 205–22.

Kull, Irving S. "Presbyterian Attitudes toward Slavery." *Church History* 7 (June 1938): 101–14.

Ledbetter, Patsy S., and Ledbetter, Billy D. "The Agitator and the Intellectuals: William Lloyd Garrison and the New England Transcendentalists." *Mid-America: An Historical Review* 62 (October 1980): 173–85.

Levy, Ronald. "Bishop Hopkins and the Dilemma of Slavery." *Pennsylvania Magazine of History and Biography* 91 (January 1967): 56–71.

Lewit, Robert T. "Indian Missions and Antislavery Sentiment: A Conflict of Evangelical and Humanitarian Ideals." *MVHR* 50 (June 1963): 39–55.

Loveland, Anne C. "Evangelicalism and 'Immediate Emancipation' in American Antislavery Thought." *JSH* 32 (May 1966): 172–88.

Bibliography

Lyons, Adelaide A. "Religious Defense of Slavery in the North." *Trinity College Historical Society Historical Papers* 13 (1919): 5–34.

Maclear, J. F. "The Evangelical Alliance and the Antislavery Crusade." *Huntington Library Quarterly* 42 (Spring 1979): 141–64.

McElroy, James L. "Social Control and Romantic Reform in Antebellum America: The Case of Rochester, New York." *New York History* 58 (January 1977): 17–46.

McFaul, John M. "Expediency vs. Morality: Jacksonian Politics and Slavery." *JAH* 62 (June 1975): 24–39.

McKivigan, John R. "The American Baptist Free Mission Society: Abolitionist Reaction to the 1845 Baptist Schism." *Foundations* 21 (October–December 1978): 340–55.

_____. " 'The Gospel Will Burst the Bonds of the Slaves': The Abolitionists' Bibles for Slaves Campaign." *Negro History Bulletin* 45 (July–September 1982): 62–64, 77.

_____. "Prisoner of Conscience: George Gordon and the Fugitive Slave Law." *Journal of Presbyterian History* 60 (Winter 1982): 336–54.

Marshall, Curtis. "Eleutherian College." *Indiana History Bulletin* 25 (November 1948): 200–203.

Mathews, Donald G. "The Abolitionists on Slavery: The Critique behind the Social Movement." *JSH* 33 (May 1967): 163–82.

_____. "The Methodist Schism of 1844 and the Popularization of Antislavery Sentiment." *Mid-America: An Historical Review* 51 (January 1968): 3–23.

Maynard, Douglas H. "The World's Anti-Slavery Convention of 1840." *MVHR* 47 (December 1960): 452–71.

Mohler, Mark. "The Episcopal Church and National Reconciliation, 1865." *Political Science Quarterly* 41 (December 1926): 567–95.

Moorhead, James H. "Social Reform and the Divided Conscience of Antebellum Protestantism." *Church History* 48 (December 1979): 416–30.

Murphy, Robert J. "Catholic Church in the United States during the Civil War Period, 1852–1866." *American Catholic Historical Society of Philadelphia Records* 39 (December 1928): 272–346.

Norton, L. Wesley. "The Methodist Episcopal Church in Michigan and the Politics of Slavery, 1850–1860." *Michigan History* 48 (September 1964): 193–213.

Pearson, Samuel C. "From Church to Denomination: American Congregationalism in the Nineteenth Century." *Church History* 38 (March 1969): 67–87.

Pease, Jane H., and Pease, William H. "Confrontation and Abolition in the 1850s." *JAH* 58 (March 1972): 923–37.

Perkal, M. Leon. "American Abolition Society: A Viable Alternative to the Republican Party." *Journal of Negro History* 65 (Winter 1980): 57–71.

Perry, Lewis. "Versions of Anarchism in the Antislavery Movement." *American Quarterly* 20 (Winter 1968): 768–82.

Pope, Liston. "The Negro and Religion in America." In *The Sociology of Religion: An Anthology,* edited by Richard D. Knudten. New York: Appleton-Century-Croft, 1967.

Posey, Walter B. "The Slavery Question in the Presbyterian Church in the Old Southwest." *JSH* 15 (August 1949): 311–24.

Bibliography

Purifoy, Lewis B. "The Methodist Anti-Slavery Tradition, 1784–1844." *Methodist History* 4 (July 1966): 3–16.

——. "The Southern Methodist Church and the Pro-Slavery Argument." *JSH* 32 (December 1966): 325–41.

Raines, Edgar F., Jr. "The American Missionary Association in Southern Illinois, 1856–1862: A Case Study in the Abolition Movement." *Journal of the Illinois State Historical Society* 65 (Autumn 1972): 246–68.

Ratner, Lorman. "Northern Concern for Social Order as a Cause for Rejecting Anti-Slavery." *Historian* 27 (November 1965): 1–18.

Richardson, Joe M. "The Failure of the American Missionary Association to Expand Congregationalism among Southern Blacks." *Southern Studies* 18 (Spring 1979): 51–73.

Rockwood, George I. "George Barrell Cheever, Protagonist of Abolition; Religious Emotionalism the Underlying Factor in the Cause of the Civil War." *American Antiquarian Society Proceedings* 46 (1936): 83–113.

Rosen, Bruce, "Abolition and Colonization, the Years of Conflict: 1829–1834." *Phylon* 33 (June 1972): 177–92.

Roth, Randolph A. "The First Radical Abolitionists: The Reverend James Milligan and the Reformed Presbyterians of Vermont." *New England Quarterly* 55 (December 1982): 540–63.

Russell, C. Allyn. "Rhode Island Baptists, 1825–1931." *Rhode Island History* 28 (May 1969): 34–48.

Sandeen, Ernest R. "The Distinctiveness of American Denominationalism: A Case Study of the 1846 Evangelical Alliance." *Church History* 45 (June 1976): 222–34.

Short, Kenneth R. "New York Central College: A Baptist Experiment in Integrated Education, 1848–1861." *Foundations* 5 (July 1962): 250–56.

Simms, Henry H. "A Critical Analysis of Abolition Literature, 1830–1840." *JSH* 6 (August 1940): 368–82.

Singleton, Gregory H. "Protestant Voluntary Organizations and the Shaping of Victorian America." *American Quarterly* 27 (December 1975): 549–60.

Sokolow, Jayme A. "Henry Clarke Wright: Antebellum Crusader." *Essex Institute Historical Collections* 3 (April 1975): 122–37.

——. "The Jerry McHenry Rescue and the Growth of Northern Antislavery Sentiment during the 1850s." *Journal of American Studies* 16 (December 1982): 427–45.

——. "Revolution and Reform: The Antebellum Jewish Abolitionists." *Journal of Ethnic Studies* 9 (Spring 1981): 27–41.

Staiger, C. Bruce. "Abolitionism and the Presbyterian Schism of 1837–1838." *MVHR* 36 (December 1949): 391–414.

Stange, Douglas C. "Compassionate Mother to Her Poor Negro Slaves: The Lutheran Church and Negro Slavery in Early America." *Phylon* 29 (Fall 1968): 272–81.

Stewart, James B. "The Aims and Impact of Garrisonian Abolitionism, 1840–1860." *CWH* 15 (September 1969): 197–209.

——. "Peaceful Hopes and Violent Experiences: The Evolution of Reforming and Radical Abolitionism, 1831–1837." *CWH* 17 (December 1971): 293–309.

Stirn, James R. "Urgent Gradualism: The Case of the American Union for the Relief and Improvement of the Colored Race." *CWH* 25 (December 1979): 309–28.

Sweet, William W. "Some Religious Aspects of the Kansas Struggle." *Journal of Religion* 7 (October 1927): 578–95.

Thomas, John L. "Antislavery and Utopia." In *The Antislavery Vanguard: New Essays on the Abolitionists,* edited by Martin Duberman. Princeton: Princeton University Press, 1965.

———. "Romantic Reform in America, 1815–1865." *American Quarterly* 17 (Winter 1965): 656–81.

Thompson, J. Earl, Jr. "Lyman Beecher's Long Road to Conservative Abolitionism." *Church History* 42 (March 1973): 89–109.

Tise, Edward. "The Interregional Appeal of Proslavery Thought: An Ideological Profile of the Antebellum American Clergy." *Plantation Society in the Americas* 1 (February 1979): 63–72.

Tyler, B. B. "History of the Disciples of Christ." *American Church History Series* 12 (1894): 1–170.

Walters, Ronald G. "The Boundaries of Abolitionism." In *Antislavery Reconsidered: New Perspectives on the Abolitionists,* edited by Lewis Perry and Michael Fellman. Baton Rouge: Louisiana State University Press, 1979.

Watkins, Richard H. "The Baptists of the North and Slavery, 1856–1860." *Foundations* 13 (October –December 1970): 317–33.

White, Marie S. "The Methodist Antislavery Struggle in the Land of Lincoln." *Methodist History* 10 (July 1972): 33–52.

Yinger, J. Milton. "The Present Status of the Sociology of Religion." In *The Sociology of Religion: An Anthology,* edited by Richard D. Knudten. New York: Appleton-Century-Crofts, 1967.

Dissertations, Theses, and Typescripts

Bannan, Phyllis M. "Arthur and Lewis Tappan: A Study of Religious and Reform Movements in New York City." Ph.D. diss., Columbia University, 1950.

Buys, John W. "An Ante-Bellum History of the Indiana Yearly Meeting of Friends." Master's thesis, Purdue University, 1968.

Carter, George E. "The Use of the Doctrine of Higher Law in the American Anti-Slavery Crusade, 1830–1860." Ph.D. diss., University of Oregon, 1970.

Cook, Lester H. "Anti-Slavery Sentiment in the Culture of Chicago, 1844–1858." Ph.D. diss., University of Chicago, 1952.

Davis, Hugh H. "The Reform Career of Joshua Leavitt, 1794–1873." Ph.D. diss., Ohio State University, 1969.

Ellsworth, Clayton S. "Oberlin and the Anti-Slavery Movement up to the Civil War," Ph.D. diss., Cornell University, 1930.

Engelder, Conrad J. "The Churches and Slavery: A Study of the Attitudes toward Slavery of the Major Protestant Denominations." Ph.D. diss., University of Michigan, 1964.

Bibliography

Evans, Linda Jeanne. "Abolitionism in the Illinois Churches, 1830–1865." Ph.D. diss., Northwestern University, 1981.

Gamble, Douglas A. "Moral Suasion in the West: Garrisonian Abolitionism, 1831–1861." Ph.D. diss., Ohio State University, 1973.

Harrold, Stanley C., Jr. "Gamaliel Bailey, Abolitionist and Free Soiler." Ph.D. diss., Kent State University, 1975.

Hennings, Lloyd V. "The American Missionary Association: A Christian Anti-Slavery Society." Master's thesis, Oberlin College, 1933.

Howard, Victor B. "The Anti-Slavery Movement in the Presbyterian Church, 1835–1861." Ph.D. diss., Ohio State University, 1961.

Jentz, John B. "Artisans, Evangelicals, and the City: A Social History of Abolition and Labor Reform in Jacksonian New York." Ph.D. diss., City University of New York, 1977.

Johnson, Clifton H. "The American Missionary Association, 1846–1861: A Study of Christian Abolitionism." Ph.D. diss., University of North Carolina, 1958.

Johnson, Howard G. "The Free Presbyterian Church: A History of an Abolitionist Sect." Senior independent study, Wooster College, 1970.

Keller, Ralph A. "Northern Protestant Churches and the Fugitive Slave Law of 1850." Ph.D. diss., University of Wisconsin, 1969.

Kraut, Alan Morton. "The Liberty Men of New York: Political Abolitionism in New York State, 1840–1848." Ph.D. diss., Cornell University, 1975.

Myers, John L. "The Agency System of the Anti-Slavery Movement, 1832–1837, and Its Antecedents in Other Benevolent and Reform Societies." Ph.D. diss., University of Michigan, 1961.

Ndukwu, Maurice Dickson. "Antislavery in Michigan: A Study of Its Origin, Development, and Expression from Territorial Period to 1860." Ph.D. diss., Michigan State University, 1979.

Norton, L. Wesley. "The Religious Press and the Compromise of 1850: A Study of the Relationship of the Methodist, Baptist, and Presbyterian Press to the Slavery Controversy, 1846–1851." Ph.D. diss., University of Illinois, 1959.

Norwood, John N. "The Schism in the Methodist Episcopal Church, 1844: A Study of Slavery and Ecclesiastical Politics." Ph.D. diss., Cornell University, 1915.

Perkal, Meyer L. "William Goodell: A Life of Reform." Ph.D. diss., City University of New York, 1972.

Powell, Milton B. "The Abolitionist Controversy in the Methodist Episcopal Church, 1840–1864." Ph.D. diss., University of Iowa, 1963.

Reynolds, Todd Armstrong. "The American Missionary Association's Antislavery Campaign in Kentucky, 1848 to 1860." Ph.D. diss., Ohio State University, 1979.

Rietveld, Ronald D. "The Moral Issue of Slavery in American Politics, 1854–1860." Ph.D. diss., University of Illinois, 1967.

Senior, Robert C. "New England Congregationalists and the Anti-Slavery Movement, 1830–1860." Ph.D. diss., Yale University, 1954.

Silverman, Jason Howard. "Unwelcome Guests: American Fugitive Slaves in Canada, 1830–1860." Ph.D. diss., University of Kentucky, 1981.

Bibliography

Spicer, Carl L. "The Great Awakening of 1857 and 1858." Ph.D. diss., Ohio State University, 1935.

Stewart, J. Mark. "The Chillicothe Presbytery in Ohio's Antislavery Movement in the 1820s and 1830s." Master's thesis, Ohio State University, 1971.

Welsh, Edward B. "Notes and Extracts on the Free Presbyterian Church." 3 vols. Typescript, Presbyterian Historical Society, n.d.

Willey, Larry Gene. "The Reverend John Rankin: Early Ohio Antislavery Leader." Ph.D. diss., University of Iowa, 1976.

Index

Library of Congress Cataloging in Publication Data

McKivigan, John R., 1949–
  The war against proslavery religion.

  Bibliography: p.
  Includes index.
  1. Slavery—United States—Anti-slavery movements.   2. Slavery and the
church.   3. Abolitionists—United States—History—19th century.   I. Title.
II. Title: War against proslavery religion.
E449.M475   1984   973.6   83–45933
ISBN 0–8014–1589–6 (alk. paper)